The Urban Factor

Due: 8ᵏ Aug

The Urban Factor

Sociology of
Canadian Cities

Leo Driedger

Toronto   Oxford   New York
OXFORD UNIVERSITY PRESS
1991

To Our Children
Who Are Finding Their Way in the City

Oxford University Press, 70 Wynford Drive, Don Mills, Ontario M3C 1J9

Toronto   Oxford   New York
Delhi   Bombay   Calcutta   Madras   Karachi   Petaling Jaya
Singapore   Hong Kong   Tokyo   Nairobi   Dar es Salaam
Cape Town   Melbourne   Auckland

and associated companies in
Berlin   Ibadan

Canadian Cataloguing in Publication Data

Driedger, Leo,
   The urban factor

Includes bibliographical references and index.
ISBN 0-19-540788-1

1. Sociology, Urban – Canada.   2. Sociology,
Urban.   I. Title.

HT127.D75 1991   307.76'0971   C91-093237-9

Table of Contents

List of Tables

List of Figures

Preface

One challenge in writing this volume was to develop a clear focus on urban sociology. Canada is increasingly dominated by its metropolitan centers, especially since the second World War, and some large centers are fast winning the race for prominence. The historical development of Canada's urban centres needed to be traced and documented. Power among the various metropoli in Canada, and the extent to which they are able to compete in the larger North American and world arenas are important in the global village, where technology and communications keep all parts of the world in touch instantly. Canadian scholars have contributed to many collections of writing on urbanization, but there are very few books of the sociology of Canadian cities. *The Urban Factor* is an attempt to provide such a volume.

A second challenge was to provide a theoretical and conceptual framework for Canadian sociology; fortunately, the classical theorists such as Karl Marx, Max Weber, and Emile Durkheim were all concerned with advancing technology and its consequences, so their writings were helpful. Max Weber wrote a volume on the emergence of the European city. American social science research, beginning with the Chicago School and its ecological emphasis, has been extensive. Since then modified versions and new emphases on urban community and networks have proliferated. Our task was to focus this vast literature on the Canadian urban scene, and to present alternative theoretical contexts. Having studied in Chicago, I am sympathetic to the Chicago School's ecological approach, but realize that the new versions and alternative approaches to neighborhood networks and community planning offer important new perspectives that need to be taken seriously.

A third challenge was to discover all available empirical Canadian research, and fit it within conceptual frameworks for enlightenment and explanation. Much empirical research has been carried out during the past twenty-five years, but there are gaps, and the need for more research is all too obvious, although scholars in urban institutes and new urban area studies are working hard. For example, we have not yet begun to study any city in Canada as extensively as Chicago was studied. Although sociologists have been the leaders in researching the city, I hope the reader of this book will detect an appreciation of other interdisciplinary research in urban history, anthropology, geography, planning, economics, and political studies. Some of my training and much of my reading has been interdisciplinary; there are always students in my urban sociology classes, who are studying other disciplines, and from them I have learned much.

In addition to the many people whose writings stimulated me and who are listed in the references, I wish to thank the Department of Sociology at the University of Manitoba, which relieved me of some teaching to pursue this writing. I also wish to thank Gordon Darroch and Barry Wellman for reading the manuscript and making helpful comments. Darroch's ideas and suggestions for further conceptual improvement were especially helpful. Richard Teleky, the managing editor of Oxford University Press in Canada, took a special interest in this project, and his encouragement was greatly appreciated. Thanks also to Darlene Driedger who helped prepare and process the many versions of the manuscript as it evolved.

Leo Driedger
University of Manitoba
1990

1. Origin of Preindustrial Cities

There have been three major revolutions that have profoundly changed the course of human life. The first was the revolution that led to the development of agriculture and brought about permanent village settlements. The second was the preindustrial urban revolution, which brought cities into being. The third was the Industrial Revolution, which spawned giant industrial urban complexes. In chapter one we shall briefly review the first two revolutions, and in the rest of this volume we shall dwell on the third in detail.

The Agricultural Revolution

Our human ancestors lived for thousands of years as nomads. They lived by hunting, fishing, and by gathering edible food. The only crude tools they had were a few unpolished stone tools (Braidwood, 1960). This level of technological life is usually referred to as the Stone Age or Paleolithic (from *paleo*, old; *lith*, stone) period (Flon, 1985:24-37; 162-5). The Paleolithic period lasted from about 500,000 BC (when Neanderthal man flourished) until about 9000 BC. A few groups still live in this fashion today in "outback" desert areas such as Australia. Evolutionists claim that during much of this pre-agricultural nomadic period humans were slowly evolving. Neanderthal man was succeeded by *homo sapiens* at about 35,000 BC. But early humans were handicapped in coping with their environment. Glaciers advanced and retreated many times across the northern parts of North America, Europe, and Asia. The last of these huge continental glaciers retreated by about 10,000 BC. After the end of this last Ice Age, great changes in climate occurred. Increases in rainfall and temperature provided a more hospitable environment, and many forms of wild life proliferated.

Early Nodes of Food Production

Soon after 10,000 BC, after the retreat of the glaciers, the first of our three revolutions occurred when some *homo sapiens* turned to agriculture. Anthropologists (Childe, 1951) have classified the move from food-gathering to food-producing as a major revolution because the cultivation of crops changes other aspects of the human lifestyle so profoundly. Flon and associates (1985) call it a triumph of agriculture. In order to engage in agriculture, early humans had to select and plant seeds, they had to remain in one place to harvest their crops, and as a result they needed to build more permanent residences and to learn to live together in organized groups.

Food production seems to have begun in at least two or three separate and distinct nodes: in the Middle East, in Mesoamerica, and perhaps in China. As illustrated in Figure 1-1, the domestication of plants and animals occurred at these central agricultural nodes and then spread throughout the world. Other crops were domesticated later in various locations. The first and major agricultural development occurred in the Middle East, in the valleys of the Tigris and Euphrates rivers, and in the Nile Valley by about 7000 BC (9000 years ago). It is here that grains such as barley and wheat began to be cultivated, and sheep, goats, and cattle began to be domesticated (Flon, 1985:166-9). These agricultural developments spread into Europe, Africa, and parts of Asia somewhat later. In Africa, other grains such as sorghums, millet, and various nuts and yams were developed in various regions to supplement diets.

The second independent agricultural node, in Mesoamerica, developed in central Mexico around what is now Mexico City. Here peppers, pumpkins, bottle gourds, avocados, squash, and cotton were grown around 7000 BC. Later corn, beans, sunflowers, and tomatoes were cultivated and spread out north and especially south into South America, where regional foods such as potatoes, peanuts, and manioc were also grown.

To what extent northern China was a third independent agricultural node is not clear. Rice certainly became a staple grain important to millions; it spread south into southeast Asia and west into India (Flon, 1985:296-7). Domestication of chickens and pigs seems to have begun here as well. Each of these three agricultural nodes, then, developed a staple diet: wheat in the Middle East, corn in Mesoamerica, and rice in China. It is logical to assume that near these centers, where food had become more plentiful, people would settle and the population would grow. Certainly villages and later cities would emerge at these three places.

Beginning of Neolithic Villages

The stone tools that archaeologists have found suggest that early humans were able gradually to develop their technology and so could gather more and more food from the environment (Flon, 1985:66-7, 172-3). "By about 75,000 years ago the tools became sufficiently specialized to suggest that they corresponded to the conditions of food-getting in broad regional environments." (Braidwood, 1960:3.) The earliest stone tools were chopping tools made from stones or rocks. Gradually all-purpose "axe" tools and blade tools for cutting and skinning animals were developed. These adaptations in tools were necessary as more co-ordinated and systematic hunting in groups developed in the old world. By about 30,000 years ago these hunting techniques and the related tools also spread to the new world (Flon, 1985:176-7). Thus the successful adaptation of human communities to the environment brought about greater

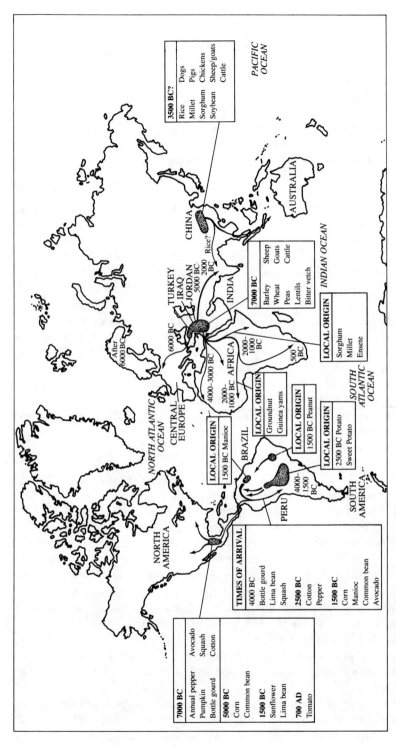

Figure 1-1 The earliest nodes of agricultural development
SOURCE: Gist and Fava (1974: 5).

cultural complexity and social organization, so that shortly after the last Ice Age (10,000 years ago) humans were at the threshold of food production (Braidwood, 1960:5). The first villages began where agriculture began (Figure 1-1). The period of early food production is known as the Neolithic period.

The first evidence of successful experimentation in food production was found by Robert Braidwood in what is now Iraq, in the Middle East area where the first agricultural revolution began. The agricultural village of Jarmo, discovered and excavated by Braidwood since 1948, was located on the hilly flanks of the fertile crescent (the fertile region between the two early civilizations anchored by Sumer and Egypt) near the Tigris River on the slopes of the Zagros Mountains (Figure 1-2). Jarmo was apparently inhabited between 7000 and 6500 BC. Other sites in the same area have been excavated. Jarmo was a permanent, year-round settlement with about two dozen mud-walled houses that were repaired and rebuilt frequently. There are a dozen distinct levels of occupancy.

In Jarmo the excavators identified domesticated grains such as barley and wheat. Goats, dogs, and possibly sheep had also been domesticated. Bones of wild animals, shells of marine animals and of nuts indicated that the people also still obtained some food by hunting and gathering. Braidwood estimates that there were 150 people living in Jarmo. The earlier period, from the lower levels of excavation, shows the use of stone vessels; these were replaced by pottery in the upper, later levels (Flon, 1985:184-7). Small clay figurines were also found, suggesting the beginnings of artwork. There was some evidence of trade: shells of marine animals were found in the village, which is distant from the sea (Braidwood, 1960:9). Many other Neolithic villages have been found in the fertile crescent area, but Jarmo is one of the earliest (Gist and Fava, 1974:8).

Jericho: Maturing Villages

Jericho and its ancient ruins lie just north of the Dead Sea in Israel. Jericho is a tiny green oasis in the glittering desert, fed by a spring of water. The site has been used by humans for a long time. Archeologist Kathleen Kenyon has excavated the many layers of the old Jericho tell, the earliest of which goes back to nearly 8000 BC and seems to pre-date Jarmo (Sjoberg, 1960:32). However, there is a great deal of controversy over when the settlement began, its size, and its level of development (Sjoberg, 1960:32-3). There was an interesting scholarly exchange between Braidwood and Kenyon about Kenyon's initial claim that the settlement dated from 8000 BC (Kenyon, 1956:184-97; Kenyon, 1957: 82-4; Braidwood, 1957:73-81; 82-4). The controversy is about where agriculture first began (in the Jericho oasis or in the river valleys of Mesopotamia) and whether Jericho had become an urban center by 5000 BC.

In the early levels at Jericho, Kenyon found well-developed mud houses and evidence of walls with fortifications. What made Jericho different from other settlements was the presence of a surrounding wall, a tower, and a large trench (a moat or a large cistern?), all suggesting an advanced division of labor and the need for defense (Spates and Macionis, 1987:31). The site was abandoned and left vacant for a millennium and then occupied again around 5000 BC by less advanced settlers with more primitive shelters. The findings of Kenyon suggest that village life occurred before Jarmo (7000 BC), soon after the last Ice Age. Gordon Childe (1957:36-8) takes Kenyon to task for her loose definition of urbanization, claiming that in addition to size and defense, evidence of other criteria such as writing and numerical notation must be found before a settlement can be considered urban. In fact, Childe considers that writing is the single definitive criterion differentiating rural villages from urban centers.

Clearly, the finds at Jarmo and Jericho illustrate that there must have been many permanent villages emerging shortly after the retreat of the last Ice Age between 8000 and 7000 BC. Jarmo appears to be an example of an early transitional village where the occupants had domesticated grains and animals, but still supplemented their diets with food gathering; settlers in Jericho had advanced further and had developed defence works and public projects. Discrepancies between the development of the two villages clearly illustrate the need to discuss which criteria should be employed to define an urban center.

Finding a Conceptual Frame

Should we first define what are the characteristics of an "urban" center or a "city," and then look at early settlements to find whether they have these characteristics? Or should we look at the early settlements first and then classify from among the early and later characteristics which ones designate a center as urban? It is a chicken-and-egg question, and one which no one can solve. We shall begin by first looking at the larger context: the preconditions necessary for cities to emerge, as described by Otis Duncan. We shall then discuss the ten criteria that Gordon Childe, having examined the literature and archeological findings, considered crucial for the definition of preindustrial cities. Once we have presented these two larger conceptual issues, we shall in the section that follows trace the development of settlements from their early beginnings.

Preconditions of Urban Growth

To define the preconditions necessary for urban growth in the preindustrial environment, Otis Dudley Duncan (1961) introduced the concept of the urban "ecosystem." He suggested that there are four basic variables in the ecosystem: 1) population, 2) environment, 3) technology, and 4) social organization (see Figure 1-2). All four variables are related, and urban development involves all four together.

Population • The size of the population is one of the most important variables for preindustrial urban development. One precondition for the growth of a

Figure 1-2 Pre-conditions of urban preindustrial growth

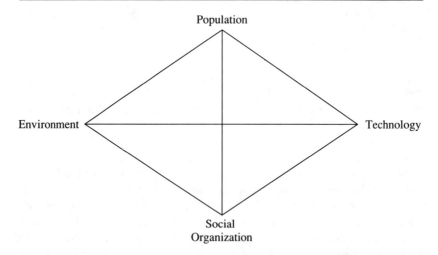

city is that there should be a population of a certain size residing permanently in one place. The environment, the level of technology, and the degree of social organization all set limits on how large such a population will grow. The early cities were relatively small; very few may have exceeded 5000 to 10,000 people.

The population density, distribution, and rates of growth or decline are all demographic variables that affect and are affected by the other components of the ecosystem (Gold:1982:13). The size of the community depended to a large degree on the extent to which the agricultural base and technological development created food surpluses sufficient to sustain a population of a given size. It is difficult to determine just how large some of the preindustrial cities were, but it does appear that few grew beyond 40,000. The criteria of size and density are still used to define industrial urban populations.

Environment • "The natural environment, including such elements as natural resources, climate, topography, soil conditions, and waterways, has always had an important bearing on the location in which cities originate and grow." (Gold, 1982:13.) Figure 1-3, introduced later, will clearly show that all early civilizations originated in the temperate zone. The earliest four Asian cities developed around rivers, and the two earliest Mesopotamian and Egyptian cities began in marshy areas where rivers naturally flooded or irrigated the land. This environment provided the most favorable living conditions. Only simple technology was needed to till the soil. The soil was fertile so there was no need to store large amounts of supplies for long periods of time. The climate was mild, so shelter requirements were minimal. Fishing and food gathering could easily be combined with the beginnings of agriculture.

In Mesoamerica the environmental features were different. The Maya built their cities in the Yucatan in forested areas that could be cleared for cultivation. The Inca built their empire along the ridges of the Andes Mountains. Animals such as the alpaca and llama, which were sure-footed climbers, were available for domestication. The Aztecs built their capital city in the middle of a lake. They were able to undertake the creative development of its foundations and of methods of communication. The Egyptian and Assyrian civilizations had to deal with desert and semi-arid environments outside the fertile areas; later civilizations around the Mediterranean found that the sea provided other resources and required new forms of invention.

Technology • The earliest cities could only develop when technological improvements in agriculture made it possible to produce large enough surpluses of food to support nonagricultural specialized populations (Gold, 1982:14). But the technology required to advance civilization in preindustrial societies was quite simple by modern standards, particularly as the favorable environment did not require advanced technology. For example, in Sumer and in Egypt the flooding of the Euphrates and Nile rivers had to be managed, for the floods posed both an opportunity (fertile soil) and a hazard (Sjoberg, 1960:29).

In contrast, the environment of the urban states around the Mediterranean offered only a poor agricultural potential. Phoenicia, Greece, and Carthage soon looked for better food supplies across the waters, which they found in places such as Sicily and the coasts of Italy and Spain. However, the Phoenicians, Greeks, and Carthaginians thus required sea-faring technology, and this caused their whole cultural and societal organization to be different from that in Sumer and Egypt. The new challenges of the Mediterranean brought about new opportunities in trade and commerce, but also problems of political conflict and the need for protection and warfare on a much larger scale. In the meantime, city populations became larger and urban organization more complex.

Social Organization • As populations grew, as technology became more efficient and increasingly capable of exploiting more difficult environments, the need for more complex organizational structures also increased. As trade increased and the population not engaged in agricultural pursuits grew, monumental public structures were built, communities developed rulers and social stratification, and the need for the formation of a larger political state emerged. For example, the building of huge pyramids in Egypt must have taken tens of thousands of workers. To plan such large projects and supervise the feeding, housing, and work assignments of such numbers required an enormously complex social organization, including a political, economic, and social infrastructure, a large bureaucracy, and leadership.

The Sumerian cities began as independent states. Ur later became the capital, co-ordinating a larger political and social structure. Later great civilizations, such as the Babylonian and Assyrian empires, arose, with huge populations covering large areas and requiring enormous armies to control.

The city-states of Carthage and Greece, the empires of Alexander the Great and Rome required complex social organizations on a grand scale. Such state powers came into conflict with each other and had therefore to develop organizations to conduct warfare. These civilizations illustrate how large and complex social organizations could become. The ecosystem of population, environment, technology, and social organization resulted in city-states that turned into national and empire states of enormous scope.

Duncan's (1961) four preconditions: concentration of population, suitable spatial environment, development of technology, and adequate social organization are all interrelated, and must be considered together as a context that may or may not be suitable for urban growth.

Childe's Preindustrial Urban Criteria

Gordon Childe (1950:4-7) has suggested ten characteristics that he considers to be essential criteria in defining an urban civilization. These are listed in Table 1-1. All ten are present in the four earliest centers in the Old World and the three in the New World that we shall be examining later, except that the Incas had not developed a written language. Childe considers language the most important feature.

Table 1.1 Childe's ten characteristics essential for defining preindustrial cities

1. Dense permanent settlement
2. Nonagricultural, specialized work
3. Taxation and tribute
4. Trade and exchange of oversupply
5. Writing and numerical notation
6. Development of the exact sciences
7. Development of works of art
8. Monumental and ceremonial buildings
9. Leadership and social classes
10. Political organization of the state

SOURCE: Childe, (1950:4-7.)

A dense aggregation of people living in a permanent settlement could describe a village. However size of population is a criterion that differentiates between village and city. The city of Ur in Sumer, with its canals, temples, and harbors, occupied only 90 ha; Childe estimated that it may have had a population of 24,000 (Childe, 1946:86-7). Most of the other early cities were smaller. Kingsley Davis (1955:430) estimates that the biggest early cities before the Roman period would have been small. In the preindustrial agricultural world, city size was determined by the availability of surplus food and the technology needed to transport it, and these were limited.

Childe (1950) defines an urban population as nonagriculturalists engaging in specialized functions. Since buildings for religious purposes, such as ziggurats, temples, and pyramids, were among the first monuments to be built, it is believed that religious practitioners were the first released from agricultural pursuits for specialized tasks. The construction of canals and waterways to enhance irrigation for agriculture was important in both the Sumerian and Eygptian civilizations, and so there must have been specialists who were engineers and planners. As food production increased, people were needed to store it.

As soon as some people are released from growing their own food, then they must have some means of obtaining their food indirectly. The means are found through taxation. Early taxes in Sumer, Egypt, and Mesoamerica may have been received in the form of agricultural products; these were stored in granaries. Later capital accumulation took the form of more durable means of exchange such as shells, gold, and eventually coinage.

As the population increased and as agriculture, public irrigation projects, and trade expanded, the need for more precise methods of measurement and control, and for the ability to make predictions based on scientific knowledge also increased. The construction of networks of canals and large buildings required accurate measurement. As trade expanded and sea travel in large bodies of water increased, the development of astronomy provided navigational aids. Exact measures of the seasons and the prediction of seasonal weather patterns, the division of time in the day, and into clusters of days (the calendar) all became important.

Sedentary life gave opportunities for improved accommodation and paved the way for architecture and artistic expression (Childe, 1951:91). Decorated pottery was one outlet for free expression of individual artistic development, and we have extensive evidence in all preindustrial societies of beautifully shaped and painted pottery as technology developed. As time went on artistic expression expanded into other fields, and specialists were released to work in public buildings; the pyramids of Egypt and Mesoamerica are notable examples.

Since the Tigris-Euphrates river delta had no stone, wood, nor metals, the early Sumerians needed to obtain building supplies and supplement their staple diet with varieties of food from elsewhere. So they traded their food surpluses with their northerly neighbors who had the resources they needed. There is evidence that trade with the Indus Valley had developed considerably (Flon, 1985:110-11).

Childe's fifth characteristic of cities follows logically. As the population grew and trade began, there was a need for some form of numerical notation to keep track of how many items were exchanged for a variety of products. Thus, writing and numerical notation emerged (Flon, 1985:72-3; 80-1; 178-9). At first writing took the form of pictographs, but soon more abstract symbols with wider application began to be used. Six of the early civilizations had invented writing, and had then turned a practical means of notation into a means of making records on their sacred temples and public buildings.

Archeological records show that the earliest public buildings were temples. Many Egyptian temples were also used as granaries for the community's surplus produce (Palen, 1982:16). The ziggurats in Mesopotamia were religious structures and also the center of urban areas; the pyramids of the Maya, the Aztec, and the Inca all seemed to have similar religious functions. The Egyptians began their huge pyramids as burial places for their pharaohs, thus bringing religious and political functions together. As the Egyptians expanded their empire, they celebrated their victories with temples such as those at Luxor and Karnak. Such monumental buildings became symbols of religious and political power.

Childe lists kingship (leadership) or a ruling class as a ninth characteristic of urbanization. As populations increased, there was a greater need for specialized leadership to provide protection; these leaders became part of a political upper class (Palen, 1982:17). It was a short step from a warrior class to kingship — the founding of a permanent hereditary dynasty. As a result, the focus of the ruling class moved from the temple to the palace, although in Egypt the pharaoh as god-king united the two. The stratification of the society and the disparity between the rich and poor can clearly be seen in the archeological digs of graves by Wooley in Ur (Adams, 1960:9). The Egyptian and Mesopotamian tombs of the ruling classes were richly furnished with ornaments, gold and other precious metals, and with important works of art.

Finally, Childe adds the formation of a state as his tenth urban criterion; the state is a last logical step after the formation of a ruling class and social stratification. Ur was the Sumerian capital of a series of cities in Mesopotamia, followed by Nineveh and Babylon. A series of empires later followed the Sumerian state. The Egyptian pharaohs, whose dynasties often lasted for centuries, developed their capitals at Memphis and Thebes. By the time Cortez captured the Aztecs, Montezuma II had subjugated the surrounding villages and cities of a large area extending from coast to coast in Central America. The vast Inca empire in South America also comprised numerous peoples who had been conquered and subdued. In many early civilizations, the formation of a powerful state with a capital city dominating the surrounding regions was quite common (Adams, 1960).

The Origin of Cities

We can now examine the earliest urban origins using Childe's ten criteria as a guide. Let us discuss the earliest four Old World and three New World civilizations in historical sequence so that we get some sense of how and where cities originated. The first four Old World centers of urbanization (Figure 1-3) (Carswell, 1981: 14, 15) arose in the Mesopotamian river valleys, the Nile Valley, and later in the Indus Valley and along the Yellow River. Urbanization (Carswell, 1981:14, 15) began independently in Mesoamerica in the Yucatan in southern Mexico, in central Mexico, and in what is now Peru (Figure 1-3).

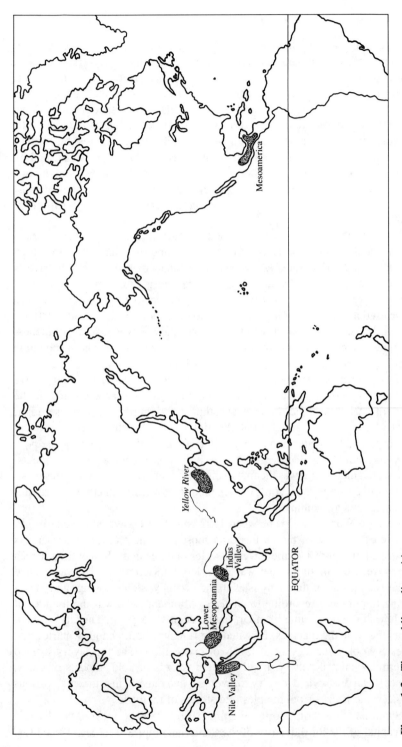

Figure 1-3 The world's earliest cities
SOURCE: Gist and Fava (1974: 17).

Mesopotamia: Tigris-Euphrates Valley

It is generally agreed that the first cities began soon after 3500 BC in lower Mesopotamia (called Sumer) along the Tigris and Euphrates rivers, in the area just north of the Persian Gulf into which these two rivers drain. This area is part of the fertile crescent, which begins in the west in the Egyptian Nile Valley and arches northwards and eastwards like a horseshoe, coming down through former Palestine (now Syria and Israel) and ending in the east in the Tigris-Euphrates delta (see Figure 1-4). It is called the fertile crescent because between the rivers at either end the first agricultural villages began, and by 3500 BC also the earliest cities were spawned. Figure 1-4 shows both the two earliest excavated villages (Jericho and Jarmo) and the earliest cities of Mesopotamia (Erech, Eridu, Ur, Lagash, and Larsa in Sumer). (Sjoberg, 1960:34.)

These urban centers were "city-states" surrounded by cultivated fields, reedy marshes, and desert. They flourished along the channels of the slow-flowing marshy Euphrates River and along canals dug to harness the river's unpredictable flow (Fishbein, 1981:40). The life-giving Euphrates provided reeds for weaving boats and mud for making bricks to build houses similar to those used in the Persian Gulf today, and to make pottery (Jacobson, 1980:71-81). As we have seen, because Sumer had virtually no wood, stone, or metals, its cities traded barley, wool, cloth, and hides with the northern mountain people for wood and metals (Fishbein, 1981:41).

These cities were surrounded by irrigation channels that permitted intensive farming. Soon domesticated livestock and crop surpluses accumulated. In the heart of each city stood the central temple or ziggurat, many stories high, made of baked bricks and decorated with mosaics. Nearby were government buildings and the better homes, while farther away the quarters for the poor were located. As early as 3200 BC, writing was recorded on clay tablets. Samuel Kramer (1956) was the first to discover Sumerian writing and describes twenty-seven Sumerian records in such fields as government, ethics, literature, medicine, and agriculture.

Leonard Wooley (1965) between 1922 and 1934 excavated the city of Ur, believed to be one of the earliest and most prominent cities in Sumer. As illustrated in Figure 1-4, there were a series of cities in the Sumer area. Erech may have been the oldest and was considered a sacred city. Ur was located on an island, one of the many isles in the swampy, slow-flowing, and meandering Euphrates. According to *Genesis*, Abraham, who was the founder of the Jewish religion, came from Ur, but no details are given. The city's inhabitants fished in the marshes, irrigated and tilled the soil, and grew barley and wheat. Wooley found several levels of civilization. The top layers yielded beautifully painted pottery, highly crafted vessels of gold, models of boats, games, head dresses and jewelry for women, and musical instruments. Various mosaics and friezes from temples told stories of their life.

Sumerian cities lasted for a long time. From 2300 BC to 2180 BC, Ur was the capital of the third dynasty of the Sumerian empire (Wooley, 1965:112).

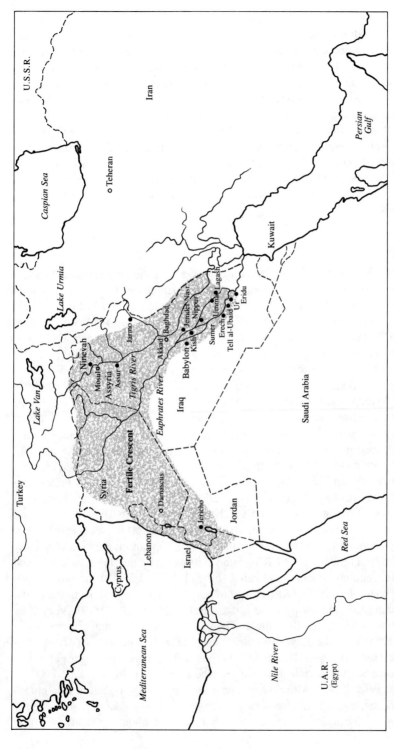

Figure 1-4 The fertile crescent and its ancient cities and villages in the Tigris-Euphrates and Nile river valleys
SOURCE: Gist and Fava (1974: 6).

The empire had expanded northwards to include cities along the Euphrates and the fertile crescent, perhaps as far as the Mediterranean Sea. Sumerian society had become stratified; the kings built monuments such as elaborate ziggurats. Each city had one of these sacred towers, the biggest and most famous, a solid mass of brickwork, was built later in Babylon, and was referred to in the Hebrew tradition as the tower of Babel (Wooley, 1965:117-20). (The Babylonians from farther north conquered Ur and the southern cities in 1885 BC). Wooley excavated many of the royal tombs of Ur, providing evidence of their well-developed culture and society, which included all the features considered essential by Childe for urban life: writing, works of art, numerical notation, social stratification, trade, population density and size, specialized labor, taxation, scientific knowledge, and formation of a state (Fishbein, 1981:40,41).

Egypt and the Nile Valley

At the western end of the fertile crescent we have the Nile River and Egypt, the second great early civilization, out of which cities evolved around 3000 BC (Flon, 1985:196). Just as the Sumerians banded together in Mesopotamia to develop irrigation projects, so the Egyptians needed to divert the Nile River's annual floods into the wheat and barley fields (Sjoberg 1960:37). Oxen and asses were domesticated for use in agriculture and for transport, and the technologies for working copper and making pottery on a wheel were developed. Boats to ply the Nile were also developed early (Walters, 1980:22-46). Writing began about 3100 BC. The earliest writings tell of a number of cities including Memphis, Thebes, Helopolis, and Nekheb, most of which cannot be excavated because of the layers of silt deposited each year by the Nile (Sjoberg, 1960:38). Few large cities developed early because the pharaohs seemed to move their capital each time their predecessor died (Walters, 1980:28-30). In Figure 1-5 we present the sequence of urban evolution: the Mesopotamian city of Eridu is first, followed by Ur; at about the same time the cities of Memphis and Thebes in Egypt also began to develop.

The Old Kingdom of Egypt, which began in 2700 BC, is considered by many scholars to be the greatest period of Egyptian civilization (Chalaby, 1981:17). During the Old Kingdom civil and religious laws, writing, and artistic cannons all came into being (Flon, 1985:200-3). During this time an early pharaoh of the Old Kingdom, Zoser, constructed great stone monuments, including the stepped pyramid at Sakkarah (Chalaby, 1981:17). Very little remains of Memphis, the capital. The pyramids and the temples provide the best records of the Egyptian culture and life at this period. At Gizeh, just outside modern Cairo, later pharaohs constructed three even larger pyramids. The largest, which rises 160 m above the desert, was built around 2600 BC (Flon, 1985:202-7). Also at Gizeh, near these pyramids, is the famous sphinx.

Thebes, which had existed as a settlement for some centuries, became the capital of the pharoahs in the New Kingdom in about 1600 BC (Walters,

Figure 1-5 The sequence of urban evolution after 3500 BC

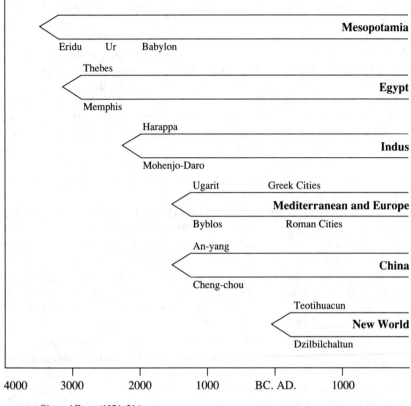

SOURCE: Gist and Fava (1974: 21.)

1980:36-9). Every victory was celebrated by building new and grandiose temples, and Thebes grew to be a large city. Two magnificent temples are still standing at Luxor and Karnak. The avenue of the sphinxes at Luxor is three kilometres distant from Karnak; it is thought that the avenue may at one time have connected the two temples. Karnak includes about two and one half hectares of monuments and temples, including the hypostyle hall, which is 102 m long by 53 m wide. The hall contains 134 massive columns, each 23 m high and laced with carvings (Chalaby, 1981:64,66). Across the Nile to the west are the Valleys of the Kings and Queens, which contained their royal tombs. The building of enormous monuments became a preoccupation of the Egyptians; such constructions required accurate scientific measurements and numeration, and included writing and many works of art. All these skills, spearheaded by an elite class, emerged in Egypt soon after they had arisen in Mesopotamia.

The Indus and Yellow River Valleys

To the east of Mesopotamia, along the valley of the Indus River of today's India and Pakistan, was a third ecosystem favorable to urban development (Flon, 1985:238-41). Excavators have found the remains of two highly developed cities whose construction began in 2500 BC (Cotterell, 1980:176,177; Spates and Macionis, 1987:40). Moenjo-Daro was located on the Indus River about 280 km from the Arabian Sea; Harappa was about 560 km farther north on the river's tributary (Flon, 1985:242-3). It is estimated that each city had a population of about 40,000, and it is thought that they were linked by trade routes with the Mesopotamian cities. Moenjo-Daro was laid out in a gridiron pattern, as are modern cities today, with a broad boulevard lined with shops and an open sewer system. Craft specialists such as potters, weavers, brickmakers, and metalworkers were located around a citadel at the city's center, which contained granaries and storage buildings (Sjoberg, 1960; Cotterell, 1980:176-81).

Cities in China go as far back as 2000 BC. Po seems to have been the earliest capital of the Shang Dynasty (Cotterell, 1980:288-91). The second and third Shang capitals have been studied in more detail. The second city, Cheng-chou, was at its height about 1600 BC. Walls 7 km long and 10 m high enclosed an area nearly 2 km^2, and contained the city's administrative and ceremonial center (Spates and Macionis, 1987:42). The political and religious elite lived inside the walls, the artisans outside. An-yang was the third Shang capital, similar to Cheng-chou but larger and closely linked with a series of agricultural villages (Flon, 1985:260-85). There seemed to be a rural-urban network: not all urban activities were located in one city, but were diffused into satellite centers that participated in the network. Most likely these Chinese cities developed independently from the Mesopotamian centers. These developments in the Indus and Yellow river valleys exhibit urban characteristics such as population density, specialized labor, taxation, trade, writing, the knowledge of exact sciences, works of art, monumental buildings, a class of rulers, and a state.

The Maya in Mesoamerica

Cities also developed independently in the New World around 300 BC in Mesoamerica in what is now the Yucatan in Mexico, Honduras, Belize, and Guatemala. Settled agricultural villages began about 1500 BC (Flon, 1985:344-53). Maize (corn) formed the agricultural base. The Maya used the slash and burn method to clear the land of vegetation and prepare it for seeding. However, they domesticated few if any animals. Tikal and Uaxactun rank among the oldest of the Mayan cities so far discovered. The numerous later ones include Chichen Itza, Mayapan, Copan, Palenque, and others (Sjoberg, 1960:46; Flon, 1985:348-51). The Mayans developed mathematics and the concept of zero; they also had an extensive knowledge of astronomy, were able to make calculations of the solar year, and developed an extremely accurate calendar. The Maya used a form of hieroglyphic writing. They did not invent the wheel, nor did they use metals. The Maya were masters of monumental stone architecture as well as of art and painting. "The ruins of the Governor's Palace in Uxmal, Yucatan, have been compared in artistic and technical perfection with the Parthenon in Athens." (Gist and Fava, 1974:15.)

The most spectacular structures were usually ceremonial religious edifices in the form of pyramids. These pyramids were not as large as those in Egypt, and were not used as mortuaries as in Egypt. The Mayan pyramids were step structures used for religious ceremonies, displaying elaborate and complex decorative art that varied from pyramid to pyramid (Flon, 1988:348-9). Steps led upwards to a small shrine at the top of the structure. Other large buildings included well-decorated palaces, planetariums, sports stadiums, and numerous other ceremonial structures. The Mayan civilization declined by about 1000 AD. The Maya seem to have abandoned their cities, not destroyed them, seemingly not because of conquest but for some other, unknown reason (Flon, 1988:352-3).

Aztec Cities

About 50 km northeast of present-day Mexico City are the ruins of Teotihuacan, which was inhabited about 150 BC to 750 AD. The Pyramid of the Sun is about 20 stories high, and is linked with the Pyramid of the Moon by an Avenue of the Dead more than one kilometre long (Gist and Fava, 1960:15). Very little is known about the people who built this vast ceremonial and administrative complex. These pyramids are much larger and taller than those in the Yucatan, and their style is quite different from that of the Egyptian and Mayan pyramids.

A later civilization was formed in the valley of Mexico by the Aztecs, whose religion was based on human sacrifice. In 1168 the Tenochas, or Aztecs as they were named in the nineteenth century, entered central Mexico from the northwest, and in 1325 began to build their capital city-state of Tenochtitlan on an island in Lake Texcoco. (Von Hagan, 1958:24.) By 1519 Tenochtitlan had a population of more than 100,000. It greatly impressed the Spanish, who under Cortez conquered the Aztecs and their ruler Montezuma II in that year (Gist and Fava, 1974:15,16). Causeways of 3 km from the mainland led to the city. Here were kept the storehouses for maize, beans, and peppers. Craftsmen and artisans worked silver and gold into works of art. The city also included a pyramidal temple. It was a city-state that extracted tribute in the form of agricultural produce from the surrounding villages. The Spaniards built a cathedral on the ruins of Tenochtitlan after they had destroyed the city. A few of the ruins can still be seen in the central square of Mexico City (Stanley, 1980: 325-31).

Inca Cities

"The only other indigenous New World civilization was that of the Inca in the Central Andes in what is now Peru, Bolivia, and Chile." (Gist and Fava,

1974:16; Conrad, 1980:348-55.) Agriculture diffused from the Mayan civilization northwards, so that by 750 BC agricultural practices and rural villages were well-established along the Peruvian coast. The Inca capital was located at Guzco in present-day Ecuador (the modern city of the same name was built on top of it). Inca cities clustered around stone pyramids covered with beaten gold in honour of their sun god (Conrad, 1980:349). "The Inca conquered various independent local kingdoms between 1100 and 1400 AD and formed a vast empire . . . linked together administratively by a centralized governmental bureaucracy under a god-king and by a stupendous, 16,000-km system of highways." (Von Hagen, 1955:295.) The Inca developed elaborate public works: roads with bridges, canals, and terraces on the mountain sides. They erected works of art out of gold, silver, and copper, and by 1000 AD they used bronze (Flon, 1985:268-9). The Inca were conquered by Pizarro and the Spanish in 1532. The Spanish were interested only in their gold, and destroyed this great civilization, subjugating the Inca people.

A review of Mesoamerican cities illustrates that the Maya, the Inca, and the Aztecs had developed all Gordon Childe's urban criteria. The only exception was that the Inca had not developed writing.

Early Mediterranean Urban Beginnings

These descriptions of urban origins in seven regions are only broad outlines. Asians might wish to know more about the Indus and Yellow river valley developments; Latin Americans would want to know more about Mesoamerican origins. As westerners, let us briefly trace the developments that moved from the fertile crescent along the shores of the Mediterranean. Egypt, the second earliest urban civilization, was based on the Nile River; its waters empty into the southeastern Mediterranean. Thus Egypt was an important Mediterranean civilization. Ugarit and Byblos, part of the Phoenician civilization, emerged in 1500 BC at the eastern end of the Mediterranean (at the same time as An-yang and Cheng-chou in northern China). Urban settlements developed after 500 BC westwards along the north side of the Mediterranean in Greece and Italy. These Mediterranean civilizations have had profound effects on western urban development.

Pirenne's Mediterranean Theory

Henri Pirenne has a fascinating theory about the importance of the Mediterranean Sea and the Greek and Roman civilizations that developed around it (Figure 1-6). Pirenne (1925:v) considered that the economic awakening and urban civilization of western Europe depended on the mastery of the sea. By the time Greece began, after 500 BC, technology had advanced sufficiently to permit ships to ply this small body of water fairly comfortably. As a result, cities and civilizations flowered on the northern, southern, and eastern shores. By the time of the Romans, the Mediterranean had become a commonwealth of trade; a familiar, almost "family" sea. This "commonwealth" included

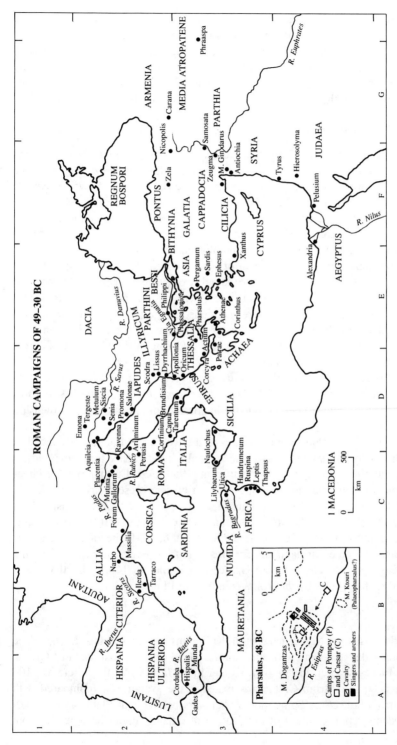

Figure 1-6 Pirenne's early Mediterranean civilizations
SOURCE: Talbert (1985).

the great cities of Constantinople and Rome, which later became centers of the Christian religion — the official religion of Europe (Pirenne, 1925:16).

After the fall of the Roman Empire, Europeans began to look inland away from the sea, and the Mediterranean Sea commerce declined. Let us briefly review the Phoenician, Greek, and Roman urban developments to gain some perspective on the emergence of the later, western urban civilizations.

The Phoenicians and Carthage

The seven urban developments discussed earlier began along rivers or inland waters, or grew out of agricultural communities. Later urbanization developed northwestwards from the Sumerian cities; the Babylonian, Assyrian, Hittite, and Syrian empires were also largely inland civilizations (Flon, 1985:190-3). After 1000 BC, sea-faring technology had developed sufficiently so that three important civilizations (Phoenicians, Greeks, Romans) could use the Mediterranean for trade, commerce, and colonization (Flon, 1985:194-5).

Phoenicia consisted of a chain of cities located along the coastal strip of what is now Lebanon and northern Israel, from around Tripoli in the north to Akko (Acre) in the south. It included Tyre, Sidon, and Byblos (Culican, 1980:129). Tyre and Sidon were mentioned in the writings of Homer; they seemed around 1000 BC to be a cluster of trading cities rather than a nation. Egyptian literature recorded that Byblos traded with the pharaohs of Egypt (945-842 BC). Tyre had treaties with kings David and Solomon of Israel (1000 BC to 922 BC). Israel traded foodstuffs for Tyre's wood, and for craftsmen to help build Solomon's temple (I *Kings*, 7; II *Chronicles*, 2; Culican, 1980:130). Both the Bible and Homer attest to the importance of Phoenician craftsmenship and commerce.

"The earliest Phoenician voyages in the west were traditionally dated to the late second millennium BC but no archeological evidence for them is earlier than the ninth century BC" (Warmington, 1980:233). Carthage was a Phoenician settlement on the coast of North Africa near present-day Tunis. It was founded by Tyre in 814 BC, or later according to some archaeologists (Warmington, 1980:233). Carthage became a powerful nation. It traded with colonies in much of Spain, Corsica, and Sicily. In fact, Mediterranean trade was dominated by the Carthaginians for three centuries. Eventually Carthage came increasingly into conflict with Greece and Rome. In 146 BC Carthage was razed to the ground by the Romans in the third Punic War.

The Greek City-States

The Minoans and Mycenaeans built the first urban settlements in Europe. The Minoans developed a civilization on the island of Crete just south of Greece and Turkey (Talbert, 1985:4-7). Homer in his *Iliad* wrote that Crete had 100 towns; 80 ships from Crete participated in the Trojan War (compared with 100 from Greece). "Some modern scholars believe that Plato (430-350 BC) based his report of the lost civilization of Atlantis upon the legends about

Minoan Crete (Willets, 1980:204). The Minoans and Mycenaeans had all of Childe's urban characteristics, including pictographic and hieroglyphic scripts, which have been found on thousands of clay tablets.

The Greeks traded throughout the Mediterranean countries, penetrating the western Mediterranean by the eighth century, and establishing colonies such as Sicily and Magna Graecia in southern Italy between 750 and 600 BC (Warmington, 1980:240). During the archaic age of Greece (700-500 BC), a series of city-states, including Corinth, Athens, and Sparta, traded with each other. Later these states banded together as leagues, especially when threatened by enemies (Hooker, 1980:215-16).

By the fifth century BC Athens had become the center of a well-organized city-state and a widespread trade network (Talbert, 1985:45-9). While it had only a limited amount of soil suitable for agriculture, its harbors were good. Growing numbers of craftsmen, merchants, sailors, and emissaries set the character of the city (Gold, 1982:38). Athens was built around a fortified hill, called an acropolis, where temples were often located. It was surrounded by large defensive walls (Gold, 1982:39). Athens is best known, however, for its social organization and cultural development.

While Sparta became a disciplined military state, Athens is better known for its achievements in philosophy, architecture, poetry, the plastic arts, and science (Talbert, 1985:27-36). Socrates, his pupil Plato (430-350 BC), and Plato's pupil Aristotle (384-322 BC) have become well known in western civilization.

After 500 BC classical Greece was often at war with Persia. By 336-323 BC Alexander the Great had overthrown the Persian empire and created a Greek empire that covered most of the area adjacent to the eastern Mediterranean and reached as far east as the Indus River.

The Roman Empire

Meanwhile in Italy north of the Tiber River, the Etruscans developed a remarkable civilization between 800-300 BC. Later the Romans absorbed these Etrusean cities into their state (Talbert, 1985:83-9). The traditional date for the founding of Rome is 753 BC, but some think it may have been as early as 850 BC (Ogilive, 1980:245). Carthage, a major competitor of Greece earlier, also challenged the rise of the Roman Empire. The struggle against Carthage, however, was long, and did not end until Rome developed a powerful fleet and, with the help of the Greek colonies in southern Italy, drove the Carthaginians out of Sicily, Sardinia, and Corsica, which the Romans annexed as provinces between 264 and 241 BC. By 14 AD the Roman Empire under Augustus Caesar controlled all the countries surrounding the Mediterranean, including Spain, France, Italy, Greece, Turkey, Palestine, and northern Africa (Ogilvie, 1980:250). The Mediterranean had become a Roman pond linking Europe, Asia, and Africa. Roman control of this area lasted for centuries, until 476 AD (Talbert, 1985:91-7).

"The early Roman Empire brought prolonged peace to the Mediterranean world. City life, fine pottery, wine drinking, appreciation of the many uses of olive oil, glass vessels, window glass, artistic bronze ware, came to regions that had not know them before. . . . Cities with characteristic structures such as markets, basilicas, baths, amphitheatres, colonnades sprang up . . ." (Liebeschuetz, 1980:257-8.) Rome was the largest European city (estimates have varied from 250,000 to one million people) until the rise of Constantinople and London. Rome, as can be seen from the ruins that have come down to us, contained paved roads, walls, gates, frescoes, mosaics, bridges, aqueducts. All are evidence of the engineering and organizational skills of the Romans (Markus, 1980: 271-2).

During the Dark Ages, from the fifth to the tenth centuries, the invasions of the Muslims separated the countries adjacent to the southern and northern shores of the sea into two ideological blocks: Christian and Muslim. The Muslims "overthrew the Persian Empire (637-644). . . . [They] took from the Byzantine Empire, in quick succession, Syria (634-636), Egypt (640-642), Africa (698), and Spain (711)." (Pirenne, 1925:15.) As these centers on the North African and Middle Eastern shores became Muslim, the Christians in Europe turned away from commerce based on the Mediterranean Sea, and focused instead on developments in the interior of the continent. The Dark Ages witnessed the decline of most of the European cities.

In the Middle Ages, during the fourteenth and fifteenth centuries, the Hanseatic League began trading actively in the area around the Baltic Sea; this development encouraged European economic activity to shift to the north. By the sixteenth century the ferment in economic, religious, and political life gave birth to the religious reformation and a new form of economic organization: capitalism (Weber, 1905). The eighteenth century witnessed the beginning of industrialization, which intensified throughout the nineteenth and twentieth centuries in Europe and ushered in the modern urban age and the metropolitan explosions of today.

Summary

We began by saying that a great agricultural revolution occurred when humans turned from gathering food to producing food. The earliest nodes of agricultural development were in the Middle East, Mesoamerica, and China about 7000 BC. Examples are the earliest Neolithic agricultural villages of Jericho and Jarmo.

The earliest cities grew out of these agricultural nodes; first in Mesopotamia (around 3500 BC), in Egypt in the Nile Valley (3200 BC), in the Indus Valley (2500 BC), and in northern China (1500 BC). After 300 BC the Maya, the Aztecs, and the Inca built urban centers in Central and South America.

Duncan stated that there were four preconditions of preindustrial urban growth that worked together: a large, dense population; a favorable environment; technology; and social organization.

Gordon Childe outlined the ten characteristics of preindustrial urbanization: permanent dense populations, nonagricultural specialized work, taxation, trade, writing, the exact sciences, works of art, monumental buildings, social stratification, and the formation of a political state. All these criteria were present in the seven earliest civilizations, except that the Inca had not developed writing.

Pirenne suggested that subsequent preindustrial western urbanization was centered around the Mediterranean. The Phoenicians were a seafaring people who began trade and colonization around the Mediterranean Sea. Athens and Greek civilization flowered in philosophy, law, architecture, literature, and art. The Greek influence was carried far and wide into the rest of Europe. The Romans organized one of the greatest empires, which not only enveloped the Mediterranean countries but also reached into most of northwestern Europe and as far north as England.

2. A World Urban Perspective

Early urban developments centered in the fertile crescent of Sumer and Egypt fanned eastwards into India and China and westwards into the Mediterranean area. With such an early start, we would expect that these preindustrial urban civilizations would be the largest and most dynamic urban areas today. However, this is not the case, because of later developments in Europe.

It was not until after 1492, when Columbus first discovered the Americas, that Europeans began to look beyond their own continent and their religious preoccupations. A series of discoveries around the 1500s culminated in Gutenberg's development of the printing press, which introduced a new form of communication. New ideas spawned religious reformation. Trade in the spices and goods from the great Asian civilizations greatly increased. European attempts to sail to Asia via the Atlantic resulted in the discovery of the two Americas and the Pacific Ocean. The new continents presented new challenges and potential for trade and for colonies. Britain and France, and later other European countries, began to settle the Americas, Australia, South Africa, and the Asian seaport rim. World-wide commerce developed: raw materials were shipped home, processed, and traded abroad. Capitalism and the Industrial Revolution spawned the factory system in England, which in turn led to increasing urbanization; both spread to other parts of Europe.

Urban Change in the World System

Daniel Chirot's (1977, 1986) works on social change within the world system can be used as a conceptual framework to discuss urban demographic changes throughout the world. Using this historically based framework, we shall trace the rise of industrialization and urbanization. Then we shall examine demography and its relationship to the development of the urban world system.

Chirot's World System

In the 1960s theories that attempted to explain problems of underdevelopment focused on the internal conditions within the undeveloped countries. It was held that these countries had outdated traditional values, antiquated political structures, and inadequate supplies of skilled labor; in addition they lacked the financial and human capital to develop their economies. Such a view places the onus for the lack of development on the individual societies, without taking into account international relationships between the developed and the developing world. But according to Daniel Chirot, there is a core of powerful states that dominate world politics to their advantage (Chirot, 1977:7).

Immanuel Wallerstein (1974) uses the term ''core societies'' for those rich, western societies that in 1900 were the centers of world power. For much of the twentieth century these core societies were the United States, the United Kingdom, Germany, and France; they were also the most heavily industrialized and urbanized societies. These ''core nations,'' along with smaller industrialized societies such as the Netherlands and Belgium, colonized almost all of Africa and huge parts of Asia. The Netherlands, Belgium, and the Scandinavian countries were ''minor core'' powers. Spain, Italy, Austria-Hungary, and Russia also had colonies, but were less industrialized, they could be seen as ''semi-peripheral'' societies. While less powerful countries such as Canada, Australia, and New Zealand were not part of the core, they were linked to the core societies of Britain and the United States.

At first these core nations controlled the capitalist world system and most of the means of production. However, since 1917 a counter-system comprised of Russia, China, and the east European countries has emerged to challenge the capitalist economic system. When Chirot was writing in 1977 and 1986, no one could have foreseen the upheavals that would take place in Russia and its eastern allies in 1990. What will happen in this communist economic network in the future is not yet clear. After the second World War, Japan opted for the capitalist system, and by 1990 became part of the core. Eastern Pacific rim Asian countries such as Korea, Taiwan, and Hong Kong seem to be going in the same direction. Where the Middle East oil-rich countries will emerge is not clear.

In 1900 four countries: Great Britain, the United States, Germany, and Russia, produced three-fourths of all of the world's manufactured goods, even though they had only one-eighth of the world's population (Chirot, 1977:24). If five minor core nations are added to these four, it can be said that 15 percent of the world's population manufactured 80 percent of the world's goods. These were the most urbanized nations, and had greater division of labor, more internal economic specialization, and smaller populations engaged in agriculture, which was highly mechanized. Their populations were also more educated and wealthier.

By 1986 Chirot (1986:iii) had decided that the Third World countries and the communist countries were not as pivotal to world social change as he had thought might be the case earlier: the changes in eastern Europe in 1990 seem to confirm that view. Chirot (1986) emphasizes the important role that the rationalization of law and religion has played in the expansion of the European core nations, and this seems to support Max Weber's contention that rationalization goes hand in hand with urbanization. Now that Japan has joined the core, Chirot (1986:244) suggests that perhaps this country may become the corporate model for the future, blending as it does the past with the present. Japanese capitalism exhibits a higher degree of group spirit, cohesion, and kinship ties in businesses and in its bureaucracies. Japanese companies show more loyalty to their workers, and there is greater communication between management and unions, which seem to have more integrated goals.

Index of Industrialization

We contend that industrialization has become a driving force for increased urbanization. We have found that a variety of industrial indicators show a close correlation with a high degree of urbanization. We would expect the core societies of northern Europe, which were at the center of the Industrial Revolution, to exhibit a high degree of industrialization. We would also expect the countries that were colonized by these core nations to be industrialized: the USA, Canada, Australia, New Zealand, and South Africa. How do the other countries of the world compare with these nations in their level of industrialization? In Table 2-1 we compare 33 or almost one-fourth of the world's countries, using nine indicators of industrialization grouped under four main factors. These 33 countries are ranked from high to low according to their level of industrialization, with Canada and the USA at the top and Afghanistan, Bangladesh, and Ethiopia at the bottom. In the first column — per capita consumption of energy — we see that the two North American countries clearly have a very high level of consumption. A second group of nine countries (mostly European) have a middling level of consumption; the remaining countries form a third group with very low levels of consumption — less than 3 percent as much as North America. This energy-consumption indicator shows that countries tend to rank by continents, with North Americans and Europeans on top and Africans at the bottom. The top consumers are "core societies" and their advanced colonies.

The next indicator of industrialization, column 2, is the Gross National Product (GNP), which represents the value of goods and services produced within each country; it is closely associated with energy consumption; the two indicators show a high degree of correlation. The third indicator, life expectancy at birth, is also connected with the first two because of the ability to use energy to produce goods and services for a safer, healthier lifestyle.

The quality of life factors, columns 4-7, are related to size of income. The wealthy countries spend a relatively low percentage (less than 20 percent) of total income on food, while families in countries that have a low average income must spend two-thirds of their total income on food, leaving little for health, shelter, education, transportation, communication, and entertainment. One-fourth to one-half of the people in the nine countries at the bottom of Table 2-1 are malnourished, and in countries such as Ethiopia and Afghanistan very few have access to safe water. These countries are mostly rural, and have only a limited access to the capital that would be necessary for industrialization and a higher standard of living.

Education is a third factor (columns 8 and 9). While almost all children and youth attend secondary schools in North America and Europe, fewer do so in South America and Asia, and less than one-fourth of the children do so in many parts of Africa and Asia.

We would expect that populations in countries with low incomes, low GNP, health problems, and poor educational facilities would also live in more crowded conditions. These indicators of industrialization show clearly that people in "core societies" have much higher standards of living than people in other countries.

Levels of Urbanization

Figure 2-1 shows the range of urbanization of the more than 150 countries of the world, based on the percentage of the population living in urban areas. We would expect from Chirot's world systems theory that industrialization and urbanization would correlate highly. To find out whether this is so, we can examine the general trend to urbanization by continent in Figure 2-1.

In Figure 2-1 we see that North America is in the highest category of urbanization, with more than 75 percent of the populations in urban centers. A majority of northwestern Europe is also in the highest category; only a few countries on this continent are in the medium range. The Australasian continent is also in the highest category. Thus we see that the north European countries, where industrialization began, and their former colonies, the USA, Canada, Australia, and New Zealand, are among the most urban areas of the world. The eastern and central European countries tend to be somewhat less urban; southern European countries are in an even lower category on the urban scale; these countries are the farthest away from northern European industrialization and Chirot's (1977, 1986) capitalist "core societies."

The Latin American countries were discovered and colonized by Spain and Portugal, two less industrialized countries of southern Europe. Latin America tends to fall into the middle range of urban levels on the whole. The countries of Oceania in the Pacific that were not colonized by Britain: New Guinea, Vanuatu, and Samoa, are at the extreme lower end.

African countries are clearly at the lowest level of urbanization, many having less than 15 percent urban population. South Africa, a former British colony where many Europeans also settled, is an exception, and the countries of northern Africa, part of the earlier Mediterranean flowering of the Roman Empire, are also more urban. But the middle African countries south of the Sahara were severely decimated by the slave trade of some European countries and some of their colonies; the African countries were exploited rather than developed.

Scale and Pace of Urbanization

In industrially developed countries where populations are now largely urban, the pace of urbanization is levelling off. Populations are still largely rural in Asia and Africa, so that we can expect an enormous explosion of cities on

Table 2.1 Selected countries rank ordered by industrialization[a] and measures of the quality of life in these countries

SELECTED COUNTRIES	PER CAPITA ENERGY CONSUMPTION[b]	GNP PER CAPITA[c]	LIFE EXPECTANCY AT BIRTH[d]	PERCENTAGE OF INCOME SPENT ON FOOD	PERCENTAGE MALNOURISHED[f]	PERCENTAGE WITH ACCESS TO SAFE WATER*	POPULATION PER PHYSICIAN	PERCENTAGE ENROLLED IN SECONDARY SCHOOLS[g]		AVERAGE NUMBER OF PERSONS PER ROOM
								BOYS	GIRLS	
Canada	288	$13 670	76	15	—	—	550	102	102	0.6
United States	280	16 400	75	13	—	—	500	95	95	0.6
Australia	180	10 840	76	17	—	—	500	92	95	0.7
USSR	176	7 400	69	—	—	—	270	77	82	1.3
West Germany	163	10 940	74	24	—	—	420	90	93	1.5
Belgium	145	8 450	73	19	—	—	370	85	87	0.6
United Kingdom	138	8 390	74	18	—	—	680	76	78	0.6
Sweden	137	11 890	77	19	—	—	410	79	88	0.7
Poland	133	2 120	71	—	—	—	550	75	80	1.4
France	114	9 550	75	19	—	—	460	84	96	1.3
Hungary	112	1 940	70	—	—	—	300	73	73	1.1
Japan	111	11 330	77	26	—	—	740	94	94	1.1
Venezuela	96	3 110	69	39	7	—	1 000	40	49	1.5
Italy	90	6 520	75	31	—	—	750	74	73	0.9
Yugoslavia	73	2 070	71	—	—	—	700	84	80	1.4
Israel	69	4 920	75	23	—	—	400	70	78	1.5
Argentina	50	2 130	70	—	2	63	—	62	69	1.4

Mexico	50	2 080	67	—	8	74	1 200	56	53	2.5
South Korea	44	2 180	67	44	4	62	1 390	94	88	2.3
Malaysia	26	2 050	67	37	—	80	3 920	53	53	2.6
Turkey	26	1 130	62	—	7	63	1 530	47	28	2.2
Brazil	19	1 640	65	—	13	76	1 300	—	—	1.1
Egypt	19	680	59	—	8	75	760	70	46	1.8
China	19	310	66	—	—	—	1 730	43	31	—
Bolivia	10	470	53	—	45	43	2 000	40	34	—
Indonesia	8	530	58	—	30	33	12 300	45	34	1.5
India	7	250	55	58	30	54	3 700	44	23	2.8
Pakistan	6	380	50	—	26	39	2 910	20	7	2.8
Kenya	3	290	54	—	30	28	10 140	22	16	2.5
Sudan	2	330	49	65	30	48	9 800	23	16	2.5
Afghanistan	2	—d	39	—	37	10	—	23	4	—
Bangladesh	2	150	50	—	38	42	9 700	26	11	—
Ethiopia	—b	110	41	—	38	6	88 120	14	8	2.7

a Measured by per capita energy consumption of 0.163 "U.N. standard" barrels of oil equivalent, 1984.

b Less than one.

c U.S. dollars, 1985. Gross National product is the total value of goods and services produced within a country during one year.

d Data not available.

e Life expectancy is the average number of years a newborn baby can expect to live given that country's current mortality rate.

f Percentage of the population below the critical minimum limit of nutrition as determined by the U.N. Food and Agricultural Organization.

g Number enrolled in school as a percentage of age group; number enrolled may be larger than total of "school-age" group due to older people enrolling as well.

* [It is assumed that where figures are not given, the majority have access to safe water.]

SOURCE: Hedley (1990:444).

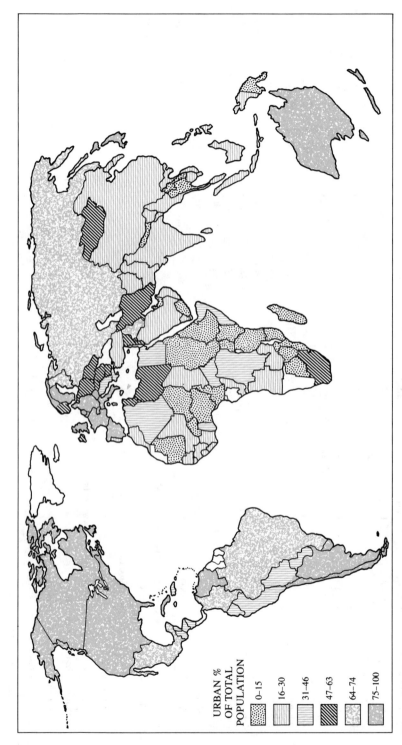

Figure 2-1 Urban population as a proportion of total population
SOURCE: World Bank (1985).

URBAN %
OF TOTAL
POPULATION

0–15

16–30

31–46

47–63

64–74

75–100

these continents. This urban explosion is also correlated with the great population increase that is occurring in these continents, which will not moderate in the near future. To provide some context for a better understanding of the rate of urbanization, we must review ideas about the demographic population transition and discuss problems related to over-urbanization.

Demographic Transition Model

The demographic transition theory has been developed on the basis of observed changes in population growth in western European societies (Coale, 1973; Stolnitz, 1964). This theory describes the three stages of change and transition that populations go through as technology and industrialization are introduced (Gee, 1986:211). The preindustrial society is in the first stage of transition. In this stage, birth rates are high and death rates are also high, so that births and deaths tend to cancel each other, preventing the population from growing. Industrialization began in the north European countries, and these were the first to enter stage two, during which new discoveries in medicine and public health helped to control diseases, resulting in a sharp decline in the death rate. Family and religious values kept the birth rate high in this stage, so the population increased substantially. However, as people moved to the cities, children were no longer an economic asset, as they had been in an agricultural, rural society, but an expense on the family budget: births dropped, so that deaths and births again were more aligned, resulting in little or no growth in stage three. During the second stage of population explosion, Europeans were fortunate to discover relatively scarcely populated continents such as the two Americas and Australia, which they colonized with their surplus population.

While the Europeans and North Americans have passed into stage three, South and Central Americans are still in stage two of population explosion. Rural migrants are flocking to their cities which have mushroomed in the past several decades. Many of these countries — Brazil, Argentina, and Mexico — have borrowed heavily to industrialize, but huge debts now force them to pay such high levels of interest that they cannot accumulate capital to build industry to compete internationally.

Many Asian countries such as China and India have entered stage two. Death rates have begun to decline dramatically with the introduction of medical technology; China has begun to force birth rates down by restricting family size. In India birth controls are much less effective, and this is also true in many other Asian countries such as Indonesia, Pakistan, Bangladesh, and southeast Asia. While their populations are exploding, their rural agricultural technology is not changing very fast, the land available for agriculture or development is severely limited, and increasingly the population can no longer be sustained on the land. Thus, many flock to the cities, which find it almost impossible to cope. Many of these Asian countries lack capital to expand their economies, and jobs are scarce, forcing many to remain unemployed. Since a majority of the migrants from the rural areas are illiterate, their opportunities for getting technical jobs are limited, and they have no means of educating their children, resulting in cycles of poverty.

Most African countries south of the Sahara are still in the first, preindustrial stage, living mostly in rural environments at subsistence level. In the meantime the Sahara Desert is expanding into agricultural areas during cycles of drought, forcing many former inhabitants to flee to the cities. Many of these countries have recently been freed from colonialism and have newly formed governments, so they lack capital, skills, and resources for development, and their cities are just beginning to tap the technology available. However, many African countries will soon enter stage two (some already have), and their populations will explode, resulting in push factors away from agriculture and pastoral communities to the attractions and pull of the city. In the city they are pressured to detribalize so as to be able to compete and live with associates from many other religions and tribes.

Longitudinal Continental Comparisons

To document the scale of urbanization over time, we need to compare urban development by continents. One of the best ways to compare world urbanization is to compare cities of 100,000 population and over. Larger cities are denser and more heterogeneous, and thus provide a better measure of the quality of urban living. Many villages in India, for example, could be as large as 20,000, but still present many rural features. Cities with a population of 100,000 or more are more typical of urban lifestyles. These cities are metropolitan centers.

The world metropolitan population has escalated, as shown in Table 2-2. Two centuries ago, in 1800, there were 16 million people in such centers — only 1.7 percent of the global population. By the middle of the twentieth century they included 314 million, or 13 percent of the world's population. Based on 1980s figures, demographers project that by the year 2000 there will be 2.7 billion people in metropolitan centers, or 42 percent of the world population. An enormous urbanization explosion has been occurring since 1950 along with the population explosion.

Metropolitanism began in industrial Europe; by 1850 there were 13 million or 5 percent living in centers of 100,000 or more. By 1950, 20 to 23 percent of the populations in Europe and North America were metropolitan, and by the year 2000 they will be levelling off at somewhat over 50 percent. However, the metropolitan explosion is occurring in South America, followed closely by countries in Asia. The population is exploding in Asian countries such as India and China, who together will contain almost half of the estimated 1990 world population of 5 billion. These masses are leaving their rural areas and moving to the cities. Some of these cities are developing their industry, which would be one factor in attracting people to urban areas, but general population growth is now an additional factor contributing to metropolitan explosion (Pannell, 1984).

Table 2.2 Population in large cities (100,000 and over) by major continental regions: 1800–2000*

AREA	1800		1850		1900		1950		2000	
	IN MILLIONS	AS % OF TOTAL POPULATION IN REGION	IN MILLIONS	AS % OF TOTAL POPULATION IN REGION	IN MILLIONS	AS % OF TOTAL POPULATION IN REGION	IN MILLIONS	AS % OF TOTAL POPULATION IN REGION	IN MILLIONS	AS % OF TOTAL POPULATION IN REGION
World	15.6	1.7	27.5	2.8	88.6	5.5	313.7	13.1	2,700	42
Asia	9.8	1.6	12.2	1.7	19.4	2.1	105.6	7.5	1,509	39
Europe	5.4	2.9	13.2	4.9	48.0	11.9	118.2	19.9	454	48
Africa	0.6	0.6	0.2	0.2	1.4	1.1	10.2	5.2	129	25
America	0.1	0.4	1.8	3.0	18.6	12.8	74.6	2.6	536	60
Oceania	—	—	—	—	1.3	21.7	5.1	39.2	16	55

*Including the U.S.S.R.

SOURCE: Davis and Hertz (1957). Table reproduced in United Nations, *Report on the World Social Situation*, including studies of urbanization in underdeveloped areas, prepared by the Bureau of Social Affairs, United Nations Secretariat, in cooperation with the International Labor Office, Food and Agriculture Organization, World Health Organization, and the United Nations Educational, Scientific, and Cultural Organization (New York: United Nations, 1957), p. 114, Table 3. The 1960 data are based on Hoyt (1962: 31, Table 3.) Data are approximately comparable with those for 1800–1950 updated for year 2000.

Populations in countries in middle Africa south of the Sahara have remained rural until recently, but with increasing problems of drought, here too people are beginning to arrive in large cities, often as refugees and squatters on the outer rims of metropolitan centers. While there were only 10 million in metropolitan centers in Africa in 1950, their numbers are rising and will continue to explode for a long time. With limited industrial development, lack of capital and resources, and heavy debts, the prospects for the metropolitan future in these middle African countries looks bleak.

Over-urbanization

Over-urbanization often occurs in developing countries where industrial technology has difficulty keeping up with natural population increase and the migration of rural populations into cities (Breeze, 1966:134). Some claim that it is a problem first of over-ruralization—populations grow so large that there is no longer land available to support the rural population, and so many leave the country in search of jobs in the city, creating an imbalance between population and resources because there are not enough jobs created by the economic system (Nagpaul, 1988:281). There are for example 600,000 agricultural villages in India, where the infant mortality rate is still 100 per 1000, literacy is less than 40 percent, malnutrition is widespread, the supply of drinking water is inadequate, electricity is lacking, and half the population live in mud huts (Nagpaul, 1988:281). India is trying to persuade people to remain in the country by undertaking rural reconstruction projects, because half of India's national income continues to come from the agricultural sector. Harley Browning (1958:117) claims that there is a high correlation between over-urbanization and over-ruralization, saying that it is important to keep people on the land by developing better agricultural technology for greater food production. There is usually a tendency to divert disproportionate shares of the nation's capital, labor, and talents to cities because they have greater political influence for obtaining resources; but this leaves the rural agricultural base unsupported.

Some attempts have been made by Davis and Hertz (1954:16-30) to measure over-urbanization. They calculate the percentage of males engaged in non-agricultural occupations as an index of industrialization, and the percentage of population in cities over 100,000 as an index of the degree of urbanization. They found that the coefficient of correlation between the two variables was .86 when calculated for a number of large cities. They found that most developing countries were over-urbanized compared to developed industrial countries. Over-urbanization occurs when the development of urban technology is inadequate to absorb the influx of rural immigrants. Similar conditions occurred when the European nations were in the process of industrializing in the nineteenth century; there were miserable living and working conditions in many British cities, for example (Gist and Fava, 1974:133).

In 1960 about one-third of North Americans lived in giant cities of one million, and 60 percent in centers of 100,000; estimates are that by the year

2000 this will have changed to 40 percent and 77 percent respectively. These changes are much more dramatic in Asia, where the population in centers of 100,000 will change from 12 percent in 1960 to 39 percent in 2000; and in cities of one million in 1960 from 6 percent to 20 percent in the year 2000. What is most interesting is that in 1960, four out of five in Asia (79 percent) lived in rural areas; by 2000 it is estimated that only one in two (50 percent) will be rural. Thirty percent of the Asian population will move to the city in 40 years, which will cause an enormous urban explosion. In Africa 85 percent were still rural in 1960, and 68 percent will remain rural by 2000. Africa is not yet urbanizing quite as fast, and a large majority are still rural, but this will likely change as the demographic transition also reaches there. Table 2-3 gives a summary of world population by urban size in 1960, 1975, and projections for 2000.

Table 2.3 World population by urban size groups: estimated 1960, and projected for years 1975 and 2000

POPULATION	1960	1975	2000	1960	1975	2000
METROPOLITAN AREAS		MILLIONS			PERCENT	
1,000,000 and over	285	496	1,285	9.6	13.0	20.5
500,000–999,000	88	181	465	3.0	4.7	7.4
300,000–499,000	66	143	355	2.2	3.7	5.7
100,000–299,000	151	257	539	5.1	6.7	8.6
Total 100,000 and over	590	1,077	2,644	19.9	28.1	42.2
Total cities and towns 2,000–99,000	413	538	772	13.9	14.1	12.3
Total urban	1,003	1,615	3,416	33.9	42.2	54.5
Total rural	1,959	2,213	2,851	66.1	57.8	45.5
WORLD TOTAL	2,962	3,828	6,267	100.0	100.0	100.0

SOURCE Hoyt (1982;50.)

Exploding Giant Cities

In early preindustrial urban development, cities remained relatively small. Populations were not large, and they did not have the transportation, communication, and sanitation facilities to cope with very large populations. Athens, the center of Greek civilization, may have had less than 100,000 people, and population estimates of Rome, the center of the Roman Empire, vary from 500,000 to a million. Large cities of a million or more began to occur only after the Industrial Revolution, when steam power became available for improved transportation, and better means of communication, improved sanitation, and the use of steel in buildings were developed. The development of multi-million giant cities has occurred mostly in the twentieth century.

Table 2.4 World's 35 largest metropoli ranked by population size (in millions), 1950–2000

RANK	METROPOLIS	1950 SIZE	METROPOLIS	1985 SIZE	METROPOLIS	2000 SIZE
1	New York/Northeastern NJ, USA	12.4	Mexico City, Mexico	18.1	Mexico City, Mexico	26.3
2	London, United Kingdom	10.4	Tokyo/Yokohama, Japan	17.2	São Paulo, Brazil	24.0
3	Shanghai, China	10.3	São Paulo, Brazil	15.9	Tokyo/Yokohama, Japan	17.1
4	Rhein-Ruhr, Federal Republic of Germany	6.9	New York/Northeastern NJ, USA	15.3	Calcutta, India	16.6
5	Tokyo/Yokohama, Japan	6.7	Shanghai, China	11.8	Greater Bombay, India	16.0
6	Beijing (Peking), China	6.7	Calcutta, India	11.0	New York/Northeastern NJ, USA	15.5
7	Paris, France	5.5	Greater Buenos Aires, Argentina	10.9	Seoul, Republic of Korea	13.5
8	Tianjin, China	5.4	Rio de Janeiro, Brazil	10.4	Shanghai, China	13.5
9	Greater Buenos Aires, Argentina	5.3	Seoul, Republic of Korea	10.2	Rio de Janeiro, Brazil	13.3
10	Chicago/Northwestern IN, USA	5.0	Greater Bombay, India	10.1	Delhi, India	13.3
11	Moscow, USSR	4.8	Los Angeles/Long Beach, CA, USA	10.0	Greater Buenos Aires, Argentina	13.2
12	Calcutta, India	4.4	London, United Kingdom	9.8	Cairo/Giza/Imbaba, Egypt	13.2
13	Los Angeles/Long Beach, CA, USA	4.1	Beijing (Peking), China	9.2	Jakarta, Indonesia	12.8
14	Osaka/Kobe, Japan	3.8	Rhein-Ruhr, Federal Republic of Germany	9.2	Baghdad, Iraq	12.8
15	Milan, Italy	3.6	Paris, France	8.9	Teheran, Iran	12.7
16	Rio de Janeiro, Brazil	3.5	Moscow, USSR	8.7	Karachi, Pakistan	12.2
17	Mexico City, Mexico	3.1	Cairo/Giza/Imbaba, Egypt	8.5	Istanbul, Turkey	11.9
18	Philadelphia/Western NJ, USA	3.0	Osaka/Kobe, Japan	8.0	Los Angeles/Long Beach, CA, USA	11.2
19	Greater Bombay, India	2.9	Jakarta, Indonesia	7.9	Dacca, Bangladesh	11.2

Table 2.4 (continued)

RANK	METROPOLIS	1950 SIZE	METROPOLIS	1985 SIZE	METROPOLIS	2000 SIZE
20	Detroit, MI, USA	2.8	Tianjin, China	7.8	Manila, Philippines	11.1
21	São Paulo, Brazil	2.8	Delhi, India	7.4	Beijing (Peking), China	10.8
22	Naples, Italy	2.8	Baghdad, Iraq	7.2	Moscow, USSR	10.1
23	Leningrad, USSR	2.6	Teheran, Iran	7.2	Bangkok/Thonburi, Thailand	9.5
24	Manchester, United Kingdom	2.5	Manila, Philippines	7.0	Tianjin, China	9.2
25	Birmingham, United Kingdom	2.5	Milan, Italy	7.0	Paris, France	9.2
26	Cairo/Giza/Imbaba, Egypt	2.5	Chicago/Northwestern IN, USA	6.8	Lima/Callao, Peru	9.1
27	Boston, MA, USA	2.3	Istanbul, Turkey	6.8	London, United Kingdom	9.1
28	Shenyang (Mukden), China	2.2	Karachi, Pakistan	6.8	Kinshasa, Zaire	8.9
29	West Berlin, Federal Republic of Germany	2.2	Lima/Callo, Peru	5.7	Rhein-Ruhr, Federal Republic of Germany	8.6
30	San Francisco/Oakland, CA, USA	2.0	Bangkok/Thonburi, Thailand	5.5	Lagos, Nigeria	8.3
31	Leeds-Bradford, United Kingdom	1.9	Madras, India	5.2	Madras, India	8.2
32	Glasgow, United Kingdom	1.9	Hong Kong, Hong Kong	5.1	Bangalore, India	8.0
33	Jakarta, Indonesia	1.8	Madrid, Spain	5.1	Osaka/Kobe, Japan	7.7
34	Hamburg, Federal Republic of Germany	1.8	Leningrad, USSR	5.1	Milan, Italy	7.5
35	Vienna, Austria	1.8	Dacca, Bangladesh	4.9	Chicago/Northwestern IN, USA	7.2

SOURCE: United Nations (1985: Table A-12.)

Explosion of Giant Metropoli

The increase in urban size and density was in its early stages in 1950 immediately after World War II. At the turn of the century, in 1900, most of the largest cities were in northern Europe, especially Britain, the heart of industrialization. Table 2-4 lists the 35 largest metropoli of the world, ranked by size. In 1950, more than one-third (thirteen) of the largest metropoli were still located in Britain, Germany, France, Italy, and European Russia (White, 1984). London was the largest metropolis for a long time, well into the first half of the twentieth century.

By 1985 London had dropped to twelfth and only four European metropoli were still listed in the top 35. Estimates show that by the year 2000 no European metropolis will rank in the top 24. Five American cities appear in the 1950 list, but by 2000 there will be only three in the top 35. In 1950 there were eight Asian cities represented in the top 35. By 1985 Tokyo/Yokohama ranked second, and over half (eighteen) of the 35 were in Asia. Obviously some new phenomena, in addition to the original industrial impetus, are influencing the growth of giant cities.

Estimates are that by the year 2000 well over half (eighteen) of the giant cities of the world will be in Asia, and only three in Europe. The center of urban growth has shifted from northern Europe to China and India, the two most populated countries, who together make up almost half of the entire world population. Asia, the largest and most populous continent, where cities in Sumer first began, is beginning to get its original momentum back again.

Whereas in 1950 only four metropoli in Latin America were among the top 35, by 1985 Mexico City was the largest giant city in the world, and estimates are that by 2000 Mexico City and Sao Paulo will be the two largest. Urban size and density are increasingly occurring in Latin America. Cairo, the north African metropolis, is the only African metropolis listed in 1950 and 1985; it moved up from twenty-sixth to seventeenth place, and will move to twelfth place in the year 2000. From the rest of Africa, only Kinshasa of Zaire and Lagos of Nigeria will rank among the top 35 in the year 2000. This is another indication that urbanization in Africa is developing more slowly.

Distribution of Giant Cities

Giant cities of one million population or more may have occurred as early as Rome two thousand years ago. What is new is that there are now more than 500 metropoli in the world, and a majority of these have developed during the last fifty years, since World War II. Mattei Dogan (1988) has arranged the giant metropoli into four categories and has plotted these cities by continent. In Table 2-5 we have summarized his research, showing the distribution by continent and by size. This Table puts the frequent misconception that most urbanization occurs in the USA and Canada into perspective.

Some continents have much larger populations than others (Asia, for example, contains more than two-thirds of the world's population). Half of the very largest metropoli (16 out of 32) are located in Asia; three-fourths (23) are located in the third world (Asia, South America, and Africa). Few of the giant metropoli of eight million or more are now located in the most industrial countries. Many of these large metropoli, such as Calcutta, Bombay, Bangalore, Madras, Shanghai, Cairo, Jakarta, Karachi, Manila, Bangkok, and Mexico City, do not have the technology needed to keep such large populations employed, housed, and fed. They do not have the industrial, transportation, and communications infra-structures to deal with their mounting problems. Millions live in slums. Increasing world over-population is turning into world over-urbanization. Almost half (25 out of 57) of the metropoli of four to seven million are also located in Asia. In Figure 2-2 we present the blizzard of 188 urban giants to illustrate this urban density (cities under 1 million are not shown).

Table 2.5 Urban populations in giant cities of the world

CONTINENTS	8 MILLION OR MORE	4–7 MILLION	2–3 MILLION	ABOUT 1 MILLION	TOTAL
Asia	16	25	52	95	188
Europe	6	8	20	78	112
North America	3	7	17	46	73
South and Latin America	5	8	10	22	45
Africa	2	9	19	40	70
TOTAL	32	57	118	281	498

SOURCE: Adapted from Dogan (1988a:30–55).

Table 2-5 shows that as yet not as many urban giants have developed in South America and Africa, but already there are a dozen more or less over four million in each of the two continents. There are 70 metropoli of over one million in Africa, and of these, the 40 with about one million will most certainly explode into much larger giants. With many African countries near the Sahara struggling with famine and drought, with relief having to come from abroad to feed their millions of refugees, the prospects for the future are not encouraging.

Effects of Urban Primacy

Wherever urban growth has accelerated, some cities in each country have grown faster than others, leading to differing prestige and influence among cities. In some regions or countries giant cities explode, leaving all others far behind and creating an imbalance even between the largest and the next largest ones. "Vienna for example, exceeds the population of Linz seven times, and Budapest is ten times as large as Miskolc, the second largest Hungarian city." (Gist and Fava, 1974:127.) Toronto and Montreal were almost the same size

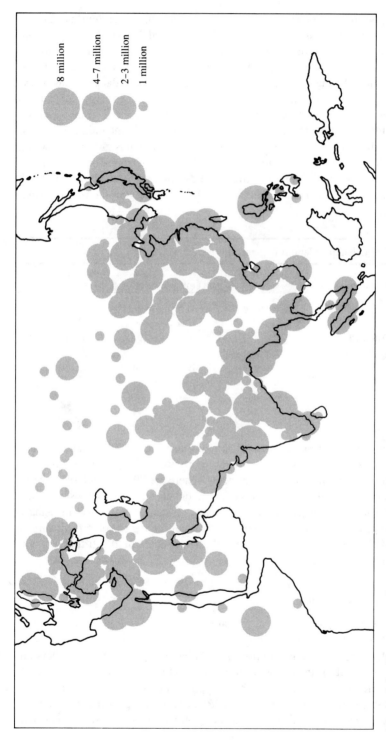

Figure 2-2 Giant metropolitan centers of one million or more located in Asia
SOURCE: Dogan and Kasarda (1988a: 39).

during the 1980s, although Toronto is now growing considerably faster. On the other hand, Winnipeg (640,000) dominates the province of Manitoba; it has 53 percent of the provincial population and it is 20 times as large as Brandon (35,000), the second largest city.

A number of methods have been devised to determine primacy ratios between cities. The simplest ratio would be between the two largest cities in a country or region: the ratio between Toronto and Montreal in 1986 would have been 1.1, while the ratio between Winnipeg and Brandon in 1986 would have been 20.0. Kingsley Davis (1969) employed a more complex method using a four-city index; he divided the population of the largest city by the combined population of the next three cities. Toronto's population of 3.4 million in 1986, divided by the combined populations of Montreal (3 million), Vancouver (1.4 million), and Edmonton (0.8 million), would result in a four-city index of 0.65. Toronto does not dominate Canada in nearly the same way as Vienna, for example, dominates Austria, especially since the populations of Toronto and Montreal have been so similar since World War II.

Cities with high primacy seem to be especially characteristic of societies in which the level of urbanization is low. Very often the capital city becomes the primate city, as Calcutta, for example, did in India before 1912. There are many exceptions to this trend, however, in more industrialized countries; consider for example the capital cities Washington, Ottawa, Canberra, and The Hague. Political capitals have advantages in that very often they include both economic and cultural features, so that such cities over time become magnets of influence and prestige. Examples are London, Paris, Vienna, Brussels, Madrid, Stockholm, Moscow, and Tokyo. These cities begin to function as national headquarters. The same is happening in developing countries, where Bangkok, Mexico City, Buenos Aires, Lima, Rangoon, Teheran, Caracas, Seoul, and Istanbul begin to overshadow their national rivals in size, economic dominance, and cultural resources. There are exceptions: Shanghai, China's primate city, had a strong economic head start, but the political influence of Beijing is growing considerably. Rio de Janeiro was the political and cultural capital of Brazil, but Brasilia is now the newly formed capital, and Sao Paulo has recently passed Rio de Janeiro in size. Delhi is now the political capital of India, but it is outdistanced in size by Calcutta and Bombay, earlier British colonial economic centers.

High primacy has both advantages and disadvantages. On the positive side, a primate city may function as a focus of national integration, making the most concentrated use of available resources. It can become a creative center of innovation, a leader that will benefit all. However, so many resources may be located in a primate city that resources are kept from the rest of the country, which may have a stifling effect. It may also act as a magnet for disproportionate loads of migrants, for which it may not always be able to find employment. It can become parasitic when a primate city receives an undue share of the national investment. To some extent this has happened in Egypt — Cairo and Alexandria have attracted most of the manufacturing, financial institutions, and communication facilities, leaving too little for the rest of the country.

Giant Primate Metropolitan Magnets

Much of our discussion in this chapter has focused on the demographic size and comparisons of urban centers. Let us now focus briefly on some of the social characteristics found in three of the largest giant metropoli in the world: Calcutta, Tokyo, and Mexico City. These metropoli are expected to have populations between 17 and 26 million by the year 2000 (Hall, 1984).

Calcutta, a Colonial Capital

Calcutta originated in 1690 as a trading center, and it was the capital of the British India Company's empire from 1772 until 1912, when the capital was moved to Delhi (Nagpaul, 1988:255-6). During the 140 years that Calcutta was a British colonial capital, it became and still is today India's chief port for international trade, the gateway to the most populated region of northeast India. "Calcutta is the world center of jute production and it has many important industries including cotton mills, tanneries, iron works, railway coach and automobile assembly plants, metal goods and manufacturing, electrical equipment, shoe factories, cement making and glass works." (Nagpaul, 1988:258.) Despite its prominence as a manufacturing and shipping port, it also is one of the most poverty-stricken centers.

Calcutta is a good example of an over-urbanized metropolis. Between 1951 and 1971 the population of Calcutta increased by 2.4 million, from 4.6 million to 7.0 million, and by 1981 it had increased by another million. Projections are that by the year 2000 there will be 16.6 million residents in Calcutta, making it the fourth most populous urban area in the world. This massive growth is a result of natural increase and in-migrations from rural villages and other cities. The rural land can no longer sustain mushrooming population growth, so many people move to the cities looking for work. Most of these migrants are destitute and are without education or marketable skills. As a result, slums filled with mostly unemployed inhabitants dependent on charity or part-time jobs have burgeoned (Gist and Fava, 1974:134). Many obtain small incomes selling rags or other things they have found picking through garbage. Some are desperate and resort to prostitution. An estimated 300,000 are homeless "street sleepers"; nearly half the families live in a single room. Many people are dependent on relatives and friends for survival, and many are forced into begging.

The economy has not been expanding rapidly enough to afford employment for all, nor have the institutions capable of providing shelter, sanitation, educational, or health and welfare services. Most institutions are burdened beyond their capacity. Still migrants continue to come by the hundreds of thousands, and there is little end in sight. In Table 2-6 we see that the same problem is occurring in nine of the other largest cities of India, in cities such as Bombay, Delhi, and Madras, which are already giant cities. What is true of Calcutta and the other Indian cities is true of many other cities in developing countries, and as they pass through the stages of demographic transition, things will only get worse.

Table 2.6 Population growth in ten largest cities — India, 1901–1981 (in millions)

CITY	1901	1931	1941	1951	1961	1971	1981
Calcutta	1.5	2.0	3.5	4.6	5.5	7.0	9.1
Bombay	0.8	1.3	1.7	2.8	4.1	6.0	8.2
Delhi	0.2	0.4	0.7	1.4	2.3	3.6	5.1
Madras	0.5	0.6	0.8	1.4	1.7	2.5	4.2
Bangalore	0.1	0.3	0.4	0.8	0.9	1.6	2.9
Ahmedabad	0.2	0.3	0.6	0.8	1.5	1.6	2.5
Hyderabad	0.4	0.4	0.7	1.8	1.2	1.8	2.5
Kanpur	0.2	0.2	0.5	0.7	0.9	1.3	1.7
Poona	0.8	0.2	0.3	0.6	0.7	0.8	1.7
Lucknow	0.2	0.3	0.4	0.5	0.7	0.8	1.0

SOURCE: Census of India and United Nations (1981); Department of Economic and Social Affairs (1983). Nagpaul (1988a:254).

Most Indian cities show a combination of Indian and European patterns. The Indian sector is congested; there is a main market place, irregular, narrow, and crowded streets, and little open space; the Indian sector contains the poorest people. The European sector has wider streets, more parks, and large homes with spacious grounds; it is undergoing enormous change. The grandeur of the public spaces and buildings of past colonial power is fading and the sectors of squatter slums have been enlarging for decades. The unemployed live in squalid squatter slums. Here the people are unskilled, and unemployment is rampant. The average annual income is estimated at $360 US in Calcutta, creating vicious cycles of poverty. Surveys show that 58 percent of the adult population are illiterate in large centers like Calcutta. Infant mortality exceeds 100 deaths per 1000 births (Nagpaul, 1988:268-9). The disparities between the rich and poor are vast and growing: 5 percent of the population command a large proportion of the wealth.

Dominique Lapierre, in his bestseller *The City of Joy* (1985), captures the suffering in the impoverished section of Calcutta. It is the heart of the poorest of the poor. Mother Teresa and her Missionaries of Charity have served in Calcutta since 1950. By 1985 the Mission had grown to 285 houses, supported by several thousand charitable foundations around the world. Her many houses provided the poorest of the poor, the destitute, and the dying with food, clothing, shelter, medicine, and above all love and hope. Calcutta is seeking to survive stage two in the demographic transition.

Tokyo, a Recent Industrial Giant

Tokyo is also located in Asia, but the contrasts between Calcutta and Tokyo are enormous. Tokyo was never dominated by a colonial power as Calcutta was. In contrast to Calcutta, the greatest slum in the world, Tokyo has no slums. While Calcutta's prominence as a world center is fading, Tokyo's is on the rise because Tokyo is the capital of a country making a successful industrial comeback after defeat in World War II. In 1985 it was the second largest giant urban area; projections are that it will remain in third place with a population of 17 million by the year 2000. Why the enormous difference between Tokyo and Calcutta?

"Tokyo, called Edo in Japan's feudal period, was the seat of the Shogun's government and in his day comprised more than one million people — the world's largest city." (Nakamura and White, 1988:223). In 1868 Japan's capital was transferred from Kyoto to Edo (renamed Tokyo), and by 1889 the city's population had reached 1.4 million; it continued to grow until World War II: it had reached over 7 million in 1940, as shown in Table 2-7. The war brought poverty, privation, and near famine, and reduced its population to less than half (3.488 million in 1945). But recovery was very fast because the Japanese accepted their defeat and proceeded to rebuild; by 1955 Tokyo exceeded its prewar size. While Japan's population was less than 40 percent urban in 1950, by 1965 it was 70 percent urban (Nakamura and White, 1988:124-5). Japan had been opened to westernization and industrialization before World War II, which made it competitive economically and a formidable industrial foe during the war. After the war it continued to be the most industrialized nation in Asia, and by the 1980s it was one of the most competitive internationally. Tokyo has been and is the center of this industrial expansion.

Table 2.7 Population of Tokyo, 1920–1980 (in thousands)

YEAR	TOKYO PREFECTURE	WARD DISTRICT
1920	3 669	3 358
1925	4 485	4 109
1930	5 409	4 987
1935	6 370	5 897
1940	7 335	6 779
1945	3 488	2 777
1950	6 278	5 385
1955	8 037	6 969
1960	9 684	8 310
1965	10 869	8 893
1970	11 408	8 841
1975	11 674	8 647
1980	11 618	8 352

SOURCE: Tokyo-to Somu-kyoku Tokei-bu Jinko Tokei-ka (1975:68–69); Japan, Prime Minister's Office, Statistics Bureau (1982c:58–59). Nakamura and White (1988b:124.)

Japan consists of a chain of islands. As a result, the Japanese are oriented towards the ocean even more than the English are. Almost all Japanese cities

are situated on the coast, partly because 70 percent of Japan's inland is moun-
tainous (Dogan, 1988:41). Eight of Japan's giant cities are located on coastal
alluvial plains. The Tokaido megalopolis along central Japan's Pacific coast
(Tokaido means "east coast road"), within which lie Tokyo, Kawasaki, Yoko-
hama, Osaka, Kyoto, Nagoya, and Kobe, contained about 60 million people
in 1985 (Dogan, 1988:42). This chain of urbanization along the center island
has been able to absorb the rural in-migration because numerous cities shared
in the influx, and their many industries and expanded economy provided jobs
for most. Japan was also twice as urbanized (40 percent) as India (20 percent)
in 1950, so the rural influx had begun much earlier. The Japanese means of
birth control were also much more effective. Japan has recently passed through
stage two of the demographic transition into stage three, while India is only
beginning stage two. Thus, Tokyo has weathered the rural influx very well,
since the influx consisted of fewer people, and the cities were also more
industrialized and able to provide jobs. That is why Tokyo has no slums, while
Calcutta is the world's largest slum.

The technology that helped to create jobs was also extended to transportation. Japan's bullet trains are the fastest in the world; they run along the
dense Tokaido megalopolis, and are used by many commuters, providing
opportunities for expansion of the suburbs. This has also slowed urban growth.
Thus, the day-time population of one city area, Chiyoda ward, is 170 times
greater than at night; in Chuo ward it is 79 times greater in day-time, and in
Minato it is 35 times greater than at night (Nakamura and White, 1988:129).
Tokyo's central business district (CBD) contains the famous Ginza shopping
district, where offices are also heavily concentrated; it is easily accessible by
rapid transit. Tokyo's commuter hinterland is the largest of any of Asia's giant
cities.

Tokyo's explosion of technology and urbanization is not without its problems, however. Tokyo's car ownership rose sharply towards the end of the
1960s, creating formidable congestion, because demands for transportation
are growing despite the excellent rapid transit system. Tokyo's position in
Japan, with over 15 percent of Japan's GNP, continues to be important despite
urban rivals elsewhere. Tokyo's workforce is concentrated in manufacturing,
wholesale and retail trade, as well as communications and services. Tokyo's
manufacturing industry is still the largest in the country, although factories
are beginning to disperse and service industries are increasingly taking their
place, as has been the case for other giant cities, New York for example.
Tokyo's dominance is clearest in commerce: it accounts for almost one-third
of all sales in Japan (Nakamura and White, 1988:134-5). Its share of retail
trade has declined, but wholesale trade has fared much better. With roughly
10 percent of Japan's population, greater Tokyo has roughly one-fourth of all
head offices, 94 percent of the offices related to the stock market, and 41
percent of the largest corporate offices.

Tokyo is the seat of the national government and is the political control
center of the nation, which gives it advantages in information services, communications, and transportation facilities. More than one-fourth of Japan's

colleges and universities and almost half of its college students are located in Tokyo. It is the main consumer of printed material, resulting in a proliferation of publishing and printing industries and writers; as well it has many musicians, actors, painters, photographers, scientists, and lawyers (Nakamura and White, 1988:137).

Since Japan is a homogeneous society (only one percent Korean and 1 or 2 percent Burakumin), Tokyo has few ethnic and racial problems. Crime is so infrequent that it is perhaps the safest giant city in the world (Nakamura and White, 1988:139-41). However, the rise of industrialization and urbanization here caused severe problems with water pollution, and Tokyo's sewer systems are still inadequate (Bestor, 1985:121-35). Land prices have soared so that housing is very expensive—twice as expensive as London and almost three times as expensive as New York. Rents and hotel prices are correspondingly high. To find cheaper housing, many commute one or two hours from Tokyo to live. A small house can easily cost five times the annual net income of a worker, so the Japanese learn to live in much smaller spaces than most North Americans and Europeans. Until recently there were very few houses more than a storey or two high because of the threat of earthquakes (Bestor, 1987). Recently stronger materials permit building up to ten or more storeys, and even skyscrapers of 30 storeys are beginning to be built. In contrast to Calcutta, Tokyo is an industrialized Asian city where jobs are plentiful and standards of modern living are rising. But it is one of the most expensive cities in the world.

Mexico City, Current Exploding Giant

If the two Asian cities of Calcutta and Tokyo fall at opposite ends of the urban quality continuum, Mexico City falls in between the two. While Mexico City ranked seventeenth among world urban giants in 1950, it escalated to first place with a population of 18.1 million in 1985, and estimates are that by 2000 its population will be 26.3 million and will still exceed that of all others. Why has Mexico City become such a giant and how is it coping compared with Calcutta and Tokyo?

The Spanish leader Cortez and a small party of soldiers first discovered the city of Tenochtitlan in 1519. The vast Aztec civilization extended over marshy islands on a 2400-m high plateau surrounded by mountains. Tenochtitlan was a thriving, beautiful city that covered the area which is now the large central square in Mexico City called the Zocalo. Here, where once Montezuma had his palace and gardens, are the old Cathedral, the National Palace, various government offices, and the National Archives. Mexico City, the largest urban giant today, was founded on one of the first urban civilizations of the New World, as we showed in chapter one. Since then the marshy lake has been filled and Mexico City built on top. Many of the buildings built almost 500 years ago by the Spaniards have sunk down some 3 m or more, creating interesting street level variations.

In 1900 Mexico City had only 344,000 inhabitants. It had grown to 1.7 million by World War II. "From 1940 to 1970 the city experienced growth rates of over 5 percent, almost doubling its population with each decade." (Schteingart, 1988:269). By 1980 its population had exploded to more than 14 million (Table 2-8), and estimates are that it will be somewhere between 26 and 30 million by the year 2000. It is also estimated that by 2000 almost one-fourth (23 percent) of the population of the country will be located in Mexico City.

Table 2.8 Concentration of population and index of primacy of Mexico City, 1900–2000 (in thousands)

YEAR	NATION	POPULATION MZMC(a)	%	PRIMACY INDEX(b)
1900	13 607.3			3.4
1910	15 160.4			3.9
1920	14 334.1			4.3
1930	16 552.6	1 263.6	7.6	5.7
1940	19 649.2	1 670.3	8.5	6.5
1950	25 779.3	2 952.2	11.4	7.2
1960	34 923.1	5 125.4	14.7	6.1
1970	48 381.1	8 882.8	18.4	6.1
1980	71 387.0	14 445.0	20.3	6.0
1990	99 669.0	21 841.7	21.9	5.6
2000	135 089.0	30 860.7	22.8	4.9

SOURCE: Garza and Schteingart (1978b); Unikel et al. (1976); MZMC data for 1980 from Centro de Estudios Economicos y Demograficos (1975).
(a) Metropolitan Zone of Mexico City.
(b) Index for Mexico City and Guadalajara.

Industrialization greatly expanded in Mexico after 1940; industrial GNP units increased from 3,180 in 1930 to 34,543 in 1975, and the GNP climbed from 3.8 percent to 29 percent of the national total; Mexico City had nearly half (45.4 percent) of the national GNP by 1975 (Steingart, 1988:269). The largest increase in employment occurred in the service sector, especially in the public sector. In the 1940s and 1950s increased borrowing of capital from abroad funded the discovery of oil and the development of industry, and these attracted many workers away from agriculture into the cities. However, this expansion of the economy slowed when the public debt rose, when oil prices dropped drastically, and when more and more profits went into servicing the national debt (Ward, 1981). The expanded public administration was politically difficult to cut, and the escalation towards greater indebtedness began to affect new-job creation. As a result, unemployment has doubled each decade since 1940, jumping to 220,000 in 1974 and rising more drastically since.

Rural-urban migration has been an important cause of urban growth in

Mexico. From 1940 to 1970, 6.2 million rural migrants moved to the city, half of them to Mexico City (Schteingart, 1988:271). With the dissolution of the Mexican peasant economy and the modernization of agriculture, thousands of people arrive in the cities in search of work. Even though economic times are now difficult, it is not possible to turn off the tap of rural migrants to the city. Many women can still find low-paying jobs in manual service, but these are increasingly fringe jobs that do not support families adequately.

In the meantime the population of Mexico City is growing and income and investment are being concentrated in the city at the expense of other regions of the country. About half of all non-agricultural activity is now located in Mexico City, and the city also absorbed about half of the national demand for industrial products and 43 percent of all durable goods. About 68 percent of the banking capital, stock and reserves are concentrated in Mexico City, as well as 42 percent of short-term loans and 93 percent of long-term loans (Schteingart, 1988:272). In addition this giant city has a large concentration of political power and of people engaged in public administration (about 35 percent of federal public employees work in Mexico City). The city is plagued by the problems of a high level of primacy.

Mexico City, unlike Tokyo, is not however a global decision-making center where one-third of the industrial decisions affect production outside the country. Very few headquarters of international companies are located in Mexico City. The city is the most dominant center in Central America, but its influence does not reach much beyond that region.

At the same time as the country is plagued by low oil prices and the accumulation and servicing of the national debt, the problems in Mexico City accelerate. Unemployment and underemployment is growing, housing is becoming scarcer, transportation facilities are becoming older and more over-loaded, and as the number of cars increase, pollution is escalating. Partly because of its location in a valley surrounded by mountains, Mexico City is now one of the most polluted areas in the world. Smoke and fumes from poorly maintained automobiles tend to settle in the valley. The Texcoco Lake bed on which the city is located has very sandy, loose, salty soil, scant vegetation, and arid eroded zones where dust can easily be whipped up. In addition, water problems add to the threat of pollution. The extensive lake system of the Valley of Mexico has disappeared, and underground springs have been over-used so that the water table has dropped about nine metres. Water costs have increased so much that Mexico City's population is drinking the world's most expensive water.

Summary

To gain a perspective on contemporary world urbanization we began by exam-ining the influence of industrialization, which has affected some countries and continents more than others. Industrialization began several centuries ago in northern Europe and has spread since to North America and the eastern Pacific rim. Industrialization is also beginning in South America and in some countries of Asia; it has affected central African countries south of the Sahara least of all. Urbanization usually accompanies industrialization. Populations of many countries in Africa are less than 20 percent urban, while in many industrialized regions of Europe and North America countries are more than 70 percent urban.

The scale and pace of urbanization also varies enormously. Industrialized populations have passed from the stage of incipient growth (with high birth and death rates) into the stage of population explosion (dropping death rates and high birth rates) followed by a third stage of population stability through low birth and death rates. However, many South American and Asian countries are in the midst of their population explosion; in these countries migrants flock to cities to find work, and over-urbanization is rampant.

The population explosion in developing countries in Asia and Latin America has spawned giant metropoli, some having over 15 million people; projections are that by the year 2000 some of these giants will have populations of more than 25 million. There are already more than 500 metropoli with over one million people, and the problems these cities face in the future is enormous. Many primate cities are absorbing the bulk of their nation's wealth like veracious monsters that cannot be satisfied. The need for capital, jobs, housing, welfare, protection, pollution control, more transportation, and investment in communications seems astronomical.

To illustrate the varied needs of our urban world, we focused on three giant metropolitan magnets: Calcutta, Tokyo, and Mexico City. Calcutta, a former colonial capital, is today the largest slum in the world, where human suffering because of over-urbanization is out of control. Tokyo on the other hand, blessed with industrial development and the latest technological innovations, and buoyed by Japan's economic development, is coping much better. Mexico City, the largest urban giant in the world, is trying to develop its economy, but is mired in debt and seems to be losing the battle to absorb the influx of millions of migrants from rural areas.

3. Canadian Urban Demography

Canadian urbanization must be seen in the larger context of North America and the world. Cities developed relatively late in Canada in this context. Let us trace the early origins of Canadian cities, the rural-urban trends over time, and the development of metropolitan centers so that we get some perspective on how urban networks in Canada have grown and where industrial dominance is concentrated.

Canadian Urban Origins

While cities began in the Old World around 3500 BC, they did not occur in the New World until about AD 300 in Mesoamerica. Agricultural developments in Mesoamerica spread north into the United States and the southern Ontario peninsula and the St. Lawrence Valley. By the time the Europeans arrived in the early sixteenth century, the Hurons and Iroquois lived in villages and cultivated the land, but their settlements did not exhibit any of the criteria of urban centers. In the rest of what is now Canada, the aboriginals were food-gathering peoples. On the West Coast the Amerindians fished extensively, and on the Prairies they hunted the buffalo. We cannot examine the historical beginnings of all 25 metropolitan centers in Canada, but we shall review samples from each region.

Colonial Maritimes: St. John's and Halifax

The Norsemen or Vikings arrived on the shores of Labrador and Newfoundland around AD 1000; there is evidence that Lief Erikson settled there briefly at what he called Vinland. Archaeologists have found remains of Norse settlements at L'Anse aux Meadows and Port au Choix on the northern tip of Newfoundland. However, as far as we know none of these Europeans remained for long.

The three metropolitan (100,000 plus population) centers in the four Maritime provinces (St. John's, Halifax, and St. John) were established primarily as bases to support the needs of European colonial powers. British and French explorers made landfall on the east coast when attempting to find a northwest passage to Asia. The discovery of coastal waters teeming with fish encouraged fishing expeditions; sometimes the fish were cured on land before the long voyage home was undertaken. Later land explorations discovered other valuable natural resources: furs and wood products.

St. John's, Newfoundland, is the oldest inhabited site in North America. Its harbour was used by European fishermen in the early 1500s. By the end of the sixteenth century a few settlers had taken permanent residence there (Nader, 1976:1). "In 1583, when Sir Humphrey Gilbert visited St. John's and formally claimed the island . . . for England, Newfoundland became the first colony of the British Empire." (Nader, 1976:2.) At that time, Gilbert noted, there were 36 fishing ships in the excellent harbour of St. John's, which is near the Grand Banks where fish were plentiful, and also was easily accessible from Europe. The English fishermen used little salt to cure their fish, and preferred to dry their catch on land, which it was easy to do in this protected harbour. "By the 1640s the number of visiting English fisherman had reached close to two thousand winter residents." (Nader, 1976:4.) The fishing captains did not encourage permanent settlers because they wanted to keep it mainly a fish drying and supply outpost. It was not until 1834 that representative government was granted Newfoundland; St. John's became the colonial capital.

St. John's was established as a colony by Europeans as a base for fishing, mining, and lumbering. The settlement was not a natural product of an indigenous agricultural base that might give rise to villages and eventually to cities. The buildings in St. John's were and still are constructed mostly of wood, the streets are the result of the random locations of various fishing interests. The city is located at the extreme east end of the island, which is comprised largely of rock and has very little agricultural hinterland. Although it is the first of all Canadian cities, it has grown very slowly. Its population of 155,000 in 1981 is dependent mostly upon the processing of natural resources; industry has hardly developed, and because the city is isolated in the extreme east of the country, transportation and connections with the rest of the country are a problem.

Halifax was founded in 1749 as a British military base to counter the French stronghold at Louisbourg (Nader, 1976:28). Earlier the French had established Port Royal in the Annapolis Valley northwest of Halifax; the British took it from the French and continued to settle it. They established Halifax on the east coast of Nova Scotia so they could more easily protect their coastal fishery. Again the area was not conducive to agriculture, and the settlers had to be supported by government grants. By 1767 there were 3,022 residents in Halifax, largely military personnel and related persons (Nader, 1976:30). By 1815 Halifax had profited from some forty years of war (out of a total of sixty-six years). The completion of the Intercolonial Railway between Montreal and Halifax in 1876 brought the city more firmly into the orbit of Montreal and Toronto. It became an important eastern seaport for Canada, especially as a port of entry for immigrants (Nader, 1976:34).

By 1900 most of the city's financial institutions had been transferred to central Canada. The Halifax economy depended on national defence during World War II; one-fourth of its residents were still in defence-related work in the 1950s and 1960s (Nader, 1976:37). Because inland ports are frozen in winter, Halifax is an important winter seaport, and in 1970 a container terminal was opened there. By 1981 its population had grown to 278,000. Halifax, like St. John's, was never an important manufacturing center. Neither St. John's nor Halifax were natural outgrowths of settler populations surrounded by an agricultural hinterland (Abdul-Karim, 1983).

New France: Quebec and Montreal

Quebec City and Montreal had very different beginnings. Both originated in New France. Here the French, not the British, dominated. Quebec City and Montreal were each founded where an Amerindian village — Stadacona and Hochelaga — was located; at each site there was land suitable for agriculture and therefore more opportunity for natural population growth. There were also similarities with St. John's and Halifax in that both cities were located on an important waterway; they were the major power centers of a European power; and they became colonial centers dominated by European interests.

Quebec City was founded in 1608 by Samuel de Champlain. It is the oldest continuously settled community in Canada (Nader, 1976:77). It is situated on a rocky promontory overlooking the St. Lawrence River, and for 150 years it became a major fortification in the French struggle for supremacy in North America. Quebec City was the earliest and largest political, commercial, and cultural center of New France, and had a population of 2000 in 1700. Today, with 576,000 residents, it is still the capital of the province of Quebec.

Quebec City was the headquarters of the major timber firms and the terminus for transatlantic shipping. In the early nineteenth century, "239 ships with a total tonnage of 42,000 were cleared in 1807; by 1808 this had increased to 334 ships and 70,000 tons; and by 1810 to 661 ships and 144,000 tons." (Nader, 1976:84.) The opening of the Erie Canal in 1825 diverted much of this shipping to New York, and the immigrants who began to settle west of Quebec City shifted the center of trade farther west to Montreal and Ontario. Although it is not the fastest growing city, Quebec City is one of the most "old-European-like" tourist centers in Canada today.

Montreal began as a mission colony of Ville-Marie in 1642 (Nader, 1976:118). In 1535 Jacques Cartier had discovered the large Huron village of Hochelaga at the base of Mount Royal; its population may have numbered as many as 3500, although when Samuel de Champlain first arrived in 1603 there was no trace of the settlement. Hochelaga in 1535 seemed already to be an important fur-trading terminus operated by Indians (Sancton, 1983:58-62). Located at the confluence of the St. Lawrence and Ottawa rivers, Montreal became an important fur-trading center; from here the *coureurs de bois* were outfitted to trade for furs with the Amerindians in the western interior, and here they returned to sell the furs. Famous explorers such as LaSalle, Jolliet, Marquette, and LaVerendrye set out from Montreal, and by 1650 it had replaced Quebec City as the market for furs (Nader, 1976:119). The fur trade expanded along the Great Lakes and Mississippi waterways, and Montreal became the most influential and important center for the fur-trading network in North America. The fur trade was controlled by two companies, the North West Company and the British Hudson's Bay Company; these two companies increasingly came into conflict with each other as they expanded westwards. By 1821 the two companies had amalgamated; the fur trade was diverted through Hudson's Bay, and Montreal ceased to be an important fur-trading center.

Canada's first bank, the Bank of Montreal, was established in 1817; because of the capital accumulated from the fur trade, Montreal became the largest and most important center for capital and business (Nader, 1976:123-4). The opening of the Erie and Welland canals diverted more business to New York, but manufacturing expanded in the later 1800s (Sancton, 1983:58-65). In 1870, 65 percent of central Canada's banking institutions had their headquarters in Montreal; increasingly it also became dominant in manufacturing and transportation as the headquarters for the CNR, the CPR, and Air Canada were located there (Nader, 1976:129-31). Expo 1967 symbolized the dominant position of Montreal as Canada's largest metropolis, a position it had held for more than 300 years. However, by 1981 the population of Toronto surpassed that of Montreal. The urban center of influence had again shifted farther west as immigration to the West increased.

Upper Canada: Toronto and Ottawa

Toronto is now the largest metropolitan center in Canada; by the 1980s it had a population of well over three million. In contrast to the Maritime and Quebec regions, which have been developing for more than 350 years, southern Ontario has developed only during the last 200 years (Magnusson, 1983:94-7). The French used the northerly Ottawa River route for their fur trade; the fur-trade forts established in the Toronto region in the early 1700s were of less importance than those in the north. However in 1792 Toronto (York) was selected as the provisional capital of Upper Canada (Nader, 1976:193); in 1800 the population of York was only 403 (Nader, 1976:193); by 1820 Kingston was still the largest urban center of Upper Canada both in population (2,336 versus York's 1,240) and in commercial importance (Nader, 1976:194). The north-south trade with the Americans increasingly favored Toronto, which was more strategically located than Kingston (Darroch, 1983:381-410). By 1831 Toronto had outstripped Kingston, and in 1867 Toronto became the capital of the newly created province of Ontario.

Toronto had a large hinterland suitable for agriculture, and this later supported natural population growth. The Northern, Great Western, and Grand Trunk railroad systems soon gave a boost to Toronto's development, as did its fine position as a port on the Great Lakes (Magnusson, 1983:94-9). Manufacturing was not of great importance at first, but agricultural machinery companies such as Massey Harris located in the city in 1879. After 1890 other types of manufacturing expanded greatly. The Toronto Stock Exchange was incorporated in 1878 (Nader, 1976:200). The rich mineral deposits north of Toronto provided opportunities for mining. Agriculture, manufacturing, and mining, with the facilities provided by a lake and canal port at the hub of a rail network, contributed to Toronto's population growth. While the city, with a population of 31,000 in 1851, ranked third behind Montreal (80,000) and Quebec City (46,000), by 1901 Toronto, with a population of 271,000, ranked second after Montreal (392,000). In 1941, at the beginning of World War II, Toronto still had less than one million population, but by 1981 its three million residents constituted the largest metropolis in Canada.

Ottawa-Hull, Canada's national capital, began later and, although it has not grown as fast, has become Ontario's second largest city. In 1810 there were only about 150 people within the Ottawa area, almost all of them on the Hull side (Nader, 1976:165). The 200-km Rideau Canal from Kingston to Ottawa was completed in 1832; Ottawa was named Bytown after Colonel By, who was in charge of building the canal (Nader, 1976:165). Bytown was best known for its saw mills and lumbering. In 1855 it was incorporated as a city and its name was changed to Ottawa, a variant of the Indian name *Outaouais*, meaning "meeting of the rivers." (Nader, 1976:166). In 1878 Queen Victoria chose Ottawa, on the border of Ontario and Quebec, as the capital for the united Province of Canada because it was a safe distance from the American border (Andrew, 1983:140-7). At this time there were only about 10,000 residents in Ottawa. By 1981 Ottawa-Hull had become the fourth largest metropolis in Canada, with a population of 718,000.

Ottawa-Hull was located in the forestry area and had a limited agricultural base; its major role as the capital has been to carry out the functions of government. It is the most bilingual metropolis in Canada, and has large populations of both francophones and anglophones (Andrew, 1983:147-60). In 1969 the federal government decided to relocate additional federal employees in central Hull, so that the metropolis and its federal buildings are now located substantially on both sides of the Ottawa River in Canada's two most populous provinces, Ontario (largely anglophone) and Quebec (largely francophone).

The West: Winnipeg, Edmonton, Vancouver

Winnipeg is located at the confluence of the Red and Assiniboine rivers in the narrow 160-km corridor between the American border and Lake Winnipeg. Winnipeg was the gateway to the West. The French fur traders first established Fort Rouge at the forks of the two rivers in 1738, later followed by Fort Gibralter, built by the North West Company. Fort Garry, center of the Hudson's Bay Company's fur trade, was built on the same site (Artibise, 1977:1-20). Because the West was isolated from eastern Canada by the enormous 2000-km stretch of the rocky Canadian Shield, trade routes south from Winnipeg into Minnesota and the Dakotas were established in the early 1800s. In 1869 the Hudson's Bay Company sold its vast western territories to the federal government; Manitoba became a province in 1870. Thereafter, European immigrants planning to settle on agricultural land in the West were funnelled through Winnipeg, which was incorporated as a city in 1874. Eastern businesses opened branches in Winnipeg, and the city became a wholesale servicing center for the western agricultural expansion (Kiernan and Walker, 1983:222-5). The Canadian Pacific Railway in 1881 built a station, shops, and freight sheds and yards in the city, facilitating western agricultural expansion and making Winnipeg the dominant center of the West (Artibise, 1977:9-19).

Between 1900 and 1914 the city grew very quickly, from a population of 49,000 in 1901 to become the fourth largest metropolis in Canada by 1941 with a population of 302,000 (Bellan, 1978:1025). Two new transcontinental railways (the Canadian Northern and the Grand Trunk) were built between 1900 and 1915, and both routed their main lines through Winnipeg; they also located their major freight terminals and repair shops in the city (Nader, 1976:271). Winnipeg's control of transportation enabled it to dominate the grain trade and the economy of the prairie region. The Winnipeg Stock Exchange was founded in 1903. Manufacturing, which started by providing the equipment needed by agriculture and the railways, has now expanded into clothing, furniture, printing and publishing, metal fabricating, and machinery.

Edmonton's history began with the establishment on Sturgeon Creek by the North West Company of a fur trading post, Fort Augustus, in 1794. The Hudson's Bay Company built Fort Edmonton on the North Saskatchewan River about 30 km away in 1795. (Nader, 1976:354.) Both were destroyed by Amerindians; later Fort Edmonton was rebuilt at the present-day site of Edmonton. The settlement soon became a North West Mounted Police post, from which the police kept order in the vast fur-trading West. When Alberta became a province in 1905, Edmonton was selected as the provincial capital and the site of the University of Alberta. In 1901 Edmonton's population was only 2,626, but by 1916 there were 53,846 people; in 1941 (Lightbody, 1983:255-62), Edmonton's population of 125,000 was less than half as large as Winnipeg's, but in 1981 it became the fifth largest metropolis in Canada with a population of 657,000, the largest on the Prairies.

The discovery of oil at the Leduc oil field escalated urban growth in Alberta; Edmonton and Calgary have been the fastest growing cities in Canada for the last three decades. Crude oil production in Alberta increased from six million barrels in 1947 to 497 million in 1974, and natural gas production increased from 53 to 2,080 billion cubic feet (Nader, 176:360). Since Edmonton's economy is not as diversified as Winnipeg's, the slump in oil revenues in the 1980s hit hard, but there has been a gradual recovery. Calgary has experienced a similar period of expansion and growth followed by a decline. Calgary became the headquarters for many oil companies, while Edmonton, being closer to the oil fields, became more of an outfitting center for the oil industry (Stone, 1990:45-9).

Vancouver, in its magnificent setting of mountains, rivers, forests and the sea, is Canada's major seaport on the Pacific coast. Its mild winters, large parks, bathing beaches, nearby skiing slopes, and its cosmopolitanism contributed by its Asian peoples, all add to its attractions. In 1792 Captain George Vancouver visited the site of Vancouver, and later whites came during the Fraser River gold rush in 1856-7 (Nader, 1976:378). The first settlement, Granville, began in 1862. When the Canadian Pacific Railway line was completed in 1885, Coal Harbour was selected as the terminus and in 1886 was renamed Vancouver (Roy, 1980:11-16). By 1901 Vancouver had grown to 29,000 people; it and the rest of the West were firmly within the influence of Winnipeg (Gutslein, 1983:189-96).

The opening of the Panama Canal in 1914 changed Vancouver's role. Supplies could now reach Vancouver more easily by boat than by rail via Winnipeg. Vancouver's population exceeded that of Winnipeg by 1921, and the city became the most important metropolis of the West. By 1981 it had become the third largest metropolis in Canada, with 1,268,200 people (Hardwick, 1974:1-24). Vancouver, the largest port on the west coast of North America, has specialized as a bulk-export center of wheat, one of the major exports from the Prairies. Earlier Victoria was the largest urban center in British Columbia and became the provincial capital. But soon Vancouver's advantage of being on the mainland offset Victoria's advantage as the center of provincial power. The University of British Columbia is located in Vancouver (Gutslein, 1983:190-4). The Fraser Valley hinterland has also been an important boost to the economy of these two metropoli.

Urban Population Shifts

Our historical survey of urban populations began with the earliest centers in the Maritimes and then moved to the West as immigrants moved westwards. In Table 3-1 we have plotted eight urban centers and their populations. In 1851 Montreal (80,000) and Quebec City (46,000) were clearly the largest. By 1981 Toronto had become the largest urban center in Canada. However, Quebec City declined steadily, so that by 1981 it ranked eighth. Montreal is still clearly the dominant center in Quebec. Three Maritime centers ranked fourth, fifth, and sixth in 1851. Since then all three have declined in rank, Saint John fading fastest; Halifax is still in thirteenth place in 1981, and is the major metropolis in the Maritimes.

Three Ontario urban centers appear in the top eight in 1851. While Toronto has become the largest in Canada, Hamilton has remained in the top ten, and Kingston has never reached metropolitan (100,000) status. There were no urban centers ranked west of Toronto in 1851. By 1901 almost half (seven) of the sixteen largest urban centers were in Ontario, which illustrates the shift westwards into Ontario. By 1981 ten of the largest 24 metropolitan centers were still located in Ontario, and four ranked in the top ten.

By 1901 two out of sixteen of the largest urban centers were in the West. However, by 1941 Vancouver and Winnipeg ranked third and fourth, and four western cities ranked in the top ten. Vancouver held third place into the 1980s,

Table 3.1 Population shifts in the Canadian urban system

1851	1901	1941	1981	RANK BY POPULATION
MONTREAL (79.7)*	Montreal (392.1)	Montreal (1193.2)	Toronto (2999.9)	1
QUEBEC (45.5)	Toronto (270.9)	Toronto (865.7)	Montreal (2828.3)	2
TORONTO (30.8)	Quebec (88.6)	Vancouver (338.3)	Vancouver (1268.2)	3
ST. JOHN's (30.5)	OTTAWA (85.3)	Winnipeg (302.0)	Ottawa-Hull (718.0)	4
SAINT JOHN (23.7)	Hamilton (83.3)	Hamilton (224.7)	Edmonton (657.0)	5
HALIFAX (20.7)	LONDON (51.6)	Ottawa (208.9)	Calgary (592.7)	6
HAMILTON (17.6)	Saint John (51.2)	Quebec (196.7)	Winnipeg (584.8)	7
KINGSTON (11.6)	Halifax (51.0)	Windsor (128.6)	Quebec (576.1)	8
	WINNIPEG (48.5)	EDMONTON (124.9)	Hamilton (542.1)	9
	VANCOUVER (43.4)	CALGARY (111.6)	St. Catharines (304.4)	10
	St. John's (40.0)	Halifax (98.6)	Kitchener-Waterloo (287.8)	11
		London (97.2)	London (283.7)	12
	KITCHENER (36.0)		Halifax (277.7)	13
	SYDNEY-GLACE BAY (35.7)	Sydney-Glace Bay (96.7)	Windsor (246.1)	14
	VICTORIA (23.5)	Kitchener (82.8)	Victoria (233.5)	15
	WINDSOR (22.4)	Victoria (81.0)	Regina (164.3)	16
	Kingston (19.8)	Saint John (70.9)	St. John's (154.8)	17
		St. John's (60.9)	Oshawa (154.2)	18
		REGINA (58.8)	Saskatoon (154.2)	19
		THUNDER BAY (56.3)	Sudbury (149.9)	20
		TROIS RIVIERES (56.3)	CHICOUTIMI-JONQUIERE (135.2)	21
			Thunder Bay (121.4)	22
			Saint John (114.0)	23
			Trois-Rivières (111.5)	24

*Population in thousands (000).

SOURCE: Census of Canada for various years, using the 1961 spatial definition of a census metropolitan area.

but Winnipeg dropped from fourth to seventh place, while Edmonton and Calgary have taken fifth and sixth places. While Winnipeg was the gateway to the West in the first half of the nineteenth century, Vancouver became the major Canadian seaport on the west coast, and Edmonton and Calgary grew faster than any other Canadian city for three or four decades in the twentieth century because of the oil boom. The largest urban concentration in 1990 is clearly located in Ontario. To what extent it may shift farther west is uncertain. Southern Ontario is at present the industrial urban center, and it will most likely remain the major urban heartland for a long time to come. Canada has become an urban system with competing centers of power; these require further elaboration.

The Canadian Urban System

A review of Canadian metropolitan centers shows that there is a vast network of cities spread across the nation, varying in size and degree of power and influence, in a variety of locations, and which over time have not all been equally competitive. In chapter two we discussed Chirot's (Chirot, 1977, 1986) world systems theory and the concept of "core societies" applied to nations. This concept of core entities may also be applied to urban centers within a single nation. In Canada there seem to be large, dominant metropoli such as Toronto and Montreal, and "minor core" urban centers such as Ottawa and Vancouver. Other, smaller metropoli take their place outwards towards the periphery according to factors such as size, growth patterns, strategic location, and various other factors; small cities, towns, and villages are increasingly distant from the core.

Let us discuss Canada as a system of cities. We must clarify what is urban and what is rural by introducing the definitions that are in use in Canada. Our review of selected cities shows that growth rates have varied over time and by region, so first we need to gain some sense of what the larger urban system looks like.

A Canadian System of Cities

James Simmons (1974, 1983a, 1983b) has developed a theory of Canada as an urban ecological and political system with a network of urban nodes that are highly interrelated and interdependent. Earlier scholars such as Bourne (1975), Bourne and MacKinnon (1972), and Berry (1964) were the first to research urban systems; Simmons has tried to develop their ideas further using Canadian data. The urban system involves a complex form of ecological and social organization that has a number of levels; an individual city and its rural hinterland; a group of cities in a region; and all the cities within a country, which together combine to make up a national system (Burke, 1990b:38). Thus each region will have its dominant city; Halifax in the Maritimes; Montreal in Quebec; Toronto in Ontario; first Winnipeg and then Vancouver in the West (Hedley, 1990: Hooper et al, 1983). These cities in turn are part of the national complex; in Canada for many years Montreal was the dominant urban center; more recently it is Toronto.

Simmons (1983a, 1983b) has suggested that cities in Canada need to be studied more carefully so that we can better understand the range of relationships between cities of different sizes and functions. Data on the characteristics of cities, their patterns of growth, how they are integrated into the national system, and the pattern of city linkages are needed. Can growth be predicted on the basis of the function of a city or its place in such a system? Economic, political, and social activities must be plotted and compared with national and international urban centers of influence.

There are clearly urban subsystems within the larger national network, such as the Windsor-Quebec urban axis, which includes the two largest centers, Toronto and Montreal, and comprises a heartland of cities in the form of an urban belt (Yeates, 1980). This subsystem, according to McGahan, contains an area of almost 27 000 km^2, more than 1800 municipalities, half of Canada's total population, and much of its manufacturing employment (McGahan, 1986:69). Lesser urban axes, such as the Edmonton-Calgary corridor and the Vancouver-Victoria strait are clearly emerging in the West. The Alberta corridor is fueled by the oil industry. In contrast, the West Coast urban strait has thrived on shipping as the window to the Asian Pacific rim. Let us look more clearly at some of the elements of urban systems, beginning with urban definitions and rates of urban growth.

Industrial Urban Definitions

In Louis Wirth's (1938) classic essay "Urbanism as a Way of Life," he suggested that three criteria: size, density, and heterogeneity, should be used in discussing industrial urbanization. Shevky and Bell (1955:7-8) developed this into a schematic version that we present in Table 3-2.

With respect to *size*, Wirth suggests that beyond a certain size, human relations in a community change. Using Wirth's work, Eshref Shevky and Wendell Bell (1955:7-12) contend that as the number of people in a community increase, there is a greater range of interaction, but the intensity of interaction declines because it is not possible to interact with 1000 or 2500 people as intensely as with a small group or with family members. The urban person becomes dependent upon a greater number of people and less upon particular people. As urban size increases, secondary contacts also increase.

Density reinforces size in producing diversification and more complex social structures. Differentiation and specialization separate home and work, and segregate urban functions so that the city becomes a mosaic of social worlds.

When peoples of many origins move to the same city, *heterogeneity* of occupations, social status, ethnic and racial origin, religions, and values converge in the same space. Thus, common backgrounds, values, ethical standards, and controls and norms are harder to establish. Urbanites expect greater diversity, accept it more readily, and live in close proximity to many with whom they have little in common. Mass educational, recreational, and cultural services are required, and politicians must often appeal to these diverse masses on the basis of the least common denominator.

Table 3-2 Louis Wirth's sociological definition of the city

A SCHEMATIC VERSION

SIZE An increase in the number of inhabitants of a settlement beyond a certain limit brings about changes in the relations of people and changes in the character of the community	Greater the number of people interacting, greater the potential differentiation
	Dependence upon a greater number of people, lesser dependence on particular persons
	Association with more people, knowledge of a smaller proportion, and of these, less intimate knowledge
	More secondary rather than primary contacts; that is, increase in contacts which are face to face, yet impersonal, superficial, transitory, and segmental
	More freedom from the personal and emotional control of intimate groups
	Association in a large number of groups, no individual allegiance to a single group
DENSITY Reinforces the effect of size in diversifying people and their activities, and in increasing the structural complexity of the society	Tendency to differentiation and specialization
	Separation of residence from work place
	Functional specialization of areas — segregation of functions
	Segregation of people: city becomes a mosaic of social worlds
HETEROGENEITY Cities products of migration of peoples of diverse origin Heterogeneity of origin matched by heterogeneity of occupations Differentiation and specialization reinforces heterogeneity	Without common background and common activities premium is placed on visual recognition: the uniform becomes symbolic of the role
	No common set of values, no common ethical system to sustain them: money tends to become measure of all things for which there are no common standards
	Formal controls as opposed to informal controls. Necessity for adhering to predictable routines. Clock and the traffic signal symbolic of the basis of the social order
	Economic basis: mass production of goods, possible only with the standardization of processes and products
	Standardization of goods and facilities in terms of the average
	Adjustment of educational, recreational, and cultural services to mass requirements
	In politics success of mass appeals — growth of mass movements

SOURCE: Shevky and Bell (1955:7–8.)

It is difficult to apply these three urban criteria. Size is usually used as the most accessible criterion, but it is difficult to decide what the dividing line between urban and rural should be. The assumption is that density and heterogeneity will follow when the population grows beyond a certain size, provided that the population is within a compact area. The Canadian census has used 1000 population or more as the criterion that defines an urban settlement; in the USA 2500 or more is considered urban. Countries do not agree on the criterion for urban size, so that world urban census data are often not comparable. Canadian census definitions also make distinctions between rural farm and rural non-farm, as well as various fringe populations adjacent to urban areas but not necessarily within the incorporated boundaries of cities. When we discuss urban ecology in Part II, we will discuss some of these problems of definition.

National Rural-Urban Growth Rates

While the urban population has grown steadily during the past 100 years, rural populations have declined (Burke, 1990:50-51). In 1851 only 13.1 percent of the population of Canada was urban, living in centers of 1000 population or more (Stone, 1967:16). Shortly after confederation (1871) the urban population had grown to 18.3 percent urban (Figure 3-1). Canada was indeed a land of "drawers of water and hewers of wood." By 1901 roughly one-third (34.9 percent) of Canadians were urban, and by 1931 over half (52.5 percent) lived in centers of 1000 or more. The Depression, which began after the 1929 economic crash, practically halted urban expansion, so that growth between 1931 and 1941 (52.5 to 55.7 percent) was very small (Cross and Kealey,

Figure 3-1 Percentage of Canadian urban population, 1871 to 1991

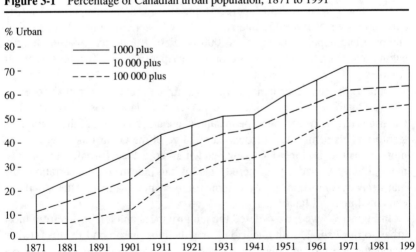

SOURCE: Statistics Canada (1984b: Chart 1, pp. 3, 15); 1991 projections made on the basis of the 1986 data in Mitchell (1989: 22.)

1985:11-17). However, World War II accelerated industrial expansion, and in the next several decades urbanization increased greatly. By 1971 three-fourths (76.6 percent) of all Canadians lived in cities of 1000 or more. Since then urban growth has been relatively dormant.

Since the Canadian census criterion for the definition of an urban settlement — 1000 population size or more — is very low, we have also plotted in Figure 3-1 the percentage of Canadians living in centers of 10,000 or more as well as metropolitan centers of 100,000 or more. In 1851 only about 10 percent lived in centers of 10,000 or more, and there were no metropolitan centers of 100,000 in Canada (Mitchell, 1989:13-17). By 1901 more than one-fourth lived in centers of 10,000, but only 12 percent lived in metropoli of 100,000 or more. At the beginning of World War II (1941) roughly one-half lived in cities of 10,000 and about one-third lived in a metropolis of 100,000 or more; by 1991 the proportions were two-thirds and well over half respectively (Mitchell, 1990:19-24). Thus, using different criteria for urban definition provides us with the assurance that we are indeed talking about greater urban density and complexity—the other two criteria that Wirth considered essential for definition of urban settlement.

Rates of Urban Growth by Region

Growth rates have varied considerably by region in Canada. One reason is that urbanization began much earlier in eastern Canada. However, other factors, such as where cities are located with respect to the Toronto-Montreal center, are also important. Some regions of Canada are much more urban than others. Although 76.5 percent of all Canadians are urban, three regions of Canada are more rural than urban. Two-thirds (61.9 percent) of Prince Edward Islanders are rural, and over half (53.7 percent) in the Northwest Territories and in New Brunswick (50.6 percent) are also rural (Figure 3-2). The first two regions each have only one small city: Charlottetown and Yellowknife, and both had populations under 25,000 in 1986. Rural areas, based on agriculture and natural resources, are on the periphery of the Toronto-Montreal complex.

Ontario, on the other hand, is the most urban region: more than four out of five Ontarians live in cities (82.6 percent). In fact, most of those urban Ontarians live in the southeast peninsula, in about ten percent of the province's territory. This peninsula, surrounded by three of the Great Lakes, is also the most industrial region of Canada, and it is here that Toronto, the largest metropolis of Canada, is centered. This urban-industrial concentration, the industrial dynamo that runs the industrial-urban Canadian system, will be examined in detail later.

In Figure 3-3 we have ordered the ten provinces and territories from most urban to most rural, with Ontario clearly the most urban and Prince Edward Island the most rural. Four provinces, the two central and the two most westerly, (Ontario, Quebec, British Columbia, and Alberta) were more urban

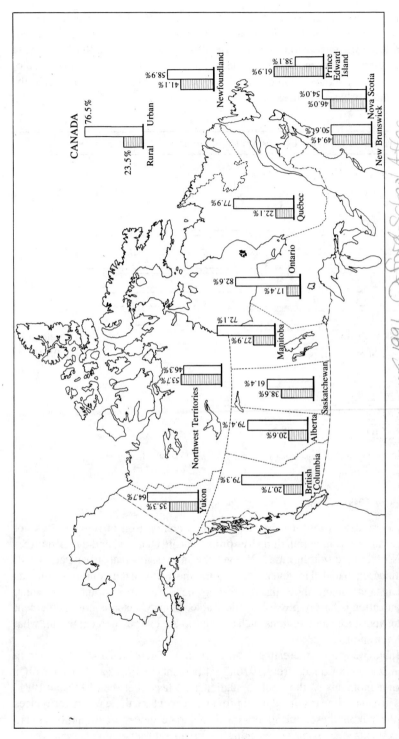

Figure 3-2 Distribution of rural and urban populations by province, 1986

SOURCE: Statistics Canada (1984a). Reproduced by permission of the Ministry of Supply and Services Canada; Mitchell (1989: 23).

than the Canadian average of 76.5 percent in 1986; the other eight are less urban than the average. Note that the Maritimes and Northwest Territories tend to be the most rural. The Prairies (except Alberta) and the Yukon tend to rank in between. Interestingly, the six largest metropolitan centers (Toronto, Montreal, Vancouver, Ottawa-Hull, Edmonton, Calgary) are located in the four most urban provinces.

Figure 3-3   Rank order by urbanization of provinces and territories, 1986

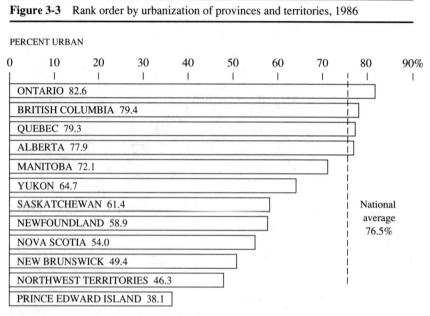

SOURCE: Statistics Canada, *Urban Growth in Canada* (1984a:8); Mitchell (1989: 23).

Rates of Urban Growth

A general discussion of urban trends and a comparison of regions does not show variations in population size, proportionate changes, and detailed directions of change within cities. We get the impression that urbanization will continue unabated. However, some of the most urbanized countries, such as Britain and Japan, show that there may be a saturation point after which urbanization is hardly possible or desirable. Since Canada is now 76 percent urban and since some regions such as Ontario are over 80 percent urban, what does the future hold?

Table 3-3 shows interesting detailed figures. There was a slight decline in urbanization in Canada from 1976 (76.4 percent) to 1981 (75.7 percent). Or to put it another way, the rural population grew faster between 1976 and 1981. This urban decline occurred in all provinces except the three prairie provinces and the Yukon; these four regions continued to become more urban. It appears that Canada may soon be reaching an urban saturation point, or with the downturn in the economy in the latter seventies, more people may have tried

Table 3-3 Percentage change of Canadian rural and urban populations, 1976–1981

	1976[1]		1981		PERCENTAGE CHANGE 1976–81
CANADA	22 992 604	(100.0)	24 343 181	(100.0)	5.9
urban	17 566 196	(76.4)	18 435 927	(75.7)	5.0
rural	5 426 408	(23.6)	5 907 254	(24.3)	8.9
NEWFOUNDLAND	557 725	(100.0)	567 681	(100.0)	1.8
urban	331 504	(59.4)	332 898	(58.6)	0.4
rural	226 221	(40.6)	234 783	(41.4)	3.8
PRINCE EDWARD ISLAND	118 229	(100.0)	122 506	(100.0)	3.6
urban	46 346	(39.2)	44 515	(36.3)	−4.0
rural	71 883	(60.8)	77 991	(63.7)	8.5
NOVA SCOTIA	828 571	(100.0)	847 442	(100.0)	2.3
urban	468 155	(56.6)	466 842	(55.1)	−0.3
rural	360 416	(43.4)	380 600	(44.9)	5.6
NEW BRUNSWICK	677 250	(100.0)	696 403	(100.0)	2.8
urban	362 479	(53.5)	353 220	(50.7)	−2.6
rural	314 771	(46.5)	343 183	(49.3)	9.0
QUÉBEC	6 234 445	(100.0)	6 438 403	(100.0)	3.3
urban	4 966 316	(79.6)	4 993 839	(77.5)	0.6
rural	1 268 129	(20.4)	1 444 564	(22.5)	13.9
ONTARIO	8 264 465	(100.0)	8 625 107	(100.0)	4.4
urban	6 771 309	(81.9)	7 047 032	(81.7)	4.1
rural	1 493 156	(18.1)	1 578 075	(18.3)	5.7
MANITOBA	1 021 506	(100.0)	1 026 241	(100.0)	0.5
urban	726 253	(71.1)	730 659	(71.2)	0.6
rural	295 253	(28.9)	295 582	(28.8)	0.1
SASKATCHEWAN	921 323	(100.0)	968 313	(100.0)	5.1
urban	514 627	(55.9)	563 166	(58.2)	9.4
rural	406 696	(44.1)	405 147	(41.8)	−0.4
ALBERTA	1 838 037	(100.0)	2 237 724	(100.0)	21.7
urban	1 393 486	(75.8)	1 727 545	(77.2)	24.0
rural	444 551	(24.2)	510 179	(22.8)	14.8
BRITISH COLUMBIA	2 466 608	(100.0)	2 744 467	(100.0)	11.3
urban	1 951 247	(79.1)	2 139 412	(78.0)	9.6
rural	515 361	(20.9)	605 055	(22.0)	17.4
YUKON	21 836	(100.0)	23 153	(100.0)	6.0
urban	13 311	(61.0)	14 814	(64.0)	11.3
rural	8 525	(39.0)	8 339	(36.0)	−2.2
NORTHWEST TERRITORIES	42 609	(100.0)	45 741	(100.0)	7.4
urban	21 163	(49.7)	21 985	(48.1)	3.9
rural	21 446	(50.3)	23 756	(51.9)	10.8

[1]*Based on 1981 area and definition.*
The figures in brackets represent the population count as a percentage of the total population.

SOURCE: Statistics Canada (1982:6). Reproduced by permission of the Minister of Supply and Services Canada.

to find jobs in the country, or at least to live in rural areas (Burke, 1990a:50-1). The 1986 data confirm this downward trend in urbanization in Nova Scotia (55 to 54 percent) and New Brunswick (51 to 50 percent), while three provinces remained the same from 1981 to 1986 (Newfoundland, Quebec, Ontario). Three provinces became more urban by one percent between 1981 and 1986, and urban Saskatchewan grew by three percent (58 to 61 percent) in these five years.

We also note that Prince Edward Island and the Northwest Territories, which are still the most rural, together comprise less than one percent of Canada's entire population. On the other hand, Ontario, the most urban region, contains more than one-third of the total population of Canada; its population is mostly located in one-tenth of the area of that province, in the southeastern peninsula. It is clear that the twelve regions vary in spatial extent and demographic size; the urban, industrial, dense population concentration is clearly located around Toronto and southern Ontario, confirming Chirot's (1977, 1986), Berry's (1964), and Bourne's (1975) hypotheses.

Metropolitan Canada

Comparisons of metropolitan populations are useful because such large urban concentrations assure us that we are also working with Wirth's other two criteria: density and heterogeneity. Let us look first at the larger continental metropolitan scene and then explore the variations within Canada.

Continental Metropolitanism

Our discussion so far has illustrated how several European powers influenced the development of urban centers in the east, and how the opening of canals diverted trade to the eastern United States and to Vancouver on the west coast. So far we have not discussed the influence of the American urban complex on Canada, something that Canadians are always keenly aware of. Former Prime Minister Pierre Trudeau commented that Canada is like a mouse sleeping next to an elephant, aware of every twitch the giant makes.

Figure 3-4 shows the metropolitan centers of one million or more (more than 0.5 million) in North America. There are nine centers of over half a million in Canada, and 65 in the United States. If numbers and concentrations of large urban centers are viewed as power centers, then we clearly see that Canada's nine compared with the 65 in the United States clearly resemble a mouse next to an elephant (and the elephant is not sleeping either)! The American influence often felt by Canadians is clearly illustrated in the dominance of American urbanism on the continent. Canadian metropolitan centers are part of this urban continental web, and must compete within it.

Almost half of these urban metropolitan giants are located in the northeastern and midwestern United States, near where five of Canada's largest nine metropolitan centers are. Thus, Toronto, Montreal, Ottawa-Hull, Ham-

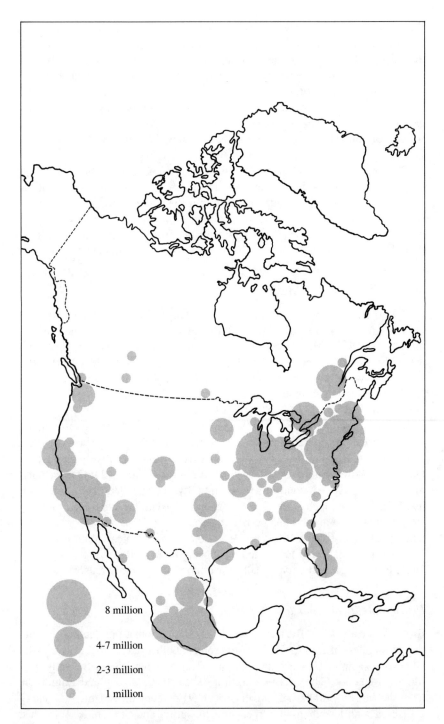

Figure 3-4 Metropolitan centers of one million or more in North America
SOURCE: Dogan and Kasarda (1988: backcover).

ilton, and Quebec City must compete with New York and Chicago, which are much larger and part of a gigantic metropolitan network. Originally Montreal extended its fur trade dominance well into American territory, but now it is only on the fringes of the northeastern North American metropolitan network. Toronto, part of the largest Canadian industrial heartland in southern Ontario, nevertheless has to compete with the larger American midwestern and northeastern complexes. The free trade agreement has thrown the doors open more widely for competition. It remains to be seen how Toronto and Montreal will fare.

The smaller metropoli in the Canadian west (Vancouver, Edmonton, Calgary, and Winnipeg) have relatively little American western competition nearby, so that there is considerable room for them to expand their influence, especially in oil and natural resources; however the West is relatively sparsely populated, and this factor may reduce their opportunities. The situations just described may explain Ontario's dislike of Alberta's openness to free trade.

Metropolitan Areas in Canada

In 1901 there were only four centers larger than 100,000 population, two in Quebec and two in Ontario (Table 3-4). None of these had reached half a million. By 1941, there were ten metropolitan centers; and two had reached the million mark. There were no metropolitan areas in the Maritimes. By 1986 there were 25 metropolitan areas, almost half of them in Ontario. In 1986, 15,183,000 Canadians lived in 25 centers of 100,000 and over (Mitchell, 1989:25-8).

It is interesting to observe that the rate of growth of Canada's metropolitan centers varied considerably. In the Maritimes Halifax grew quickly between 1941 and 1961; Saint John and St. John's have grown relatively slowly. In Quebec, Montreal also grew after World War II (1941 to 1961); Quebec City grew more slowly; Chicoutimi's population exploded between 1961 and 1971 but did not grow much after 1971. In Ontario Toronto has continued to grow steadily and more quickly than other centers. In the West, Winnipeg's population exploded between 1901 and 1921; Vancouver has grown more quickly since 1921. Calgary and Edmonton have been the fastest growing cities since 1941. Rates of growth vary, usually for important economic reasons.

Urban Mobility in Canada

Birth and death rates affect the growth of urban populations, and so too do migration rates. In Table 3-5 we present some mobility data that help to explain why, for example, Calgary and Edmonton have grown so fast recently and Montreal has not. The first two columns show that Calgary and Edmonton have the largest number of movers (over 60 percent moved in five years) compared with less than 40 percent in Chicoutimi and St. John's. Why this enormous difference? There seem to be push and pull factors operating.

Table 3.4 Metropolitan development in Canada, 1901–1986[a]

METROPOLITAN AREAS	YEAR OF INCORPORATION	1901	1921	1941	1961	1971	1981	1986
St. John's	1888				91	132	155	162
Halifax	1841	51	75	99	184	223	278	296
Saint John	1785	51	61	71	96	107	114	121
Chicoutimi-Jonquière						43	134	158
Sherbrooke							111	130
Trois-Rivières								158
Quebec	1832	117	158	241	383	480	576	603
Montreal	1832	415	796	1 216	2 156	2 743	2 828	2 921
Ottawa-Hull	1855	103	168	236	430	453	718	819
Oshawa							154	204
Toronto	1834	303	686	1 002	1 824	2 628	2 999	3 427
Hamilton	1846	79	154	207	359	499	542	557
St. Catharines-Niagara					95	303	304	343
Kitchener-Waterloo	1912	53	75	99	155	227	288	311
London	1855	52	74	97	181	286	284	342
Windsor	1892	22	66	129	193	259	246	254
Sudbury	1930	16	43	81	111	155	150	149
Thunder Bay					91	112	121	122
Winnipeg	1873	48	229	302	476	540	585	625
Regina	1903				112	141	164	187
Saskatoon	1906				95	127	154	201
Calgary	1893	8	78	136	279	403	593	671
Edmonton	1904	15	84	136	338	496	657	785
Vancouver	1886		224	394	790	1 082	1 268	1 381
Victoria	1862		64	86	154	196	233	256
CANADA CMA POPULATION						11 725	13 924	15 183
PERCENT						57%	58%	60%

[a]Figures represent population in thousands.

SOURCE: *1986 Census of Canada*. Data Collected from all Households. Summary Tabulations, Census of Population Areas (CMAs), 1987.

Table 3.5 Mobility status of population (5 years and over) by metropolitan areas, 1976–1981 (percentages)

CMA	NON-MOVERS	MOVERS	IN-MIGRANTS		OUT-MIGRANTS		NET INTERNAL MIGRATION[a] 1976–1981
			FROM SAME PROVINCE	FROM DIFFERENT PROVINCE	TO SAME PROVINCE	TO DIFFERENT PROVINCE	
Calgary	34.9	65.1	19.8	80.2	48.3	51.7	+66 460
Chicoutimi-Jonquière	61.5	38.5	95.6	4.4	89.7	10.3	−3 005
Edmonton	38.8	61.2	29.1	70.9	55.8	44.2	+34 975
Halifax	50.2	49.8	33.0	67.0	31.5	68.5	−4 755
Hamilton	55.9	44.1	79.2	20.8	73.1	27.0	−3 230
Kitchener	50.1	49.9	82.2	17.8	74.1	25.9	−1 585
London	48.4	51.6	82.5	17.5	72.8	27.2	−1 930
Montreal	49.7	50.3	78.0	22.0	44.6	55.4	−105 585
Oshawa	48.0	52.0	89.4	10.6	80.6	19.4	+9 300
Ottawa-Hull	48.7	51.3	52.9	47.1	51.7	48.3	−8 010
Quebec	55.6	44.4	91.4	8.6	83.3	16.7	−1 290
Regina	47.4	52.6	53.0	47.0	46.5	53.5	+1 780
Saint John	52.6	47.4	44.5	55.5	42.3	57.6	−2 725
Saskatoon	43.0	57.0	55.5	44.5	47.4	52.6	+7 770
St. Catharines-Niagara	59.3	40.7	77.1	22.9	72.1	27.9	−5 495
St. John's	60.3	39.7	56.0	44.0	39.1	60.9	−3 065
Sudbury	58.2	41.8	85.9	14.1	72.6	27.4	−12 805
Thunder Bay	56.6	43.4	71.5	28.5	47.0	53.0	−935
Toronto	50.0	50.0	58.9	41.1	63.1	36.9	−18 240
Trois-Rivières	56.0	44.0	96.8	3.2	94.3	5.7	−460
Vancouver	45.7	54.3	35.8	64.2	63.2	36.8	+18 825
Victoria	44.8	55.2	43.5	56.5	64.9	35.1	+8 725
Windsor	58.1	41.9	84.7	15.3	72.8	27.2	−12 290
Winnipeg	51.8	48.2	40.4	59.6	25.6	74.4	−22 975

[a](From Different Province) − (To Different Province) = (Net Internal Migration, 1976–1981).

SOURCE: 1981 Census; catalogue 10-137, table 3. Reproduced by permission of the Ministry of Supply and Services Canada.

Columns 3 and 4 of Table 3-5 show that Calgary and Edmonton drew the largest numbers of in-migrants from other provinces, largely because of the oil boom. The three Quebec cities drew most of their in-migrants from Quebec province. French Quebekers in these core French areas presumably did not want to work outside Quebec. Thus economic and cultural factors may affect willingness to move. The last column shows that Calgary and Edmonton gained many more in-migrants from other provinces than they lost to other provinces; Montreal lost many more to other provinces. Because of turmoil related to the French language, many (especially English-speaking Montrealers) left Montreal. This factor helps to explain why Montreal has increasingly fallen behind Toronto's growth. Trends, of course, change, so that a look at the 1981 to 1986 period shows that Alberta's drawing power declined during the oil slump.

Primary Metropolitan Dominance

In the previous section we began by examining Canada's place in the metropolitan network of North America. In this section we need to examine the pattern of metropolitan dominance in Canada. Industrial power, socio-economic influence, and the economic roles of metropolitan centers affect metropolitan dominance.

Industrial Power

Manufacturing is a key factor in modern industrial urban power. Figure 3-5 shows the distribution of the labor force engaged in manufacturing in 1986. As expected, it is obvious that Toronto and Montreal have the largest number of Canadians employed in manufacturing. Not only does Toronto have the largest population and the most workers in manufacturing, but it is surrounded by numerous other industrial metropolitan centers, which form a network of urban power unmatched elsewhere in Canada. The metropolitan corridor begins with Windsor in the southwest, runs through London, Kitchener-Waterloo, St. Catharines, Hamilton, Oshawa, Ottawa-Hull, Montreal, Trois-Rivières, and is anchored in the northeast by Quebec City; half the metropolitan centers of Canada lie within this strip. A look at Figure 3-5 shows the extent of industrial dominance in central Canada. The Atlantic and western urban wings pale in light of this massive accumulation of urban power.

To illustrate further Toronto's and Montreal's dominance, Figure 3-6 shows that one-half of the urban population of Canada lives in Toronto, Montreal, and Vancouver, with the other half in the other 22 metropolitan centers. Both demographically and industrially, Toronto and Montreal dominate Canada. Because of Toronto's strategic location in industrial southern Ontario, and because it attracts most of the immigrants from abroad as well as from other parts of Canada, it will increasingly become the dominant metropolis in Canada.

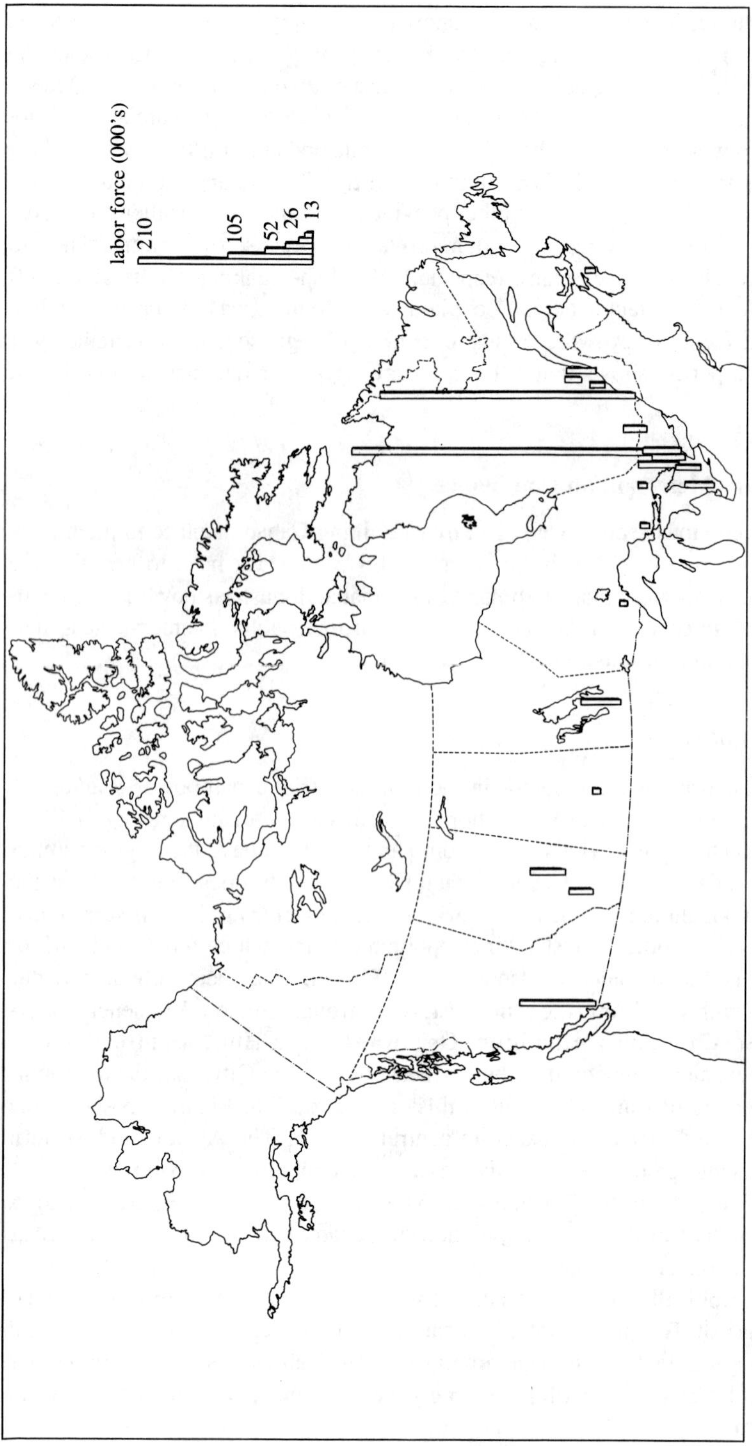

Figure 3-5 The distribution of the labor force in manufacturing, 1986
SOURCE: Statistics Canada (1989).

Urban Socio-Economic Influence

Occupation is one indicator of socio-economic status, income and education are also usually considered as indicators. In Table 3-6 we see that Toronto and Montreal rank third and thirteenth respectively in average household income; Calgary and Edmonton rank first and second. While the two largest metropolitan centers dominate Canadian manufacturing, the two fastest growing have higher average household incomes. Alberta's power, derived from its oil and gas resources, has been felt in Canada for several decades now, and it will likely increase. The smaller metropoli all tend to have considerably lower average household incomes; both their small populations and their low incomes reflect their lack of influence.

Table 3.6 Education and income levels, CMAs, 1981

POPULATION 15 YEARS AND OVER	% LESS THAN GRADE 9	% UNIVERSITY WITH DEGREE	AVERAGE HOUSEHOLD INCOME
Toronto	16.2	11.6	$28 765
Montreal	23.7	9.1	24 038
Vancouver	11.9	10.4	27 688
Ottawa-Hull	13.2	15.1	27 179
Edmonton	10.8	11.5	28 887
Calgary	8.1	13.2	30 597
Winnipeg	16.1	9.6	23 206
Québec	20.8	9.9	24 511
Hamilton	17.4	7.9	25 549
St. Catharines-Niagara	19.7	6.0	23 311
Kitchener	18.4	8.5	24 330
London	13.1	11.0	23 679
Halifax	12.8	12.1	23 807
Windsor	18.6	7.6	23 773
Victoria	9.3	10.6	24 212
Regina	14.0	9.6	25 828
St. John's	18.5	8.4	24 989
Oshawa	14.1	5.5	26 620
Saskatoon	13.6	11.3	23 956
Sudbury	21.3	6.3	23 764
Chicoutimi-Jonquière	21.1	6.2	22 960
Thunder Bay	18.9	6.8	26 165
Saint John	19.7	6.7	22 948
Trois-Rivières	24.9	7.0	20 652

SOURCE: 1981 Census. Reproduced by permission of the Ministry of Supply and Services Canada.

Education is usually important for higher-paying and professional jobs. Quebec's four metropoli are among the bottom five in education levels, with

Figure 3-6   Ratios of populations of giant metropolitan centers to all other metropolitan centers in Canada, 1986

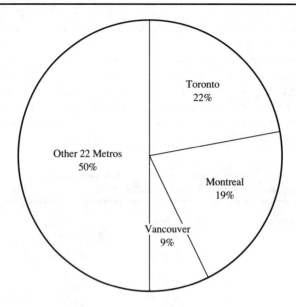

20 to 25 percent of their population having less than grade nine education.
Ottawa-Hull, Calgary, Halifax, Toronto, and Edmonton have the highest number with university degrees, which shows that different metropolitan centers
do seem to play different functions in Canada. Ottawa-Hull has a concentration
of political expertise; Calgary and Edmonton have specialists in the oil
industry.

Urban Economic Roles

Our discussion so far has suggested that the various Canadian cities may play
different economic roles. Can we plot their specializations in a way that will
help to understand their roles? In Figure 3-7 we have plotted cities that tend
to concentrate on one of three urban economic roles: 1) resource exploitation
industries; 2) trade, services, and finance; and 3) other special activities such
as transport, public service, or defence. We note that the larger metropolitan
centers: Toronto, Montreal, and Vancouver, all tend to be in the middle of the
diagram, which means that they are diversified and provide all three of these
clusters of services.

    Many eastern towns and cities, such as Oshawa, Welland, Timmins, and
Sudbury, tend to specialize in resource exploitation and industry. Then there
are special service centers, such as Ottawa in federal government, Halifax in
the military, and Thunder Bay in wheat shipping, that fall into the special

Figure 3-7 Economic roles of Canadian cities

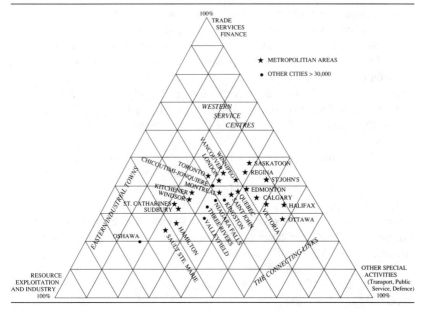

SOURCE: Statistics Canada, *Census of Canada;* Simmons (1974: 73).

activities corner, opposite the eastern industrial cities. Saskatoon, Regina, Edmonton, and Calgary are engaged in special trade and services related to the wheat industry or the oil industry. Figure 3-7 does confirm that while some of the larger metropolitan centers have diversified into a full range of economic activities, smaller urban centers in the various regions have specialized in resource exploitation, industry, trade, finance, transport, or defence.

Summary

We began a discussion of Canadian urban origins by focusing on the history of urban development in four regions. The first European landings occurred at St. John's when fishing expeditions from several countries fished off the shores of Newfoundland and began using its harbours for drying fish. Halifax became one of the first British military strongholds. Quebec City and Montreal were important settlements of New France; Quebec City has since become the capital of the province. Montreal became the hub of the Northwest Company's fur trade and held the dominant metropolitan position in Canada until recently. Toronto emerged as the major center in Upper Canada, and has now become the largest metropolis in Canada. Ottawa has become Canada's capital. As the Canadian population expanded westwards, Winnipeg became the gateway to the West; later Vancouver on the Pacific coast emerged as the third ιt metropolis, and Edmonton has become Alberta's oil capital. Over the 100 years numerous urban shifts have resulted in some cities becoming ε dominant and others declining in influence.

Size, density, and heterogeneity are usually used as criteria for the definition of "urban." Canada defines urban as a concentration of 1000 or more people. Since 1871, when only about ten percent of Canada's population was urban, the urban population has grown to three-fourths of the total population, and well over half are located in metropolitan centers of 100,000 or more. The distribution of this urban population varies enormously; Ontario is the most urban, the Northwest Territories and Prince Edward Island the least urban. Rates of urban growth also vary over time.

The 24 metropolitan centers of 100,000 or more in Canada are clearly part of a much larger North American network, and have to compete with urban industrial power in the USA. Toronto and Montreal are the dominant metropoli in Canada, representing almost half of the entire metropolitan population. Toronto especially has become an attractive industrial magnet, but centers like Calgary and Edmonton have grown even faster because people have been attracted by the Alberta oil industry.

Toronto is clearly the industrial manufacturing core of southern Ontario, where one-third of Canada's metropolitan centers are located. Urban centers in central Canada have engaged in resource exploitation and industry, western urban centers have developed trade and services, and other centers such as Ottawa, Halifax, and Thunder Bay have developed specialized roles in public service, defence, or transportation. Canada has a diverse urban network, with central Canada dominant in economic and political power, while the western and eastern wings follow trends set by the metropolitan giants of Toronto and Montreal.

4. The Ecological Approach

In part one we discussed the four preconditions for urban growth: size and density of population; a favorable ecological environment; technology; and social organization; all of these are interrelated. We also discussed the first of the four elements of the ecological system — population size. In part two we shall focus on urban ecology, the second element of the urban system. (Organization and technology will be discussed in parts three and four.) This ecological focus became the major focus of early urban studies in the United States. Numerous urban sociologists have followed the urban ecological approach.

Urban populations exist in specific locations that include climate, topography, and the natural environment with its natural resources. This natural environment was subject to geological change, and may still be subject to natural disasters, all of which shape the space used by humans. Location and available space may affect the size and density of a population. The city is one way in which people, by using technology and social organization, adjust to their environment.

Human Ecology

"Everything is connected to everything else. This is the basic principle of ecology whether it is applied to plant ecology, animal ecology, environmental ecology or urban ecology." (Commoner, 1971:39.) Ecologists describe and analyze interdependence among the various elements of an environment. Urban ecology deals with human relationships in the city; human ecology looks at human interrelationships in a larger context. Much of the sociological literature on human ecology is concerned with the distribution in space of people and institutions. More recently, human ecology has also increasingly looked at the cultural, racial, ethnic, economic, and political relationships among individuals and groups.

Early Ecological Beginnings

Human ecology is based on three main sources: plant and animal ecology, geography, and sociological studies of the spatial distribution of social phenomena. The first source stemmed from biological writings of the late nineteenth century—the works of Darwin and his followers, and of the plant and animal ecologists (Theodorson, 1982:3). Early sociologists were carrying out studies on the spatial distribution of social problems: in France on the distribution of crime, suicide, and other social phenomena (Elmer, 1933:8-10); on crime in England in the nineteenth century (Levin and Lindesmith, 1933:801-16). It was only at the Chicago School in 1921 that Park and Burgess introduced their term "human ecology" when they attempted to apply the basic ideas of plant and animal ecology to the study of human communities. Robert Park (1936:1-15), in his classical article on human ecology, began to set up a conceptual framework. This gave rise to studies in the 1920s and 1930s that led to development of classical human ecology as it is described today.

Changing Approaches to Ecology

According to this classical framework, people are in competition and struggle for space. However, human social interdependence and the division of labor requires considerable co-operation among people as well, so that there is a need for competitive co-operation at both the biotic and cultural levels (Theodorson, 1982:4).

> The biotic level involves basic, non-thoughtful adjustments made in the struggle for existence. This level is regarded as subsocial and is based on the organization of symbiotic relationships. The struggle for existence, based on competitive co-operation, and resulting in the organization of the biotic level of society, also determines the spatial distribution of persons. . . . The cultural level, based on communication and consensus, is seen as a superstructure resting upon the biotic level. The biotic level is referred to as community, and the cultural level as society.

Severe criticisms of the classical school were begun in the late 1930s by Milla Alihan (1938:81-91), who had difficulties with the biotic and cultural distinctions. Paul Hatt (1946:423-7) continued his criticism of the Chicago school in the 1940s, saying that the concept of natural areas did not apply to his study in Seattle, and A.B. Hollingshead (1947:194-204) also wanted a broader definition of ecology, linking spatial and cultural elements of ecology (Theodorson, 1982:5). By the 1950s the distinction between the biotic and the cultural levels was no longer accepted.

By the sixties, "neo-orthodox" and "sociocultural" versions of ecology vied with each other in attempts to define the field; the first was a new version of traditional ecology, and the second increasingly involved social and cultural values as their primary explanatory thrust (Theodorson, 1982:5). Amos Hawley (1944, 1955) tried to reconcile conflicting conceptions of neo-orthodox and sociocultural approaches, and he has now emerged as one of the leading urban ecologists. Hawley rejects the cultural and biotic distinctions and considers them all social, suggesting that nonspatial aspects of social organization are also within the scope of human ecology.

More recently Leo Schnore, Otis Duncan, Walter Firey, Gideon Sjoberg, and many others have modified and developed the field of human ecology. Schnore (1958:620-34) argues that ecological theory can be linked to Durkheim's conception of social morphology concerned with the social organization of a population and its environment, bringing in population characteristics. Otis Duncan (1961:140-9), concerned to connect population (P), environment (E), social organization (O), and technology (T), developed his ecological complex, which he labelled POET. Walter Firey (1945:140-8) probed the connections between symbolism and ecological variables, enlarging the sociocultural discussion to symbolic interactionism. Recently, Walter Firey and Gideon Sjoberg (1982:150-64) discussed neo-orthodox and sociocultural ecologists, suggesting that the neo-orthodox tend to look more for quantitative and the latter more for qualitative research.

The Chicago School

Urban ecology has been developed over the past sixty years by American sociologists, and the Chicago School has become famous for its urban ecological work. The University of Chicago opened the first Department of Sociology in North America before the turn of the century, and the city of Chicago soon became its social laboratory. Four of the sociologists working in Chicago became particularly noted for their work in urban ecology. Robert Park expounded the idea of natural areas within the city; Robert McKenzie investigated urban mobility; Ernest Burgess is well known for introducing the concept of concentric patterns of urban growth; Louis Wirth studied the urban way of life.

Concentrations of Natural Areas

Robert Park, who established the first urban studies center in the United States and served as the first president of the Chicago Urban League, had an unbounded fascination with the city. In his classic article, "The City: Suggestions for the Investigation in the Urban Environment" of 1916, he argued that the city was a social organism with distinct constituent parts; this idea led to his concept of "natural areas."

> Every great city has its racial colonies, like the Chinatowns of San Francisco and New York, the Little Sicily of Chicago, and the various other less pronounced types. In addition to these, most cities have their segregated vice districts . . . their rendezvous for criminals of various sorts. Every large city has its occupational suburbs, like the stockyards in Chicago, and its residential enclaves, like Brookline in Boston, the so-called 'Gold Coast' in Chicago, Greenwich Village in New York, each of which has the size and character of a completely separate town, village or city, except that its population is a select one. (Park: 1967:10.)

Park looked for cohesive sub-communities within the city, and he encouraged many of his students to study various components of the city such as the slums, the suburbs, various ethnic communities, and areas where elite groups resided. Chicago became the laboratory for these studies of ecological areas, and books that became classics grew out of these studies. Park based his ideals on concepts developed earlier by other sociologists. 1) Like Weber, Park saw the modern city as a commercial structure that sprang out of the market place; 2) like Durkheim, he found that division of labor, driven by industrial competition, was important; and 3) with Toennies, he thought that this dominance of the market economy would result in the erosion of traditional ways of life (Spates and Macionis, 1987:112-13).

Like Toennies, who saw the forces of disorganization in the city everywhere, Park recognized these forces as problems, but unlike Toennies, he also saw them as having the potential for greater human freedom, variety, and tolerance. Park also felt that "most if not all cultural changes in society will be correlated with changes in its territorial organization, and every change in the territorial and occupational distribution of the population will effect changes in the existing culture." (Park, 1952:14.) Thomlinson (1969:9) says "an intimate congruity between the social order and physical space, between social and physical distance, between social equality and residential proximity is the crucial hypothetical framework supporting urban ecological theories."

When people live together in spaces or "natural areas," as Park called them, there are forces such as competition, dominance, invasion, and succession in operation (Michelson, 1976:8). People compete to get a fair share of the available space. Some gain more influence and power, and then dominate others who are unable to hold on to their share of the available space. It is similar to hogs at the feeding trough: the runts get crowded out and are increasingly left with less food as time passes. In addition to these changing relationships within the area, outsiders move into the space as invaders, and others, moving out of one area and invading new areas, are succeeded by others moving into their former space. Many of Park's students and colleagues devoted themselves to applying this model to real situations in the city, especially Chicago (Persons, 1987).

The Chicago School has been very influential in the development of urban sociology; classical human ecology and its links to theories in the biological sciences has had its followers, but also its critics. The sociocultural school of urban sociology has been most critical of classical human ecology. Sociocultural scholars think that early human ecology theories overemphasized economic factors and ignored sociopsychological variables. Walter Firey (45:140-8), in his land-use study of central Boston, pointed out that valuable land near the central business district remained in use for non-economic purposes such as parks and cemeteries, as for example the 40-acre Boston Commons in the heart of downtown Boston. Other areas were also never developed commercially, such as Beacon Hill, a largely upper class residential area near the center of Boston. Firey thought that sentiment and symbolism played important parts in city development. Later sociologists, such as Amos Hawley, Otis Dudley Duncan, and Leo Schnore, see merits in the classical human ecology framework, but also take into consideration sociocultural variables. William Michelson (1976:3-32) suggests that social variables have received too much attention and that again the physical environment should receive more emphasis.

Ecological Processes of Change

Roderick McKenzie, a student and colleague of Park, examined the complexity of ecological change. McKenzie separated the ecological factors into four areas:

> 1) *Geographical*, which includes climatic, topographic and resource conditions; 2) *economic*, which comprises a wide range and variety of phenomena such as the nature and organization of local industries, occupational distribution, and standard of living of the population; 3) *cultural* and *technical*, which include, in addition to the prevailing condition of the arts, the moral attitudes and taboos that are effective in the distribution of population and services; 4) *political* and *administrative measures*, such as tariff, immigration laws, and rules governing public utilities. (1968:23)

These four categories considerably enlarged the boundaries of urban ecology, and took it beyond its base in biological ecology, which McKenzie thought Park had relied on too heavily. The geographical category recognized spatial and environmental factors, while the economic, cultural, and political categories enlarged the human factor considerably. McKenzie (1968:23) also stressed that economic activity would vary within a city, different ethnic or cultural groups would also congregate together in different areas within the city, and centres of political power (or the lack of them) would also vary within an urban area.

McKenzie suggested that the five processes of concentration, centralization, segregation, invasion, and succession all contributed to different human spatial arrangements.

Concentration refers to groups of people or activities that tend to concentrate in some parts of the city more than in others. Low-income groups would find cheaper affordable housing in older sections of the city, while the well-to-do would concentrate in newer, more expensive areas. "McKenzie argued in addition, that an important concomitant of such a process is the development of territorial specialization through existing transportation and communication facilities" (McGahan, 1986:29).

Centralization implies that each city has a center, and that other parts are less central. A city's age would be a factor in the development of a center: business begins in a small way in the center, and as the city grows, new businesses are started. Growth is affected by transportation facilities. The location of harbors for boats along rivers or lakes, stations for the railroads that appeared roughly a hundred years ago, and more recently bus services and bus depots, all are related to the spatial development of cities, because industry and factories locate where the transportation is, and vice versa. Thus businesses, transportation, and residential housing are located according to needs such as access to shopping, transportation, and other services. These services, McKenzie suggested, tend to be centralized for more easy access, giving cities urban centers.

Segregation refers to the tendency of various groups of people to live together in a specific area separately from other groups. Ethnic and racial groups often tend to be segregated. Segregation may be voluntary, as with the Chinese in Chinatowns, or Jews living around a synagogue. Or it may be involuntary, as with Blacks in many North American cities because they may not be permitted to live in certain areas. Segregation implies that there is a high concentration in one area of a specific group, and that the group develops a community with its own language and culture and with distinct institutions.

Invasion. While the three processes of concentration, centralization, and segregation have to do with the spatial location of populations, the last two processes focus on flow into and out of urban spaces. When an important group tends to mold and dominate a space, such as Italians in a "Little Sicily," Chinese in a "Chinatown," or Blacks in a "Blackbelt," we think of these as "natural areas" as Park saw them. When individuals of other groups enter such "natural areas" or spaces in considerable numbers, bringing with them their own values, cultures, and institutions, they are seen as invading the area. Also business sections of a city often invade old housing areas and replace them.

Succession takes place when a new group invades an ethnic "natural area" and replaces it or "succeeds" it. Some areas within a city may have gone through a series of such replacements, particularly if a group becomes upwardly mobile and moves out to another, better area. Many of the Jews who came to Montreal, Toronto, and Winnipeg at the turn of the century were from relatively poor *shtetls* in eastern Europe. Several generations later, they have moved out to the suburbs to live in improved circumstances, taking their synagogues with them. Business areas often succeed slum areas when owners remove the housing and sell the land to new businesses. McKenzie suggested that all five of these ecological processes are in operation as changes in spatial areas occur.

Predicting Patterns of Growth

Park's concept of "natural area" and McKenzie's description of the five processes of ecological change naturally call for some attempt at predicting how these various areas will change and in which direction.

Ernest Burgess (1967) picked up on McKenzie's concentration and centralization processes and used them to predict urban growth, using Chicago as his model. Burgess said the city began with the core business district in its center. Other functional areas of the city, such as residential areas, grow outwards from the centre each year in concentric circles like the growth rings of a tree. Burgess said that "the Loop," Chicago's earliest and largest business district, was in the center and grew over the years, invading old housing areas.

There has been considerable discussion about whether various cities in North America and in the world would all have the same growth pattern as Chicago's, or whether there are different patterns depending on additional factors. Unlike Park, whose interest lay very much in "natural areas," often of ethnic and racial origin, Burgess seemed to concentrate mostly on the economic factors of industrial and business growth, and on social class. He used income and occupational factors, but he did not discuss areas of segregation much, even though Chicago at the time had considerable areas of ethnic concentration and segregated Black belts. His basic assumption seemed to be that the industrial, economic factor was dominant (Theodorson, 1982:3-7). Other urban sociologists continued to work with this basic assumption; we shall discuss their work later when we look at social area analysis and factorial ecology.

Plotting Urban Ways of Life

In part one we mentioned that Louis Wirth considered that three dimensions of population (size, density, and heterogeneity) are important variables of urban life. Wirth (1928) carried out a "natural area" study in Chicago of a Jewish community, and wrote a book entitled *The Ghetto*, in which he was able with careful analysis to draw together many strands of empirical data into larger theoretical tenets. Like many other Chicago sociologists, Wirth was pessimistic about industrialized urban life. "He saw the city as an acid that, in time, ate away traditional values and undermined the formation of meaningful institutions and relationships." (Spates and Macionis, 1987:116.)

In 1938 Wirth published his essay on "Urbanism as a Way of Life," which has since become a classic. European theorists had a tendency to produce a great deal of theory, but it was often not backed up by empirical data. Urban scholars of the Chicago School tended to collect a lot of descriptive data, but it took someone like Louis Wirth to gather these studies into a general theoretical framework of urban areas. While other Chicago School sociologists emphasized ecology, Wirth moved the discussion increasingly to broader sociocultural issues of demography and the quality of life. Wirth's contribution to urban sociology was his systematic organization of insights into a sociological theory of the city.

> The second main contribution was Wirth's theory, which became a persuasive, almost mesmerizing document that would dominate the field for the next 20 years. Tying the main insights of the European tradition to the observational studies of the Chicago group, Wirth showed for the first time that true urban theory was possible. All in all, the Chicago group was almost solely responsible for the early growth of urban sociology in America. (Thomas, 1983:490.)

In his famous essay "Urbanism as a Way of Life," Wirth attempted to delineate the characteristics of the large modern city.

> Wirth stated that among the distinguishing features of the metropolis, aside from large size and relative density of population, are heterogeneity of people and

cultures: anonymous, transitory, and impersonal relationships; occupational specialization; secularization of thought; and the predominance of segmental and secondary contact. (Gist and Fava, 1974:45.)

Morris (1968:169) has argued that Wirth implicitly assumed an urban society in which economic rationality is highly valued and in which large bureaucracies are possible. Wirth seemed to be torn between life in natural areas, such as the Jewish life he wrote about in *The Ghetto*, and the exciting characteristics of a larger city, which offer freedom and lead away from a communal lifestyle.

We have reviewed the contributions of four Chicago sociologists to the major urban ecological issues. Each was concerned with different aspects of complex modern urbanization. Throughout the remainder of this volume we shall refer back to many of the basic issues they raised. In the next section we discuss further Burgess's concepts concerning urban growth patterns.

Patterns of Urban Growth

Are there uniformities in the growth patterns of cities? If so, can these patterns be plotted and predicted? Can principles be developed so that generalizations can be made that will apply to cities around the world? Increasingly urban ecologists have tried to go beyond description to formulate a set of hypotheses and theories that will systematize our expectations and make planning for the future possible. Are there ideal growth patterns that can be developed and then applied to most cities? There are three well-known theories of urban ecological growth patterns: 1) the concentric zone theory; 2) the sector theory; and 3) the multiple nuclei theory. We shall examine these theories and see to what extent they apply to actual North American cities.

Burgess' Concentric Zones

In our discussion of the Chicago School we introduced Ernest W. Burgess and his attempt at ordering and predicting growth patterns of a city, using Chicago as his laboratory. Burgess thought Chicago had grown like a tree, with concentric circles growing around a center where the main business district was located. These circles grew ever larger as they expanded towards the periphery. In Figure 4-1 we have plotted the concentric zone design; Burgess suggested that each of these zones had a different land usage. Let us discuss each of these zones.

The Central Business District is the innermost zone, the oldest business section; here business first began when the city was small. This zone also includes department stores, hotels, restaurants, and theatres. This concentration of business, commerce, and services meets the needs of downtown shoppers. This inner zone is the main area for retail trade, light manufacturing, and commercialized recreation. Museums, sports stadiums, art galleries, as well as government buildings might often be located in the center.

The Zone of Transition, zone number two in Figure 4-1, surrounds the

Figure 4-1 Schematic illustrations of three early theories of urban growth

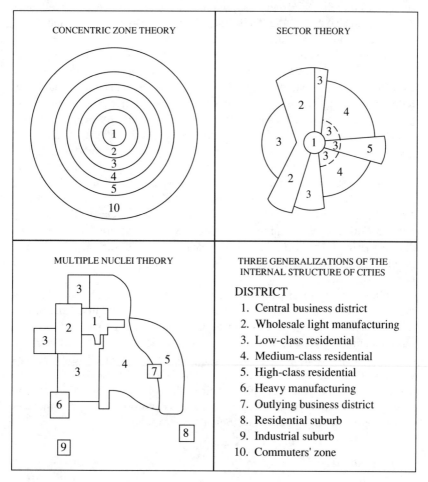

SOURCE: Harris and Ullman (1945: 7-17).

business district and is often referred to as the slum. This zone still contains the oldest housing of the early days of the city; housing which has begun to deteriorate, and which is in the immediate path of business and industrial expansion. This area tends to be heavily populated by lower income classes, by Old World immigrants, rural migrants, racial groups, and social outcasts such as criminals and prostitutes. Burgess called it the zone of transition because the people living there were often transient, and the housing would soon be demolished to make room for business expansion.

The Zone of Workingmen's Homes is the third zone moving out towards the periphery. In fact zones two to five were all residential zones, with the oldest and least desirable housing in zone two and the best housing located in zone five. Housing for blue-collar workers in zone three would be better than the housing in zone two. Zone three would have fairly small, older houses, sometimes on relatively small lots, but they would mostly be quite well kept. Taxes would also be low, but facilities such as sewers would be old and would often break down, and park areas might often be quite limited.

The Zone of Middle Class Dwellers would be even farther out from the center, and would consist of very good older housing or modest newer homes. Here professional, small business, managerial, and clerical people would live. Later, when we discuss suburbanites, we shall differentiate among these groups, which range from lower- to upper-middle-class residents (Schnore, 1972). When Burgess (1925) devised this schema, the suburbs had not yet greatly expanded, so his classification was still quite general and broad.

The Commuters' Zone is on the outer periphery of the city, often beyond its political boundaries, and consists of satellite towns and suburbs that exist in a mutually dependent relationship with the metropolis (Gist and Fava, 1974:163). These towns and communities could be seen as "bedroom communities" that house commuters during the night but are largely vacated during the day. This zone has also expanded since World War II and has proliferated into different types that we shall need to discuss and reclassify later as well.

Burgess' theory of urban growth patterns was based mainly on data from the city of Chicago collected in the 1920s. His data show that "in passing from the center or loop of Chicago to the periphery, delinquency rates, sex ratios and percentages of foreign-born persons tended to decrease, while home ownership was inclined to increase." (Burgess, 1927:178-84.) These gradients were also observed by Shaw and McKay (1942) in their studies of delinquency and by Faris and Dunham (1939) in their studies of the ecology of insanity in Chicago (Gist and Fava, 1974:164-5). Later, as cities changed, new theories of urban growth were developed, to which we turn next.

Hoyt's Sector Theory

Homer Hoyt (1959:114-16) was one of the first to attempt to modify the zonal theory. He noticed that some cities conformed to the Chicago zonal model more than others, and he also found that segments of Chicago, including the Black Belt and the German ghetto, tended to cut across some of the zones.

Hoyt took his work seriously, studying 142 cities block by block. The scope of the study, compared with Burgess' main reliance on findings in Chicago, was a major advance that provided a diversified comparative base from which Hoyt could draw conclusions. Hoyt also examined all these cities in three different time periods (1900, 1915, and 1936), because he suspected that the time factor was also important. Hoyt's finding can be summarized as follows (Spates and Macionis, 1987:174-5): 1) most of the areas varied in size; 2) although some cities provided evidence of concentric zones, in no case did the zone form an entire ring, and many sectors were pie-shaped; 3) sometimes fashionable districts were located beside lower-income districts or were surrounded by lower-class districts; 4) over time, sectors seemed to change radially along a path begun in earlier years; and 5) fashionable areas were seldom found in only one location in the city. Hoyt found, for example, that Boston's Beacon Hill was located on high ground "above" others; in some cities some fashionable areas were located near, for example, aesthetic waterfronts.

Hoyt suggests that "industrial areas develop along river valleys, water courses, and railroad lines instead of forming a concentric zone around the central business district . . ." Hoyt likened the American city to an octopus with tentacles extending in various directions along transportation routes (Gist and Fava, 1974:164). Hoyt also suggested that high-rental residential areas tended to be located near transportation routes on higher ground. In Chicago he saw a string of high-class suburbs reaching along the lake front and stretching from the Loop northwards into Evanston and beyond, connected by rapid transit to the central city and therefore easily accessible to it.

As a result of his findings, Hoyt developed what he called the sector theory of urban growth. As illustrated in the second diagram in Figure 4-1, most cities might have a central business section, but it was not usually surrounded evenly by a concentric circle representing the slums. Rather, many cities might have sections that are pie-shaped, and follow for example railroads or rivers. Many cities, such as Winnipeg for example, have older sections along the Canadian Pacific Railroad with small houses built on small lots designed for workers in the railroad system; these are represented by section three in the diagram. Wholesale and light manufacturing also follow the railroad because companies want easy access to the rail system. On the other hand, housing in Winnipeg on the south side of the Assiniboine River made Wellington Crescent the elite section of the city in the 1920s and 1930s; North Kildonan also tends to have pleasant housing areas with large lots along the river; these areas of better housing are represented by sector five in the diagram. Other, more medium residential areas would tend to fill in between the extremes of sector three and sector five in sector four.

Hoyt's data from 142 cities, with their many variations, provided clear alternatives to Burgess' concentric zone theory, backed by the famous Chicago School. Hoyt's convincing, well-documented research provided insights that called for more exploration of a variety of growth formations, especially because as time went on and new forms of transportation became dominant, there was an increasing need to continue to examine the intricacies of the growth patterns over time. Harris and Ullman helped to offer a third alternative to urban growth patterns.

Harris and Ullman's Multiple Nuclei

Hoyt's study was a major advance over the work of the Chicago ecologists, but it was still limited, like the work of Burgess, by being based on sectors. Hoyt suggested that industry, especially, tended to move outwards radially from the center of the city along rivers and railroad lines, but he did not develop a theory of these radial movements. In 1945 Chauncey Harris and Edward Ullman developed another theory of land use in an attempt to broaden Hoyt's findings. They suggested that as a city grew it diversified considerably, and this resulted in the diversification also of land use (Harris and Ullman, 1965).

Harris and Ullman agreed that a city will begin with a major central business district (CBD), which is an important sector in most cities. This central district however, developed along locational, cultural, and economic lines that the concentric zone and sector theories often did not explain.

> For example, while wholesale and light manufacturing (2) [in the third diagram of Figure 4-1] might be near the CBD, low-income residences (3) might be in various separate districts around it. A medium-income residential district (4) might abut the CBD and be bordered on its outer edge by a high-income residential area (5). Between the two might exist a secondary business district (7), and farther out might exist a completely separate residential suburb (8). Heavy manufacturing (6) might be a relatively large distance from the CBD and evolve an industrial-residential suburb (9) near it. (Spates and Macionis, 1987:175.)

Why did these more complex patterns develop? Dealing with zones and sectors seemed too rigid, especially in 1945 when the specific land uses were being more carefully considered. In earlier years, when North American cities began, industry was often near the center of town where people concentrated so they could walk to work. However, as land costs in the center escalated and as transportation became more flexible, heavy industry especially began to move out of the center into the periphery where land prices were cheaper and offered considerable savings in taxes and rents. Much of the industry that used to be near the CBD in Chicago in the 1920s moved to the south side into Gary, Indiana.

Another reason for differentiation of land use is that the various activities are not always compatible and therefore separate themselves into nuclei some distance from each other. Residential and industrial areas become separated and this separation is reinforced by zoning laws. Prostitution and X-rated movies are distasteful to suburbanites, who do not want their children exposed to them, and so these specialized services concentrate in parts of the central city away from the suburbs. Transients living near the older slum housing areas might avail themselves of these services.

Third, different racial and ethnic groups such as East Indians and Sikhs may enter a city and begin to concentrate in one area where a cluster of businesses provide specialized foods and clothing, and then become a node attracting more immigrants of the same cultural background. In some American cities and as well in Halifax, there may be informal restrictions on where Blacks may find housing. Realtors and building companies might informally encourage ownership and renting of specific ethnic and racial groups in some parts of the city rather than others, resulting in minority enclaves.

Fourth, people want to separate themselves for economic and social class reasons. Some can afford only older and less expensive housing and tend to look for the cheapest residential areas. Others can afford newer or better housing and pay more attention to prestige and status, often escaping to the suburbs. Suburbanites also try to locate close to traffic beltways that will permit easy commuting to their work. Commuting involves transportation costs that not all can afford. Industrial suburbs may spring up close to the industries in which blue-collar workers are employed, saving transportation costs as well as traffic hassles.

Basically, Harris and Ullman (1945) suggested in their multiple nuclei theory that land use can not always be predicted. Historical, cultural, and socio-economic values will have differing impacts on cities, and the exact location of an economic or ethnic nucleus cannot be determined for all cities. The formation of these nuclei depend on a variety of factors—topographical, historical, cultural, racial, economic, and political—that do not result in the same combination for each urban area. The Burgess zonal pattern, and to a lesser extent the Hoyt sector pattern, suggested inevitable predetermined patterns of location. Harris and Ullman suggest that these patterns vary depending on circumstances, and these patterns may also vary over time so that a city's ecological patterns may change also.

Making Sense out of Divergent Theories

Burgess and Hoyt were trying to gather together many fragments of empirical knowledge into a comprehensive whole. It is inevitable that there would be critics who would say that they did not go far enough. Milla Alihan (1938:225) thought that Burgess' gradients and boundaries between zones should be more distinct. She also criticized his theory for being too focused on ecological land use and insufficiently on sociocultural factors. It is true that he might have taken greater note of sociocultural factors, and those who followed did expand the role of these factors. But the fact that Burgess ordered ecological patterns seriously is a contribution that must be acknowledged.

Perhaps the most penetrating critique was that of Walter Firey. Firey (1947:41-86) demonstrated that both the concentric-zone and sector theories were not adequate to explain the spatial patterning in Boston. He pointed out that the distribution of groups was less orderly and more complex, and "that Beacon Hill and the West End, situated in what would be the zone of transition, are populated by sharply contrasting people." (Gist and Fava, 1974:166.) Beacon Hill is a fashionable residential district; adjacent to it, within the same concentric zone, is a population of lower-income immigrants and their descendants. Firey pointed out that these two areas represent a sharp contrast in lifestyles: they are polar opposites. Firey (1947:41-86) also demonstrated that in Boston both the highest and lowest rental areas were located within the inner zone of the city. "Not a single concentric zone reveals any homogeneity in its rental classes." (Firey, 1947:77.) Firey's Boston study implied that the multiple nuclei theory that Harris and Ullman (1945) were just developing at that time fit the Boston pattern better.

Of what value are these theories if they seem to be 1) so specific to individual cities, and 2) so different in their general outcomes? I think all three theories are useful because all three tend to describe general patterns within specific time periods. The dominance of the mode of transportation at a certain period seems to be an important factor. Cities in Europe are much older than those in North America, so many European cities first took shape during a period when walking or using animals were the only forms of transportation. Thus, the older European cities were fairly small, had a central marketplace, and most had surrounding walls. Streets were narrow, mostly leading towards the center where the economic, political, and religious activities took place. Roman Catholic cathedrals still dominate many of these old European city centers.

Older cities in the eastern parts of North America, including Boston, Quebec City, and Montreal, were built like European cities with a major central core. Access to the central core was important because travel by foot had a limited range. Chicago, which began in the early 1800s, and many other cities that developed before the coming of the railroads in the 1880s, were shaped largely by a concentric zone pattern because this enabled people to live as close to the center of activity as possible. Chicago's center (now the Loop) was located on the shore of Lake Michigan, and expanded outwards later.

Other cities, such as Boston, were also shaped at first by their location on a waterway—a bay or a river—that provided a method of transportation, and their populations tended to spread out along shorelines. In such cities, concentric-zone development was hardly possible or practical. Development following a natural shoreline seemed more functional, and thus these cities tended towards sector development. Montreal and Vancouver are good examples of such cities. When the steam locomotive and the railroads became a dominant form of transportation about a hundred years ago, they too reinforced the sector pattern. Now people wanted to live near this dominant means of transportation. Thus, water and rail transportation between the 1880s and 1940s molded many city patterns along sectors.

A third form of transportation, the automobile, arrived before the First World War, but its main impact did not occur until after World War II in 1945, when car ownership became nearly universal in western countries. Los Angeles is often cited as a city that has been shaped extensively by the automobile. The car is not confined to water channels or rails, but is flexible and free to roam in all directions. Cities such as Calgary and Edmonton, which have tripled and quadrupled their populations in the past 40 years, have been shaped largely by the automobile. Since the car can easily go in all directions, multiple nuclei, especially shopping centers throughout the metropolitan area, have emerged. The major shopping centers outside the Central Business District were mostly built after 1945.

In summary, we suggest that each of these theories is applicable to some cities. Older cities that developed on fairly level ground before the advent of mechanized forms of transportation tended to follow the pattern of concentric zones. Ancient European cities and Chicago are good examples. Cities that have mostly developed since the arrival of the automobile in 1945 are patterned into multiple nuclei. Los Angeles and Calgary are good examples. Most Canadian cities have been shaped by all three forms of transportation (animal power, rail, and automobile); however, some have been shaped more by one form of transportation than another. Thus, some cities contain patterns of concentric zones, others conform more to sector pattern theory, and still others are dominated by multiple nuclei. For many cities all three patterns are evident, but which pattern dominates depends on the time factor. Other factors, such as immigration, have also had an impact.

Recent Ecological Methodological Advances

The concentric zone and sector theories were useful in beginning to understand the spatial arrangements of urban activities, but they tended to be too uni-dimensional in their basic assumptions. The multiple nuclei theory did intro-duce more factors, but did not investigate the origins of these factors nor describe them in detail. With newer, more advanced statistical techniques such as factor analysis, it is now possible to include multiple dimensions and sources of change, and to work with them more carefully and seriously. Recent studies have taken multiple dimensional factors and used them to construct new the-ories: social area analysis and factorial ecology.

Shevky-Williams-Bell Social Area Analysis

Eshref Shevky and Marilyn Williams (1949) did some important trailblazing in Los Angeles (the city where the car became a dominant multiple nuclei factor). They focused on "social areas" of Los Angeles, seeking to sort out the major factors that might have given rise to different types of population clusters. They suggested three major factors: 1) social rank or socio-economic status based on occupation and education; 2) family status based on size of family, number of gainfully employed women, and type of residence; and 3) segregation, especially of ethnic and racial groups into clusters (Shevky and Williams, 1949). Shevky and Williams suggested that as a society becomes more urbanized or a city grows larger, it becomes more specialized, popula-tions are segmented socio-economically and ethnically, and families are smaller and more nuclear.

Shevky and Williams began with census data of metropolitan Los Angeles and computed composite indices from social rank, family status, and ethnic segregation for each census track. They divided the Los Angeles population into low, middle, and high socio-economic status, and into low, medium, and high urbanization (family status) categories. They then plotted these categories so that clusters of census tracts of low social rank became differentiated from medium and high ranks, and they did the same for the three types of family status as well. In addition they used dots to superimpose over the socio-economic and family status categories tracts that had high concentrations of Blacks, Hispanics, or other visible minorities. There was a convergence of minorities of low socio-economic status and large families in the center of Los Angeles, while Caucasian, well-to-do, smaller families were concentrated towards the periphery.

Shevky and Williams (1949) summarized their findings in Los Angeles with a scattergram (Figure 4-2). As shown in Figure 4-2, visible minorities that were segregated were more heavily located in the lower social rank category (left side) and in all three family status sections. They concluded that these three factors — social rank, family status or urbanization, and minority segregation — were major factors that needed to be taken into consideration by researchers when differentiating population clusters. Sometimes all three factors converged, but sometimes they did not, and clusters could occur in a variety of patterns. There could be multiple nuclei, each with a different combination, providing a variety of outcomes.

Figure 4-2 Scattergram of social areas showing social rank, family status, and segregation (largest dots) in Los Angeles

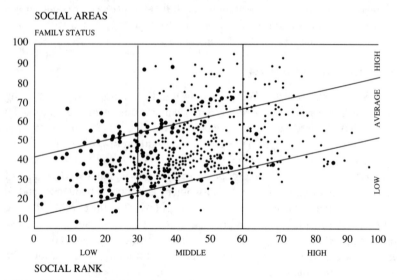

• Census tracts with high indexes of segregation

SOURCE: Shevky and Williams (1949:70-71).

Later Eshref Shevky and Wendell Bell (1955) did a similar study in San Francisco, using the research based on Los Angeles as a guide, but with a more sophisticated conceptual framework. As summarized in Table 4-1, they began with three postulates concerning change in an industrial urban setting. As a city grew, they expected greater intensity and range of change, greater differentiation in functions, and greater complexity of organization. These changes caused changes in the structures of social systems (shown in columns two and three), which provide a rationale for the three constructs of social rank, urbanization, and segregation shown in column four. Column six shows the index for each of the three factors shown in column five. Each index includes indicators: the index for social rank includes three indicators or measures — occupation, schooling, and rent; the urbanization index includes the measures of fertility, women in the work force, and type of family dwelling; and the third index, for segregation, includes racial and national distinctions. The six columns in Table 4-1 trace the rationale and sequence used to arrive at the three indices (rank, urbanization, and ethnicity) in social area analysis.

This new, more sophisticated social area analysis spawned a number of other studies. Van Arsdol, Camilleri, and Schmid (1958a, 1958b, 1961) studied ten cities using the factors of social rank, family status, and segregation, and found these factors more useful in some cities than in others. Others, however, were severely critical. Hawley and Duncan (1957) claimed that the study lacked a theoretical framework and so did not provide a basis for making predictions. Otis Dudley Duncan (1955) suggested that Shevky and associates had not provided enough reasons for selecting these three factors and that others should have been considered. Scott Greer (1956:19-25) followed up on the study of some of the census tracts in Los Angeles and found that neighborhood status was related to family status, for example. However, the work of Shevky, Williams, and Bell generated considerable interest, and it led to the use of factorial ecology.

Frederick Hill (1976) and Michael Ray (1977) did an extensive survey of the 1971 Canadian census data of the 21 metropolitan areas in Canada. They used average family income (social status), family life cycle (family status), and ethnic diversity (ethnic status) indices, which are similar to the three factors used by Shevky and Bell. They mapped these three factors for each of the 21 metropolitan areas to illustrate the variations in each census track, and published the data in tables. What is striking about this comparison of cities is that they vary so considerably. For example, St. John's has only low scores on the ethnic diversity index because most of the population is British; Montreal shows a clear east/west split down the middle between francophones and anglophones; Toronto seems to follow the Chicago pattern with non-British minorities in the center; Winnipeg seems to have multiple ethnic nuclei; and Vancouver seems to follow a sector pattern. We certainly cannot therefore assume that the other growth patterns apply uniformly to Canada's metropolitan centers; more careful exploration and analysis is needed.

Factorial Ecology

Factorial ecology uses factor analysis aided by computer technology to determine how social characteristics cluster. All census data characteristics thought to be potentially important are fed into a computer; the computer compares all these characteristics by census tracts, and shows how they are related and where they cluster. Thus, this technique tries to speak to Duncan's criticism that factors should not be pre-selected, as the factors used by Shevky and

Table 4.1 Shevky and Bell's social rank, urbanization, and segregation indicators of social area analysis in San Francisco

POSTULATES CONCERNING INDUSTRIAL SOCIETY (ASPECTS OF INCREASING SCALE) (1)	STATISTICS OF TRENDS (2)	CHANGES IN THE STRUCTURE OF A GIVEN SOCIAL SYSTEM (3)	CONSTRUCTS (4)	SAMPLE STATISTICS (RELATED TO THE CONSTRUCTS) (5)	DERIVED MEASURES (FROM COL. 5) (6)	
Change in the range and intensity of relations	Changing distribution of skills: Lessening importance of manual productive operations— growing importance of clerical, supervisory, management operations	Changes in the arrangement of occupations based on function	→ *Social Rank* (economic status)	→ Years of schooling, Employment status, Class of worker, Major occupation group, Value of home, Rent by dwelling unit, Plumbing and repair, Persons per room, Heating and refrigeration	→ Occupation, Schooling, Rent	Index I
Differentiation of function	Changing structure of projective activity:	Changes in the ways of living—	→ *Urbanization* (family status)	→ Age and sex, Owner or tenant, House structure, Persons in household	→ Fertility, Women at work, Single-	Index II

Index
III

Complexity of organization → Lessening importance of primary production—growing importance of relations centered in cities—lessening importance of the household as economic unit → movement of women into urban occupations—spread of alternative family patterns → family dwelling units

Changing composition of population: → Redistribution in space—changes in the proportion of supporting and dependent population—isolation and segregation of groups → *Segregation* (ethnic status) → Race and nativity Country of birth Citizenship → Racial and national groups in relative isolation

Increasing movement —alterations in age and sex distribution —increasing diversity

SOURCE: Shevky and Bell (1955:4).

associates were. Interestingly, even with this more sophisticated computer technique, the factors of social status, family status, and segregation often emerged as the most important ones (Hamm, 1982). R.J. Johnson (1976) used factorial ecology to examine Whangarei, a city in New Zealand, and found that socio-economic status, family status, and ethnic factors were all important in determining location of residence in Whangarei. In Copenhagen, Denmark, Pedersen (1967) found socio-economic status and family status to be important factors; Sweetster (1965) found similar results in Helsinki, Finland and in Boston; and Latif (1973) found the same in Alexandria, Egypt.

Nicholson and Yeates (1969:162-79) looked at the ecological and spatial structure of the socio-economic characteristics of Winnipeg, and found that the three factors of social rank, family status, and ethnicity appeared to be fairly similar to findings in Los Angeles and San Francisco. Hunter and Latif (1973:308-33) examined the findings of Nicholson and Yeates and detected contaminating statistical artifacts. Hunter and Latif (1973) therefore compared the 1951 and 1961 census data from Winnipeg, using four different factor categories. First of all, they found that whether they used principal factor, principal component, alpha factor or image analysis made very little difference: all four approaches gave roughly the same results, and these did not seem to vary very much when 1951 and 1961 were compared (Davies and Barrow, 1973). Hunter and Latif (1973:316-27) found that in Winnipeg there was a well-defined and robust factor — social rank. They also found that the number of people in the family, the number of women working outside the home, and the fertility ratio made up a second factor; this factor applied to English, French, and to immigrants, but it did have certain similarities to the ethnicity factor. These Winnipeg findings show that Shevky and Bell's findings in the USA also tend to apply to Canadian cities, with some variations and differences in the make-up of the factors.

Linking Factorial Ecology to Growth Models

Do the recent advances and more sophisticated analyses of the complexity of urban social areas fit into the earlier concentric-zone, sector, and nuclei theories, or must we abandon all previous attempts? Brian Berry and Phillip Rees (1969) suggest that they are related, but each of the earlier theories explained only some elements of change. Berry and Rees reasoned that if socio-economic status was the sole factor in urban location, cities would tend to divide themselves into sectors; if family status were the dominant social characteristic, then the spatial ordering would be in concentric zones; and if ethnicity were the major factor, then the major ordering would be in the form of multiple nuclei. Each of the three theories was partially correct, because each did consider at least one of the factors; however, all of these factors, and perhaps more, are operating at the same time (Berry and Rees, 1969:445-91).

Recently, Delbert Erwin (1984:59-75) did a comparative factorial ecology analysis of 38 American cities that showed that socio-economic status, family status, and ethnicity explained most of the patterning within these cities. Using

1970 census data, Erwin concluded that American cities in general shape themselves in zones, sectors, or nuclei depending on the variables of socio-economic class, family status, and ethnicity. To what extent do these patterns also apply in Canada, a neighboring country?

At the same time that Berry and Rees (1969) were working at comparing Chicago and Calcutta, Robert Murdie (1969) did a factorial ecological analysis of metropolitan Toronto using 1951 and 1961 census data; his results were similar to those of Berry and Rees (1969). Murdie (1969:7) sought to test the following general hypothesis:

> Over time, the economic status pattern tends to expand sectorially, the pattern of family status tends to move outwards from the city center in a wave-like concentric fashion, and minority groups expand according to "spatial diffusion" process such as Morrill has described for the Negro ghetto, into zones of least resistance based upon economic status, and therefore sectorial.

Figure 4-3 (Murdie 1969:9) demonstrates how each of the three factors of social layers fits the physical space. Economic status tends to follow sectorial lines, family status follows the concentric-zone pattern, and ethnicity follows the multiple-nuclei pattern. Murdie found that this model went a long way in explaining the spatial and social patterning of the population in metropolitan Toronto during 1951 and 1961.

Using the three factors of social status, family status, and ethnicity, Murdie (1969:91, 92, 98, 99, 100, 104, 105) then plotted the patterns for 1951 and 1961. In Figure 4-4 we show only one of these: family status in 1961, using factor scores (designating high interval relationships). Family differences (using the indicators of fertility, type of household, and participation of women in the labor force) vary considerably, from factor scores of plus 150 to minus 150. That is, larger families in smaller houses and women working outside the home were located in the center of the figure. Moving away from the center, families became smaller, they lived in larger houses, and fewer women worked outside the home. The family status pattern tended to follow the concentric-zone model. In a similar way Murdie showed, with maps and statistics, that when using social status, the population divisions followed the sector pattern; and when using ethnicity, multiple nuclei patterns emerged. More studies of other Canadian cities are required to determine whether the Toronto patterns also apply to other Canadian cities, especially as new trends develop.

Summary

This chapter deals with urban ecology, one of the most important concepts of the sociology of urbanization. Early American sociologists carried out some pioneering work on urban ecology, particularly those at the University of Chicago. This chapter reviewed the important contributions of five of them. Park developed the idea of "natural areas" where people of similar ethnic, cultural, and economic backgrounds cluster. McKenzie suggested that the five

Figure 4-3 Murdie's model of the urban ecological structure using indicators of physical space, and economic, family, and ethnic status

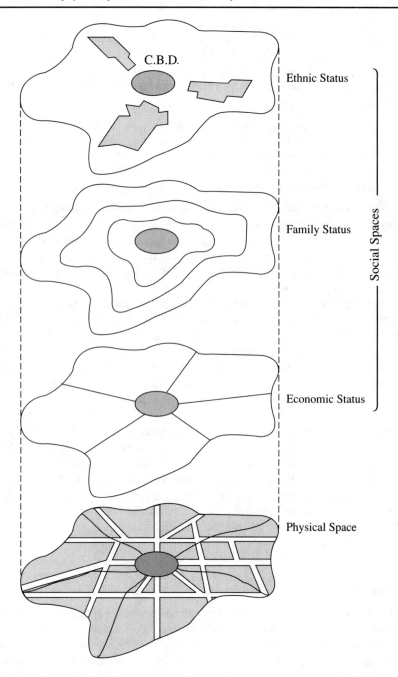

SOURCE: Murdie (1969: 9).

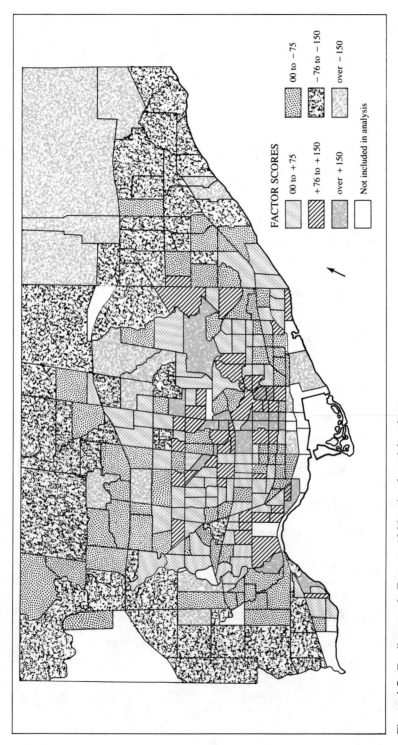

Figure 4-5 Family status in Toronto, 1961, using factorial ecology
SOURCE: Murdie (1969: 92).

processes of concentration, centralization, segregation, invasion, and succession operate within all cities as sub-communities emerge, change, and succeed each other. Burgess attempted to put these two concepts—of natural areas and of change—into a more comprehensive concept to predict where the various types of groups would locate, and how each would fit into a larger metropolitan whole. Wirth concentrated on the social factors within a city, and tried to tie the many factors together while describing "an urban way of life." These scholars and their students, known as "the Chicago School," have since the 1920s had an enormous influence on both urban sociology and North American sociology in general.

Burgess developed the concentric-zone theory, the first comprehensive attempt at predicting urban growth patterns within the city. Using Chicago as his model, he suggested that cities began with a central focal point and then grew by adding additional concentric zones over time as metropolitan area grew. Later Hoyt studied Boston, and found that the patterns of growth formed a sector pattern, following transportation routes such as the railroad or a waterway. Later still, Harris and Ullman suggested that urban ecological growth patterns conform rather to multiple nuclei; many business areas, many socio-economic foci, and many concentrations of ethnic and racial groups. We suggested that each of the three theories has merit, and that transportation may have been a major factor in shaping cities. Early cities were shaped by concentric zones around a center because people had to get there by foot or by animal power. Later, railroads were built, populations settled near these transportation lines, resulting in sectoral patterns of growth. Finally, with the introduction of the automobile, which can move in all directions, multiple shopping centers and ethnic communities emerged.

Recently more sophisticated methodological advances have been developed that can examine and compare complex ecological spatial patterns. Shevky and Williams in Los Angeles and Shevky and Bell in San Francisco used social area analysis to show that social rank, family status, and ethnicity seem to be major factors according to which population groups cluster. Factorial ecology permitted scholars to sort hundreds of variables into clusters, called social factors. These more sophisticated statistical methods show that sub-populations are indeed formed in most North American cities according to social status, family status, and ethnicity. There is additional evidence that social rank tends to correlate with the sector model of ecological growth, family status correlates with the concentric-zone pattern, and ethnicity with the multiple nuclei theory. Methods of controlling the many variables operating in a complex metropolitan society are improving, and urban sociologists are now increasingly able to deal with its complexity and diversity and gain a more thorough understanding of ecological trends.

5. Social Class Shaping Space

In part one we discussed Daniel Chirot's (1986) theory that a core of powerful, industrial, urban nations are dominating the world system. This concept of a core and a periphery was also applied in a smaller context—that of a country or nation. James Simmons (1983) suggested that in Canada, Toronto and Montreal are clear leaders in economic and political influence; other metropolitan centers within this Canadian industrial system are less powerful. In this chapter we suggest that the same concept of dominance can be applied in an even smaller context—within metropolitan centers. Urban ecological areas contain some residential locations and some activities that have a higher status or more power than others, resulting in differential spatial arrangements. Our discussion in the latter part of chapter four clearly showed that socio-economic status is an important factor in determining spatial patterns, as demonstrated by factorial ecology and social area analysis (Erwin, 1984; Murdie, 1969; Hunter and Latif, 1973).

Spatial Ordering of Social Class

Social class involves social stratification. Different social strata have differing levels of influence and power, resulting in social inequality. Karl Marx was among the first to analyze the effects of social class and show that it results in inequality. Other scholars have continued his research into social inequality (Coleman and Rainwater, 1978; Bell and Robinson, 1980; Hunter, 1981; Grabb, 1984; Reitz, 1990). Max Weber was greatly concerned with power, which he claimed originated in numerous interest groups (Grabb, 1984:6,7). Many urban scholars (Duncan, 1961; Theodorson, 1982) have explored the relationship between social class differences and the spatial patterns in urban areas. We saw that development of urban social growth patterns has varied over time, and they were greatly affected by the available means of transportation. When humans were confined to walking and animal transport, commercial centers within cities were compact and easily accessible. The development of the railroad changed those patterns somewhat; more flexible transportation by the automobile made greater ecological mobility possible and again changed spatial patterns.

In this chapter we shall discuss how social class has helped to reshape

ecological patterns in the city. First, we focus on the extent to which centralization is still possible; then we discuss the degree of suburbanization that is
taking place, and then look at how these patterns vary in the United States and
Canada. The downtown areas and the suburbs have quite different uses of
space, and quite varied patterns of socio-economic status and power as well.

Duncan and Centralization

The concentric zone, sector, and multiple nuclei theories of urban growth all
begin with a central business district (CBD) universal to all cities. It is true that
some CBDs face severe competition from business nuclei elsewhere in the city,
but even Los Angeles, which is one of the most nucleated cities, also has a
central business district. Otis Dudley Duncan (1961:140-9) and Theodorson
(1982:122-8) looked at urban spatial patterning in Chicago from a socio-
economic perspective, and found that growth tended to be in concentric zones.
They therefore assumed that cities grew from the center outward, that the
major business activity would be concentrated in the downtown central business district, and that residential areas would contain groups of differing socio-
economic status, beginning with the lowest in the innermost zone and increasing in status farther from the center (Theodorson, 1982:3-7). Spatial patterns,
therefore, were determined largely by economic factors. The degree of centralization was an important feature of urban spatial patterns. The idea of
decentralization is related to centralization in that residents of higher socio-
economic status move away from the center (decentralize) into the suburbs.

Recently, however, older suburbanites seem to be moving back into high
status apartments near the downtown after they have raised their families in
the suburbs. Thus, a recentralization or back to the center movement seems
to be taking place, especially in larger metropoli. It is difficult to show all
these movements on a diagram. Figure 5-1 represents the essential parts of a
metropolitan ecological system. There is the inner central city with a core
area that includes the central business district and slums. The numerous suburbs, most of which are politically independent (Winnipeg's being an exception), are located in the outer suburban zone, each with its business centers
and residential areas. Then there is the urban fringe still farther from the center
of the metropolis, containing exurbias and satellite cities. Residents of the
fringe and suburbs relate to the central city in distinctive ways.

Schnore's Index of Suburbanization

Using the educational attainment of the American male population 25 years
and older, Schnore (1964:164-76) developed an index of suburbanization
based on 1960 data from 200 urbanized areas in the USA. The USA has ten
times as many metropolitan centers as Canada, and therefore provides more
variety for comparative analysis. He then contrasted the central city with the
suburban outer area, as shown in Figure 5-1. In Schnore's index, levels over
100 indicated over-representation in the central city, when the central city and

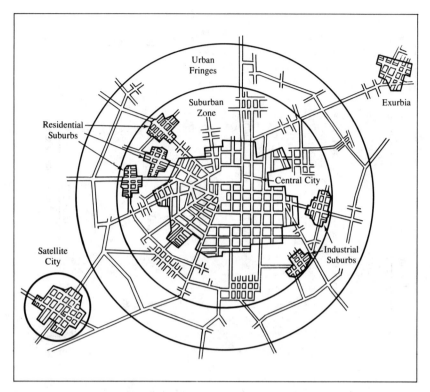

Figure 5-1 Ecological diagram of the metropolitan regions
SOURCE: Boskoff (1962: 132).

suburban outer areas were compared, and levels of education under 100 indicated under-representation in the central city. All but 12 of his 200 urbanized areas fell into one of the six patterns presented in Table 5-1.

In Type A, represented by Tucson, the four educational groups with the least education are under-represented in the central city and higher educated people are over-represented. This pattern is in complete contrast to the concentric zone theory (Gist and Fava, 1974:255-60). Type B, represented by Albuquerque, is similar to Type A but the range of educational levels is larger. Type C contained the largest group (70 of the 200 cities). In this group, represented by Los Angeles, both the lower and higher levels of education are over-represented in the central city. Type D, represented by Baltimore, shows almost perfect conformity with the Burgess model; and Type E, depicted by New York, conforms completely with the Burgess model (67 of 200 urban areas conformed to this pattern). Type F, represented by Miami, is the reverse of Type C: here groups with the lowest and highest education are over-represented in the central city. Type X, Memphis, does not show any differentiation of education with the central city.

One-third of the urban areas conform to the Burgess model. These include New York, the largest city in the USA, and Chicago, the second largest city

Table 5.1 Six patterns of residential distribution of educational classes based on indexes of suburbanization*

	(1) "A"	(2) "B"	(3) "C"	(4) "D"	(5) "E"	(6) "F"	(7) "X"
	HIGHEST EDUCATIONAL CLASSES ARE OVER-REPRESENTED IN THE CITY	HIGHEST EDUCATIONAL CLASSES ARE OVER-REPRESENTED IN THE CITY	BOTH HIGHEST AND LOWEST EDUCATIONAL CLASSES ARE OVER-REPRESENTED IN THE CITY	LOWEST EDUCATIONAL CLASSES ARE OVER-REPRESENTED IN THE CITY	LOWEST EDUCATIONAL CLASSES ARE OVER-REPRESENTED IN THE CITY	INTER-MEDIATE EDUCATIONAL CLASSES ARE OVER-REPRESENTED IN THE CITY	NO SYSTEMATIC VARIATION
Pattern label	"A"	"B"	"C"	"D"	"E"	"F"	"X"
Name of area used in example	Tucson	Albuquerque	Los Angeles	Baltimore	New York	Miami	Memphis
School years completed							
None	90	85	131	128	129	83	98
Grade: 1–4	93	81	113	124	119	137	101
Grade: 5–6	96	88	110	117	111	136	101
Grade: 7–8	99	93	99	104	107	115	101
High school: 1–3	100	97	94	98	100	100	100
High school: 4	101	103	97	86	91	89	99
College: 1–3	102	106	102	86	87	81	100
College: 4 +	103	110	106	87	84	81	100
Number of areas represented by example shown	14	10	70	23	67	4	12

*index of suburbanization: over 100 means educational class is overrepresented in city; under 100 means educational class is overrepresented in suburbs.

SOURCE: Schnore (1964:170).

(the city that provided the data for the development of the theory). Another one-third, represented by Los Angeles, the third largest city, has a U-shaped pattern with the educational extremes in the center. Miami, an important tourist center, is the reverse of the Los Angeles pattern, and has a bell-shaped pattern with the middle educated groups most highly represented in the central city. All in all, there is quite a range of patterns, although Burgess' zonal model is well represented in Types D and E; these two comprise about half of the 200 urban areas. Spatial distribution by social class, as measured by education, seems to take many forms.

Balakrishnan's Centralization Index

T.R. Balakrishnan and George K. Jarvis (1976:204-16) studied the socio-economic differentiation in 23 metropolitan centers in Canada using 1961 census data. They used a composite score of occupation, education, and income as indicators of socio-economic status, and they measured the ecological distance from the center of the urban area of groups who scored high. They grouped the 23 centers by size into four distinct groupings. There are distinctly different patterns when the four are compared. They found that Montreal, Toronto, and Vancouver (the three largest centers) clearly follow the Burgess zonal pattern, as do New York and Chicago in Schnore's study (Type F). Socio-economic status is lowest in the city centers and rises steadily out towards the suburbs.

In contrast to the pattern of the three largest Canadian cities, the seven centers with populations under 100,000 (most of them are now over 100,000) seemed, as with Schnore's Type X, to have no clearly defined pattern variation, although Saskatoon followed the Burgess zonal pattern. It seems that in small cities, spatial arrangements are relatively undifferentiated by socio-economic class, but as cities grow, they increasingly follow the Burgess zonal patterns. When an urban population reaches one million or more, the lower socio-economic residents tend to live in the inner city and higher status residents increasingly are located towards the suburbs. When Balakrishnan and Jarvis (1976:208) analyzed spatial patterns using a quartile zone system (SES distributed in four equal groupings of 25 percent each) rather than physical distance, they found a similar pattern. This Canadian study shows that size of urban area seems to be an important factor in the way socio-economic status groups cluster.

Using 1986 Canadian census data, maps of twelve of Canada's 25 metropolitan centers (Calgary, Edmonton, Halifax, Hamilton, Montreal, Ottawa-Hull, Quebec, Regina, St John's, Toronto, Vancouver, Winnipeg) have been drawn showing population distributions by education, income, and occupations (Census of Canada, 1989). The maps show that socio-economic spatial patterns vary considerably. Winnipeg, for example, has a clear division between north and south, with residents of levels of higher education, occupation, and income in south Winnipeg (Census of Canada, 1989:29,47,53). Some cities follow more centralized patterns, as shown in Table 5-2, and

Table 5.2 Socioeconomic status index by distance from city center

METROPOLITAN AREA	LESS THAN 1.5 KM	1.5 TO 3 KM	3 TO 4.5 KM	4.5 TO 8 KM	8 TO LESS THAN 15 KM	15 KM OR MORE
Population size						
500 000 or more						
Montreal	37.6*	42.4	44.7	49.8	51.7	51.3
Toronto	38.0	44.1	48.7	51.1	55.7	56.6
Vancouver	49.4	51.6	53.9	53.4	55.0	48.4
TOTAL	39.6	44.6	47.1	50.6	54.3	53.1
200 000–499 999						
Winnipeg	41.4	47.6	52.2	57.6	49.9	—
Ottawa-Hull	47.7	50.0	51.4	59.9	58.8	—
Hamilton	44.7	48.0	46.7	48.5	51.0	—
Quebec City	43.2	46.7	47.5	52.4	47.0	—
Edmonton	44.4	50.1	52.9	55.4	51.2	—
Calgary	43.6	50.5	56.1	60.2	47.4	—
TOTAL	44.1	48.4	51.1	54.8	52.1	—
100 000–199 999						
Windsor	42.8	46.4	46.6	49.7	53.0	—
Halifax	43.5	55.2	53.2	47.8	—	—
London	45.3	50.5	53.3	55.5	48.6	—
Victoria	47.2	48.4	55.6	53.3	51.2	—
Kitchener-Waterloo	47.7	49.4	52.9	42.9	45.4	—
Regina	49.6	51.0	47.4	—	—	—
Sudbury	46.4	47.4	46.3	43.6	41.1	—
TOTAL	46.1	50.2	51.0	49.4	49.6	—
Less than 100 000						
Saskatoon	46.5	52.5	50.0	45.3	—	—
Saint John, NB	47.0	44.7	53.0	48.4	—	—
Sherbrooke	42.8	44.8	47.1	49.6	—	—
St. John's, Nfld.	49.6	53.7	46.6	42.6	42.9	—
Kingston	47.2	55.7	54.8	49.7	—	—
Oshawa	43.8	46.8	51.7	50.2	47.6	—
Trois-Rivières	44.6	49.3	40.8	44.3	—	—
TOTAL	46.2	48.2	49.2	46.1	45.8	—

*Percent who scored high on SES.

SOURCE: Adapted from Balakrishnan and Jarvis (1976:207).

others form more nucleated patterns. Assuming that all metropoli contain a central business district (CBD) that has economic and political power, slums where the lower socio-economic status residents live, and suburbs with higher status residents, let us compare and contrast each of these distinct ecological areas.

Downtown: The Inner Commercial Heart

How long the downtowns of cities will remain viable and dynamic is under considerable debate, but most Canadian cities still have dynamic central city business areas. Until recently the central business districts have been centers of commercial power, of services, and of influential communications media.

CBD Characteristics

Most central business districts (CBD) still retain some of their traditional structures and functions and many are still major centers of political and economic power. "Here, in the large city, are located the captains of industry, merchant princes, publishers of metropolitan newspapers, leaders of labor, and high-placed bureaucrats and executives who find it expedient to be near the center of power." (Gist and Fava, 1974:231.) In the CBD, business offices employ workers such as accountants, private secretaries who perform endless paperwork, and salespeople, and service outlets employ receptionists, hotel workers, restaurant personnel, skilled technicians, maintenance workers, janitors, cleaners, and security people. All these workers and a host of others are needed to keep the institutions located in the CBD running well.

The central business district is also a center of communications and of information flow. The media — television, radio and telecommunications — locate here because the CBD is the most concentrated point of activity in the daytime. Financial institutions, including the stock market, boards of trade, and civic and provincial institutions seek to stay close to the centers of political power.

To summarize, the downtown is 1) the commercial center of the city; 2) the center for retailing, wholesaling, and warehousing; 3) the area where manufacturing used to be concentrated and where light manufacturing often still exists; 4) the area where service industries, business offices, and financial institutions are located; and 5) an area that has only a small quantity of residential housing. The CBD is the heart of the city. In most metropolitan centers in Canada this heart remains intact, although for several decades institutions have begun to decentralize. The city center "is the most accessible point, the most intensively developed area, the largest employment district, the largest generator of traffic, and it has the highest land values." (Nader, 1975:89.) It is the main financial, commercial, governmental, cultural, and entertainment center within the metropolis, and its buildings constitute a unique record of the city's history.

"The central city" can be defined as the area enclosed by the political boundaries of the original municipality, which is the historic core of the metropolitan area (Nader, 1975:89). The central business district, in contrast, is usually defined as the smallest geographical area within the city center where commercial uses are dominant. Delineating the CBD is difficult; planners usually try to designate a compact area, eliminating as much residential area as possible without leaving out too much of the commercial areas. Since the commercial areas usually expand and invade old residential areas at the periphery, the CBD area needs to be enlarged from time to time. Thus, the designated CBD in 1990 is usually not the same as it was in 1950.

In addition to changes in physical size, there have been changes in functional specialization. For example, retailing is no longer the primary function of most CBDs. "Since 1961 nearly all new department stores in Canadian cities have been located in the suburbs, and for the nine largest metropolitan centers, the CBD's share of total department store sales declined from 84.6 percent in 1961 to 57.4 percent by 1966 and 39.0 percent in 1971." (Nader, 1975:92.) However, those who plan conventions still prefer to hold them in the city center. In 1972, 350 conventions and trade shows were held in Toronto, attracting a total of almost 245,000 out-of-town delegates. The number of conventions has risen since then. Downtown hotel space is also expanding because of such activities. In Figure 5-2 we see the generalized land-use areas in downtown Toronto. Office, retail, hotel, wholesale, governmental, and institutional functions cluster in their distinctive areas. George Nader (1976) has plotted the historical development and the profiles of fifteen metropolitan downtowns in Canada, and these six functions are usually present in each one. However, the patterns and shapes of downtowns vary considerably, depending on topological features (some are located on the coast, others along lakeshores, and still others along rivers).

Waning Commercial Dominance

Since World War II and the introduction of the automobile, CBDs have increasingly been forced to compete with the large shopping centers located in the suburbs, which include the large department stores for shoppers. This battle for shoppers has been escalating in recent years, and the downtown is losing its dominant commercial attraction. Can the downtown area survive as land costs increase, parking becomes more expensive, and congestion gets worse? Some planners, such as Jane Jacobs, think the CBDs can compete, but only if they change and make greater use of their historic potential and strategic ecological place. Jane Jacobs (1958:140-66) says that downtown is for people and that too often city planners forget to plan for human diversity. Jacobs says downtowns must be revitalized, not by building more uniformly and incorporating more open space, but by providing more diversity of function; plans should be organized around people, not around buildings. "There is no magic in simply removing cars from downtown, and certainly none in stressing peace, quiet, and dead space." (Jacobs, 1958:146.) Alleys could become animated and streets made more interesting, more variegated, and busier than before. Tourists must be attracted, and tourists mean crowds, Jacobs says. In order to compete with suburban shopping centers, many downtown areas seek to revive "local color," and Jacobs (1958:149) thinks that the gaiety and activity of the old market square can be brought back as it used to be, and as it still is in many European and Asian cities.

The historical part of Quebec City shown in Figure 5-3 illustrates the tourist

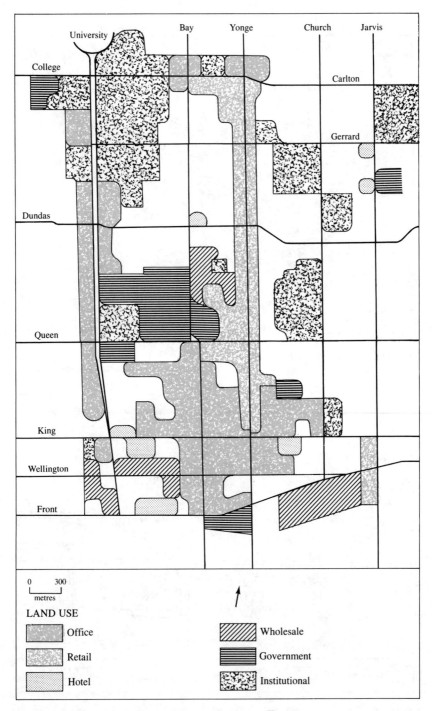

Figure 5-2 Generalized land-use zones, downtown Toronto
SOURCE: City of Toronto Planning Board.

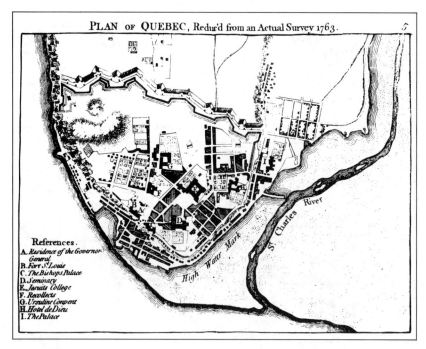

Figure 5-3 Québec City, 1763
SOURCE: Courtesy Cartographic & Architectural Archives Division, National Archives of Canada, Ottawa.

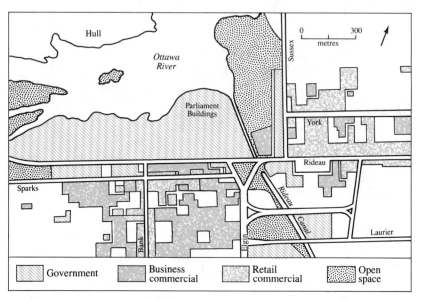

Figure 5-4 Generalized land use, Ottawa city centre
SOURCE: City of Ottawa, Planning Department, 1970.

interest created by the old city walls, the old fort, the palaces, the Catholic seminary, the college and other old buildings, and the narrow, winding streets and cobblestone paths. Of course few cities in Canada have as lengthy a past as Quebec City and Montreal, but all cities have some historical features that can be highlighted. Figure 5-4 shows land use in Ottawa-Hull. Here recent building, especially on the Hull side, has incorporated the Ottawa River and its bridges as an integral part of the city, including adjacent park areas. The Parliament buildings are also a tourist attraction in the central area. Sparks Street in the business section has been made into a pedestrian mall, making it more attractive to tourists and people generally.

While Quebec City has history and Ottawa has the national capital as tourist attractions, Vancouver has an advantage in its physical setting. The entire peninsula shown in Figure 5-5 supports the central city area and its central business district. The retail section in the middle is expanding eastwards towards Gastown, the old renovated business area (Hardwick, 1974:43-4). Gastown, with its street musicians, cobblestone streets, and interesting eating places, together with the largest Chinatown in Canada combine to make the area a good tourist attraction (Lundgren, 1973:211-14). Remnants of Japan-town add to the surprises and uniqueness of shopping in the area (Hardwick, 1974:46,70).

Howe Street, Robson Street, Pender Street, and Water Street all add color to different parts of downtown Vancouver (Hardwick, 1974:71). The two major functions of business offices and wholesaling are separated. The office buildings in the north of the CBD overlook Burrard Bay with its mountain background; the wholesaling area in the south is close to the railyards to the east. These run through the center of the city, as is the case in other cities such as Toronto and Winnipeg. Stanley Park, one of the largest urban recreation areas, provides a beautiful area for relaxation. The West End, with its high-rise apartments, has many advantages: the downtown within walking distance, Stanley Park next door, and the marina, English Bay and its beaches only blocks away (Gaylor, 1973:199-200). Unfortunately, as is so often the case, industry lines most of the shores of both Burrard Bay to the north and False Creek to the south. Access to the Pacific for commercial purposes is what triggered Vancouver's growth, but now commerce has cut off the downtown area from access to the water (Smith, 72). Since Burrard Bay and False Creek provide the best access to the Pacific for ocean-going ships, there is less likelihood that industry will retreat elsewhere, as it is beginning to do in many other cities.

In addition to historical sites, Jane Jacobs (1958; 1963) recommends adding attractions such as fountains, beaches, and boat trips. These are meeting places of delight, joy, wonder, and surprise; they can be beautiful when lit at night as well as places where people meet during the day. European cities especially have created many such fountains in parks and small areas; these appeal to the senses: sight, sound, touch. Jacobs suggests that more open parks and squares will help to provide visual appeal and opportunities for people of all

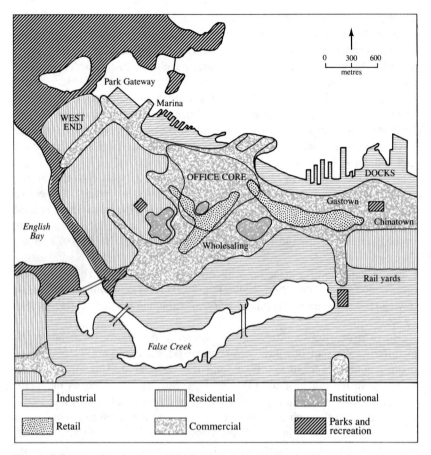

Figure 5-5 Functional areas within the downtown peninsula, Vancouver
SOURCES: Smith (1972), and City of Vancouver.

ages from a variety of socio-economic and ethnic backgrounds to mix together, adding color and interest in food, dress, and behavior.

Jacobs (1963:29-89) proposes that sidewalks could be used for contact: mobile carts selling various things and stands offering a variety of foods add to a sense of action. Streets can be unifiers rather than dividers. A good example is Sparks Street in Ottawa: it was closed to cars, and trees and shrubs were planted, fountains and playgrounds were built, and plenty of places to sit were provided. Jacobs (1963) calls for smaller shops, which stock surprising and interesting items for tourists, as do the shops at the historic "Forks" site opened in 1989 in Winnipeg. Yorkville in Toronto provides such a variety of shops selling artwork, crafts, and books. Such variety and excitement usually attract tourists and help to sustain the downtown commercial areas in their competition with the larger, more accessible suburban shopping centers. Eaton Centre in Toronto is another example of such variety, but roofed in to make it comfortable in winter; Winnipeg's Portage Place has been built for the same purpose.

The Automobile as Agent of Change

Studies have been carried out to assess the extent to which the downtown is still a place where large numbers work, as it was in the past. In metropolitan Toronto, for example, it was assumed that 90 percent of the people entering the central area between 7 a.m. and 9 a.m. were on their way to work, and it was found that traffic flow remained fairly constant between 1951 and 1971 (Nader, 1975:95). The West End of Vancouver, with its high rise apartments, alleviates some automobile travel since it is within walking distance of some CBD jobs (Hardwick, 1974:63). These automobile traffic figures suggest that downtown remains an important place to work, even though in Toronto traffic may be levelling off. T.A. Wier (1961:76-86) plotted the daytime population flows in Winnipeg, and the automobile commuting from the suburbs to downtown was considerable.

In 1970 in Toronto there were 78,890 office workers, 59 percent of all who worked downtown, and 37 percent of all the office workers in the whole metropolitan area; another 30 percent of downtown workers worked in the retail and service fields (Nader, 1975:108). There were 13,396 workers in manufacturing and construction in downtown Toronto in 1964, a decline of 12 percent since 1960, and there was a 21 percent decline in the same period in transportation storage and wholesale workers (from 13,956 to 11,064). In the meantime government and community service workers increased by 10 percent, financial, insurance, and real estate workers rose by 4 percent, and retail and personal services by 1 percent (Nader, 1975:112-13). Since then, manufacturing, wholesale storage, and transportation seem to be decreasing, and retail stores are also leaving for the suburbs. On the other hand, governmental, community, and financial services seem to be on the rise, so that while many people continue to work in the downtown area, they are engaged in different kinds of work. Office space has increased considerably ever since 1960, and downtown Toronto is a much more popular area for business offices than midtown or suburban areas. Toronto's skyline has also dramatically changed since 1960; a number of new skyscrapers have been constructed, including the 600-m CN Tower, which, when it was completed in 1975, was the world's tallest free-standing structure.

Jane Jacobs (1971:204-8), A.J. Dakin (1971:209-10), and Ralph Cunningham (1971:211) joined the debate that has raged over freeways in Toronto, deploring the negative impact of freeways. As the population of Toronto passed well over the three million mark, the pressure to get easier and faster access to downtown greatly increased. Boyce Richardson (1972:129-42) debates the alternatives — whether workers should come to the downtown area by car or bus — and suggests that more planning is needed to control the negative features of traffic. While many workers in the past were able to live near their work, the increase in the population and the growth of the city mean that many workers must now live in the suburbs and commute to work downtown. As could be seen from car registrations, the number of cars more than doubled in one decade after 1945, and cars have multiplied since then. Many choose to come by car to work downtown (Jacobs, 1958:33). To accommodate the cars, many cities are building larger and wider freeways into the downtown area, carving so much space out of the city that the land and tax base is seriously eroded (Bello, 1958:33). The increasing flow of automobiles into the city center also means that more parking is needed, which again leaves less space for human activity.

Lewis Mumford (1964) criticizes the heedless demolition, tasteless reconstruction, and deadly traffic congestion that clogs the urban arteries of European and North American cities. Some European cities, such as Amsterdam, have created a better mix of transportation: boat, train, car, bicycle, and walking are all used. Toronto began building freeways in the seventies, but some were halted. Generally, Canadian cities have not constructed as many freeways as have cities in the USA, but then Canada's population is only one tenth that of the USA, and Canada has fewer very large cities. As manufacturing and wholesaling move out of the center, and railroads increasingly give way to trucks, fewer workers in these industries will need to come to work downtown, which seems to be distributing the traffic flow over the entire metropolitan area. On the other hand, new businesses emerge downtown, which also require transportation.

Slums: The Older Core Area

The slum area is a core area of older housing usually adjacent to or near the CBD. There is an interesting sequence of spatial invasion and succession between these two core areas. As the metropolitan area grows, the CBD usually expands into the older housing area. Many entrepreneurs buy up older houses on the periphery of the CBD, holding these properties until they can be sold to business entrepreneurs who are planning to expand. These old and small houses are then demolished, making room for commercial and retail enterprises. Thus, residents living in these old houses, usually from the lowest social class, are constantly being pushed back away from the CBD, and the CBD continues to invade the slums as business expansion takes place.

Characteristics of the Slum

"The term 'slum' is an evaluative, not an analytic concept. . . . Current definitions of the term include two criteria—the social image of the area, and its physical condition." (Gans, 1962:308.) The criteria imply poor quality housing occupied by lower classes. Slum areas typically contain run-down housing, small stores selling goods geared to the preferences or needs of the local residents, and narrow, cluttered streets (Gist and Fava, 1974:275). Slums are usually located near the center of the city (second concentric zone), or along transportation lines such as railroads or rivers (sector pattern), the only means of transportation when the city first began. Slum areas are the least attractive areas in the city, but since the houses are old, rents are cheapest here, and so the slums attract those who cannot afford to pay very much, including the impoverished, the dispossessed, new immigrants, and racial minorities.

"The convenience of the area downtown, coupled with its low rents, also attracts students, artists, 'bohemians', and some intellectuals, as well as criminals and social deviants of various types who welcome the anonymity provided by the slum's density of population and by its lack of organized resistance to their residence." (Gist and Fava, 1974:276.) The variety of people often gives rise to distinct subareas within the slum such as Skid Row and racial or ethnic ghettoes. Charles Stokes (1962:187-97) makes the distinction between "slums of hope," often inhabited by newcomers and recent immigrants looking for a better life, and "slums of despair," which mark the end of the line for many racial minorities, the aged, and social outcasts. John Seeley (1959:7-14) classifies these dwellers into four types: 1) the permanent necessitarians who are social outcasts and the long-term poor; 2) temporary necessitarians who are poor for the short term, such as students or recent immigrants; 3) permanent opportunists such as prostitutes who work there, fugitives and criminals; and 4) temporary opportunists such as short-term sellers and purveyors of shady goods or services. Both the social organizational and disorganizational forms of slum activity deserve some discussion and differentiation.

Social Order of the Slum

Gerald Suttles' *The Social Order of the Slum* (1968) is a classic study of ethnicity and territory in the inner city of Chicago. Suttles studied the Addams area shown in Figure 5-6 (named after Jane Addams' Hull House), south of skid row and "The Loop," the central business district. Black (Negro), Italian, Hispanic (Mexican), and Puerto Rican immigrants surrounded the Addams area and were also represented within the study area. Blacks lived in housing projects in the south part of Addams, an extension of Blacks living in "The Village" and "Jew Town" areas. The Italians, the largest group and the longest residents in the area, were located on the west side of Addams; the Puerto Ricans were also located on the west side and the Hispanics in the northwest corner (Suttles, 1968:13-19). Peanut Park, located right in the middle of the Addams area, was the residential area around which the various groups revolved.

The subtitle of Suttles's book is *Ethnicity and Territory in the Inner City*, which accurately describes the Addams territory: ethnicity was an important factor in ordering spatial arrangements. The various ethnic groups also were ordered by size and influence. The Italians had the most economic and political power. In chapter six we shall develop this theme of ethnic segregation further; here we wish to show briefly how an ethnic social order was created among

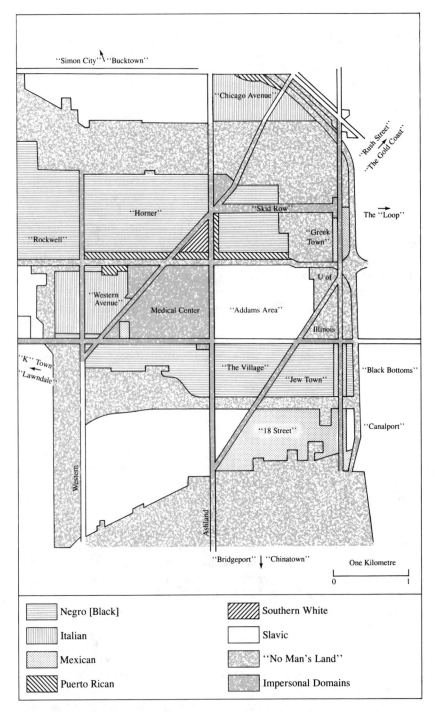

Figure 5-6 Neighborhoods adjacent to the Addams area
SOURCE: Suttles (1968: 14).

the poor. Suttles describes the ethnic institutions in the area, such as the churches, schools, and stores, and the patterns of use of these institutions. The Blacks were Protestants, the other three groups Roman Catholics; sometimes Italians, Hispanics, and Puerto Ricans would worship in the same Catholic church, but there were also some churches dominated by a particular ethnic group, depending on where it was located. Different churches catered to different groups.

There were 267 commercial establishments, the majority of which (166) were located in the Italian area; only 18 were located in the Black area. Thus, the Italians had enormous power advantages in that they entered the area first, they were still the largest group (although some were beginning to leave), they were Caucasian, and the largest number of institutions were located in their area, most of which they operated themselves. This dominance of the Italians was also apparent in the recreational establishments: Italians had more parks, social centers, clubs, and playgrounds, and sometimes had exclusive "rights of usage" of some of them. The Blacks, who were the most recent arrivals, had few institutions in their area: they ranked at the bottom of the status system. Of the fourteen schools, some "belonged" to each of the groups; the Blacks gaining ground in numbers over time. The Italians had the greatest access to connections of political influence, and controlled the patronage of the First Ward, giving rise to suspicions and fears (Suttles, 1968:99). Ethnicity was therefore an important factor of the lifestyles of the residents of the area. Social stratification was real; invasion and succession forces were at work, with the Italians gradually moving out and the Blacks increasingly moving in. Suttles called it ordered territorial segmentation by ethnic groups.

The Slum as Social Disorganization

Sociologists of the Chicago School such as Robert Park and his students focused on the social disorganization of the slum. Nels Anderson (1923, 1934, 1940) concentrated on men on the move in Skid Row. Edwin Sutherland (1937) published his book *Professional Thief*, and Frederick Thrasher (1963) in *The Gang* wrote about the many delinquent groups in Chicago. They saw the slum as the area where social disorganization was most blatant.

We have gleaned ten forms of social disorganization from the literature; these are listed in Table 5-3. Since the slum is the oldest part of the city, the schools there are old and difficult to maintain, and it is hard to attract the best teachers to teach children whose parents do not always see the need for education. Since housing in the slum is old and cheap, the unemployed, who have little education and few skills, are attracted to this area (Metropolitan Corporation of Winnipeg, 1967). Being unemployed and on welfare, they lack adequate food, shelter, and health care. It is hard to create trust within a community when many of the people are transients or of diverse backgrounds. The pressures on the families are great so that there are high levels of separation, divorce, and illegitimate births. Many troubled people turn to drink and drugs, and to get these resort to robbery and theft (Metropolitan Corporation of Winnipeg, 1967). In a community lacking in organized activities, youth gangs are common, and some turn to violence. Slum residents are often targets for unscrupulous politicians and graft. Fly-by-night religious sects set up their store-front churches, and new religions find adherents among those who are desperate.

Table 5.3 Forms of social disorganization in the slum

1. Poor educational facilities (run-down schools, few teachers with insufficient qualifications, lack of facilities such as books and equipment).
2. High rates of unemployment (lack of skills, low levels of education).
3. Many dependent on welfare (for health care, food).
4. Lack of sense of community (transients, ethnic and racial diversity).
5. Family problems (high rates of divorce, separation, illegitimacy).
6. Personal degradation (drinking, drugs).
7. High crime rates (robbery, theft, violence).
8. Numerous delinquent gangs (social and violent).
9. Opportunities for political graft (gang leaders, and politicians).
10. Numerous religious sects (store-front churches, new religions).

Skid Row: Heart of the Outcasts

Skid Row is a special area of the slum, usually located on the edge of the central business district, often in a former business section that has deteriorated while a newer CBD has emerged elsewhere. Most of the ten forms of social disorganization described in Table 5-3 are heavily concentrated in Skid Row. Demographically, Skid Row is comprised mostly of homeless men. Nels Anderson (1923), considered by some as the ''skid row sociologist'' (Wallace, 1965:viii), is well known for his early volume *The Hobo: The Sociology of Homeless Men*, which he published in 1923; it was followed by *Men on the Move* (1940). Most large metropolitan centers in North America have Skid Rows, some of the most famous being Harlem in New York and the Black Belt in Chicago.

Samuel Wallace (1965) wrote *Skid Row as a Way of Life* when he was one of nine graduate students studying the Minneapolis Skid Row by participant observation. The students took on various roles such as hobo, ex-G.I., alcoholic, confidante of a prostitute, and casual laborer, and they slept, ate, drank and participated in Skid Row activities. They found that Skid Row was a deviant community that provided a distinctive way of life. In his book Wallace (1965) described where these male ''vagabonds, rogues and sturdy beggars'' slept, the charity and welfare organizations they frequented, the bars that were their social centers, how they found jobs, and how they related to the legal and justice systems. He also described the various routes that led people to Skid Row, and their subsequent existence there. Many Skid Row residents are of the very lowest social class, without alternatives, and Skid Row was for them at least a familiar place that met their few needs.

Canada's cities are relatively small compared to those in the USA, so slums in Canada are less extensive and less well known compared to those in New York and Chicago. However, Toronto's lower ward has been studied by W.E. Mann (1970) and its Skid Row has been researched by Keith Whitney (1970). When Mann (1970:33-64) studied Toronto's blighted area south of Queen Street and west of University Avenue, it had been in the news because of the bookmaking, prostitution, and juvenile delinquency there. Mobility among the residents was very high, some people moving three and four times a year, educational qualifications were low, and people were often unemployed because they lacked saleable skills. Membership in teenage gangs was high. There were many pubs, which were important meeting places, especially for the men, where sports, sex, and drinking were the focus of conversations. These pubs, where the manager acted as "head of the household," served as neighborhood or community centers—where the residents could get to know each other, exchange information on jobs, borrow money before payday, and watch television, which was not available in their small hotel rooms. Professional deviants such as bookmakers, bootleggers, and prostitutes often used the pub as their base (Mann, 1970:61).

Keith Whitney (1970:65-74) studied Skid Row in Toronto, a specific part of the lower ward that Mann researched. Whitney claimed that Toronto's Skid Row, with a population around 10,000, was one of the largest in North America. It was bounded by Yonge Street on the west, the Don River on the east, Carlton Street to the north, and King Street on the south. "Here the majority of hostels, flops, soup kitchens, bars, pawn shops, and other 'supporting' services are located." (Whitney, 1970:66.) Fifty percent of the men on Skid Row were fifty years or older (many being pensioners), but a fifth were under twenty-five. Whitney (1970:67) said that contrary to expectations, only one-third had problems with drinking, and only a small number were actually chronic alcoholics.

Whitney (1970:70-2) described the ten missions, including the agencies operated by the United Church, the Roman Catholic Church, the Salvation Army, and other social clubs and agencies. These organizations spent considerable funds and effort trying to feed, clothe, and house these men. It was a self-perpetuating system that included pawn shops, jails, wine shops, flophouses, small roominghouses, the social work agencies, churches, and the police department. As Wallace suggests, Skid Row for many becomes "a way of life" where they feel comfortable and secure. Skid Row is the stereotype many people have of all slums. Many of the ten disorganizational features listed in Table 5-3 are found here. There are actually many organizational features in Skid Row also, which are often not mentioned.

Let us now turn to a discussion of the social organization of the larger slum, concentrating on the other residential areas. In his classic *Street Corner Society*, William Foote Whyte (1943) studied two youth gangs in an eastern

American city slum that he called Cornerville. This slum was inhabited almost exclusively by Italian immigrants and their children. Whyte learned Italian, lived with an Italian family in Cornerville for eighteen months, and became a part of the activities of two men's gangs, one called *Doc and his boys*, and the other called *The Nortons*. Whyte (1943:xvi) found that Cornerville was a highly organized and integrated society, and these gangs had important places in this social organization. "The North Italians, who had had greater economic and educational opportunities, always looked down upon the southerners, and the Sicilians occupied the lowest position of all." (Whyte, 1943:xvii.) Doc and his corner-boy gang and Chic [Norton] and his college-boy club demonstrated the contrast between the southerners and the northerners, although when Whyte was studying them in the latter 1930s, during the Depression, most of them did not have jobs.

When the Italians first came as immigrants to Cornerville there were numerous clashes with the Irish who lived there, but eventually the Irish moved out. Whyte describes the social structure of Doc's gang, which had its internal ranking system; Doc was leader, and he had several close advisors; the rest of the gang were followers. Doc's gang occasionally got involved in racketeering, especially alcohol-trafficking, and also got involved with assisting politicians to get elected—by means not always within the law. Whyte's study was among the first to show that social organization is clearly evident in the residential ethnic slum; This had been evident to some extent in Whitney's study of Skid Row in Toronto. Leadership, stratification, organization of activities, spatial social patterns, social networks, norms and values, all were at work within the slum community. James Lorimer and Myfanwy Phillips (1971) showed that the people living east of Parliament Street in Toronto also lived in an inner city neighborhood where lifestyle and social institutions brought a sense of order to many working people.

Suburbia: The Outer Metropolis

The suburbs, or the outer suburban zone, the third segment of a metropolitan area, are usually made up of numerous independent urban areas surrounding the central city. In cities in the western world, suburbanites are usually middle- and high-status residents. The suburbs, together with the urban fringe, make up the urban ecological area that is called a metropolis if it has a population of 100,000 or more.

Alvin Boskoff (1962:133) defines "suburbs as those urbanized nuclei located outside, (but within accessible range), of central cities that are politically independent but economically and psychologically linked with services and facilities provided by the metropolis." By "urbanized nuclei" we mean those areas outside the central city (Figure 5-1) that have substantial populations, mostly in non-rural occupations, with distinctly urban forms of recreation, family life, and education (Duncan and Reiss, 1956:117-19; Duncan and Reiss, 1958). Cities tend to expand by political annexation of existing or potential suburban areas.

Suburban Types and Characteristics

Alvin Boskoff (1962:134-7) has classified North American suburbs according to three major functions into residential, industrial, and recreational or resort suburbs. Residential suburbs are most common; he divides these into three subtypes: 1) traditional upper-class; 2) stable middle-class; and 3) "package" suburbs. The traditional upper-class suburb attracts high status families. Housing is most expensive here, and there is comparatively little mobility and turnover. Upper-class suburbs are most common in fashionable cities such as Boston, New York, Philadelphia, Montreal, and Toronto.

The stable middle-class suburbs are the most common. Humphrey Carver (1948) was among the first in Canada to plan suburban housing communities. Thorncrest Village, built in 1948 in the Toronto suburb of Etobicoke, was one of the first well-known, self-contained and self-governed suburban communities in Toronto (Sewell, 1977:25-7). It is this type of suburb that symbolizes the typical suburb today. Usually professionals, medium-level proprietors, and executives live here.

The "package" suburb is the residential suburb that has the least expensive housing, often mass-produced with fewer individual architectural designs, on smaller lots. These suburbs have fewer parks and fewer services. Residents here are more mobile than in the other two types of residential suburbs, families are usually younger, and include junior executives who are on the rise but cannot yet afford to live in more expensive places. As housing gets more expensive, as it has done in Toronto and Vancouver, package suburbs can be designed according to need, building smaller houses on smaller lots to make them affordable to the less affluent middle class.

The industrial suburb is the blue-collar workers' residential area of the outer city (Boskoff, 1962:135). These "employing" suburbs tend to have residents of the skilled and semi-skilled lower and lower-middle status groups. These suburbs are often located in somewhat less desirable areas near factories and industry, easily accessible to blue-collar workers. Houses and lots are small, so initial costs, mortgage payments, and taxes are low. These suburbs do not grow as quickly as the middle-class residential suburbs, but they are increasing.

Recreational or resort suburbs are usually extensions of metropolitan areas near lakes or large parks where people can go to relax. Many buy cabins as second homes or retirement homes. These areas include cottages, curio shops, and a variety of entertainment facilities. The population is usually transient; many live there part-time, leaving for the south in the winter and returning to work or relax in summer. This type of suburb is even less common than the two discussed earlier.

Alvin Boskoff (1962:136-8) has also outlined some of the basic features and roles of suburbs. The period after World War II, when the car came into its own, was the period of suburban growth, so the highest *rate of population increase* takes place on the outer rim of the metropolis. The *sex ratio* is usually balanced in the suburbs, because mostly families live there. A higher proportion of *married adults* live in the suburbs than in the central city. Suburbanites are *younger* because young families with children like to live in the suburbs. Suburbs are the best places for families. Suburbs *attract whites*; there are fewer foreign-born and visible minorities in Canada's suburbs. Adult suburbanites are *better educated* and have more years of formal schooling. *Professional, managerial, and business* occupational groups tend to be disproportionately highly represented in the suburbs. The *median income is higher* in the suburbs, because people have more education and therefore access to higher status jobs. The suburb acts as *a frontier* for many who want to try new things, build, plant a garden, or find new social groups. A new community waits to be created in a suburb. Suburbs mostly have one- or two-storey housing, so the suburb is *less congested* and population density is lower than in the central city.

Basically the suburb provides new opportunities for newcomers from many places who have the income, education, political connections, and energy (youth) to create a new community.

Suburban Potential for Neighborhoods

While the suburbs, like the slums, have their problems, the suburbs are a more stable place to raise a family, especially one with small children. Schools, parks, recreation centers, and homes are relatively new and attractive. Younger, better educated professional families with good incomes are sources for community leadership and creative social networking and friendships. Several intensive community studies (not all suburban) have been done by William H. Whyte (1954; 1956) of Park Forest, by Herbert Gans (1967) of Levittown, and by Seeley, Sim, and Loosley (1956) of Crestwood Heights. Thorncrest Village in Etobicoke and Don Mills in Toronto were among the first planned suburbs in Toronto, and require similar intensive study (Sewell, 1977:19-38).

William Michelson (1976:17-23) is critical of the work of earlier American human ecologists because of 1) their incomplete conceptualization of the environment; 2) their fixation with aggregates; 3) their erection of disciplinary boundaries; and 4) their ecological determinism or lack of acceptance of intervention. Space, Michelson says, has been utilized by early ecologists as a medium, seen on a flat plane, without enough concern with the linkage between humans and their environment. Their focus on large, natural area aggregates has not recognized suburbs as neighborhoods. As human ecology was formalized into a discipline, it created disciplinary boundaries that did not take into account the concerns of psychologists, sociologists, anthropologists, and geographers sufficiently (Michelson, 1976:20,21). More recently large, diverse social relations within an entire environment have been the focus of study, with new emphases on neighborhoods.

William H. Whyte's (1954) study of the town of Park Forest, Illinois, nearly 40 km south of Chicago (although not a suburb), was a study of young, highly mobile professionals with many upper-middle-class suburban characteristics. Whyte (1954) studied the 17,600 homes in Park Forest, and plotted these within their environmental context, as shown in Figure 5-7. Park Foresters lived in both detached homes and garden apartments grouped into courts, and these courts developed individual cultures or styles of life of their own. "One would be known for its wild parties; another, for its emphasis on church going; a third would be actively involved in community affairs . . ." (Michelson, 1976:180). Whyte observed that there were clusters of friends and activities, illustrated in Figure 5-7. Whyte plotted these activities three years later, and found that some of these clusters had shifted as some people moved away and new ones took their place. Thus, within one large area, there were a variety of ways of life.

Whyte found that several factors brought these people together, including children, because parents met while tending to the needs of their children; driveways and stoops provided opportunities for social contact; and gardening resulted in exchanges of ideas and helped to develop friendships (Michelson, 1976:180). Whyte also found that where residents were located on the block —whether at a corner or in the middle—also made a difference in the number of opportunities for contacts and friendships.

Herbert Gans' (1967) study of Levittown, New Jersey, found that space was less important in suburban living than Whyte's study of Park Forest suggested. Contact with close neighbors seemed less important than living in similarly priced homes, because the latter seemed to produce greater homogeneity of owners (Michelson, 1976:184-5). Families with children look for other couples with children so that there are potential playmates. Being in the same stage of the family life cycle also seemed to be important, because couples without children, families with children, and older families where the children had already left had different needs and social patterns.

Herbert Gans (1967) found that a street can become a barrier between neighbors because the cars keep children and their parents on their own side of the street. A dead-end street with a bay and no sidewalks becomes a playground where boys play hockey and girls walk their doll carriages; and bay motorists respect the dual functions of the street. "Deviants," couples without children both of whom are away working all day, have few opportunities for development of social webs compared to those who are around all day looking out for their children. Spatial placement and the formation of friendship webs complement each other.

Seeley, Sim, and Loosley's (1956) study was of a suburban community in Toronto located on the heights above the older city; it was a classic Canadian suburban study. This study of an upper-middle-class suburb focused on the demographic structure, the family, school, and social institutions in depth. It took the reader behind the scene to what went on inside the homes, schools, clubs, and churches, and told how the commuters and their families thought, felt, and acted (Seeley, Sim, and Loosley, 1956:506). Seeley et al (1956) present the symbolic, social psychological, and social aspects, best demonstrated by the setting of the home and the functions and uses of its rooms.

Seeley et al (1956) described the living room where these upper-middle-

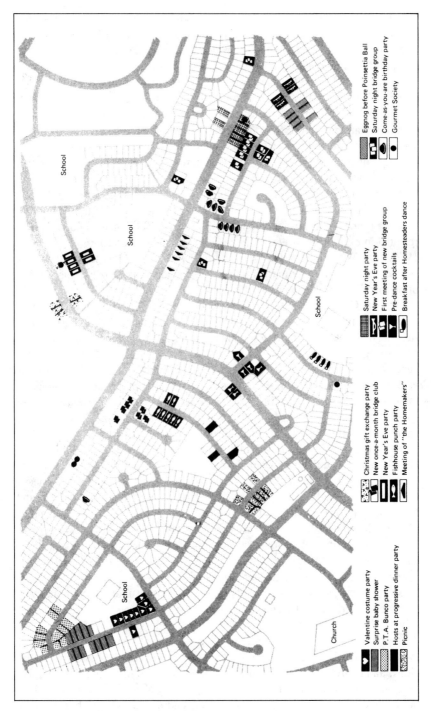

Figure 5-7 Sampling of social groupings in Park Forest
SOURCES: Whyte (1956: 374–7); and Michelson (1976: 181).

class Crestwooders met and entertained their guests as "the stage" in "productions" intended to enhance their social status. These living rooms are "charmingly arranged, harmoniously matched in color, but rather empty and cold of life." (Seeley *et al* 1956:51.) These front rooms seem like museums with their paintings, sculptures, and rugs, where children were strictly forbidden to enter during the week. Family living was done in "family rooms" designed more for relaxation, which the living room did not provide. More will be said about Crestwood Heights when we discuss the family in chapter nine.

The Fringe and its Satellites

The urban fringe illustrated in Figure 5-1 is the area out beyond the suburbs (Russwurm, 1971). It is the area into which suburbs may expand in the near future, thus becoming a part of the metropolis, although sometimes metropolitan governments do extend their annexations considerably into the fringe even before such expansion has taken place. The land use pattern of the fringe is often a varied and unco-ordinated mix of residences, commerce, manufacturing, special services, and even farming, and has many plots of vacant land waiting to be bought and used for suburban expansion. Such fringes are usually not too attractive: they contain buildings that are in need of repair or are abandoned and used as dumping grounds; they usually lack gas, sewer, water, and street services.

Satellite cities located a short distance from the metropolis but not yet incorporated into the metropolitan complex are miniature versions of the central city. The origin of such small cities is independent of the larger city, but they slowly become engulfed into the larger whole. Satellite cities are politically independent; they serve as a source of workers who want to live in a small town but work in the metropolis. Satellites usually provide a normal range of frequently needed services, and easy access to the greater variety and opportunities in the central city close at hand (Kneedler, 1951:49-53).

Exurbias, also shown in Figure 5-1, are a relatively recent form of urban living; these are only attached to the very largest cities such as New York, Chicago, and Los Angeles (Boskoff, 1962:144-5). Exurbias are really suburban outposts that are unattached to the metropolis in the way a satellite city is unattached. The "creative" branches of urban communication services such as advertising, commercial art, television, films, magazines, and publishing may be easily carried out in such exurban places in a country-like environment away from the city, but with all the suburban amenities and with easy access to the central city when needed (Spectorsky, 1955). Now that computers and fax facilities are increasingly available, exurbia may well become more popular, particularly as the metropolis becomes increasingly larger and more difficult of access. Exurbia can become working environments that are close to the land, where the pacesetters of urban fashion live in artistic colonies and drive special foreign cars. It looks as if exurbia will be new satellite suburbs of the future, adding to urban sprawl.

Summary

Social class or status is an important factor in the spatial ordering of an urban population. Working with the concentric zone perspective, Duncan sought to measure centralization or decentralization of populations from the CBD. Leo Schnore tested this centralization concept by comparing 200 urban areas in the USA, and developed seven types of spatial arrangements; only one-third tended to conform to the concentric zone pattern. T.R. Balakrishnan examined 23 urban centers in Canada using a socio-economic index to order centralization, and found that for the largest centers socio-economic status increased as distance from the centre increased. However, in smaller urban centers, there was less differentiation in socio-economic status, so that centers of less than 100,000 showed hardly any differences.

Next, we examined the downtown business district, the slums, and the suburbs as three different zones of urban life. We found that with the increasing use of the car as a form of transportation, it is increasingly harder for CBDs to survive. Jane Jacobs has some important suggestions for revitalizing downtowns, which some are beginning to follow. Controlling the use of the automobile in the CBDs is an important part of managing the detrimental features of auto transportation.

Most large North American cities have slums located in the older sections of the city that are considered by many to be a blight on the metropolis. Slums have poor educational and housing facilities and are the depository of people with low incomes, or who are unemployed; family disorganization, delinquency, crime, gangs, and lack of a sense of community are common features of slums. Skid Row is the part of the slum that is inhabited by homeless men and social outcasts. However, the work of William Whyte illustrates that low socio-economic residents do form various social structures and organizations. As Suttles shows, there is a social order among immigrant and ethnic groups in the slums. Thus slums may reveal both disorganization and social organization.

Suburbs in the outer parts of the metropolis are more pleasant places to live, but only higher status residents can afford to live in these newer parts of the city. Like slums, suburbs have their advantages and disadvantages. The younger, higher-income and more educated suburbanites have more resources to build communities from scratch in new and creative ways. However, a homogeneous population may induce boredom and a sense of being trapped.

6. Segregation: The Ethnic Mosaic

The three ecological growth models discussed in chapter four suggest that ethnicity is a major factor in shaping internal urban growth. In this chapter we want to focus on the ethnic factor as it contributes to the ecological mosaic. Ecological studies suggest that the multiple nuclei that Harris and Ullman (1945) predicted, and that Shevky and associates found in Los Angeles and San Francisco, were strongly related to ethnic enclaves in the city. In this chapter we wish to examine the dimensions of ethnic segregation; the various approaches used to delineate these nuclei; and comparative ethnic data; and finally we shall zero in on some in-depth studies of ethnic communities. Ethnicity, a concern of Jane Jacobs, is an important addition to the human element of cities, in contrast to industrialization, which tends to dehumanize.

Canadian Origins of Segregation

While much of the early research into segregation took place in the United States, there are some early Canadian descriptions by Roderick McKenzie and Charles Dawson. We must also distinguish between the various racial, cultural, and occupational clusters of urban populations; some are voluntary, but others are involuntary and are brought about by discrimination and segregation. Clusters of segregated populations change over time because of mobility, invasion, and succession.

McKenzie: Natural Units of Dominance

Roderick McKenzie entered the University of Chicago Ph.D. program in sociology in 1913 with the full intention of working with W.I. Thomas, who was in the process of publishing his five volumes on the Polish peasant in Chicago. Unfortunately, Thomas had to leave, so McKenzie worked with Robert Park. McKenzie had grown up in Brandon, Manitoba, and had studied at the University of Manitoba in Winnipeg, where he had been influenced by the influx of immigrants, the heterogeneity of the Winnipeg and Manitoba populations. and the dominance of some groups over others. By dominance we mean the controlling position that a person, or a group, or an area acquires over competing people, groups, or areas (Shore, 1987:110). McKenzie

(1923:287) argued that all humans and human institutions become integrated into dynamic relations of dominance and subordination, leaders and followers. He saw areas within the city that were dominated by ethnic groups or groups based on social class in competition for survival with other groups, forming many different ethnic and/or class nuclei.

Having grown up in a small town in southwestern Manitoba, McKenzie was a part of a solid rural community of British background. This community was deeply aware of the rural Ukrainian community centered on Dauphin, north of Brandon, part of the rural Ukrainian Aspen Belt that extended west through Saskatchewan north of Saskatoon all the way into Alberta north of Edmonton. In addition, people of French background were located east of the Red River in southeastern Manitoba, Icelanders dominated the interlake region around Gimli, and the Mennonites were entrenched on their reserves to the west and east. Each of these ethnic groups lived in isolated rural communities that seldom interacted with each other. When McKenzie went to university in Winnipeg, he found that these groups were again segmented into "natural areas" within the city, the French east of the Red River in St. Boniface, the Jews, Poles, and Ukrainians in the North End, Icelanders and Germans in the west of the city, Mennonites in North Kildonan, and the British in western St. James and southern Winnipeg. When he came to the University of Chicago to study, he found that Chicago was also segmented into a variety of "natural areas" where an ethnic group was dominant. McKenzie's early causal observations now spawned theories about ethnic dominance in a natural area where an ethnic group was numerically, economically, and politically influential.

Dawson: Segregation in Montreal and the West

Charles Dawson was born and raised in the Maritimes, attended Acadia University, and began his studies at the University of Chicago in 1914; he also was working with Robert Park (Shore, 1987:xiv). Like many in the Chicago School, Dawson saw the city as a social organism. Dawson went to McGill University in 1922, and could be considered the founder there of the first department of modern sociology in Canada. At that time Montreal was exploding with activity and growth; by 1928 it had at least 1,400 industries, stockyards, and packing houses, all of which Dawson and his students were busy categorizing according to the Burgess concentric zone model learned in Chicago. In 1929 Dawson and Gettys (1929:130) published some of the patterns of growth they had discovered in Montreal; these are shown in Figure 6-1.

Dawson was mostly interested in describing the general growth pattern of Montreal and the extent to which it conformed to the Chicago concentric zone model. He made "no attempt to account for . . . the division of the city, straight through the center, into French and anglophone groups." (Shore, 1987:136.) Examination of Dawson and Gettys' drawing of Montreal in Figure 6-1 shows that indeed the English are clearly located in the west, segregated from the French. Immigrants from other countries — Negroes, Italians, Russians, and Chinese — are concentrated near the central business section

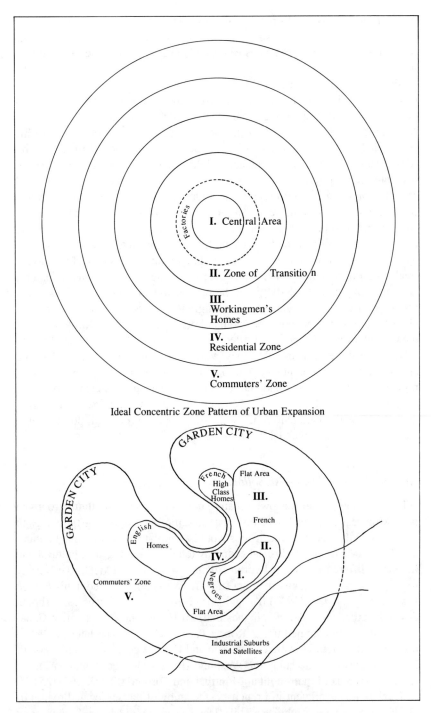

Figure 6-1 Dawson's study of segregation patterns in Montreal
SOURCE: Dawson and Gettys (1929: 130).

between the English and French solitudes. Dawson's students later began to examine the effects of transportation lines on population patterns, and the location of ethnic groups such as Blacks, Chinese, Italians, and recent immigrants in the city.

From his earlier studies of Montreal, Dawson turned to the larger issues of dominance in Canada. Dawson's early article on Canadian settlement in general appeared in the same issue of the *American Journal of Sociology* as McKenzie's well-known article on dominance (Shore, 1987:150). In his research Dawson combined the concepts of dominance, introduced by McKenzie, and regionalism, and applied them to Canada, which he suggested had four major physiographic regions. The most important was the central region containing southern Ontario and Quebec. To the east were the Maritimes, separated from the central region by the Appalachian Mountains. The western plains represented a third region, separated from the central region by the Canadian shield; and British Columbia, the fourth region, was separated by the Rockies from the Prairie region. The urban centers of Halifax, Montreal/Toronto, Winnipeg, and Vancouver dominated their regions. A natural laboratory in which to study group interaction was the newly settled western region with its bloc settlements of immigrants. Dawson's *Group Settlement* (1936) study explored how the Doukhobors, Mennonites, Mormons, Germans, and French Canadians settled the West, how they segregated themselves, and the extent to which they were able to retain distinct and viable ethno-religious communities. Dawson saw the Maritimes and the West as regions dominated on the national level by the metropolitan centers of Montreal and Toronto. He applied the concepts of regional dominance discussed in part one to the national scene, suggesting that metropolitan power was a major influence that must be taken into account.

Hughes: The French-English Solitudes

While Dawson's studies showed many nuclei of segregated ethnic groups in both Montreal and the West, his basic assumption, following the Chicago School, was that these ethnic groups would assimilate to the dominant culture eventually because the industrial economy tended to homogenize cultural and linguistic differences. It was Everett Hughes, who came to McGill University to join Dawson as a faculty member in 1927, who demonstrated in his *French Canada in Transition* (1943) that industrialization does not necessarily break down the ethnic boundaries. Hughes married Helen MacGill, a native Canadian, and the two studied under Robert Park in Chicago and later published together. At McGill University, Dawson and Hughes decided on a division of labor—Dawson would study the West and Hughes Quebec, both considered to be hinterlands of metropolitan Montreal and Toronto (Shore, 1987:254).

Hughes was proficient in French, so the study of the segregated region of Quebec was a natural choice, while Dawson never did learn French even though he taught in Montreal. Before Hughes started on his Quebec study, he had supervised the study by Horace Miner of rural Quebec, *St. Denis* (1939), which described the evolution of French society from a peasant society to a transitional industrial community. Hughes himself studied in Cantonville, which had been invaded by a number of new industries initiated and managed by English-speaking people, while the French constituted the labor force. At the time of the study, 768 of the largest corporations with headquarters in Montreal were managed or owned by residents of English origin and only 93 were headed by residents of French origin (Shore, 1987:258).

In the preface to his book, Hughes (1943:x) says he chose Cantonville, the first of a series of French towns he had planned to study, because "it stands in between the two extremes" of Horace Miner's traditional, rural, French parish prototype of St. Denis on the one hand, and of Montreal, the largest metropolis in Quebec on the other hand. Industries, all started and managed by English-speaking people, had both "enlivened and disturbed" Cantonville. The English and French were very much segregated within Cantonville spatially, socially, and in terms of division of labor on the job. In 1941 Cantonville had a population of 20,000, of whom 95 percent were Catholic and French. The industrial invasion of English-speakers was in many ways alien to French Quebec, and the fact that the English held the top industry positions, while the French in their own territory worked at lower status jobs, created potential French-English conflict. These ethnic relations caused Hughes to explore minority-majority relations earlier than many other sociologists.

The ethno-religious symbolism of the huge Roman Catholic church of the French, overlooking the public park, illustrates the dominance of the 95 percent who were French in Cantonville. The English went to "the 1911 Anglican church, a time-weathered monument of the English past." Both language and religion separated the two ethnic communities; children were also segregated into Catholic schools where the teaching was in French and Protestant schools where the teaching was in English. This separation of the two groups is very well illustrated in Table 6-1, which shows French and English segregation by the horizontal axis, and Catholic and Protestant segregation by the vertical axis. The various institutions within the community fall along a downward-sloping curve; each group had its separate social institutions and there was very little mixed or shared activity (Hughes, 1943:124).

The French and English were socially segregated also:

> When English and French women meet socially, there is something of a barrier between them. Golf club and other semipublic bridge parties furnish the chief occasions for female mixing. Most of the English women cannot converse in French and accuse the French women of chattering away among themselves: 'The French are much freer. They laugh and giggle, while the English sit quietly and talk. . . . ' These apparently trivial complaints reveal a wide and deep gulf between French and English manners. It is a difference which appears in men's sports as well. . . .   (Hughes, 1943:166).

While socially, politically, and demographically the French dominated Cantonville, the English had the highest positions in industry. These managerial

Table 6.1 French Catholic and English Protestant affiliation with voluntary associations

RELIGIOUS AFFILIATION	ETHNIC AFFILIATION						
	FRENCH BY DEFINITION	FRENCH IN FACT	MOSTLY FRENCH	MIXED	MOSTLY ENGLISH	ENGLISH IN FACT	ENGLISH BY DEFINITION
Catholic by definition	Insurance* (1) Fraternal (1)	Church† Savings and loan† Drill corps (1) Insurance (1) Fraternal (1) Charity† Youth (3) Labour (1)					
Catholic in fact	Political (1) Insurance (1)	Business (2) Drama and music (3) Political (1) Insurance (1) Drill corps (1) Fraternal (2) Sports (3)					

Mostly Catholic					Sports (3) Musical (2)
Mixed				Business (1) First-aid (1) Sports (1)	
Mostly Protestant			Business (1) Sports (1)		
Protestant in fact	Fraternal (2)	Sports (1) Drama (1) Boys (1)			
Protestant by definition		Church			

*The insurance associations are all fraternal insurance orders.
†Parochial organizations found in some or all of the Catholic parishes.
SOURCE: Hughes (1943:124).

positions paid well, so that their families lived in spacious, comfortable homes along streets shaded by tall elms and maples. The wide, newly-paved streets led to the larger factories. In contrast, the French blue-collar workers who worked in the factories lived in ramshackle tenements where poverty was evident. Thus, the two ethnic groups lived side by side, each in its own solitude, separated by differences both of ethnicity and of social class. Dawson had found similar French-English ecological segregation in Montreal; it still exists to some extent today.

Dimensions and Perspectives on Segregation

The early Chicago sociologists were interested in the ecological segregation of humans in cities. They wanted to plot the spatial arrangements of humans by race, culture, occupation, religion, and the like. Some of these human spatial patterns where segregation happened voluntarily were influenced by political power, but other patterns occurred involuntarily because of coercion. Let us sort out some of these dimensions of spatial arrangements, and then discuss two perspectives on how human ecological segregation may be studied.

Dimensions of Segregation

The American human ecologists such as Robert Park worked extensively with Blacks in the Deep South. Blacks were moving into Chicago in droves in the 1920s, resulting in the Black Belt, which has now surrounded the University of Chicago where these sociologists taught. In many American cities, such as Washington, D.C., over half the population now consists of Blacks, and Whites and Blacks are divided into racial solitudes similar to the French and English solitudes in Montreal. The Canadian population is about 95 percent Caucasian, so other racial minorities are small, but in cities such as Toronto, Montreal, and Vancouver visible minorities such as Chinese, East Indians, and Native Indians are becoming more numerous and more visible. Native Indians and Chinese, especially, are highly segregated in Canadian cities.

Canada has always been much more aware of its British and French, cultural and linguistic charter groups, who make up two-thirds of the population. In 1971 it was acknowledged that Canada is a bilingual and multicultural nation. Linguistic and cultural differences have become a major factor in the segregation of urban peoples in Canada. The English-speaking and French-speaking populations in Montreal are highly segregated spatially; the Jews, Italians, Greeks, and Portuguese are highly segregated in Toronto and Montreal; Ukrainians and Poles are segregated in Winnipeg's North End.

Urban populations are also segregated by social class and socio-economic status groups. The suburbs contain disproportionate numbers of professionals and managers, while blue-collar workers live in older sections closer to the center. The higher income groups are usually separated from those of lower income; more highly educated populations are separated from those of lower education. Cities have their elite sections as well as their slums. Some ethnic groups are more heavily located in some areas than others.

Voluntarism is also a factor. Race and social class often combine to force many visible minorities to live in deteriorated sections of the city where it is difficult to raise families because of limited resources and disorganized social environments. Early Chinese bachelors clustered together in Chinatowns to survive and protect themselves against prejudice and discrimination (Ramcharan, 82:75). Jews in Montreal, Toronto, and Winnipeg were and still are highly clustered together to support their Jewish institutions, family life, and distinctive religion. However, Native Indians in Canadian cities are forced to live in the inner cities because of unemployment, low incomes, and often discrimination. Descendants of northern Europeans usually have the greatest freedom from discrimination because they have the jobs, the means, and therefore the opportunities to live where they choose (Anderson and Frideres, 1981:299-304). Let us turn to two theories or perspectives that help us to understand how and why the various nuclei in the city are formed and sustained.

Duncan's Zonal Segregational Model

Two well-known models have been developed that examine urban residential segregation, one by the Duncans (1957) and the other by Shevky and Bell (1955). The Duncans' (1957) model is oriented to social class as the major factor that determines where people live in the city based on the concentric zone theory of urban growth. The Duncans assume that the lower class residents live close to the center where the oldest, cheapest housing is; because socio-economic status rises towards the outer zones, the Duncans predict that the higher status families such as the British, other northern Europeans, and Jews will live in the suburbs, and recent immigrants from low status, nonwhite racial groups will live near the center. The Duncans (1957) used occupational mobility data as the basis for their study. Much work was devoted to social rank.

In their study, *The Negro Population of Chicago*, the Duncans plotted the distribution of Blacks in Chicago in 1920, 1930, 1940, and 1950, using census tract data. The Black Belt, which began between 10th and 40th streets in 1920, spread westwards and extended southwards to 70th street by 1950. While Harris and Ullman's multiple nuclei theory had been proposed earlier, the Duncans preferred to think in zonal terms and tried to fit the Black Belt phenomenon into socio-economic (income, education, occupation) patterns. They also focused their discussion largely on invasion and succession trends, thinking that the larger racial patterns had resulted from these trends. They focused on crowding, education, unemployment, home ownership, and rental costs, all of which were socio-economic factors. While the Duncans were busy looking at Blacks in Chicago in socio-economic terms, trying to fit the racial pattern into the zonal model, Shevky and Bell were beginning to follow the multiple nuclei perspective; this was more useful in predicting racial and ethnic patterns.

Shevky and Bell's Multiple Nuclei

Shevky and Bell (1955), in their studies of Los Angeles and San Francisco, were able to break out of past thinking based on the zonal and sector theories and to pursue the multiple nuclei theory proposed by Hoyt *et al.* Duncan (1955:84-5) recognized their novel, comparative approach and the opportunities it provided for both economic and social research; however, he severely criticized their conceptual framework and their methodological measures. It is true that their methods could have been improved, but their multiple nuclei conceptual framework offered many possibilities, which others have since used with considerable success. By using factor analysis, Shevky and Bell could incorporate and control for more variables; we have already outlined the potential for factorial ecology.

In addition to their three factors of social rank, family status, and ethnicity, Shevky and Bell (1955) developed indices of isolation and segregation that others have found useful (Driedger, 1974, 1978, 1979, 1980). Shevky and Bell (1955:44) defined ecological isolation as "the residential concentration of the members of a particular group with other members of the same group"; their isolation formula proceeded from this definition. The assumption is that the greater the probability that members of the same ethnic group will meet each other, the more likely it is that a larger number of the group live in close proximity and are then likely to create their own ingroup institutions that will reinforce their ethnic identity and perpetuate their distinct ethnic culture. Thus, Shevky and Bell (1955) turned the focus of study from zones and sectors in the context of the city as a whole to nuclei within the city, their relative size, and the intensity of the interaction of members of the group within the spatial enclave.

The Shevky and Bell (1955:45) segregation ratio was used to measure a second dimension of interaction, that involving the probable interaction between members of a subordinate ethnic group with members of all other subordinate groups in the metropolis. The reasoning here was that minorities within spatial enclaves or minorities in proximity to each other could band together to strengthen their specific interests when negotiating with majority groups. An example is the co-operation that occurred in the North End of Winnipeg among the Jews, the Poles, and the Ukrainians (Driedger and Church, 1974:3052). Shevky and Bell's R* value represented the probability that an individual of a minority group would meet another member of his/her group or of another minority group in a given census tract. Many ethnic minorities on the Canadian Prairies can band together to support multiculturalism, so as to reinforce the status of their own cultural contributions. Shevky and Bell's formulae recognized the salience of social rank or socio-economic status as a strong factor (assumed to be the major factor in the work of the

Duncans), but also provided a logical framework to explain the survival of multiple ethnic nuclei. Shevky and Bell's approach is helpful because it shows that ethnicity is an independent influence on spatial location, and results in ethnic nuclei that do not necessarily conform to zonal or sector patterns.

Ethnic Residential Concentration

To gain some insights into the extent to which the Duncan and the Shevky and Bell approaches to research on segregation have been applied to Canadian cities, we focus first on the work of Stanley Lieberson and of T.R. Balakrishnan, who has done the most work in a national context. Anthony Richmond (1972) was among the first to focus on segregation in Toronto, and Leo Driedger and Glenn Church (1974) did the same in Winnipeg. We shall therefore examine these two cities in more detail to see how other factors influenced residential segregation.

National Segregation Trends

Stanley Lieberson (1970) was one of the first sociologists to study residential segregation in Canadian cities; he focused especially on language. He used a slightly modified form of the segregation index proposed by Bell (1954), and worked with 1941, 1951, and 1961 census data. Comparing thirteen metropolitan centers in Canada, he found that there was a considerable correlation between residential segregation and retention of the French language. A score of 1.0 on the index means that the correlation between residential segregation and language maintenance are perfect; a score of 0.0 means that there is no correlation between the two. French language retention was highest in Quebec City (1.0), Montreal (.99), Trois Rivières (.98), and Ottawa (.81); the concentrations of the French-speaking population in these cities was also highest; in cities where French language retention was low, such as Regina (.18), Calgary (.21), and London (.20), the French populations were also sparse. He concluded that French retention ratios will vary inversely to the degree to which French Canadians encounter people who speak only English (Lieberson, 1970:216).

T.R. Balakrishnan (1976, 1979, 1982, 1987, 1990) has done the most extensive work in Canada on comparing large numbers of ethnic groups in most of the metropolitan areas. His work is also the most recent and uses the latest available census figures. In his first work with Jarvis, (Balakrishnan and Jarvis 1979:218-27) they used 1961 and 1971 census data to compare all metropolitan centers in Canada; they found very little change (1961 to 1971) in segregation patterns. They also found that socio-economic status was predominantly sectoral, family status was zonal, and ethnic status followed neither pattern—similar to findings in the USA where ethnic groups seemed to follow multiple nuclei.

Balakrishnan also (1979:487-96) compared sixteen metropolitan centers

using 1951 and 1961 census data, and found that Montreal (.516 in 1951 and
.504 in 1961) and Toronto (.408 in 1951 and .398 in 1961) had declined
slightly, but were still the most residentially segregated ethnic populations,
and Victoria (.241 in 1951 and .215 in 1961) and Calgary (.263 in 1951 and
.205 in 1961) were the least ethnically segregated. (Segregation scores range
from 0 to 1.0 with 1.0 being high.) In all but two cases the 1961 indices were
lower than the 1951 indices. In Montreal the French and non-French are highly
segregated from each other; Toronto has had a large influx of new immigrants,
and these tend to segregate themselves. Balakrishnan (1979:496) also found
that northern Europeans—the British, Scandinavians, Germans, and Dutch—
were least segregated from each other, and the Italians and Asiatics were
segregated from the northern Europeans. Balakrishnan (1982:92-110) also ran
indices for the same centers and groups using 1971 census data and found
very similar results.

Balakrishnan (1990) has now updated his work on ethnic segregation for
selected metropolitan centers using 1981 data; we present the results in Tables
6-2 and 6-3. The 1981 results are not that different from the 1951, 1961, and
1971 results. Hill (1976:84-92) found very similar results for 1971. We see
in Table 6-2, using two types of segregation indices, that Montreal (.574 and
.507) and Toronto (.433 and .331) are again the most highly segregated cities,
with Ottawa-Hull (.345) running second on the second index. Calgary (.233
and .177) and Victoria (.282 and .208) are again the least ethnically segregated

Table 6.2 Mean segregation indices for the selected metropolitan areas of Canada,
1981

METROPOLITAN AREA	NUMBER OF CENSUS TRACTS	INDEX * 1	INDEX ** 2
Halifax	62	.386	.268
Montreal	657	.574	.507
Ottawa-Hull	177	.426	.345
Toronto	602	.433	.331
Hamilton	146	.377	.275
St. Catharines-Niagara	73	.383	.278
Kitchener-Waterloo	62	.331	.240
London	71	.333	.234
Windsor	56	.352	.253
Winnipeg	134	.386	.294
Calgary	115	.253	.177
Edmonton	139	.299	.219
Vancouver	245	.331	.250
Victoria	53	.282	.208

* Mean based on all possible pairs (all single origins only)
** Mean based on each group with the rest of the population

Rank correlation between indices 1 and 2 = .96

SOURCE: Balakrishnan and Selvanathan (1990).

in 1981 as they were in the previous three censuses. Montreal is clearly the most and Calgary the least segregated. There is a high correlation between indices 1 and 2 in Table 6-2 (.96), meaning that the rank order of cities in each index is almost identical (close to 1.0).

Balakrishnan (1990) also ran the 1981 census data for the sixteen metropolitan centers shown in Table 6-3; he then presented a composite score for each ethnic group and found that nationally the Native Indians (.491) and Italians (.439) are most segregated, and the British (.293) and Germans (.314) least segregated on average in Canadian cities (Ramcharan, 1982). We present this data in Table 6-3. It is clear that, with very few exceptions, all ethnic groups in Montreal are more segregated than anywhere else. It is also clear (with a few exceptions) that the Native Indians are among the most segregated in all cities. Except for Montreal, where they are also highly segregated, the British tend to be least residentially segregated. Calgary is the least segregated city, and its most segregated group (Native Indian .386) is still less segregated than Montreal's least segregated group (British .480). The francophone and anglophone solitudes in Montreal are split like nowhere else in Canada. Balakrishnan (1990) also shows that in Montreal and Toronto, lower socio-economic status individuals in each ethnic group are also (with few exceptions) considerably more segregated than higher status groups.

Segregation of Visible Minorities

Having looked at the segregation patterns of metropolitan areas generally, let us examine the three largest (Toronto, Montreal, and Vancouver) more closely to get a better picture of how these ethnic nuclei cluster. John Kralt (1986a; 1986b; 1986c) has published extensive materials on the concentrations of numerous ethnic groups in Montreal, Toronto, and Vancouver for 1981. In Figure 6-2 we have plotted Toronto and Vancouver, showing census tracts in which certain ethnic groups cluster. In Toronto over half of the Portuguese (56 percent), the Jews, (53 percent), and the Italians (51 percent) are located in small clusters of tracts (Balakrishnan and Kralt, 1987:148). The Chinese and Portuguese are located closer to the center, and the Italians and Jews farther towards the periphery.

In Vancouver over half the Chinese (52 percent) are located in Canada's oldest and largest Chinatown near Burrard Inlet, close to where the largest Japantown used to be located (now only a few blocks long). The Indo-Pakistanis, Italians, and Jews also have their distinct areas.

In their study, Balakrishnan and Kralt (1987:151) used the dissimilarity index as well; this is the sum of either the positive or negative differences between the proportional distributions of two ethnic populations. It ranges from zero (complete similarity) to unity (dissimilarity) between the residential distributions of two ethnic populations. The Gini index measures similar correlations. Comparing the three largest metropolitan centers in Canada, we see in Table 6-4 that the Jews (.832) are the most highly dissimilar in Montreal,

Table 6-3 Mean index of segregation for ethnic groups, 1981

METROPOLITAN AREA	BRITISH	GERMAN	OTHER SINGLE	UKRAINIAN	POLISH	FRENCH	DUTCH	SCANDI- NAVIAN	ITALIAN	NATIVE INDIAN
Halifax	.291	.319	.347	.473	.439	.297	.350	.367	.453	.522
Montreal	.480	.497	.562	.553	.524	.585	.603	.647	.675	.615
Ottawa-Hull	.327	.349	.363	.393	.385	.605	.420	.408	.484	.530
Toronto	.342	.355	.416	.427	.460	.360	.436	.441	.560	.532
Hamilton	.299	.328	.322	.330	.360	.320	.440	.416	.418	.535
St. Cath-Niagara	.298	.357	.314	.307	.341	.406	.404	.434	.435	.528
Kitchener	.268	.311	.290	.327	.303	.266	.324	.415	.360	.449
London	.254	.278	.283	.334	.330	.275	.361	.375	.366	.476
Windsor	.273	.287	.322	.306	.334	.335	.342	.412	.357	.545
Winnipeg	.329	.331	.374	.347	.358	.462	.366	.345	.428	.520
Calgary	.195	.200	.231	.218	.240	.231	.247	.225	.355	.386
Edmonton	.247	.274	.298	.270	.270	.266	.302	.270	.420	.383
Vancouver	.271	.275	.359	.271	.305	.294	.328	.278	.488	.439
Victoria	.227	.231	.288	.229	.292	.256	.298	.242	.342	.412
Mean	.293	.314	.341	.342	.353	.354	.373	.377	.439	.491

SOURCE: Balakrishnan and Selvanathan (1990).

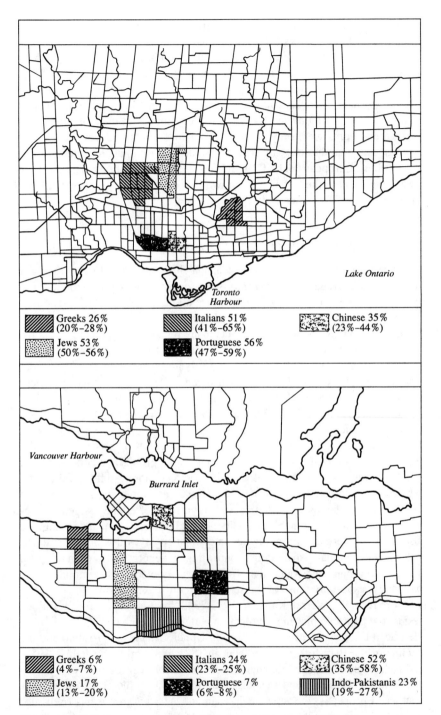

Figure 6-2 Ethnic concentrations in Toronto and Vancouver: 1981
SOURCE: Balakrishnan and Kralt (1987: 148).

followed by the Greeks (.658) and the Portuguese (.603) in a generally highly segregated city. The Jews (.740) also have the highest dissimilarity score in Toronto and the second highest in Vancouver (.562). The Portuguese (.633) rank second in Toronto and first in Vancouver (.589). The German-Austrians rank lowest on the dissimilarity index in all three cities. Interestingly, visible minorities such as Blacks, Chinese, and Indo-Pakistanis ranked in the middle. Blacks especially had dissimilarity scores very similar to the British in Montreal; their scores were only slightly higher in Toronto and Vancouver. The Chinese had high dissimilarity scores also, usually ranking after the Jews and the southern Europeans. The Chinese ranked third highest on dissimilarity in Vancouver, where the largest Chinatown is located and where past Chinese-White relations have often been difficult.

Ethnic Segregation in Toronto

Our survey of ethnic segregation in Canada shows that Montreal is the most residentially segregated and Toronto is the second most segregated city. The Portuguese, Jews, Italians, and Indians are all highly segregated in Toronto. Since Toronto is located in the industrial heartland of Canada, it is also among the fastest growing centers, and attracts many recent immigrants to new jobs. This has changed Toronto from an urban center largely created by Canadians of British origin, to one of the most ethnically and racially diverse in Canada. Fortunately, ethnicity in Toronto has also been researched extensively (Richmond, 1972; Kalbach, 1980; Kallen, 1977; Balakrishnan and Kralt, 1987; Breton *et al*, 1990).

Anthony Richmond (1972) was among the first to focus specifically on residential segregation in Toronto. Richmond used 1961 census data to plot indices of dissimilarity between the various ethnic groups and concluded that ethnicity was a salient factor along with socio-economic status in differing residential patterns. Richmond (1972:14) used a sample survey in 1969 to 1970 to ask questions about the causes and effects of ethnic residential segregation and patterns of mobility. He found that Jewish, Italian, and Portuguese Torontonians were highly segregated in distinct enclaves. He studied residential and occupational distributions, controlling by generation for each religious and ethnic group, and found that Toronto's Jews were highly mobile occupationally, especially those of the second and third generations.

More recently, Warren Kalbach (1980; 1990) has focused on Toronto ethnic residential patterns, plotting segregation patterns for each decade since 1871. He traced the early British dominance in Upper Canada and Toronto and the decline of the British from 96 percent in 1871 to slightly over half in 1971. Kalbach (1980:9-17) used the index of dissimilarity over this 100-year period (1871 to 1971) and found that dissimilarities among the British and other southern Europeans, the Jews, and Asian and African groups has risen substantially. Kalbach did computer mapping of many of these groups to trace the extent of their concentration and segregation. He also traced the ecological

Table 6-4 Indices of dissimilarity of each ethnic group from all other groups and Gini indices of concentration

ETHNIC GROUP	MONTREAL DISSIMILARITY	GINI	TORONTO DISSIMILARITY	GINI	VANCOUVER DISSIMILARITY	GINI
British only	.459	.539	.261	.229	.176	.145
French only	.472	.460	.198	.220	.210	.249
German-Austrian	.409	.504	.192	.205	.157	.174
Jewish	.832	.931	.740	.867	.562	.715
Italian	.565	.689	.506	.627	.448	.566
Greek	.658	.823	.461	.589	.480	.643
Portuguese	.603	.763	.633	.777	.589	.752
Black & Caribbean	.463	.582	.376	.474	.325	.419
Indo-Pakistani	.579	.712	.401	.520	.379	.496
Chinese	.595	.738	.447	.577	.502	.622
Mean	.564	.674	.422	.509	.382	.478

SOURCE: Balakrishnan and Kralt (1987: 151).

mobility of groups over time to show their invasion and succession patterns; the mobility patterns of the Italians and Jews are shown in Figure 6-3. Both groups began roughly in the center of Toronto in 1950 and then proceeded to move towards the suburbs, establishing segregated enclaves en route. The Jews, who are more upwardly mobile socio-economically, have also travelled farther towards suburban nuclei such as North York.

A number of these clusters of ethnic concentrations have been studied at different times. Seeley, Sim, and Loosley (1956) studied the family and community patterns of Crestwood Heights, which was the suburb where the largest concentration of Jews was located in the 1940s (see Figure 6-3). Evelyn Kallen (1977) followed the Jews to North York and did an extensive study of their changing socialization and identity patterns over several generations. These are two in-depth studies of the Jewish community in two different locations in time. These ethnic multiple nuclei are moving and changing. Grace Anderson (1974) did an extensive study of the Portuguese, who are the most segregated of all ethnic groups in Toronto. This in-depth Portuguese study shows the channels of immigrant arrivals, and their adjustments and beginnings in a large metropolis, which we will describe in more detail in the next section. All these studies enrich the general census data, so that we now have a larger understanding of what some of these ethnic nuclei are like and how they change.

Breton, Kalbach, Isajiw, and Reitz (1981; 1990) studied a large sample (1840) of adults in Toronto in 1978; Reitz (1981) did some extensive work on ethnic segregation in jobs. He found that 71 percent of the West Indian males and 65 percent of the females were among the most segregated in occupations. Jews were heavily segregated in white professional occupations, and Italians were heavily segregated in blue-collar jobs. Reitz's (1981) findings suggest that education, income, and occupation are closely intertwined, that some ethnic groups are in higher status occupations, and that this is also correlated with place of residence. Ethnicity and socio-economic status are independent but influence each other with regard to residential segregation (Isajiw and Driedger, 1987).

Segregation in Winnipeg

In the early seventies, when Anthony Richmond was beginning his studies of segregation in Toronto, Leo Driedger and associates (1974) also began research on ethnic segregation in Winnipeg. Using some of Shevky and Bell's (1955) ethnic concentration, isolation, and segregation indices, Driedger and Church (1974:30-52) compared the Jewish, French, Ukrainian, German, Polish, and Scandinavian groups; they found the Jews and French most segregated, and the Poles and Scandinavians least segregated. They used a variety of methods to distinguish between the dimensions of segregation such as concentration, isolation, and mobility over three decades, 1941 to 1971. By examining ethnic clustering of census tracts in 1941, they found that 69 percent

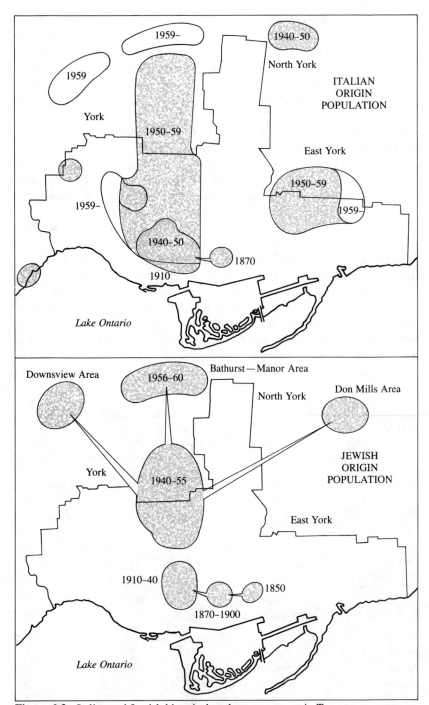

Figure 6-3 Italian and Jewish historical settlement patterns in Toronto

SOURCE: City of Toronto Planning Board, "Report on the Ethnic Origins of the Population of Toronto," 1961 (adopted from Figures D-1 and D-3); and Kalbach (1980).

of the Jews were located in a cluster of six census areas in the North End, and 42 percent of the Ukrainians were also clustered in the North End adjacent to the Jews (Driedger, 1978, 1979). However, the French were highly concentrated across the river in the older parts of St. Boniface. Examination of these same areas in 1961 showed that most of the French remained in St. Boniface, but the Jews had moved, and 58 percent now lived in two distinctly new suburban areas in North Kildonan and River Heights. Of the remaining Jews, one group had remained largely in its original area, and the other had moved out to the suburbs (Driedger and Church, 1974).

To document these changes in residential segregation over time, Driedger and Church (1974) used Shevky and Bell's (1955) isolation and segregation indices; the results are presented in Figure 6-5. The ecological isolation index shows the "residential concentration of the members of a particular group with other members of the same group." (Shevky and Bell, 1955:44.) The Shevky and Bell segregation ratio was used to measure the probable interaction among members of a subordinate ethnic group with members of all subordinate (non-British) groups in Winnipeg. As shown in Table 6-5, the Jews were the most segregated of all groups in 1941 (.71), and they still remained highly segregated in 1971 (.60), although their movement into the suburbs in the interval had resulted in a slight decline over the three decades. The French were also highly segregated, and by remaining in their St. Boniface area over time, their segregation scores actually increased. The Scandinavians, who in Winnipeg are largely Icelandic, always scored the lowest among the six groups studied.

Table 6-5 A comparison of ethnic group isolation and segregation in Winnipeg, for 1941, 1951, and 1961, with 1971 estimates

ETHNIC GROUPS	ISOLATION 1941	1951	1961	1971
Jewish	.31	.21	.18	.19
French	.19	.20	.18	.15
Ukrainian	.23	.16	.12	.14
Polish	.05	.04	.02	.02
German	.08	.04	.04	.03
Scandinavian	.02	.01	.00	.01

ETHNIC GROUPS	SEGREGATION 1941	1951	1961	1971 (ESTIMATED)
Jewish	.71	.64	.62	.60
French	.43	.52	.57	.60
Ukrainian	.64	.58	.56	.53
Polish	.61	.60	.59	.58
German	.48	.47	.48	.45
Scandinavian	.26	.37	.47	.44

SOURCE: Driedger (1980).

Driedger (1978, 1979, 1980, 1987) also investigated the patterns of ecological mobility of each of the six ethnic groups. He took a sample of residents
in the North End and St. Boniface, where the Jews and French were concentrated in 1951, and traced their whereabouts a decade later in 1961. He found
that seven out of ten French movers located in the same north St. Boniface
area, and of the remaining three, most located in newer areas of St. Boniface
as well. As in Montreal, the French in Winnipeg tend to stay in their French
area of residence. The Jews, on the other hand, were among the poorest
eastern European immigrants when they first arrived, but were more upwardly
mobile than any other groups; two-thirds moved out of the aging North End
to establish new, distinct Jewish communities in West Kildonan and River
Heights.

Driedger (1978, 1979, 1980) also predicted that the Jews and the French
in Winnipeg, who were the most isolated and segregated, would also be the
most institutionally complete, which in fact was the case. He found that north
St. Boniface was a francophone center that had French churches, schools, and
other social institutions. The Jews, on the other hand, took their synagogues,
schools, and social institutions with them to the suburbs, where they were
replanted and supported. The Toronto and Winnipeg studies provide further
qualitative data that show the variations among ethnic groups in mobility,
institutional completeness, concentration of their ingroup, as well as segregation from others. These ethnic nuclei are diverse, ever-changing and
dynamic, showing that invasion and succession is an important part of urban
ethnic ecological patterns and change. The multiple nuclei theories allow for
more change than the concentric zone and sector hypotheses.

Studies in Segregation

To get some feel for the diversity of ethnic residential segregation in Canada,
we shall examine studies of Blacks in Halifax segregated because of race;
Jews in Montreal and their religion; the Chinese in Vancouver, engaged in
business in the largest Chinatown; and the Portuguese, who are new and first-
generation immigrants in Toronto. Each study shows that there are a variety
of social reasons why minorities become spatially segregated into nuclei. Let
us illustrate how the theory of multiple nuclei presented by Hoyt and the
multiple ethnic patterns of residential segregation found by Shevky and Bell
can also be found in Canada.

Africville: Blacks in Halifax

Donald Clairmont and Dennis Magill (1974) have documented the life and
death of a Canadian Black urban community, called Africville, that no longer
exists. "Africville was a Black enclave within the city of Halifax, inhabited
by approximately 400 people, comprising 80 families, many of whom were
descended from settlers who came over a century ago." (Clairmont and
Magill, 1974:19.) It was tucked into a corner of Halifax, where it was rela-

tively invisible, and was referred to as "shack town." The ghetto was isolated from the rest of Halifax behind the railroad and city dump, and was surrounded on three sides by water (Bedford Basin). Most of the Black families had squatter rights; those who did not, rented.

"Slavery was never instituted by statute in Nova Scotia, yet slavery was practised in Halifax a year after the city was founded and, over the next five decades, it was not uncommon in other parts of the province." (Krauter, 1968:40; Krauter and Davis, 1978:41-68.) At the outbreak of the American Revolution, there were approximately five hundred slaves, many of whom had come with their New England masters. Slave-holding Loyalist immigrants increased the number by approximately a thousand. There were also refugee Blacks who settled at Preston near Halifax on small lots of rocky soil and scrubby forest ranging from three to four hectares (Clairmont and Magill, 1974:42).

The area that eventually came to be known as Africville was settled by the slaves who had settled at Preston but could not make a living because of the poor land. They came to the shore of Bedford Basin in the area that is just below the recently built A. Murray McKay bridge. This area was convenient for fishing and also near opportunities for wage labor. The Africville population increased tenfold between 1850 and 1964. The people had little education and very low incomes; a third of the adult population was unemployed, another third had irregular work, and the final third worked in low paid jobs as porters, domestics, laborers, clerical workers, and dockworkers. Sewerage, lighting, and other public services were conspicuously absent in Africville (Clairmont and Magill, 1974:19). The people obtained water from improvised wells that were often in a poor state. There were no paved roads.

The Africville land seemed to be a prime site for potential industrial development. The city of Halifax owned properties near it, the railway was close by, and the shoreline was valuable for harbor development. Discussions began after 1955 about removing the Black community. After numerous studies and reports it was decided to relocate the residents of the community in 1964 (Clairmont and Magill, 1974:180).

Once relocation was agreed on, the Halifax City Council accepted the responsibility of providing the relocatees with safe, sanitary, and decent housing. About 75 percent were relocated in urban renewal projects within walking distance of their former dwellings. They received better housing but they lost a lot of freedom because they were now renters instead of landowners or owners of dwellings; only one-third owned their own homes after relocation. The lack of a regular income made it difficult to pay mortgages and service and maintenance bills. Most families of Africville were relocated in Uniacke Square; this was two-storey public housing. Clairmont and Magill (1974:223) interviewed many relocatees. Two-thirds said they had more difficulties making ends meet in their new homes. Over half said they were able to stay in contact with their former Africville friends; but over half also thought they could no longer count on their neighbors for help. A majority felt they had lost a feeling of belonging, that the friendliness and trustworthiness of neighbors had declined. These were the social costs of relocation. Now Africville is a public park where formerly there was a segregated block community.

Jewish Segregation in Montreal

Until recently the largest Jewish community in Canada lived in Montreal; "almost all (98 percent) of Quebec's Jews live in or near Montreal." (Waller and Weinfeld, 1981:415.) The first congregation (Spanish and Portuguese Jews) was established in Montreal more than 200 years ago in 1768; German Jews arrived later. By 1901 the Jewish population had climbed to almost 7,000, and by 1971 there were 109,000 (Waller and Weinfeld, 1981:416). These Jewish Montrealers usually identified with the English-speaking population, although recently Sephardic Jews from French-speaking Africa have arrived to form a small francophone minority. The Quebec school system has been based on religious preferences: Roman Catholics attended Catholic schools (these are also mostly French); non-Catholics (including Jews) attended non-Catholic schools.

"In the 1971 census, 77 percent of Montreal Jews listed English as the language most often spoken at home (10 percent listed French, 7 percent Yiddish, and 6 percent 'other')." (Waller and Weinfeld, 1981:417.) The Jews of Montreal are not only segregated from the French, but they are also a "Jewish Solitude" that has not integrated with other English-speaking Montrealers; this is a similar situation to Louis Wirth's (1928) Chicago ghettos. The Jews have developed their own organizational infrastructure, which includes social, cultural, and welfare services. There is also a high degree of social segregation: 87 percent indicated that all their neighbors were Jewish, and 35 percent that almost all their business associates were Jewish (Weinfeld and Easton, 1979).

As the oldest and most organized ethnic community, the Jews of Montreal were relatively happy in Quebec, content to ignore provincial politics as long as they could do business and make a living. They were concerned about a separatist Quebec, which would be isolated from the large North American market, including English Canada. Between one-fifth and one-fourth are Holocaust survivors. Because of their past experience of anti-Semitism, they are afraid that strong separatist feelings may also spill over into anti-English-speaking anti-Semitism. Any signs of prejudice against anglophones, who are a small minority but control banks and large corporations, alarm many Jews, because such prejudice could easily extend to religious prejudice as well. A few incidents of public anti-Semitism can always be found.

Quebec separatist politics are seen as possibly detrimental to business. After a separatist-leaning government was elected in Quebec, private capital started to leave Quebec and moved to Toronto. Many Jews, especially younger ones, also moved to Toronto, so that the Jewish community in Toronto is now the largest in Canada, and they are again residentially segregated. A disproportionate number of older Jewish people remained in Montreal; this left a shrinking base for funds to keep Jewish institutions going. "Parents expect

46 percent of the next biological generation will not be in Montreal by 1983." (Waller and Weinfeld, 1981:433.) Montreal's Jewish schools teach Judaic studies conducted in Hebrew and Yiddish for half the day, and secular studies conducted in English for the other half of the day, but pressures to include French are increasing. Thus, in addition to studying Hebrew, Yiddish, and English, Jews are faced with learning more French. The fact that the religious curriculum is developed in Toronto and New York, to be taught in English, makes inclusion of more French a problem.

Shaffir (1981:12-17) summarizes the distinctiveness of Canadian Jews by saying that they are: 1) more geographically concentrated than their American counterparts (over two-thirds of Canadian Jews live in Montreal and Toronto); 2) more "Jewish" than American Jews in that they speak more Yiddish, provide their children with more Jewish education, make more visits to Israel, are more orthodox, and have lower rates of intermarriage; 3) a generation closer to the Old World (in the 1970s, at least 40 percent of the households were foreign-born). They say that Jewish identity is doing well in the two cities of Canada, and that ecological and cultural segregation are important.

Shaffir (1981:17-19) also compares the uniqueness of Canadian Jews with other minorities in Canada. 1) Canadian Jews are both a religious and an ethnic group; religious and cultural traditions reinforce each other, including the use of as many as three Jewish languages (Yiddish, Hebrew, Ladino). 2) Jews in Canada are relatively affluent, so they have both the will and the means to support Jewish education and Jewish institutions. 3) Jews have significant ties with Israel. Radio, television, and the newspapers daily remind Jews of Israel's problems. 4) Finally, many experienced the Holocaust personally; their off-spring are deeply aware of these experiences. That they are different they remember daily, and their identity has considerable salience through ingroup loyalties. To live in a natural area where other kin and their community are a support is important to them. Thus, Jews in Montreal, Toronto, and Winnipeg are voluntarily segregated socially and ecologically.

To illustrate the extent to which conservative Jewish religion is entrenched in some parts of Montreal, William Shaffir (1974) studied the Lubavitcher Chassidim in Montreal, and reported his findings in *Life in a Religious Community*. The Lubavitcher are but one branch of the Chassidim; they are ultra Orthodox, and focused on the teachings of a leader called a Rebbe. All males wear black hats and black clothes, and adult males wear beards, which make them highly visible. Although the Lubavitcher Chassidim are a small group that started only in 1941, they run orthodox schools to which many other Jews also send their children; these reinforce the social and ecological segregation of Jews.

The Chinese: Segregated Chinatowns

"Emigration from China to Canada began in 1858." (Wickberg, 1982:7; Morton, 1974). These early Chinese immigrants were mostly men seeking to do business during the gold rush in British Columbia. In 1881 Chinese men were brought in from the USA and Asia to help with the building of the Canadian Pacific Railway (Lai, 1988:3-33). By 1885, there were 10,000 Chinese in Canada, all in British Columbia (Wickberg, 1982:27); more than one-fourth (2,900) in railroad construction. When the building of the railroad ended in the 1880s, thousands of Chinese were left unemployed. While many Chinese settled in Victoria, Vancouver was to be the western terminus of the Canadian Pacific Railway. Large groups of Chinese were employed to clear the area, and these workers became a threat to the Whites, because they were cheap labor that took much-needed jobs. "In 1884 the Chinese in Burrard Inlet comprised five merchants, ten store employees, thirty cooks and laundrymen, and one prostitute, as well as sixty sawmill hands." (Wickberg, 1982:61.) By 1886 many Chinese in the Burrard Inlet area began to raise vegetable gardens and started truck farming, and soon they supplied most of the vegetables for the Vancouver settlement. By 1886 they began to settle in the Pender area; here the oldest and for many years the largest segregated Canadian Chinatown has existed for a hundred years, next to the largest segregated Japantown in Canada (Driedger, 1989:248-50).

In 1941 there were 35,000 Chinese in Canada; by 1981 there were 289,000. Before the Second World War the Chinese were centered in British Columbia; after 1945, the many Chinese immigrants spread across Canada. By 1981 about one-third resided in Vancouver, another third in Toronto, and the remaining third scattered mostly in other cities across Canada (Lai, 1988:118). The two largest Chinatowns in 1986 were located in Toronto (143,235) and Vancouver (109,370); these were studied in some depth by David Lai (1988).

As seen in Figure 6-2, the Vancouver Chinatown comprises some eight city blocks along Pender Street close to the downtown business section, and just off Burrard Inlet. Figure 6-4 shows more detail; hundreds of stores, shops, and businesses of all kinds are located in Chinatown, along with all the services that the Chinese need (Lai, 1988:126-35). A number of Chinese newspapers are published here, and movie houses, restaurants, clubs, voluntary organizations, churches and temples, and recreational facilities are located in Chinatown (Wickberg, 1982:254-67). The community puts on annual Chinese festivals and various attractions such as musicals, drama contests, and literary events. Chinese "bachelors" of the early days live here, as well as many families, so that it is a living Chinese community where activity never ceases (Lai, 1988:126-35). Since Chinatown constitutes a business section that attracts tourists, it has a viable economic base that has survived for a hundred years and most likely will continue for the foreseeable future.

The dissimilarity scores for the Chinese in Vancouver (.50), in Toronto (.45), and in Montreal (.60) rank them third, fifth, and fourth highest respectively, because of the differing patterns of early and later immigration. Those who still live in Chinatown are as segregated as any other ethnic group, if not more so. However, the Toronto Chinese community has been moving and has relocated recently, which has not happened in Vancouver (Lai, 1988:146-9). The Vancouver Chinatown is one of the best examples of a segregated urban community near the downtown business district.

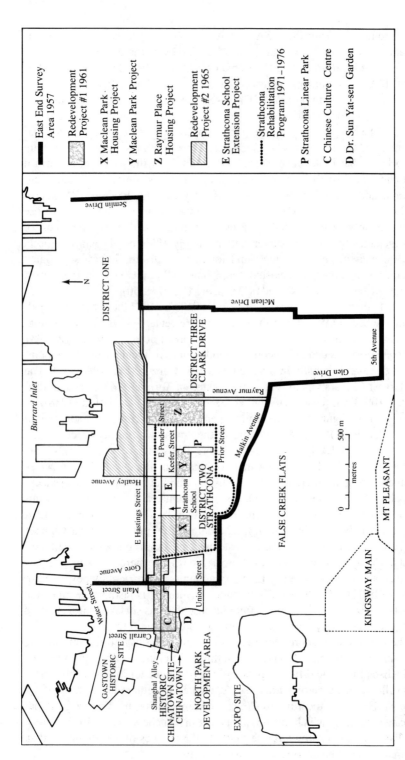

Figure 6-4 Vancouver's Chinatown and Strathcona District, 1950–1980.
SOURCE: Lai (1988: 127).

Chinatowns had their origins at the turn of the century; because the first Chinese immigrants were not allowed to bring their families, these Chinatowns met the special needs of the Chinese "bachelors" who needed each other's social support (Lai, 1980:13-21). The many Chinese immigrants who came to Canada after the Second World War came as families; they were often professional and business people who located freely in urban suburbs, and were therefore relatively unsegregated. Many are integrating fast, and are experiencing an extensive modification of their culture. Some intermarriage is taking place, but they remain physically visible and this hinders assimilation for many (Li, 1988).

The Portuguese: Immigrants in Toronto

The 1981 Census reports 188,000 Portuguese in Canada, most of whom came after World War II and especially during the 1960s. Two-thirds live in Ontario, and almost half in Toronto (89,000); there they make up 3 percent of the metropolitan population (Balakrishnan and Kralt, 1987:143). Over half (56 percent) in Toronto live in seven small census tracts near downtown Toronto in the Kensington Market area. The Portuguese are one of the most segregated ethnic groups in Toronto, with a .63 dissimilarity score. These recent immigrants were drawn to settle in the southern Ontario industrial milieu. Race is not a factor, since they are Caucasian, but social class is, since they came mostly from poor, Portuguese-held islands, and have little education or special occupational skills.

We are fortunate to have several intensive studies of the Portuguese in Toronto by Grace Anderson (1974) and Anderson and Higgs (1976). Anderson writes (1974:167):

> When the residents of metropolitan Toronto think of the Portuguese, they usually call to mind the colourful Kensington Market with its Portuguese stores spilling over onto the side-walks. Chickens can be bought, still alive, from cages. Fresh fruit stores, vegetable stands, and fish shops are there in abundance. The delicious aroma of Portuguese pastries floats from the bakeries. Everywhere there is bustle and animated conversation. The groups jostle each other. . . . blocking the free flow of pedestrian traffic on the crowded sidewalks. Occasionally a car attempts to make its way down the road. . . . Many visitors come to the area to see the 'Portuguese district'. . . .

Richmond (1972) has plotted the location of the Portuguese and other ethnic groups in Toronto; the study by Balakrishnan and Kralt (1987:148) was illustrated in Figure 6-2. The Portuguese are located adjacent to Chinatown, so that the two business areas tend to complement each other. "Between 1953 and the mid-60s, the Portuguese poured into the Kensington Market area." (Anderson and Higgs, 1976:69.)

Using Raymond Breton's criterion of the "institutional completeness" of an ethnic group, Anderson writes of the Portuguese (1974:170):

The Portuguese in Toronto now constitute in many ways a very 'institutionally complete' ethnic group. Within the Kensington Market area there are also Portuguese restaurants, real estate agents, printers. Books and records from Portugal can be purchased there. Several newspapers are available. . . . A radio station reports Portuguese programs regularly. In the ethnic press various services are offered in addition to those mentioned above — taxis, driving schools. . . . , a Portuguese bank, and services of immigration consultants, interpreters and income tax specialists.

Two Catholic churches provide services in Portuguese. Several centers provide social activities and social assistance. There are clubs and pool halls, and soccer teams with a large Portuguese contingent.

The family is very important to the Portuguese, and mutual aid is common. Relatives live within easy reach of each other. The average size of the family is 5 to 6 people, and the average education of those who come from the Azores Islands, where few went to school beyond grade four, is three to four years of schooling (Anderson, 1974:71). Half of the immigrant men were farmers, so urban life in Toronto is new to them; in addition they must deal with the cultural differences. Most of the men are happy to find blue-collar jobs.

The Portuguese in Toronto are one of the post-World War II immigrant groups (others are the Italians and Greeks) who are highly segregated in the center of the city, are of lower socio-economic status, have developed their own institutionally complete enclaves, and communicate at home and in much of their time in Portuguese; many learn to speak only broken English.

Elizabeth Bott (1957) was among the first to develop the social network perspective, beginning with the family as a small network unit. Network theory focuses on individual ties, which are more pliable and less rigid than social structures, forming nets of interchange. Ethnic groups such as the Portuguese stress the importance of the family and encourage endogamy. The ethnic family can be seen as a network that links many others. The Portuguese maintain informal relationships with colleagues, friends, neighbors, and relatives (Bott, 1957:98). Bott maintains that no urban family can survive without its network of external relationships. Bott (1957) suggests that as ethnic groups move from isolated rural communities, or as rural communities become less isolated and move to a more open urban environment, they must make sure the family remains tightly knit. Strong family ties among the Portuguese illustrate that all three of Shevky and Bell's indicators are operating — socio-economic status, family ties, and ethnicity — to bring about residential segregation.

Summary

Residential segregation is one way of examining the multiple nuclei in metropolitan areas. Canadians were among the first to study such segregation. Roderick McKenzie, who grew up in Manitoba, is well known for his work on dominance in urban areas. Charles Dawson was the first Canadian sociologist; he taught at McGill, studied segregation in Montreal, and later examined immigrant group settlement on the Canadian Prairies. Everett Hughes, who joined Dawson at McGill, studied the effects of industrialization on French-English relations in Quebec.

Ecological segregation is influenced by numerous factors, including race, ethnicity, social class, and religion. Early American sociologists explored the segregation of Blacks in ghettos. In Canada the French and English are highly segregated in Quebec, and are clustered in anglophone and francophone solitudes in Montreal. Jews, Chinese, Greeks, Portuguese, and Native Indians are all highly segregated in Canadian cities. Some cluster voluntarily; others have to live in racial or ethnic clusters because of social pressures. The Duncans' propose that residential segregation occurs in zones following social class lines, while Shevky and Bell predict multiple nuclei of racial and ethnic clusters. In Canada ethnicity seems to follow the multiple nuclei pattern, particularly in Montreal, Toronto, Vancouver, and Winnipeg.

Using census data, national research shows that ethnic segregation is highest in Montreal and Toronto, Canada's two largest cities. Calgary and Victoria in the West are the least residentially segregated Canadian cities. Balakrishnan found that Native Indians, Portuguese, Italians, and Greeks are the most residentially segregated. Jews are especially segregated in Montreal, and Portuguese, Italians, and Jews are highly segregated in Toronto. Chinese are highly segregated in Vancouver, so the patterns do vary by ethnic group. Many ethnic and religious groups also have their own churches, schools, and voluntary organizations, which support their identity.

Studies show that segregated ethnic nuclei are complex subcultures where values, culture, language, and ideals are nourished. Blacks had a segregated community in Africville in Halifax; here they were highly isolated, socially and spatially. Jews are an example of a segregated religious group. Chinatowns are highly developed in Vancouver and Toronto; here the Chinese have their businesses, institutions, homes, and social activities. The Portuguese are one of the most recent immigrant groups to Toronto, and are highly segregated.

Ethnic residential segregation conforms to the multiple nuclei theory of urban spatial patterns, and the findings of Shevky and Bell in ethnic residential segregation in Los Angeles and San Francisco are clearly demonstrated in most of Canada's cities as well. Ethnicity is an important factor in the dynamics of urban growth, and sociologists have studied it intensively.

7. Work and the Industrial Economy

In parts one and two we examined the first and second preconditions of Duncan's theory of urban development (see chapter one). We now need to discuss the third and fourth preconditions: social organization and technology. These four elements of urban growth interact with each other, so it is not possible to discuss the first two—population and environment—without also discussing social organization and technology. It is not possible to deal with all the social institutions—family, religion, education, economics, and politics —we shall therefore select three (economics, politics, family) and examine how the urban factor influences them. In chapter seven we begin with a discussion of work, a major human activity, and the one by which we make a living.

A major theme in this book has been urban dominance and influence. In parts one and two we looked at dominance in a world setting (core nations and periphery); in a national context (regional dominance by major urban centers); and within an urban center (dominant areas, socio-economic classes, and ethnic groups). In part three we want to show how economic and political power have grown, and how other social institutions such as the family are increasingly less influential in the modern urban setting.

Urban Economic Power

Industrial technology began to develop in Europe in the sixteenth century; this was also the century that ushered in the Protestant Reformation and saw the beginnings of political nationalism. The developments in technology were accompanied by the rise of laissez-faire capitalism with its emphases on individual enterprise, competition, private property, and the profit motive—attitudes that were in considerable contrast to the feudalism of the Middle Ages. The tenets of the Roman Catholic Church—including resignation and acceptance of the *status quo*—influenced, had even controlled European life and thought throughout the Middle Ages. The religious reformation freed the individual from this religious domination. We shall begin by developing a conceptual context for institutions of economic power.

Institutions of Economic Power

Jack Richardson (l986:437-56) defines economic institutions as "the set of organizations, groups and processes by which people in a society produce and distribute goods and services"; these institutions will vary depending on the mode of production, the available technology, and the central values held by the society. When an individual, a group, or a metropolis controls a significant share of a particular resource, it has power over others. This creates dependence in those who need or want the resource. Classical sociologists such as Weber and Marx were concerned with such power.

Richardson (1986:436) compares the approaches of the classical sociologists:

> Weber [1958] proposed that the distribution of benefits in an economic exchange depends on the relative market power of the parties involved. Market power, in turn, rests on two interrelated factors in Weber's analysis. The first is how much the control of a commodity is concentrated in a few hands. The second is how effectively one party to an exchange can withhold a commodity from the market.

Our discussion of metropolitan centers such as Toronto and Montreal showed that some are better able to compete in the larger Canadian economic network because they are much larger than others as well as more strategically and centrally located. Concentration of metropoli in one region will also provide some Canadian regions with more economic power than others. In the competition for such power, can some urban centers effectively control the distribution of commodities so that other urban centers become relatively dependent? To what extent are the economic power elite also concentrated in a few centers, and are there extensive overlapping networks, so that a few power elite within a few centers control large sections of the economy?

Irving Zeitlin (1972) suggests that much of Weber's work is a debate with the ghost of Karl Marx, and can therefore be seen as a positive and extensive elaboration of some of Marx's concerns.

> While Weber analyzed economic power mainly in terms of the relations of exchange, Marx focused on the relations of production. Marx [1954] proposed that those who control the means of production (the bourgeoisie) dominate and exploit those who do not (the proletariat).   (Richardson, 1986:439.)

Industrial society applies machine technology in a variety of ways, using intensive division of labor, which results in increasingly more formal occupational structures. The machines and the structured workforce both tend to alienate the workers. Capitalism, under individual ownership of the means of production, is designed to maximize profits in an economy controlled by the forces of supply and demand. Weber focused on the extent to which such market power became increasingly rationalized, bureaucratized, and secularized, and less interwoven with other social institutions such as family, religion, and education. As a result these institutions become less influential.

For Marx the "mode of production" is the foundation of his conception of history. Marx's conception involves two elements: the forces of production, and the relations of production (Richardson, 1986:442). The forces of production include the interaction among human producers, their tools, the technology, and the material environment. Class, power, and property make up the relations of production (Zeitlin, 1972). Technological developments, division of labor, and population pressures create dynamic forces for change, all of which are more exaggerated in highly urban environments (Richardson, 1986:442).

Weber extended Marx's analysis by placing it within a broader sweep of historical dynamics (Zeitlin, 1972):

> The first of these dynamics was the rise of rationality, which became institutionalized through technology, the marketplace, economic enterprise and the law. The second was the coincident development of bureaucracy, which separated the producer from the means of production, administration, science and war. Thirdly, Weber (1930) examined the influence of religion on the rise of capitalism. He proposed that early Protestantism encouraged the self-discipline, hard work and individualism that fostered competition and investment.
>
> (Richardson, 1986:444.)

In the next section we focus on economic institutions and enterprises and the relative power commanded by various sections of society such as business and labor (Smucker, 1980).

The Canadian Corporate Elite

While classical sociologists were concerned with the rise of industrial power, Canadian sociologists such as John Porter (1965) and more recently Wallace Clement (1975, 1977, 1988) have concentrated on the Canadian corporate elite and corporate power on this continent. George Grant (1965:9-10) describes the changes that have taken place since World War II:

> From 1940 to 1957, the ruling class of this country was radically reshaped. In 1939, the United Kingdom still seemed a powerful force, and the men who ruled Canada were a part of the old Atlantic triangle. They turned almost as much to Great Britain as to the United States, economically, culturally, and politically. After 1940, the ruling class found its gravity in the United States.

Rosenbluth (1954:206) writes: "In 1946, 35 percent of Canada's manufacturing was foreign controlled; by 1953, foreign control had risen to 50 percent, and by 1957 to 56 percent; in mining and smelting the corresponding increases were from 38 percent to 57 percent to 70 percent." Clement (1977:80-131) documents the consolidation of the continental economy and the extent of multinational corporations operating from the United States and Canada.

Extreme corporate concentration has also taken place within Canada. *The Toronto Star* reports (1986). . . . "Six Canadian conglomerates control 723 companies: the Weston Group with 123 corporations; the Black Group with 123; the Demarais Group, 121; the Irving Group, 121; the Charles Rosner

Bronfman Trust, 118; and the Edward and Peter Bronfman Groups with 117. . . . nine families control 46 percent of the value of the most important companies on the Toronto Stock Exchange.'' Wallace Clement (1975, 1977) has traced the extent and density of such interlocking directorships; these we need to examine further.

Corporate interlocking, usually involving senior executives, occurs when one person sits on the board of directors of two or more companies. Clement (1977:164-8) found that of the 194 dominant corporations in the United States and the 113 in Canada, the average Canadian corporation had 16.3 interlocking directorships while the American average was 12.4. Clement also found that the largest corporations tend to have the largest interlocking directorships, especially banks. Figures 7-1 and 7-2 compare the density of interlocks in the United States and Canada, illustrating the centrality of the sectors within each nation. In Canada finance is clearly the dominant sector, having the highest interlocks internally (.37), and also extensive interlocks with transportation (.72), manufacturing (.62), resources (.59), and trade (.37). In Canada the various sectors are greatly dependent on the banks for financing.

In the United States, both manufacturing (.29) and finance (.16) have the highest interlocks internally, and also the highest percentage of interlocks between two sectors (.50). Manufacturing is also strongly interlocked with trade (.31), resources (.31), and transportation (.27). These interlocks with other sectors of the economy are higher than in Canada, where the banking interlocks dominate much more. Canada's manufacturing sector is more dominated by foreign control; thus, interlocks between manufacturing and other sectors are weaker than in the United States. Interlocking directorships are only one indicator of the consolidation of economic power, and our discussion here involves national comparisons. In section three of this chapter we will examine which metropolitan centers are most economically dominant. But first let us briefly sketch how some of these urban centers have developed, and how they fit into the economic power networks of Canada and North America.

Industrial Technological Beginnings

Industrial technological cities began with the invention of steam power, which made the large factories of northern Europe, and especially of Britain, possible (Gendron 1977:40-61).

Development of Industrial Technology

Delbert Miller and William Form (1980:40-41) have plotted the development of industrial technology, and have suggested that it occurred in four different periods, as shown in Table 7-1. In chapter one we briefly showed how the Mediterranean Sea became important to trade for the Phoenicians, Greeks, and Romans. However, these civilizations declined with the fall of the Roman

Figure 7-1 Density of interlocks among the five sectors (194 dominant U.S. companies) in 1975

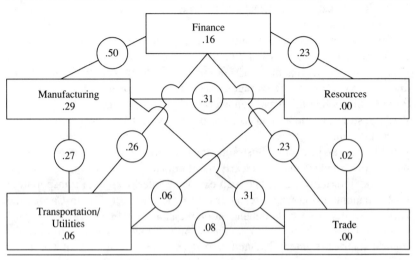

NOTE: Density of interlocks is calculated by dividing the potential number of interlocks by the actual number of interlocks per sector. The figures in the sector boxes represent the density of interlocking *within* each sector. If the density were 1.00, all potential interlocks between sectors would be active; if it were .00, there would be no interlocks. The potential number is determined by the actual number of elite positions within each sector.

Figure 7-2 Density of interlocks among the five sectors (113 dominant Canadian companies) in 1972

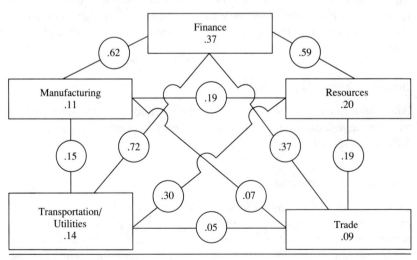

SOURCE: Clement (1977: 166).

Empire and the rise of the Muslim empire, which divided the Mediterranean into Christian (in the north) and Muslim (in the south) solitudes, so that trade and urban development were disrupted. The pre-industrial age (1500 to 1785) began with the discovery by Columbus of America in 1492. Human muscles, wind, and water were the only sources of power; the technology was available to use wood, iron, and bronze to build ships. Through the use of these ships, trade developed in the Mediterranean and Baltic-North Sea areas, which spawned new trading patterns after the Dark and Middle Ages ended and the Roman civilization collapsed.

Before the preindustrial period, Venice and Genoa, on the eastern and western coasts of northern Italy, maintained commercial trade links between India and China and western Europe, making possible the flow of silks and spices via inland trade routes going north into continental Europe, and by sea around Spain as far as England and the Netherlands. Trade by sea was crucial, so these civilizations continued to develop their sea technology; thus later they were able to tackle larger waters like the Atlantic. With the fall of Constantinople to the Ottoman Turks in 1453, Genoa's line to Asian trade was broken. The Genoans supported trade routes via the Atlantic, including Columbus and his voyages (Breasted, Huth and Harding, 1961:38).

At the same time, the Hanseatic League, numbering merchants from 70 member cities, developed around the North and Baltic Seas; the league traded as far west as England, as far east as Novograd in western Russia, in the north to Bergen, Norway, and in the south to Leipzig and Cracow in Poland (Breasted, Huth and Harding, 1961:38). The manufacture of silk and linen products soon spread from northern Italy to northern France and the Netherlands; all were important items of trade for the Hanseatic League in the thirteenth and fourteenth centuries.

In the early industrial period, England was dominant because steam power from coal was first developed there. Steam power was harnessed to machines that were able to produce superior woollen goods. From 1785 machines increasingly replaced skilled craftspeople, manufacturing processes were subdivided, and industry, using the new technology, outdistanced the competition. Cities emerged near England's coalfields (the source of energy) — Leeds, Manchester, Liverpool, Birmingham, Newcastle, and Glasgow (Breasted et al., 1961:34). Britain became the leader in industrialization and urbanization, followed by France and Germany in northern Europe. The invention of steam trains, steamships, and the steam press followed. Early industrialization had gained a major foothold between 1785 and 1870.

New England: Opening the West

At the beginning of the early industrial period, England, the dominant industrial power in Europe, had thirteen important colonial states on the east coast of the United States. Steampower improved transportation between England and its colonial states, permitting increased trade: the American colonies

Table 7-1 Ages of industrial technology

IMPORANT DETERMINERS OF TECHNOLOGY IN DOMINANT AGES	PRE-INDUSTRIAL AGE 1500–	EARLY INDUSTRIAL AGE 1785–	MATURE INDUSTRIAL AGE 1870–	EMERGENT POST-INDUSTRIAL AGE 1953–
Power	Muscle, wind and water	Steam with the use of coal	Electricity and internal combustion machines with use of oil, gas, and coal	Atomic energy supplemented with solar, geothermal, and fusion energy
Tools	Hand	Machine	Automatic machine	Automatic factory
Work skills	All-round skilled craftsmen and unskilled manual workers	Skilled craftspeople replaced by machine (semi-skilled) operatives as a result of subdividing manufacturing processes	Skilled inspector, mechanic required as operations replace need for machine feeding or tending	Highly trained engineers as designers are required; skilled technicians required for monitoring controls and for maintenance of equipment
Materials	Wood, iron, bronze	Steel	Copper, alloyed steels, light alloys, aluminum	Plastics, superalloys, use of 32 new metals, notably magnesium and titanium

Transportation	Walking, or use of animals, via dirt roads; sailboat over seaways	Steam train via steel rails; the iron steamship via ocean way	Automobile, diesel train, or prop airplane via paved highway, railway, and airway	Road and rail track; jet airplane, rocket, and helicopter; turbine and atomic train via railway; atomic ships via ocean surface and sub-surface
Communication	Word of mouth, newspaper, messenger	Mail moved faster by rail and water; newspaper printed on steam press	Telephone, telegraph, AM and FM radio, movie, television, microfilm, magnetic tape	Television telephone, video cassette, talking book or newspaper, universal two-way radio communication, high-speed computers, magnetic-tape photography, vocatypewriter, cable television

SOURCE: Miller and Form (1980: 40-41).

supplied England with cotton for its textiles mills, so that a burgeoning urban industrial Britain traded with its American colonial hinterland overseas. During the early part of the early industrial period, a network of railways using steam power developed in the eastern American states, linking places as far west as Chicago with the east coast. By the end of that age, in 1870, a series of railroads had been built across the American West, from Chicago to the west coast, opening up vast territories for immigrant settlement.

The mature industrial age began in 1870 with the development of new sources of power. The vast waterways of the North American continent provided opportunities to develop electric power, a cleaner source of energy, for travel by electric trains and buses within the city, as well as for other uses. The automobile, mass-produced in Detroit, provided an additional cleaner (than coal-burning steam engines) and more flexible means of transportation. The full impact of the car did not, however, hit North American cities until after World War II, when it became a major factor in the development of suburbs.

Other changes during the mature industrial age revolutionized the urban world of work. New materials such as copper, alloyed steels, light alloys, and aluminum were developed, which in turn permitted the development of automatic machines requiring fewer operators; these threatened to decrease the number of available jobs. Work skills needed updating because more mechanical skills were required.

With the emergence of the post-industrial age, telephone, telegraph, radio, movies, television, microfilms, and communication by magnetic tape have revolutionized the communications fields. The work environment has become faster, more flexible, requiring a more versatile workforce and highly trained engineers, designers, and technicians. Atomic, solar, geothermal, and fusion energy have been developed. New materials, new forms of transportation, and new methods of communication are revolutionizing urban life.

Lower and Upper St. Lawrence

The British and French were the two main powers that explored and exploited North America, to the extent that it became a battleground between them for raw materials. In chapter three we briefly described the development of three cities on the east coast of what is now Canada: St. John's, used by fishermen; Halifax, a British military base; and St. John, a major source of lumber for British shipbuilding. In the interior, British and French vied with each other in the fur trade. Initially the British concentrated their settlements, however, in the New England States; the northern areas were only of strategic interest.

While the British concentrated on New England (beginning with the first settlement at Williamsburg in 1607), the French settled in New France along the St. Lawrence River and in what is now Nova Scotia at the beginning of the seventeenth century. The first settlement in New France, Quebec, was founded in 1608. In 1763, as a result of the British defeat of the French, New

France came under British rule. British settlements now dominated the eastern areas of the North American continent. At this period Britain tended to see these colonies as sources of raw materials for their factories and industry back in England.

Just when the British thought they had secured major dominance in North America, the settlers in New England rebelled. By the end of the American Revolution in 1776, Britain had lost its major colonial settlements in New England, retaining only the northern part of the North American colonial empire. Settlement in Upper Canada (now southern Ontario) developed with the arrival of the British Empire Loyalists, refugees from the American Revolution, who settled there and in the Maritimes, providing the British with a new focus for their colonial interests (Armstrong, 1981). Eventually settlement, and the railways, spread west across the whole of what is now Canada. Industrialization and urbanization only developed towards the end of the nineteenth century in Canada. Toronto has since that time become the leading city in Canada in the post-industrial age (Gendron, 1977). Since 1953 Canada has evolved all the features of this post-industrial age: automated factories; highly trained engineers, designers, and technicians; solar, geothermal, and atomic sources of energy. Canada is now part of the larger American industrial giant, with which Canadians must compete under free trade.

Innis: The Staples Perspective

Harold Innis (1951) developed his perspective on Canada's economic role by studying its primary products, such as cod, furs, lumber, wheat, and minerals, and their trade within the world market. "Innis (1951) proposed that the Canadian economy was driven by the demands of raw materials of the metropolitan markets of France, then Britain and then the United States." (Richardson, 1986:451.) Exploitation of Canada's raw materials stimulated manufacturing in Europe and the USA at the expense of Canadian development. Canada did not diversify because it became caught in a "staples trap" — in good times when there was capital, there was no will to invest; and in bad times there was not sufficient capital to diversify (Richardson, 1986:452).

Being on the periphery of French, British, and American centers of power, Innis (1951, 1956) proposed that Canada's economy was prone to regionalism, each region trading its own staples. In the early days, cod, the staple of the eastern maritime coast, along with lumber, was controlled by the British. The French controlled the early fur trade along the St. Lawrence and the waterways of the interior. Later the British traded furs from the West through Hudson Bay.

Today, eighty percent of Canada's population lives within a few hundred kilometres of the USA—in a narrow 5000-km long, snake-like strip stretching along the American border. Physically, it is much easier for Vancouver to trade with Seattle and Toronto to trade with New York, than it is for St. John's to trade with Victoria, 5000 km away. The Maritimes seek to prevent Europeans and Americans from taking all their fish; Quebeckers sell electricity to the New England states; Ontario exchanges automobile parts with Americans; and Manitoba sells electricity, Saskatchewan potash, Alberta oil, and British Columbia lumber to their neighbors to the south. Wheat is sent around the world from the Prairies, and lumber is sent to Japan. Each of Canada's many regions has its staples and products to offer, and it is usually simplest to sell to the nearest buyer.

Since Canada has historically been a supplier of staples, its economy has been very dependent on the demands and fluctuations of other economies — first of the British, more recently of the American. The result has been boom-bust cycles in the Canadian economy, which have also affected Canadian immigration. During the last quarter of the nineteenth century, 500,000 more people left Canada than arrived; and during the first quarter of the twentieth century, Canada lost as many people to the United States as it allowed to enter from Europe (Richardson, 1986:452). This boom-bust immigration has affected the national identity, because this erratic pattern of population growth has produced one of the lowest ratios of "tradition carriers" in the world (Bell and Tepperman, 1979). Canada has always had many first-generation immigrants who are learning to become Canadians; it is the ones who have been in Canada longer who leave for the United States.

Despite these adversities, Canada began to develop its technology and diversified into manufacturing and industry. Value added in manufacturing as a percentage of gross national product in the United States was 23.0 in 1870 and 20.5 in Canada. By 1979, this had risen to 30.0 in the United States and to 24.6 in Canada (Richardson, 1986:453). Thus the contribution of manufacturing to the gross national product has been nearly as high in Canada as in the United States. However, Canadian industry has focused more on semi-processed goods for export and on the manufacturing of components, and less often on developing new industrial products that are leaders in the field. However, Canada's lesser role in the development of technology and industry may have advantages as well as disadvantages. Let us turn to a discussion of some of the effects of industrialization — the concerns of classical sociologists in Europe.

Trends in Industrial Dominance

There is empirical evidence to substantiate Harold Innis' (1956) concerns about the dominance of foreign powers over the Canadian economy, and of regional dominance also, and we shall examine this evidence. What is interesting is the dominance in finance, manufacturing, and services of Canada's largest urban centers over the rest of the country. Despite its past history of an economy based on staples, Canada has developed manufacturing, and Toronto is emerging as the industrial giant of the central region. John Porter (1965) led the discussion of power elites in Canada, and Wallace Clement (1975; 1977) continued that quest. Later Keith Semple (1988:343-56) has provided a cogent summary of urban dominance, foreign ownership, and corporate concentration within the Canadian economy.

Regional Financial Concentrations

Modern technological developments have accelerated in Canada since the 1950s, and giant corporations have become concentrated in a few metropolitan centers; these corporations have also increasingly come under foreign influence. Semple (1988:345) provides a breakdown of the 268 largest corporations, having over $868 billion in assets under their control. As seen in Table 7-2, the top 70 banks in Canada controlled $428 billion, almost half the $868 billion total, and these assets were largely located in their headquarters in Toronto ($218 billion) and Montreal ($206 billion).

Of the top 50 corporations in diversified finance, with assets totalling $123 billion, most are again located in Toronto and Montreal, but with significant concentrations in Ottawa and Edmonton as well. The largest insurance corporations: Sun, Manufacturers, Canada, Confederation, and Crown Life, all have their headquarters in Toronto ($68 billion out of $107 billion assets). While Toronto is dominant in life insurance, the majority of trust companies are located in Montreal ($38 billion out of $57 billion assets). Many of these trust companies trace their ownership to a few powerful families such as the Reichmanns, Bronfmans, and Belzbergs (Semple, 1988:344). Provincial crown corporations are heavily represented in the top 25 utilities, such as Ontario Hydro, Hydro Quebec, Saskatchewan Power, and Bruncor; each is located in the capital of its respective province.

If we look at the location of these metropolitan areas by region, we find that the central region controls almost half (48.6 percent) of the assets in the financial sector, the eastern region 40.5 percent, and the West 11 percent (Semple 1988:346). Toronto is clearly dominant in the central region, having $385 billion out of $433 billion; Montreal ($315 billion out of $362 billion) dominates the eastern region even more. Seventeen western cities control only $100 billion assets between them, so that no one metropolitan center dominates in this region as Toronto and Montreal do in the other two regions. Toronto and Montreal together control 78 percent of the finances in these sectors. Only 8.9 percent of these corporations are owned by foreign interests. Canada controls its financial institutions through its elite in Toronto and Montreal (Semple and Green, 1983:389-406; Semple and Smith, 1981:4-26).

Foreign Dominance in Manufacturing

On several occasions we said that Canada's manufacturing was heavily concentrated in the southern Ontario peninsula. Although Canada has been a supplier of staples throughout its history, manufacturing spilled over into southern Ontario from the United States, where the largest industrial network in the world is located.

Table 7-2 Total assets of financial, utility, and development corporations in Canadian cities in 1985 in millions of dollars

RANK	CITY	REGION	TOP 70 BANKS	TOP 50 DIVERSIFIED FINANCE	TOP 27 LIFE INSURANCE	TOP 26 TRUSTS	TOP 40 CREDIT UNIONS	TOP 25 UTILITIES	TOP 30 REAL ESTATE	TOP 268 TOTAL	PERCENTAGE OF TOTAL	TOTAL FOREIGN
1	Toronto	Central	218 021	33 627	67 918	2 970	2 287	33 452	26 475	384 732	43.00	40 873
2	Montreal	East	206 192	31 404	8 533	38 284		30 176	102	314 691	35.18	32 293
3	Quebec City	East		4 450	6 548	385	23 651			35 034	3.92	
4	Ottawa	Central		22 287	3 709		486	267	2 377	29 126	3.26	3 709
5	Edmonton	West	106	21 409		1 775	593	2 013	2 500	28 396	3.17	
6	Vancouver	West	4 515	3 749		509	3 792	12 853	1 308	26 726	2.99	1 102
7	Winnipeg	West			10 801	118	462	4 689	611	19 923	2.23	
8	Calgary	West				912	607	11 294	4 673	17 486	1.95	860
9	Stratford	Central				8 706				8 706	0.97	
10	Kitchener	Central			7 588					7 588	0.85	
11	Halifax	East		555	1 512	3 537	164	1 433	118	7 319	0.82	
12	Regina	West					1 406	2 820	35	4 261	0.47	
13	Fredericton	East						2 820		2 820	0.31	
14	St. John's	East						2 457		2 457	0.26	
15	Saskatoon	West				69	938			1 007	0.11	
16	Hamilton	Central		626		107	208			941	0.11	477
17	London	Central		685					144	829	0.09	685
18	Barrie	Central		470						470	0.05	

Table 7-2 (continued)

RANK	CITY	REGION	TOP 70 BANKS	TOP 50 DIVERSIFIED FINANCE	TOP 27 LIFE INSURANCE	TOP 26 TRUSTS	TOP 40 CREDIT UNIONS	TOP 25 UTILITIES	TOP 30 REAL ESTATE	TOP 268 TOTAL	PERCENTAGE OF TOTAL	TOTAL FOREIGN
19	Victoria	West					410			410	0.05	
20	St. Catharines	Central					327			327	0.04	
21	Chilliwack	West					188			188	0.02	
22	Steinbach	West					163			163	0.02	
23	Kelowna	West					149			149	0.02	
24	Trail	West						139		139	0.02	
25	Swift Current	West					135			135	0.02	
26	Red Deer	West					132			132	0.01	
27	Prince Albert	West					129			129	0.01	
28	Lloydminster	West					121			121	0.01	
29	Nelson	West					121			121	0.01	
30	Moose Jaw	West					88			88	0.01	
OTHERS				29				85	54	168	0.02	
Total domestic			428 834	122 533	106 609	57 372	36 557	104 498	38 379	894 782	100	
Total foreign			30 234	10 412	16 311	21 570		860	612			79 999
Percentage foreign			7.1	8.5	15.3	37.6	0.0	0.8				8.9

SOURCE: Semple (1988: 345).

Table 7-3 The revenues of manufacturing corporations in Canadian cities in 1985 in millions of dollars

RANK	CITY	REGION	TOP 50 TRANSPORT MACHINERY	TOP 70 FOOD	TOP 50 METALS	TOP 55 FOREST	TOP 55 CHEMICAL	TOP 60 ELECTRICAL	TOP 50 MACHINERY	TOP 60 MISC. MFG.	TOP 25 TEXTILES	TOP 475 TOTAL	PERCENTAGE OF TOTAL	TOTAL FOREIGN
1	Toronto	Central	39 768	12 593	6 937	5 257	9 688	11 795	9 396	4 755	3 312	103 501	53.02	72 279
2	Montreal	East	2 878	12 390	10 145	6 244	3 328	817	1 024	1 463	1 276	39 565	20.27	12 133
3	Vancouver	West	1 273	277	120	7 643		37		1 400	87	10 873	5.56	2 731
4	Windsor	Central	7 249		31		84		284			7 364	3.77	7 333
5	Hamilton	Central	925	91	2 643	234	649	784		145		5 755	2.95	3 120
6	London	Central	557	2 426		506				414		3 903	2.00	302
7	Ottawa	Central	255	18	965	107	425	717	962	103		3 552	1.82	1 140
8	Calgary	West		1 551					55	1 812		3 418	1.75	102
9	Kitchener	Central	328	648			672	154		72	71	1 945	1.00	891
10	St. Catharines	Central	465	113	104	501	62		10	77		1 332	0.68	860
11	Sarnia	Central					1 290					1 290	0.66	1 290
12	Sault Ste. Marie	Central			1 176	78						1 254	0.64	
13	Edmonton	West		750	43					192	180	1 165	0.60	180
14	Florenceville	East		1 023								1 023	0.52	
15	Winnipeg	West	182	75	58	63	20			252	46	696	0.36	449
16	Kamloops	West				561						561	0.29	500
17	Halifax	East	100	454								554	0.28	
18	Saskatoon	West		376	95		76	60				436	0.22	

Table 7-3 (continued)

RANK	CITY	REGION	TOP 50 TRANSPORT MACHINERY	TOP 70 FOOD	TOP 50 METALS	TOP 55 FOREST	TOP 55 CHEMICAL	TOP 60 ELECTRICAL	TOP 50 MACHINERY	TOP 60 MISC. MFG.	TOP 25 TEXTILES	TOP 475 TOTAL	PERCENTAGE OF TOTAL	TOTAL FOREIGN
19	Brantford	Central							139		118	428	0.22	76
20	St. Georges Beauce	East				330						330	0.17	
21	Peterborough	Central	74	242								316	0.16	316
22	Prince George	West					310					310	0.16	160
23	Regina	West			304							304	0.16	
24	St. Thomas	Central	179						73	51		303	0.16	303
25	St. John's	East		298								298	0.15	
26	Cambridge	Central						50	119		119	288	0.15	119
27	Guelph	Central						247	41			288	0.15	150
28	Woodstock	Central	13						227		33	273	0.14	
29	Kingsley Falls	Central					266					266	0.14	
30	Kitimat	West					236					236	0.12	
OTHERS				706	547	669	682		349	316	115	3 384	1.73	1 083
Total domestic			54 246	34 031	23 195	23 005	16 976	14 661	12 679	11 062	5 357	195 212	100	
Total foreign			50 057	11 534	6 153	5 245	11 044	5 745	9 792	5 009	938	105 517		
Percentage foreign			92.3	33.9	26.5	22.8	65.1	39.2	77.2	45.3	17.5	54.0		

SOURCE: Semple (1988: 347).

Table 7-4 Total revenues of service corporations in Canadian cities in 1985 in millions of dollars

RANK	CITY	REGION	TOP 60 RETAIL	TOP 50 TRANS-PORT	TOP 65 COMMU-NICATION	TOP 70 WHOLE-SALE	TOP 70 MISC. SERVICE	TOP 30 CO-OPS	TOP 90 PROFESSIONAL SERVICE	TOP 40 CONSTRUCTION	TOP 475 TOTAL	PERCENTAGE OF TOTAL	TOTAL FOREIGN
1	Toronto	Central	30 362	2 095	10 644	8 101	4 967	638	7 304	1 422	65 533	33.96	20 387
2	Montreal	East	9 926	25 459	16 744	2 881	1 282	3 212	1 255	3 154	63 913	33.12	4 627
3	Winnipeg	West	10 259	796	398	4 466	5 371	1 748	658	97	23 793	12.33	5 638
4	Vancouver	West	1 736	916	95	6 154	657	350	262	457	10 627	5.51	3 965
5	Calgary	West	324	1 025		1 228	300	2 164		557	5 598	2.90	421
6	Ottawa	Central		217	503	74	3 167		84		4 054	2.10	
7	Edmonton	West	221	518	1 314	81	80	305		1 193	3 712	1.92	174
8	Regina	West	92		423			2 023	268		2 806	1.45	
9	Saskatoon	West	82			334		1 831			2 247	1.16	
10	Hamilton	Central		556		537	230			226	1 549	0.80	836
11	Stellarton	East	908					114			1 022	0.53	
12	Quebec City	East						190	546	140	876	0.45	
13	Granby	East						759			759	0.39	
14	Victoria	West							714		714	0.37	
15	London	Central	144	40	19	259	186		40		688	0.36	255
16	Guelph	Central					79		544		623	0.32	79
17	Kitchener	Central	299						312		611	0.32	
18	Halifax	East		107	310		80	93			590	0.31	80
19	Moncton	East		191				287			478	0.25	

Table 7-4 (continued)

RANK	CITY	REGION	TOP 60 RETAIL	TOP 50 TRANS-PORT	TOP 65 COMMU-NICATION	TOP 70 WHOLE-SALE	TOP 70 MISC. SERVICE	TOP 30 CO-OPS	TOP 90 PROFESSIONAL SERVICE	TOP 40 CONSTRUCTION	TOP 475 TOTAL	PERCENTAGE OF TOTAL	TOTAL FOREIGN
20	Cornerbrook	East								328	328	0.17	
21	Drummondville	East				275					275	0.14	
22	Saint John	East			243						243	0.13	
23	Red Deer	West					71	169			240	0.12	
24	Rimouski	East						225			225	0.12	
25	Sault Ste. Marie	Central		200							200	0.10	
26	Blenheim	Central				185					185	0.10	
27	Thetford Mines	East				183					183	0.09	
28	St. John's	East	42		136						178	0.09	42
29	Kelowna	West						171			171	0.09	
30	North Bay	Central		130							130	0.07	
OTHERS				140	51		53	148		55	447	0.23	
Total domestic			54 395	32 390	30 880	24 758	16 532	14 427	11 987	7 629	192 998	100	
Total foreign			11 360	570	1 925	13 098	2 634		3 905	3 012			36 504
Percentage foreign			20.0	1.8	6.2	72.0	15.0		32.6	39.5			18.9

SOURCE: Semple (1988:348).

In Table 7-3 we see that Toronto is also dominant in manufacturing. Toronto-based manufacturing corporations accounted for over half (53 percent) of the $195 billion produced in 1985. Toronto leads seven of the nine manufacturing sectors: transport machinery, food, chemicals, electrical, machinery, textiles, and miscellaneous manufacturing. Montreal leads in two: metals and forest products, and is a close second in foods, having 20 percent of the total market (Semple, 1988:346). These two metropolitan centers have 73 percent of all manufacturing; Vancouver, in third place, is a long way behind with only 6 percent.

Over half (54 percent) of the $195 billion generated in 1985 by these 475 manufacturing corporations was foreign-owned. Foreign ownership is especially high in transport machinery ($50 billion out of $54 billion), which includes the operations of General Motors and Ford, and chemicals ($11 billion out of $17 billion). Seventy-two percent ($72 billion out of $104 billion) of the manufacturing generated in Toronto was foreign-owned. Toronto is clearly the leader in manufacturing, and it is here that foreign ownership (largely American), also has its greatest concentration.

Service and Resource Corporations

Toronto and Montreal also dominate the service sector, with 34 and 33 percent respectively of the $193 billion generated in 1985 by 475 corporations, as illustrated in Table 7-4. Toronto leads in four of the eight sectors, particularly in the largest sector, retail, as well as in wholesale, professional, and miscellaneous services. Montreal leads in the other four, particularly transportation (CP, CN, and Air Canada), as well as communications, construction, and co-ops (Semple, 1988:346). Nineteen percent of these service corporations are foreign-owned, but only wholesale is dominated (53 percent) by foreign ownership; retail and transportation are mostly Canadian-owned.

Calgary (46 percent) and Toronto (44 percent) share the leading revenues from resource corporations. Thirty billion, or 37 percent, of the $83 billion in revenues from the top 150 corporations in petroleum and mining are foreign-owned. Calgary-based resource corporations controlled $38 billion of the $62 billion revenues from petroleum; Shell, Gulf, and Petro-Canada all have their headquarters in Calgary. Toronto-based corporations controlled $15 billion of the $20 billion generated by mining in 1985 (Semple, 1988:347-9).

Dominance of Toronto and Montreal

The Canadian economy is highly centralized, as shown by the degree of control exercised by corporations located in Toronto and Montreal in the four major areas of finance, manufacturing, services, and resources. Whereas in the past Britain and France dominated the Canadian economy, using Canada as a source of raw materials, today the United States exercises a great influence, especially through foreign-owned corporations located in Toronto. In 1981 Toronto became the largest urban center in Canada, surpassing Montreal for the first time; it is obvious that while Toronto and Montreal dominate Canada economically, Toronto is fast moving ahead as the major industrial center.

As illustrated in Figure 7-3, Toronto is at the apex of the Canadian urban industrial hierarchy, and Montreal is clearly second. Toronto, with a population of 3.4 million, is now the largest metropolis, with 43 percent of the national corporate total, while Montreal is a close second with 31 percent of the national total. All other urban centers in Canada share only 26 percent among them.

Toronto gained almost $50 billion in assets through corporations moving, merging, or acquiring or establishing new headquarters there, and lost over $20 billion through corporations that left, for a net gain of $30 billion (Semple, 1988:351). Toronto, Montreal, and Calgary have gained the most through such moves, reinforcing their dominance regionally and Toronto's total dominance nationally.

It is also clear that foreign investors are helping to make Toronto dominant; they have invested $109 billion out of a total of $170 billion of their non-financial manufacturing, services, and resources investments in Toronto, $17 billion in Montreal, and $12 billion in Calgary. Seventy-seven percent ($130 billion out of $170 billion) of this foreign investment came from the United States, $13 billion from the United Kingdom, $12 billion from Japan, and the rest from numerous others. The majority of the American non-financial investments ($88 billion out of $130 billion) went to Toronto, and more than 80 percent of all these foreign investments in Toronto in 1985 ($88 billion out of $109 billion) came from the United States (Semple, 1988:352-5). It is clear that the Americans are making Toronto their primary Canadian investment center. The advantages of scale and interlocking directorships shown by Porter (1965) and Clement (1975, 1977) are clearly at work in Toronto and Montreal. Clement (1977) sees these larger urban centers interlocked with the larger continental corporate networks, which tend to cross national borders.

Work and Leisure

Having examined the industrial complex extensively, we now need to discuss the consequences of such industrial dominance in the workplace. Has the distribution of the Canadian labor force by type of industry changed? To what extent has labor organized to combat the dominance of industry in the workplace? Has job satisfaction actually declined in industrialized nations? Is unemployment and poverty a problem? To what extent do workers need more leisure time to get away from it all?

The Labor Force by Type of Industry

In 1881, fifty-one percent of Canadians were involved in primary industry, 29 percent in secondary industry, and 19 percent in tertiary occupations (Smuc-

Figure 7-3   Summary of the financial, manufacturing, services, and resource dominance of Toronto and Montreal in Canada

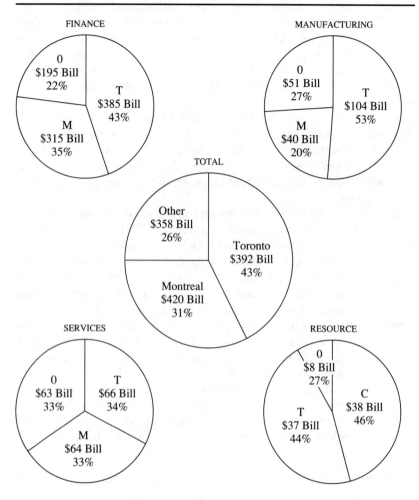

FINANCE

0
$195 Bill
22%

T
$385 Bill
43%

M
$315 Bill
35%

MANUFACTURING

0
$51 Bill
27%

T
$104 Bill
53%

M
$40 Bill
20%

TOTAL

Other
$358 Bill
26%

Toronto
$392 Bill
43%

Montreal
$420 Bill
31%

SERVICES

0
$63 Bill
33%

T
$66 Bill
34%

M
$64 Bill
33%

RESOURCE

0
$8 Bill
27%

C
$38 Bill
46%

T
$37 Bill
44%

ker, 1980:78). By 1983 this had been reversed; only 7 percent were engaged in primary industry, 24 percent in secondary occupations, and 69 percent in tertiary occupations (Hedley, 1986:500). In Figure 7-4 we see that in 1901 most of Canada's labor force was concentrated in the primary and agricultural sectors, while less than 15 percent of the workers were in white-collar work. Since then the percentage of workers in white-collar work has escalated: after World War II by far the largest number of workers were employed in this sector. Almost half the work force was white-collar in 1981, and the majority were urban (Krahn and Lowe, 1988:21-30).

Figure 7-4   Percent distribution of labor force, major occupational groups, 1901-1981

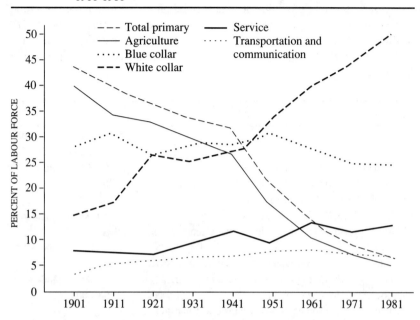

SOURCE: Based on Ostry, S. *The Occupational Composition of the Canadian Labour Force* (Ottawa: Dominion Bureau of Statistics, 1967), Table 2 [for 1901-61]; 1981 Census, *Population: Labour Force — Occupation Trends* (# 92-920, vol. 1) [for 1971-81].

Organization of Labor Unions

With the development of industrial power in Canada it was inevitable that labor would organize to protect its interests. The history of labor unions and the labor movement is one of conflict and struggle for power. In studies and analyses of labor-management relations, there are marked differences between consensus and conflict theorists (Berg, 1979). The consensus perspective asserts that management and labor have common goals, while the conflict perspective sees the goals of each in opposition to the goals of the other. Consensus proponents argue that power is shared, while conflict theorists say it is widely unequal; consensus advocates see the distribution of rewards as just and fair, while conflict theorists see it as grossly unjust (Hedley, 1986:504-505; Chaison, 1982). In Table 7-5 we list ten of the largest labor unions in Canada. These unions are of three basic types — public, industrial, or trade; each type emerged in a particular historic period (Hedley, 1986:506). After industrialization had brought about increased division of labor, semi-skilled machine operatives became the occupation of the majority of the working class. They banded together in industrial unions to increase their strength and challenge capitalist ownership (Kumar, 1986:95-6; Freeman and Medoff,

1984:228-40; Lipset, 1987). Blue-collar workers organized earlier than white-collar workers; by 1972 non-manual, white-collar, and professional workers, particularly those in government, had formed public-sector unions, at a time when white-collar workers were becoming the largest sector of the labor force, as illustrated in Figure 7-4 (Hedley 1986:506-7). Union activity in Canada is heavily concentrated in Canada's two largest urban centers, Toronto and Montreal.

Table 7-5 Ten largest unions, Canada, 1986

UNION	MEMBERSHIP 1986	TYPE OF UNION
1. Canadian Union of Public Employees	304 300	Public
2. National Union of Provincial Government Employees	254 300	Public
3. Public Service Alliance of Canada	182 000	Public
4. United Steel Workers of America	160 000	Industrial
5. United Food and Commercial Workers International Union	156 000	Industrial
6. International Union, United Automobile, Aerospace and Agricultural Implement Workers of America*	140 000	Industrial
7. Social Affairs Federation Inc.	93 000	Public
8. International Brotherhood of Teamsters, Chauffeurs, Warehousemen and Helpers of America	91 500	Industrial
9. School Board Teachers' Commission**	75 000	Public
10. Service Employees International Union	70 000	Trade

* This union became autonomous from its U.S. parent in 1986, creating the Canadian Auto Workers Union.
** Previously part of the Quebec Teaching Congress.
SOURCE: *Directory of Labour Organizations in Canada, 1986* (Ottawa: Supply and Services, 1986), p. 15.

Job Satisfaction

Numerous studies have been carried out in industrial countries of workers in various occupations and their attitudes to their jobs. Two-thirds to three-fourths of the industrial workers in Britain, the United States, Australia, and Canada were found to be satisfied with their work (Hedley, 1981:12; Hedley, 1986:509). Only 10 to 15 percent were dissatisfied; 17 percent of the workers in the USA, where technology has advanced farthest, registered dissatisfaction.

Generally, workers with higher occupational skills placed greater emphasis on intrinsic job features: challenge, interest, variety, and responsibility. They also valued performing well, and receiving respect from those they work with, as well as how the company judged them. Less skilled workers focused more on extrinsic features such as hours of work, pay levels, raises, bonuses, and vacations (Burstein *et al.*, 1975:28; Chelte *et al.*, 1982). Men more than

Table 7-6 Job satisfaction of industrial workers in four countries

JOB SATISFACTION	BRITAIN 1969	U.S.A. 1974	AUSTRALIA 1977	CANADA 1979
	%	%	%	%
Very satisfied	14	17	19	15
Satisfied	62	51	55	59
Indifferent	14	15	14	13
Dissatisfied	6	11	8	10
Very dissatisfied	3	6	4	3
Total	99	100	100	100
Number of workers	3098	649	1359	363

SOURCE: Hedley (1981).

women valued job security, employee benefits, and opportunities for promotion, while women were more concerned with getting along with others and with social relations (Hedley, 1986:509-10). Canadian workers were attached to their work, and valued responsibility, challenge, and work that interested them, and wanted to obtain a sense of accomplishment from their work.

Leisure: Decline of Work Time

There are numerous reasons why three-fourths of Canadian workers were satisfied and only 13 percent dissatisfied with their work. It may be that many no longer expect challenging and creative work, and have come to settle for less. But work conditions have been greatly improved since the Industrial Revolution first began. Wages have gone up for all workers, partly owing to the efforts of trade unions to obtain better wages for union workers. Labor unions have also been an important factor in reducing the hours of work per week and per day, especially in urban areas, so that blue-collar workers have considerably more time to use as they see fit. While professional workers often work longer hours than blue-collar workers, their work schedule and pace are usually more flexible, and often their work also allows for more creativity and identification with what they do. Industrial technology and specialization tend to lead to fragmentation and segmentation of the labor force.

In Figure 7-5 we have plotted a time chart of the 168 hours in a week; the chart shows the hours spent working, an average of 56 hours a week devoted to sleep, and the remaining free time. We have not found any time studies done for the early industry period in the nineteenth century in England, but there is sufficient literature to show that many workers worked twelve, fourteen, and perhaps even more hours per day, six or seven days a week. It is estimated that workers averaged 64 hours of work a week by 1870 (Reid, 1985:146-50; van Cleef, 1985:87). Assuming that earlier some averaged

Figure 7-5   Time spent at work during a typical Canadian employee's week

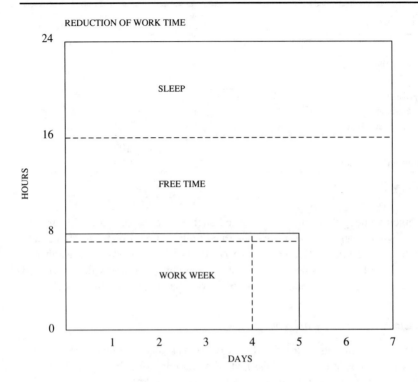

twelve hours a day, seven days a week, we could draw a line across the chart showing that half of the time was spent at work. That would have left them only four hours a day which they could use at their discretion. During such time they would have to prepare and eat meals, travel to and from work, and take care of household and family responsibilities. Life must have been almost impossible.

Since then, and especially since the second World War, the standard work week became the 40-hour, five-day week. The work week has been reduced to an average of 37.8 hours by 1984 (Krahn and Lowe, 1988:53), or less than one-fourth of the total 168 hours of time in a week (Weeks, 1980:69; Kaliski, 1985:86). Increased leisure has been an important factor in making industrial work more tolerable, and is a major reason why workers feel more satisfied with their work.

It is true that most people also have to spend some time at home coping with household and family needs, but technology and increasing affluence have helped to make these tasks less onerous, and there is much more free time in which to do them. As well as the shorter work week, with its free weekends (Saturday and Sunday), hours worked have been decreased by other features: national holidays (long weekends), vacation time (one to three or even more weeks), coffee breaks (10-30 minutes twice a day), sick leave, and retirement, usually after age 65 or even earlier, providing leisure time for many years. In many cases work weeks are now being cut to fewer than forty hours; some workers only work four days a week. These free times help a great deal to alleviate the stresses and hazards of work.

Barry Robinson (1968) defines leisure "as a period of time not devoted to work or household duties, when one has the freedom to do as one pleases, most often choosing a pleasurable, relaxing activity." But leisure time, while a pleasure for some, may be a burden for others. Many blue-collar workers with limited creative interests now have much more leisure time, but often do not know what to do with it; while professional people often work long hours and would like to have more time for the many other things they want to do.

In his study of Southdale and Fort Richmond, two middle class suburbs in Winnipeg, Robinson (1968:45) found that the most popular leisure activities were reading (98 percent), watching television (95 percent), visiting friends (91 percent), motor trips and sightseeing (81 percent), bowling, swimming, skating, skiing (79 percent), attending parties (78 percent), family get-togethers (77 percent), going for walks (77 percent), dining out (76 percent), and playing with children (75 percent). Social activities were most popular for all ages; creative activities were next most popular, and their popularity increased with age; physical recreation was third in popularity, decreasing with age; and spectator sports ranked last (Robinson, 1968:45). Females enjoyed social and creative activities most, while males enjoyed physical activities most. Lower income suburbanites were somewhat more involved in physical and spectator activities.

Unemployment: Forced Non-Work

While the capitalist economic system has been greatly modified to take into account more of the social needs of the workers, unemployment is still one of the great tragedies that modern technology has not been able to resolve. Unemployment is greatest and therefore takes its toll among the unskilled and powerless. When profit margins fall, production is curtailed and workers are laid-off, sometimes for short periods of time, sometimes permanently. It is an even greater tragedy when a worker who has served the company for 25 or more years is laid-off and is at an age where he or she lacks the skills to compete in the marketplace.

In 1966, only 3.4 percent of the women and 3.3 percent of the men in Canada were unemployed. Since then, unemployment has been rising, as shown in Table 7.7. It peaked at 12.1 percent for men in 1983, and then declined (Armstrong and Armstrong, 1983). The differences between the unemployed rates for males and females are not that great, but female unemployment has usually been somewhat higher. The proportion of women among the unemployed has risen from 31.8 percent in 1966 to 44.1 percent in 1986, largely because of the large increase of women in the labor force. In 1986, 55 percent of Canadian women worked outside the home, compared with 24 percent in 1951. According to Armstrong and Armstrong (1983:65-66, 234, 249), in 1980 24 percent of Canadian women who were working worked part-time, compared to 6 percent of the men. The average earnings in 1985 for all occupations was $13,437 for women, and for men $23,217. We shall discuss women's position in the workplace further when we discuss the family in chapter nine (Calzavara, 1988:287-301).

Table 7-7 Unemployment rates by sex in Canada, 1966–1986

| YEAR | UNEMPLOYMENT RATE | | WOMEN AS PERCENT OF UNEMPLOYED |
	WOMEN	MEN	
1966	3.4%	3.3%	31.8%
1967	3.7	3.9	31.4
1968	4.4	4.6	31.8
1969	4.7	4.3	35.1
1970	5.8	5.6	34.7
1971	6.6	6.0	36.8
1972	7.0	5.8	39.1
1973	6.7	4.9	42.6
1974	6.4	4.8	42.6
1975	8.1	6.2	43.2
1976	8.4	6.4	44.2
1977	9.5	7.3	44.1
1978	9.6	7.6	44.8
1979	8.8	6.6	46.1
1980	8.4	6.9	44.8
1981	8.3	7.0	45.0
1982	10.9	11.1	40.9
1983	11.6	12.1	40.7
1984	11.4	11.2	42.7
1985	10.7	10.3	43.5
1986	9.9	9.4	44.1

SOURCE: Armstrong and Armstrong (1983: Table 1).

These unemployment rates vary enormously by region in Canada. The manufacturing provinces had the lowest unemployment rates in 1986: Ontario with 7.0 percent and Quebec with 11 percent, while provinces distant from the manufacturing center have had greater unemployment — Newfoundland 20.0 percent, New Brunswick 14.4 percent, and British Columbia 12.6 percent (Krahn and Lowe, 1988:56). Alberta's oil industry has led to fluctuations in the unemployment rate, but in 1986 it was 9.8 percent; the prairie provinces have experienced fluctuations owing to their agricultural base, with Manitoba and Saskatchewan both having 7.7 percent unemployment in 1986 (Krahn and Lowe, 1988:56). Unemployment rates for Native Indians in the prairie provinces are much higher, sometimes as high as 30 percent. When the Canadian economy is strong, the central industrial area of southern Ontario has relatively low unemployment rates; but when the economy declines, unemployment rises. Populations distant from this industrial center, such as Newfoundland and the Maritimes, seem to be burdened with steady unemployment at high rates because so many are dependent on primary occupations. Many are also employed only part time (Armstrong, 1984:203; Bonlet and Lavallee, 1984:12; Akyeampong, 1986:144).

Summary

We have discussed in this chapter work in the industrial economy. The classical theorists were concerned with the effects of technology and industry on work: Marx focused on the relations of production, and Weber focused on relations of exchange. These economic power relations also became a major sociological focus in Canada; Porter concentrated on the power elite, and Clement had a narrower concern with the corporate elite and continental corporate power.

The Industrial Revolution began in England with the introduction of the steam engine in 1785 and spread to northern Europe. European nations used this new-found power to operate their factories to process the raw materials they obtained from their colonies abroad. The New England states, colonized by the British, were the first on the North American continent to adopt this new industrial power. The West was opened later. France and England traded in the natural resources of North America, and France developed settlements along the St. Lawrence. Later southern Ontario became the industrial center of Canada. Harold Innis proposed that Canada has always been a supplier of staples, first for the British, more recently for the Americans, so that Canada's economy has always been dominated by other industrial powers who needed our raw materials.

We focused in the third section on the extent of industrial dominance in Canada, and found that the financial institutions are mostly located in Toronto and Montreal. Manufacturing is also massively located in Toronto, and over half of the investment in this sector is from foreign countries, largely American. Service corporations are also heavily concentrated in Toronto and Montreal; and the headquarters of corporations are located mostly in Calgary and Toronto. We conclude that Toronto is clearly the leading urban center for manufacturing, finance, and service industries, with Montreal clearly an important second urban center, especially in finance and services. These two largest metropolitan centers dominate the Canadian economy.

Work and leisure have been affected by the technology in the workplace in Canada. Whereas the labor force was most heavily concentrated in primary and agricultural work in 1901, by 1981 more than two-thirds were in tertiary work, and white-collar occupations dominated the work scene. Labor has organized itself into unions to improve work conditions, hours of work, and conditions at work. These improvements have helped to keep work satisfaction high, and leisure time has greatly increased, so that on the average, workers spend less than 40 hours at work per week. Unfortunately, unemployment has also risen, as high as 12 percent nationally, and to 20 percent in some regions, showing that workers are often subject to the vagaries of the modified capitalist economic system. While some of the concerns of the classical writers have proved unfounded, many problems have become ingrained in Canadian industrial society.

8. Power, Politics, and Government

In our discussion of the urban technological economy in chapter seven, the dominance of Toronto and Montreal in central Canada became quite evident. Toronto is the political capital of Ontario, the most populous province, where more than one-third (35 percent) of all Canadians live; it is clearly in the center of Canada's industrial heartland. Montreal, the most populous Canadian metropolis through most of Canada's history until 1971, is firmly anchored in the second most populous Canadian province, French Quebec (27 percent), clearly a second bastion of industrial power. Together these two urban giants comprise almost one-half of the total Canadian metropolitan population, and they are located in the two regions where two-thirds (62 percent in 1986) of all Canadians live. Toronto and Montreal represent economic power; Toronto is clearly forging ahead faster than Montreal, gaining both in population and in industrial power. Are their political power networks similar?

Theoretical Concepts of Power

Power involves the ability to achieve ends, even over opposition (Spates and Macionis, 1987:33). Power includes the capacity or authority of an individual or group to command or influence the behavior of others. Power vested in people who are selected or appointed by a socially approved procedure is considered "legitimate," and is often referred to as "authority" (Gist and Fava, 1974:455). But people may also hold power not through a legitimate process of social approval but by persuasion or even physical force. In complex settings such as cities, economic, political, and social power is often intertwined in individuals or groups and cannot be easily differentiated. Thus, Karl Marx saw power as deriving from the linkage between economic and political forces, which joined together to pursue corporate economic ends. Coleman and Rainwater (1978) discuss the wealth and prestige, as well as the political influence, of some Boston urbanites and their ability to shape events in that city. The urban poor, on the other hand, are powerless (Clark, 1978).

There are many types of urban political structures. A city such as "Middletown," Indiana, dominated by a single industry, differs politically from a complex industrial city such as Chicago, where Mayor Daley was a long-time political boss (Lynd and Lynd, 1929, 1937). The unicity government (amalgamation of urban municipal governments) in Winnipeg today is vastly different from the powerful city government of Mayor Drapeau, who brought Expo '67 and the Olympic Games to Montreal in the 1960s and 1970s. In some cities power may be lodged largely in one individual or small group, whereas in other urban centers power may be diffused through many representatives on urban councils and several interest groups.

The Metropolitan Power Elite

C. Wright Mills (1956), in his book *The Power Elite*, demonstrated that three major power blocks (politicians, business people, and the military) dominated American society. The power structure could be represented by a pyramid, with a small elite on top of the pyramid and the rest distributed below and subject to the influence and decisions of the elite (Mills, 1956). In some cities, a small elitist structure headed by a mayor or political boss may rule behind the scenes. Richard Daley, who was mayor of Chicago for more than twenty years, is usually cited as typical of the influential North American city bosses. While cities in Canada have not had such prominent city bosses as Daley, Mayor Jean Drapeau of Montreal possessed similar traits, which we shall explore later in this chapter.

John Porter in 1965, in his book *The Vertical Mosaic*, charted the hitherto unexplored subjects of social class and power in Canadian society. People tend to be ambivalent about power because in a democratic society we emphasize equality, whereas power implies the dominance of some over others. In his chapter on ethnicity and social class, Porter focused on the two charter groups — the British and French. The British formed the majority of the population, and the French a strong minority, heavily concentrated in Quebec (Porter, 1965:91). It was these two charter groups, representing more than 90 percent of the population in 1867, who formed the Confederation of Canada, comprising Ontario, Quebec, Nova Scotia, New Brunswick, and Prince Edward Island. Both politically and economically, Montreal and Toronto dominated this Confederation; Montreal was clearly the more influential center at that time. Later immigrants were designated as entrance-status Canadians; their ethnic status gave them less economic and political power.

Porter (1965:201) emphasized the importance of the elites and the structure of power because "power means the recognized right to make effective decisions on behalf of others." Porter found that the British and French dominated the power positions; Canadians of other origins were grossly under-represented in the power structure. While he did not include mayors of Canadian cities or members of city councils in his research, the same power structure based on these charter groups has been present in a majority of cities in Canada. The power elites in Quebec cities have been largely French, while the British have dominated in the rest of English-speaking Canada. Interestingly, in the past Montreal has been a hybrid, with the British influence dominant economically, but the French dominant politically. This situation is changing rapidly, and the French are becoming increasingly dominant economically.

Wallace Clement (1975, 1977) continued Porter's research of the Canadian corporate elite, and also looked at continental corporate power and the economic linkages between Canada and the United States. Both the larger, North American economic, political, and social power systems, as well as the internal Canadian national, provincial, and urban municipal political power groups are intertwined in networks of influence, of which any one metropolitan government or governments is only one part. The power elite will try to dominate urban municipal networks and compete with other political systems around them. Sometimes powerful mayors, such as Drapeau of Montreal, emerge; more often powers are lodged in small urban councils; on still other occasions powers are distributed and shared more broadly.

Pluralist Politics: Distribution of Powers

Advocates of pluralistic powers hold that power should be diversified and diffused within communities in line with democratic principles (Magnusson, 1983). Pluralists value special interest groups and public opinion, and listen to a variety of voices with the intention of meeting the interests of as many as possible. It is assumed that urban populations are heterogeneous, differentiated by racial, ethnic, religious, and other social interests, and that economic interests are diverse. Power should be decentralized so that such voices can be heard.

David Reisman (1953:246-7) presents the case for plurality of power:

> There has been a change in the last fifty years, a change in the configuration of power in America, in which a single hierarchy with a ruling class at its head has been replaced by a number of 'veto groups' among which power is dispersed . . . The ruling class of businessmen could relatively easily decide where their interests lay and what editors, lawyers, and legislators might be paid to advance them. The Lobby ministered to the clear leadership, privilege, and imperative of the business ruling class. Today we have substituted for that leadership a series of groups, each of which has struggled for and finally attained a power to stop things conceivably inimical to its interests, and within far narrower limits to start things.

Therefore, a diversity of power groups compete in presenting their interests, some of which win and others do not (Gold, 1982:215).

Thus, communities are composed, not of single elites, but rather of a series of competing elites, forming coalitions as needed to gain their ends. Robert Dahl (1958:463-9) and Nelson Polsky (1959:232-6) carried out important studies of such pluralist politics in New Haven, Connecticut; they found that many groups were involved in urban development, in public school policy, and in getting mayors elected. They found that the number of people involved in the leadership pool was 500, but the overlap often was minimal.

The power elite tend to be representative of business and professional groups, who have greater financial means and higher levels of education and training. Thus, economic interests are usually well represented, but the poor remain powerless. Racial, ethnic, and women's groups are often among those who lack access to the power elite. Housing, social assistance, fair labor relations, equality, and justice are usually not compatible with the business interests of profits and free enterprise. It is more difficult for the poor, for visible minorities, and for the socially handicapped to organize themselves into special interest groups that can compete for representation on city councils. Thus, studies show that the monolithic power elite are much better represented on metropolitan municipal governments, often holding dominating majorities for decades without serious challenge.

We turn next to examine how various metropolitan centers in Canada emerged as centers of influence.

Canadian Metropolitan Power Development

To gain some sense of where the urban centers of influence are located in Canada, let us trace the development of domination, beginning in the east and moving westwards as the country was opened up. We briefly traced some of this westward movement in chapter three; here we shall focus on: 1) regional central place; 2) unique economic power; 3) ethnic power dynamics; and 4) urban political types. Seven metropolitan areas (Halifax, Montreal, Toronto, Winnipeg, Vancouver, Edmonton, Ottawa) will illustrate the variety of changes in power opportunities during the past several centuries. Each center represents an interesting combination of place, economics, ethnicity, and politics that will illustrate the multiple dimensions and complexity of these power relationships.

The theory of central place assumes that urban centers dominate the space in which they exist and that their influence radiates outwards into the rural hinterlands. The greater the variety of services provided from a center to a hinterland, the greater will be the centrality of its location (Hawley, 1981:235).

> Thus, urban centers form a numerical and functional hierarchy in a region. The smallest centers, providing the lowest-order functions, are most numerous; the next size class of centers, only one-third as numerous, offers all the lowest-order functions and somewhat more specialized services; at the apex is the regional capital, from which are available all lower-order services and also the most specialized or highest-order services (Hawley,1981:235).

Thus, urban places are part of a network of power, the largest being the most influential, the smaller relatively less powerful. Canadian metropolitan centers are each part of a network power complex; our examination of seven centers will illustrate some of these power relationships.

Halifax: Past British Colonial Power

"Above all else Halifax is a naval town both in appearance and employment structure; but it is now showing signs of adopting a new role as a capital of the Atlantic region." (Nader, 1976:28.) Halifax was founded in 1749 as a British military base to counter the French stronghold of Louisbourg. Strategically it was the northern extension of the British-owned New England colonies to the south. Its *raison d'être* was to protect the fishing grounds of the eastern coastal waters. Halifax was also the fortification closest to the entrance into the St. Lawrence, the French route to New France.

There were a few settlers in the early days, and "the town was sustained largely by government grants"; it had in 1752 a population of about 3,850 (Nader, 1976:30). While fishing was an important part of the economy, there was little soil available in the vicinity for agriculture. In 1758 thousands of British troops were stationed in Halifax, in preparation for the siege of French Louisbourg.

After the defeat of the French, Halifax declined in importance until after the end of the American Revolution.

When Halifax was a British naval stronghold, its population was largely British. "In 1776 the first group of Loyalists (about fifteen hundred in number) arrived in Halifax." (Nader, 1976:31.) The largest influx of United Empire Loyalists came around 1783, when about 10,000 arrived. Since agriculture, fishing, and trade provided only limited economic opportunities, many left. Many of these Loyalists, however, brought their slaves with them so that until recently Canadian Blacks were most heavily located in Nova Scotia, including Halifax (Henry, 1973; Clairmont and Magill, 1974). These Blacks, whom we examined in chapter six, have remained examples of powerlessness and discrimination.

In recent years the seaport has become an important container port, linking the transportation of goods by rail and ship, but as the railroads are now in decline and the St. Lawrence Seaway allows ships to bypass Halifax in the summer months, its importance has been somewhat undermined. Founded over 240 years ago, Halifax has become the largest metropolis in the Maritimes, and is the dominant urban influence. However, its population has not grown at the same rate as the population nation-wide; it is now ranked fourteenth of Canadian metropoli, and is the center of a have-not economic region.

The very first settlement in what is now Canada was in 1604 to 1605 in Port Royal. This early French settlement did not survive for long. Later French settlers, who came to be known as the Acadians, settled in the Annapolis Valley west of Halifax. Although the Acadians wished to remain neutral in the war between Britain and France that broke out in 1755, the British perceived them as a threat because they would not take an oath of loyalty. They were deported and dispersed, some to the American colonies, others later to France and England. After the war was over, some of the Acadians returned and settled in communities in Nova Scotia and New Brunswick. Thus, the Maritime region, while always heavily British, has some French-speaking communities. French-English and religious (Anglican versus Catholic) cleavages have remained a significant part of Halifax history, enshrined in the separate school systems (Magnusson and Sancton, 1983:171).

These regional, economic, and ethnic factors are important to an understanding of the place of Halifax in the larger political arena. Metropolitan

Halifax is made up of the political jurisdictions of Halifax, Dartmouth, and Bedford-Sackville; Halifax is the largest. The unsuitability of the terrain, consisting of rock laced with waterways, has forced development into the Bedford-Sackville region, which is growing fastest. Civic politics is non-partisan. There is a council-manager system of government, with a series of boards, commissions, and committees operating outside the regular administrative structure, on which we shall elaborate more in the next section (Cameron and Aucoin 1983:179-82). A more unified metropolitan government has not been considered. The dual Protestant-Catholic school systems are still maintained, but are declining in the core of the city, and separate schools are no longer being built in newer suburban developments. There is a regional authority that operates the transit, sanitary landfill, and jail systems; this may gradually turn into a more integrated metropolitan system as time goes on.

Montreal: Emergence of French Power Elite

Until recently Montreal was the largest metropolis in Canada; it had a blend of Latin flair and European architecture (Nader, 1976:117). Montreal began in 1642 with the establishment of the mission colony of Ville-Marie on the St. Lawrence River. It was the second settlement in New France, the first being Quebec City. Montreal was strategically situated, and gradually replaced Quebec City as the commercial center of the French fur trade because it was a transshipment point for the inland waterways. By 1700 the French fur trade had extended southwest of Lake Michigan, including the Mississippi basin, and Montreal had become the most influential metropolis in North America (Nader, 1976:119), emerging as the main center for the organization, supply, and financing of a far-flung network of French-controlled fur trading posts (Sancton, 1983:59). After the defeat of the French, British merchants were quick to seize control of the fur trade. By 1821, when the North West Company was absorbed into the Hudson's Bay Company, furs were shipped via Hudson Bay, and Montreal's dominant role in the fur trade was over. The conquest of New France left a French-speaking, Roman Catholic population under the rule of the British. New France was permitted to keep its language, its religion, and its laws, but it was ruled by an English-speaking minority who also controlled the economy and business. It is not surprising, then, that the majority on the city council were English-speaking until well into the 1870s (Sancton, 1983:60). English-speaking dominance in business is changing only recently.

As illustrated in chapter six, the French-speaking and English-speaking populations are segregated into "two solitudes," with new immigrants located between as a buffer zone (Sancton, 1983:63). In 1881 Canadians of French origin made up only 56 percent of the population of Montreal (Kralt, 1986a). Between 1881 and 1921 those of British origin dropped to 24 percent. Those of French origin have now become a majority (Sancton, 1983:65). Because of Quebec laws promoting French language and culture, English-speaking

Montrealers have been moving to Ontario, causing a further decline in the English presence. Quebec is increasingly moving towards a greater French identity; immigrants are expected to learn and to use French, and French Quebeckers are increasingly entering the highest levels of business. It is expected as a result that the English-speaking presence will continue to decline.

"John Drapeau is undoubtedly Canada's best known mayor. By sponsoring Expo 67 and the 1976 Olympics he has become an international personality." (Sancton, 1983:58.) Drapeau did his best, in his more than 25 years in office, to establish Montreal as an international and cosmopolitan city. Montreal has frequently been led by powerful, popular, charismatic leaders (Sancton, 1983:66). Mayor Drapeau and his Civic party are a good example of elite power; they completely dominated the municipal elections of 1962 and 1966, winning 87 percent and 94 percent of the vote, and 42 of 45 and 45 of 48 council seats respectively (Sancton, 1983:71). Montreal was for a long time one of the most politically fragmented urban areas in Canada, and this only changed in 1965 when the suburban areas became more consolidated (Nader, 1976:160). Because the majority of his voters were in core Montreal, Drapeau tended to ignore suburban interests, and used various political maneuvers that kept the urban area fragmented and prevented integrated metropolitan planning. Instead, Drapeau brought super-projects such as Place Ville Marie, Place des Arts, the subway system, Expo 67, and the Olympic stadium to Montreal, all part of his vision of turning Montreal into an international city. Drapeau comes closest to the Canadian version of a city boss like Mayor Daley of Chicago.

Toronto: From British to Multicultural Dominance

Toronto was selected as the site for the capital of Upper Canada in 1793. Consequently it developed later than Halifax and Montreal. The fishing and fur trade largely bypassed Toronto; the fur trade out of Montreal followed the Ottawa River farther north, although the Dutch and English did use "the Toronto Passage" between New York and the West after 1664 (Nader, 1976:191). Forts were built on the Toronto site in 1720 and 1750, but not used extensively.

After the 1776 American Revolution, large numbers of British Empire Loyalists came to southern Ontario. It was decided in 1791 to create the province of Upper Canada under British common law and with the British system of landholding, both different from Quebec. Thus Toronto and southern Ontario became a British charter group stronghold. In 1800 the population of York (now Toronto) was only 400; by 1834, the year Toronto was incorporated as a city, it was still only 9000 (Magnusson, 1983:96).

It is more recently that Toronto has become prominent because of its central location: 1) it is closer to the western frontier; 2) it is farthest south, close to the American industrial midwest and east; 3) it has a good harbor located on the St. Lawrence Seaway with access to the Atlantic; 4) it has the richest agricultural hinterland east of the Great Lakes; 5) it is also close to northern mining exploration; 6) it is now at the centre of Canada's industrial heartland; and 7) it is the capital of Ontario, the most populous province with more than one-third of Canada's population.

After World War II industrial Toronto and southern Ontario increasingly attracted the lion's share of Canada's immigrants to its factories. Before the 1940s Toronto was still 80 percent British and overwhelmingly Protestant. Breton *et al.* (1990:18-19) have done one of the most thorough studies of ethnicity in Toronto, showing that in 1981, 47 percent of the population were of British origin, and 29 percent had mother tongues other than English. By 1990 the British were in a minority, the Catholic church had become the largest in the city, and 40 percent of the residents had a mother tongue other than English (Magnusson, 1983:111-12). While the British were dominant earlier, Toronto has now turned into the most multicultural urban center in Canada, and this ethnic diversity is increasing (Kralt, 1986b). Some of the problems connected with such diversity will be dealt with in chapter ten.

Since 1971, Toronto has become Canada's largest metropolitan center with a population of 3.4 million in 1986. Toronto's southern Ontario hinterland contains a network of urban centers such as Hamilton, Windsor, London, Kitchener-Waterloo, and Sudbury. This network of smaller urban centers providing a variety of functions and services clearly fits into a hierarchy of centers with Toronto at the apex as the regional capital (Hawley, 1981:235). But Toronto has also become the industrial hub of the whole country, as we saw in chapter seven, with Montreal clearly in second place.

In 1953 the municipality of Metropolitan Toronto was composed of a federation of thirteen municipalities. In that year the Ontario legislature set in motion a royal commission to study the needs of the expanding metropolitan region. In 1967 the Ontario government consolidated these municipalities into the City of Toronto and the boroughs of York, East York, Etobicoke, North York, and Scarborough (Nader, 1976:240). Within this federation, each area municipality retained its local autonomy, but major regional services such as debenture borrowing, public transportation, wholesale water supply, trunk sewers, regional parks, expressways, major arterial roads, and police protection have become the responsibility of the metropolitan corporation (Nader, 1976:240-1). As shown in Table 8-1, the city of Toronto in 1984 had a council of 23 members in eleven dual wards; the boroughs of East York (council size of 9 in 4 wards), Etobicoke (11 in 5 wards), North York (19 in 14 wards), and Scarborough (19 in 14 wards). Non-partisan politics became more partisan in Toronto in the 1980s when independent populist mayors such as David Crombie and John Sewell were elected.

Winnipeg: Unicity Gateway to the West

Winnipeg represents a fourth, significantly different, regional setting. The city, located at the confluence of the Red and Assiniboine rivers, is the gateway to the Prairies. Fur trading forts were located on this site as early as 1738

(Artibise, 1975:7-19; Nader, 1976:267; Bellan, 1978:1-13). The Red River settlement was founded on this site in 1812. When Manitoba became a province in 1870, Winnipeg became the capital. Winnipeg incorporated in 1873, at which time it had a population of only 1867; but the population grew dramatically after 1885, when the Canadian Pacific Railway connected it with eastern Canada (Morton, 1957:166; Bellan, 1978:14-24). Located in a 150-km corridor with the American border to the south and Lakes Manitoba and Winnipeg to the north, it was the only Canadian route to the West.

Winnipeg became a warehouse and depot for the eastern goods and supplies being shipped west (Artibise, 1975:61-87). Because of its booming economy, it was billed as the "Chicago of the North." It became the fourth largest city in Canada, and retained this rank until 1971. The economy has always remained highly diversified. At the centre point of the railway routes connecting east to west, Winnipeg became a transportation repair center; it developed large stockyards and meat processing facilities, and was the home of the grain exchange. With the opening of the Panama Canal in 1914, ships from Europe and the east coast could reach Vancouver by sea, and this curbed Winnipeg's stronghold as the gateway to the West. With the Depression in the 1930s, and the beginning of the oil boom in Alberta in 1947, Winnipeg's economic influence in the West declined still further.

Soon alliances along ethnic and class lines emerged (Kiernan and Walker, 1976:222-3). Until recently Winnipeg was the most ethnically, culturally, and socially diverse of all metropolitan centers in Canada. When the West was settled beginning in the 1870s, Winnipeg was the gateway for immigrants who came from Europe via ship and rail from the east; many continued west to settle the Prairies, but many stayed in Manitoba. There were strong social class polarizations, which culminated in the 1919 Winnipeg General Strike (Bellan, 1978:163-90; Rea, 1973:1-117). In 1981, the British were the largest group, consisting of 37 percent of the Manitoba population; but there are also large populations of Germans, Ukrainians, French, Dutch, Poles, and many others (Driedger, 1990:255).

Winnipeg is culturally very diverse; the people living north of the Assiniboine River are of lower socio-economic status, and consistently elect New Democratic Party representatives; in the south live the more affluent Winnipeg residents, who are largely of British origin, and tend to vote conservative. These ethnic and class differences have divided Winnipeg politically since the turn of the century. Long-time Ukrainian Mayor Stephen Juba was notably successful in assembling a coalition of power based on ethnic groups (Sancton, 1983:302).

Winnipeg's 624,000 population in 1986 represents roughly 60 percent of Manitoba's population of slightly over one million, making the metropolis the most dominant in its region. The coalition of business and professional interests has persisted over the years, and is now lodged in the Independent Citizen's Election Committee (ICEC) (Artibise, 1975:287-319). Workers' interests are now represented by the NDP. This political polarity has lasted since the

1919 Winnipeg General Strike. Provincial governments have alternated between the Conservatives and the NDP. In 1972 the NDP provincial legislature restructured the Winnipeg municipal government in a radical and comprehensive way, forming a unicity government covering the total metropolitan area and having all local services under one unified municipal adminstration (Nader, 1976:293-4). The council was large—50 members—for greater local representation, designed to alleviate discrimination against the poorer areas (Kiernan and Walker, 1983:231-4). However, the conservative ICEC has held a majority of seats for the past 65 years, so that the system has not worked as radically as the new structure might promise. Recommendations by committees have often been ignored. The 50 seats have been reduced to 29 plus the mayor, in favor of efficiency rather than representation. The twelve community committees have been telescoped into six, consolidating power in fewer representative forums (Kiernan and Walker, 1983:238-9). This radical unification and restructuring has not yet accomplished its promised potential, largely because municipal government has been highly politicized and has remained in the hands of the conservative power elite.

Vancouver: Beautiful Terminal on the Pacific

In 1792 Captain George Vancouver visited the site of Vancouver during his exploration of the North Pacific coast, but no settlement followed until the discovery of gold in the Fraser River in 1856 to 1857 (Nader, 1976:378-9). It was the completion of the transcontinental railway to Burrard Inlet in 1885 that spurred settlement, first as the little town of Granville, incorporated in 1886, which was later renamed Vancouver by Van Horne of the CPR. The first train arrived in Vancouver in 1887, and that same year the first ship docked at the CPR wharf. These were the beginnings of Canada's Pacific coast train and ship terminal (Gutstein, 1983:190-1). Earlier Victoria was dominant in the coastal area, but by 1901 Vancouver had grown to a city of 29,000, surpassing the population of its early rival (Nader, 1976:379-80). As a rail and shipping terminal on the mainland, Vancouver had many strategic advantages over Victoria, and the latter could not compete, even though the provincial capital was located in Victoria.

British Columbia was firmly within the economic sphere of Winnipeg until the Panama Canal opened in 1914; a grain elevator was started the same year (Gutstein, 1983:192). Since ships could now come to Vancouver directly, Vancouver soon extended its economic sphere of influence eastwards, so that by the 1920s its dominance extended into Saskatchewan. By 1921 it had a population of 163,000, and regular shipments of wheat were carried via the Panama Canal to Europe (Nader, 1976:380-1). By 1929 Vancouver's population of 250,000 exceeded that of Winnipeg, and Vancouver became the third largest city in Canada (Gutstein, 1983:194). These rail and shipping activities have made Vancouver Canada's major port and terminal for trade with Asia and the Pacific rim nations.

The gold rush in the 1850s brought a variety of ethnic migrants into the

Fraser Valley, but it was the building of the CPR in the 1880s that brought large numbers of Chinese to the west coast. When work on the railroad was finished, many Chinese moved to Vancouver and formed Canada's largest Chinatown, still located on Pender Street (Lai, 1988:80-86). Until World War II Vancouver also had Canada's largest Japantown, located on Hastings and Powell streets, but this community was decimated in 1942 when the west coast Japanese were interned and sent inland (Kralt, 1986c; Petrie, 1982:11-48). In chapter six we showed the segregation patterns of the Chinese, Japanese, Greeks, Jews, Portuguese, and Indo-Pakistanis in the city, illustrating the large numbers of visible minorities, which have often been seen as a threat to Vancouverites of European origin (Balarishnan and Kralt, 1987; Hardwick, 1974:115). Race relations have not been good in British Columbia, where dominant whites have passed legislation to keep visible minorities, especially Asians, from obtaining power (Wickberg, 1982).

These unique regional, economic, and ethnic characteristics have produced many partisan political conflicts in Vancouver, especially after 1968 when Conservative and Social Credit governments were challenged by the New Democratic Party. The Non-Partisan Association (NPA) made up of the social and business elite, was formed in 1937 as a response to the CCF, which had earlier elected three of eight council members. The managers and owners of small and large business corporations dominated the NPA, which ruled for thirty years until 1968 (Roy, 1980:152). However, in 1980 Harcourt ran as an independent, but backed by the NDP, and won. The municipal structure under which Vancouver is now operating is illustrated in Figure 8-2.

Edmonton: Oil Capital of Alberta

Settlement began in 1795 with the building of fur trading forts on the Sturgeon and North Saskatchewan rivers. The RCMP arrived in Fort Edmonton in 1874. The settlement became a thriving commercial-transportation center with the coming of the CPR. In 1891 Calgary had a population 10 times that of Edmonton, and these two Alberta cities have been rivals ever since; Edmonton is now the larger of the two. It was chosen as the provincial capital when Alberta became a province in 1905. The University of Alberta is located there. The intersection of three transcontinental railways stimulated growth before World War I, so that by 1914 it had a population of 72,500, but had only increased to 93,800 by 1941 (Nader, 1976:356-7). Edmonton's northern location made it the gateway to the agricultural and mining opportunities in the Peace River area (Lightbody, 1983:260-1).

In 1942 Edmonton became the operations base for the construction of the Alaska Highway and the Canol Pipeline. The discovery of the Leduc oil well in 1947 set in motion an explosion of economic activity, making Edmonton one of the largest oilfield supply centers in Canada (Lightbody, 1983:260). For four decades, Edmonton and Calgary were the fastest growing cities in Canada, surpassing and challenging Winnipeg's position as the dominant metropolis on the Prairies. Edmonton's economy is not as diversified as Winnipeg's, but in population size it is now the fifth largest city in Canada after Toronto, Montreal, Vancouver, and Ottawa-Hull.

Lightbody (1983:255) calls Edmonton "a solid bourgeois city." From 1934 to 1960, 88 percent of the Citizen's Committee (who were 80 percent British) were successful in winning seats on the city council. *The Edmonton Journal* has been a foe of the CCF and then the NDP, supporting mostly conservative candidates. Edmonton entered the post-war period as a small city of 112,000; by 1981 its population had increased five-fold to 657,000. The oil industry attracted an ethnically heterogeneous population, so that in 1981 Edmonton was almost as diversified ethnically as Winnipeg and Toronto. Edmonton is a conservative city within a conservative province, so that candidates leaning towards the left have not been very successful.

Ottawa-Hull: Center of Federal Co-ordination

The small community of Hull was founded on the Quebec side of the Ottawa River in 1800. The Ottawa Valley had been an important Indian trade route ever since Samuel de Champlain came in 1613, and continued to be an important trade route for the North West Fur Trading Company between Montreal and the West (Nader, 1976:163-4). In 1810 there were only 150 people, living mostly in Hull. When the 200-km Rideau Canal from Kingston to Bytown, the lumber center on the Ontario side of the river, was completed in 1832, Bytown had a population of 2500 (Nader, 1976:165). It was incorporated as Bytown in 1850 and as the city of Ottawa in 1855, after the Indian name *Outaouais*, meaning meeting of rivers (Nader, 1976:166). In 1857 Queen Victoria chose Ottawa as the capital of Canada because it was on the border of Ontario and Quebec, between Toronto and Quebec City, the capitals of Upper and Lower Canada, and well inland from the American border and the danger of American raids. Thus, a sleepy lumber town became the capital of Canada.

During 1870 to 1900, Ottawa-Hull ranked as the foremost lumber center of Canada, with large mills producing both lumber and wood by-products. It also experienced population growth because of its role as the capital of Canada after Confederation. By 1979, there were 103,000 federal employees in the national capital region (84,129 in Ottawa and 18,851 in Hull) — 30 percent of the total labor force of the city. Between 1921 and 1941 the population of the city of Ottawa only increased from 107,843 to 154,951, but in the next twenty years the metropolitan population doubled to 344,214, and by 1981 it had more than doubled again to 718,000, making it the fourth largest metropolis in Canada (Andrew, 1983:146-7). The numbers of federal government employees in Ottawa-Hull have escalated, and so has the ratio of civil servants to the rest of the population, giving the city a conservative atmosphere.

Ethnically Ottawa-Hull is unique in that it straddles the two largest central provinces: anglophone Ontario and francophone Quebec. In addition to its

French-English dual location, the federal government has spent millions helping to make Ottawa-Hull one of the most bilingual urban centers in Canada.
Since the country is officially bilingual, it is important symbolically that the
nation's capital provide a bilingual model for Canadians to emulate. However,
since the federal government also functions bilingually, it is important that
leaders, members of parliament, and government officials and workers can
communicate with each other effectively. Communications with the French-
speaking and English-speaking populations have been improved by having a
greater number of French-speaking civil servants on the Hull side, and a
greater number of English-speaking civil servants on the Ottawa side.

Ottawa-Hull is unique in that it involves two provincial governments, is
the location of Canada's federal government, and in addition, 52 local municipalities in Ontario and Quebec are involved (Nader, 1976:187). The multi-
plicity of governments and the resulting fragmentation of jurisdictions is the
worst in Canada. The National Capital Commission has total jurisdiction over
the whole Ottawa-Hull capital area, and is involved in such projects as the
surrounding greenbelt, the relocation of the railway lines, expansion of Gat-
ineau Park north of Hull, development of parks and spaces, and the decentralization of government offices, especially to Hull. In 1980 Ottawa's
municipal government was changed to fifteen aldermen elected by wards and
a mayor elected at large (Andrew, 1983:154). After the failure of the Meech
Lake accord, it will be interesting to observe whether Quebec will increasingly
distance itself from the rest of Canada. If Quebec should separate or develop
some form of sovereignty-association, how will a Canadian capital located on
both sides of the Ottawa River be affected?

Urban Political Components and Structures

Having reviewed the historical developments of urban political power in Canada, we can now turn to an examination of the political power structures of
urban centers. Each city has its own environmental context, which it seeks to
exploit and dominate. What are the general components of political power in
urban centers, and how do these structures vary from city to city?

There are basically five components of urban political structures: the
mayor, the council, committees of council, the bureaucracy, and special-
purpose bodies. Higgins (1986:147-65) describes five different models used
by the various Canadian cities to organize these five basic components of
political decision-making. Let us look at each of the five components, and
then discuss the various internal structures that have evolved in Canadian
metropolitan centers.

Basic Components of Urban Decision-Making

The Mayor is the most publicly visible component of the urban structure. The
functions of the mayor are usually vague, but personality and political acumen

are essential in providing leadership and authority on the job. The role of the mayor is both legislative and administrative. The mayor should 1) see that the laws passed by the municipality are executed; 2) oversee the conduct of the civic officers, ensuring that they do their duties; and 3) the mayor should communicate with council on urban affairs, budgets, and services, making recommendations to council as appropriate (Higgins, 1986:21-9). "The American tradition of 'strong' mayors has not been transplanted to Canada," but they are more than just ordinary council members (Higgins, 1986:129). Powerful mayors such as Jean Drapeau of Montreal have exercised power in informal charismatic ways rather than by legal ways.

The Council is the legislative policy-making body; it is headed by the mayor. Resolutions and bylaws passed by the council are carried out by municipal civil servants. Council members are usually elected by the voters in city wards. Council members, who may be called aldermen, represent the majority of the voters in their constituency, and bring their concerns to council for debate and action. Urban councils normally have about a dozen representatives headed by the mayor, although larger councils are elected in some metropolitan centers.

Committees of the Council are a part of virtually all municipal councils, but there is considerable variation on the number of committees and the extent to which they are used. Often there are both standing committees and temporary, *ad hoc*, or special committees formed for specific tasks. Usually only some members of the council sit on these committees, with the mayor or board chairperson an *ex officio* member. Council members may indicate their preferences as to which committees they would like to sit on. Committees can be useful to council by scrutinizing the evaluations of the municipal civil servants; debating and preparing reports and recommendations on issues or problems that require study and thought. As a result of the work of committees, council has more assurance that all options have been explored.

The Bureaucracy includes the officials and staff who carry out the decisions of the council and the upper administration. In large urban centers local government may require numerous employees: 12,000 full-time in Edmonton; 10,369 in Calgary; 8,648 in Winnipeg; 6,000 in Vancouver; and 5,692 in Toronto in 1984 (Higgins, 1986:139). Edmonton had the largest number of full-time employees per 1000 population (22.5), followed by Calgary (17.5), Winnipeg (15.3), Vancouver (14.5), and Halifax (12.9).

Special Purpose Bodies are a fifth component. They are created for specific purposes and include police commissions, boards of education, parks boards, conservation authorities, library boards, museum boards, public transit commissions, boards of health, emergency measures organizations, electrical utilities commissions, industrial development boards, boards to operate convention centers, and public housing authorities (Higgins, 1986:142-4). Some of them, such as school boards, may often be quasi-autonomous.

These five basic components — mayor, council, committees, bureaucracy, and special bodies — are a part of all urban municipal governments. The structuring of these components, however, varies by city. We now turn to review some of the government structures in Canadian metropolitan municipalities.

The Council-Committee Structural Model

One of the simplest structures, often used by smaller urban centers, is the council-committee model illustrated in Figure 8-1. Derived from the British system of local government. and used by the Borough of East York in metropolitan Toronto, this model is one of the oldest and simplest, and serves smaller centers well. The mayor is an *ex officio* member of all committees, and has an onerous task. "The elected council meets both as a whole and in a number of committees, with each of the standing committees dealing with a particular area of both policy and administration." (Higgins, 1986:148; Plunkett, 1968:15-36.) Special committees may also be created from time to time on a short-term basis. As Figure 8-1, shows there is considerable communication between departments and committees; the frequent reporting keeps the many substructures informed about what is going on elsewhere. The model facilitates communication, tends to eliminate duplication, and keeps the council and the various administrative bodies in touch.

While this is an effective model for smaller urban centers, when centers and organizations become larger, it becomes impossible for both the mayor and the aldermen to keep up with all the meetings and work required. The fact that larger municipalities have abandoned this structure illustrates that there are serious shortcomings. Chief among the problems is the lack of any co-ordinating mechanism other than council as a whole, and this imposes too heavy a workload on mayor and council.

Council-Chief Administrative Officer Model

A more recent council-chief administrative officer model has become common in Canadian urban municipalities; this is shown in Figure 8-2. "This structure originated in the United States—in Staunton, Virginia in 1908—and was first imported into Canada by Westmount, Quebec in 1913." (Higgins, 1986:151.) This model is more in line with structures that may be found in the business world. A city manager is hired to oversee and direct the day-to-day operations of the municipality, and has the authority to recruit and dismiss staff, organize departments, assign responsibilities, control the lines of communication, and draft the annual budgets (Higgins, 1986:151; Plunkett, 1968:37-50). The sole administrative duty retained by the mayor and council is to hire and fire the city manager. This model sharply separates the executive and legislative powers, a practice common in the United States but very different from the British model common in Canada in the past.

The chief advantage of this structure is the degree of co-ordination possible. because all lines of communication go from the departmental bureaucrats

Figure 8-1 A council-committee structure of urban polity

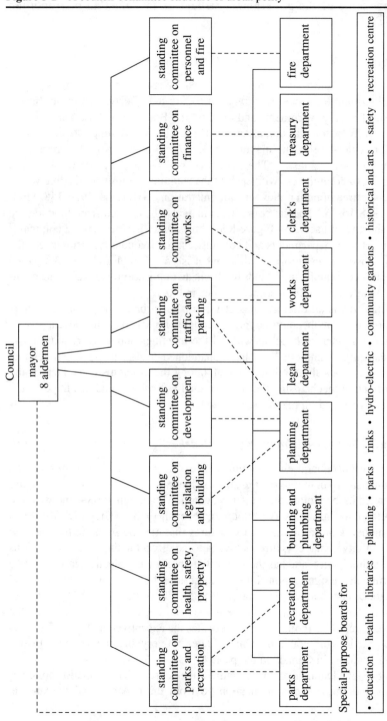

Council

mayor
8 aldermen

standing committee on personnel and fire

standing committee on finance

standing committee on works

standing committee on traffic and parking

standing committee on development

standing committee on legislation and building

standing committee on health, safety, property

standing committee on parks and recreation

fire department

treasury department

clerk's department

works department

legal department

planning department

building and plumbing department

recreation department

parks department

Special-purpose boards for

• education • health • libraries • planning • parks • rinks • hydro-electric • community gardens • historical and arts • safety • recreation centre

SOURCE: Higgins (1986:149).

Figure 8-2 Council-chief administrator officer structure of urban polity

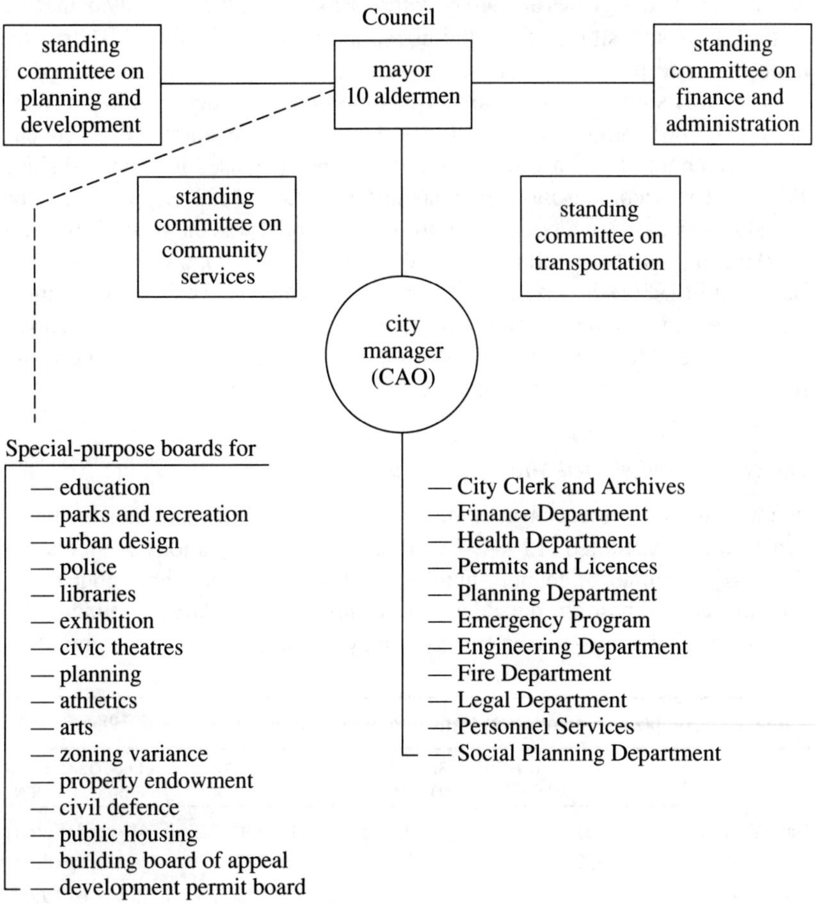

Council

| standing committee on planning and development | | mayor 10 aldermen | | standing committee on finance and administration |

standing committee on community services

standing committee on transportation

city manager (CAO)

Special-purpose boards for

— education
— parks and recreation
— urban design
— police
— libraries
— exhibition
— civic theatres
— planning
— athletics
— arts
— zoning variance
— property endowment
— civil defence
— public housing
— building board of appeal
— development permit board

— City Clerk and Archives
— Finance Department
— Health Department
— Permits and Licences
— Planning Department
— Emergency Program
— Engineering Department
— Fire Department
— Legal Department
— Personnel Services
— Social Planning Department

SOURCE: Higgins (1986:153).

through the city manager to council. A second advantage is that the members of council can concentrate on legislative functions, representing the wishes of their constituents and making policy accordingly (Higgins, 1986:152-3). But there are also risks and disadvantages with so much dependence on one person and one office. Since the city manager is in control of all information, he or she is able to select what information flows to council, and to his/her subordinates as well. The city manager must often make crucial judgements, and these may be affected by his/her personal views. This much responsibility may be too much to place on one person. As urban centers get very large, it becomes almost impossible for one individual to cope with so much power and responsibility.

To relieve the amount of responsibility that devolves on the city manager, some urban centers have modified the two models we have described so far. A council-commission structure, widely used in western Canada, as for example in Calgary, designates a board of commissioners in place of a city manager, so that the responsibility for administration and co-ordination is shared by more than one person. A council-board of control model is widely used in Ontario; it is similar to the board of commissioners model used in the West to share co-ordination responsibilities — London is an example. The council-executive committee is a fifth model, which has been used in Montreal since 1921, and is becoming more popular in Ontario. It shifts responsibility for operations away from a board of control. This model was adopted by Toronto in 1969, and has been followed by Winnipeg in 1971, Ottawa in 1980, and Hamilton in 1981 (Higgins, 1986:158-64). In Toronto, the executive committee, comprising the mayor and four aldermen, is part of a larger city council comprising eighteen aldermen. It is this model that supports powerful mayors such as Mayor Drapeau of Montreal.

Composition of Selected Municipal Councils

In Table 8-1 we present profiles of sixteen municipalities and their councils as they were constituted in 1984. The Table shows the variations in population size, size of municipal council, number of people represented per councillor, and the electoral base for the aldermen. Montreal has the largest council — 58 elected in 57 wards — and is run by a mayor and an executive committee.

Table 8-1 Compositon of selected Canadian urban municipal councils, 1984

MUNICIPALITY	POPULATION IN 1981*	SIZE OF COUNCIL	PEOPLE PER COUNCILLOR	ELECTORAL BASIS FOR ALDERMEN
East York	101 974	9	11 330	4 wards (dual)
Edmonton	532 246	13	40 942	6 wards (dual)
Etobicoke	298 713	11	27 156	5 wards (dual)
Halifax	114 594	13	8 815	12 wards
London	254 280	19	13 383	7 wards (dual)
Mississauga	315 056	10	31 506	9 wards
Montreal	980 354	58	16 903	57 wards
North York	559 521	19	29 448	14 wards
Ottawa	295 163	16	18 448	15 wards
Saskatoon	154 210	11	14 019	10 wards
Scarborough	443 353	19	23 334	14 wards
St. John's	83 770	9	9 308	at large
Toronto	599 217	23	26 053	11 wards (dual)
Vancouver	414 281	11	37 662	at large
Victoria	64 379	9	7 153	at large
Winnipeg	564 473	30	18 816	29 wards

SOURCES: Higgins (1986:133); and compiled from Statistics Canada, 1982, Table 1.

Winnipeg has the second largest council — 30 (it used to be 50) elected in 29 wards; it too is run by an executive committee. Greater Toronto, on the other hand, is divided into the five urban municipalities of Toronto, East York, Etobicoke, North York, and Scarborough; these vary in council size and the number of people represented by each councillor.

Governmental Policies and Services

Our review of urban centres earlier in this book shows that they vary in historical background, regional setting, ethnic diversity, and political structure. Let us now make some comparisons of their policies and services. It is clear that there are differences in urban governments and overlapping political jurisdictions between levels of governments. Municipal governments are constantly faced with financial problems, and the provision of all the services residents desire is a challenge that some are better able to meet than others (Flanagan, 1990).

Fragmentation and Proliferation

Goldberg and Mercer (1986:196-7) show that local governments are more fragmented in the United States than in Canada; they claim that this is related to catering to the greater American emphasis on individualism. By fragmentation they meant the proliferation of members and levels of government. They also say that Americans, as a result of local pressures, have more independent school districts and other special purpose districts, which create additional fragmentation. Canadian political culture, they say, is much more accepting

Table 8-2 Index of urban municipal fragmentation for selected metropolitan centers

Montreal	0.031
Baltimore	0.014
Minneapolis/St. Paul	0.064
San Francisco/Oakland	0.022
Toronto	0.009
Pittsburgh	0.124
St. Louis	0.102
Washington	0.050
Vancouver	0.018
Seattle	0.052
Portland	0.068
San Diego	0.012

SOURCE: Goldberg and Mercer (1986: 214).

Table 8-3 Number of urban local government units in selected metropolitan areas ranked by population size, 1972

	POPULATION 1972 (millions)	LOCAL GOVERNMENTS
New York	9.944	538
Chicago	7.085	1172
Los Angeles-Long Beach	7.000	232
Philadelphia	4.878	852
Detroit	4.489	241
Boston	3.417	147
San Francisco-Oakland	3.132	302
Washington, D.C.	2.999	90
Dallas-Fort Worth	2.446	288
St. Louis	2.400	483
Pittsburgh	2.396	698
Baltimore	2.125	29
Houston	2.124	304

Table 8-3 (continued)

	POPULATION 1972 (millions)	LOCAL GOVERNMENTS
TORONTO[1]	2.086	47
Newark	2.082	207
Cleveland	2.046	210
Minneapolis-St. Paul	1.996	218
Atlanta	1.684	86
Anaheim (etc.)	1.527	111
San Diego	1.443	151
Milwaukee	1.426	149
Seattle[3]	1.421	269
VANCOUVER[2]	1.082	60
Portland	1.007	298

[1]Municipality of Metropolitan Toronto (1971, Population); count of local governments — 1968 data.

[2]Vancouver Census Metropolitan Area (1971); local government count is an estimate.

[3]1970 Population.

SOURCES: Advisory Commission on Intergovernmental Relations, *Trends in Metropolitan America* (Washington, C.D.: U.S. Government Printing Office, 1977), Table 16; and Goldberg and Mercer (1986: 215).

of control and intervention by municipal government. Goldberg and Mercer (1986:196, 214) developed an index of municipal fragmentation based on the number of municipal governments in a metropolitan area per thousand population (the higher the score the more fragmentation). In Table 8-2 we compare American and Canadian centers and see that Canadian fragmentation scores are significantly lower.

We also see that there are variations among the three Canadian centers. In Canada, provincial governments have acted to reduce such proliferation. Goldberg and Mercer (1986:197) explain that Montreal has a higher index because it uses parishes as a geographical base for its municipalities, which has contributed to the numerical profusion of local governments. Toronto, on the other hand, has a low index because a reorganization of municipal areas has reduced the number of local governments to five in a two-tier system.

In Manitoba the NDP provincial government reorganized Winnipeg's twelve municipalities into a unicity or metropolitan-wide municipal government for efficiency and greater distribution of powers and services (Goldberg and Mercer, 1986:197-9). Such government action would be almost unthinkable in the United States, but Canadians do seem to accept more control by government. In Table 8-3 we illustrate the extent of local governmental proliferation. It is interesting to note that Chicago and Montreal, two centers with a high level of proliferation, have had strong mayors—Richard Daley and Jean Drapeau—who were dominant for many years. Presumably such proliferation of local governments needed political bosses who welded together political machines through charisma and/or power.

Overlapping Financial Jurisdictions

From our discussion of urban fragmentation it is clear that scores, even hundreds of local governments are involved in many metropolitan centers. What makes these situations even more complex is that provincial (state) and federal governments are also involved, especially in financing metropolitan operations (Schwab, 1982:481-3). Financial jurisdictions and responsibilities can therefore be extremely complex. Urban governments, including central city government, and suburban municipalities obtain their revenues from two main sources: 1) transfers from provincial or federal governments; and 2) from their own tax bases. Dependence on outside sources undermines municipal autonomy, of which local governments are usually very jealous. Thus, they are faced with a dilemma: apply for funds from other levels of government or raise taxes themselves. Neither option is desirable.

There is a second set of problems related to the interplay between the central city government and the local governments of the surrounding suburbs. As discussed in chapter five, facilities and housing in the central city are aging, and people of the lower socio-economic classes—including recent immigrants and disadvantaged racial groups—live in the central city; these people cannot afford to pay high municipal taxes. Middle and upper class suburbanites live in areas with newer facilities, and have less need of fire, police, and welfare services, yet they are best able to pay more taxes. Thus, there are often disparities among local governments in the amounts of taxes they can raise, the kinds of services they need to provide, and the costs of the physical upkeep of a safe, liveable urban environment.

Since suburbanites often use the central city for athletic and entertainment facilities, and for other services, and since many work downtown and therefore use the transportation services both for leisure and work, many people argue that suburbanites should also pay a fair share for access to these services. In addition, the construction of wider and faster freeways into the center takes up land where taxpayers used to live, thus reducing the tax-base for the central city, so central city governments try to devise ways to tax non-resident shoppers and users of their facilities. These inequalities of the means to pay and the differential use of facilities lead to pressures to integrate central city and suburban governments, as with the unicity government of metropolitan Winnipeg.

Goldberg and Mercer (1986:224) have examined the expenditures in selected Canadian and American central cities, and compared them with expenditures in their outer suburbs. They have clustered these cities roughly according to size and region; the results are presented in Table 8-4. It is striking how greatly these expenditures and ratios vary. Montreal spends more per capita in the suburbs, and this is even more pronounced in Minneapolis-St. Paul, but reversed significantly in Baltimore (170.1). Of the three, Baltimore spends the most in the central city ($1,293.90) per capita and the Twin Cities most in the suburbs ($1,033.90). Similar patterns occur in the midwest with Toronto, Pittsburgh, and St. Louis spending more in the suburbs, and

Table 8-4 Expenditures per capita (city vs. suburbs), selected metropolitan areas, 1976-77

	CITIES	SUBURBS
Montreal	541.60	624.90
Baltimore	1293.90	979.30
Minneapolis-St. Paul	361.90	1033.90
Toronto	507.40	706.80
Pittsburgh	336.60	641.80
St. Louis	511.90	631.20
Washington	2303.06	1168.20
Vancouver	622.40	822.50
Seattle	459.50	832.10
Portland	361.70	833.30
San Diego	252.40	912.60

SOURCE: Goldberg and Mercer (1986: 224.)

Washington more in the central city. In the far west all four centers spend more per capita in the suburbs.

Washington and Baltimore both have severe poverty in their central cities, so this may be one of the reasons so much is spent per capita in the central city—high levels of spending are for welfare services, and for fire and police forces. The other centers likely spend more in the suburbs because they have more tax resources and can afford to spend more on new community facilities and services. The three Canadian cities all spend somewhat more in the suburbs. per capita expenditures of Montreal, Toronto, and Vancouver are also quite similar. Through its many departments and crown corporations, the Canadian federal government assists urban transportation facilities, and itself funds public facilities such as airports, ports, and railway stations (Goldberg and Mercer, 1986:201).

Summary

Urban government is an important social institution that uses power to achieve political ends. Urban power may reside in: 1) a power elite—a mayor and his executive; or 2) a pluralist structure in which power is widely distributed across councils, boards, and committees. Conservative business and professional interests have usually tried to consolidate and control power within a small elite, while more social-minded politicians have tried to distribute power more widely in response to the needs of workers and those who are powerless.

We examined seven urban centers across Canada: Halifax, Montreal, Toronto, Winnipeg, Vancouver, Edmonton, and Ottawa-Hull. We found that there were variations in the historical and regional settings, economic opportunities, ethnic mix, and political structures among these seven urban complexes. Some dominated larger regions than others, and some were much more influential than others in the larger national economic and political arena also. But each was an important "central place" for its respective regional area.

The five basic urban political components of mayor, council, committees of council, bureaucracy, and special-purpose bodies have been structured into a variety of models. The council-committee model used in smaller urban centers keeps the five components closely integrated and involved for maximum and direct communication. However, as urban populations grow, large structures have become more pyramidal, and a hired administrative manager or managers work with small councils, boards, or executives. This leaves the larger council to concentrate on policy, while day-to-day operations are taken care of by the bureaucracy. Most large Canadian metropoli have moved to this type of structure.

Governmental policies and services must be designed to fit the needs of cities, which will vary according to their respective settings and over time. Some metropolitan areas are much more fragmented than others, involving many competing political interests. There are always too few resources to fill all the needs, and there are many overlapping financial jurisdictions and responsibilities. Federal, provincial, and local sources of income are blended to try to cover the needed services. Suburbanites with greater means and resources are often reluctant to share responsibilities with lower-income central city residents.

9. Family Networks in Urban Communities

At the end of chapter four we showed Murdie's diagram (Figure 4-4) of the three most salient social factors he found in Toronto that affect location (economic, family, and ethnic status), confirming Shevky and Bell's findings in Los Angeles and San Francisco. We have discussed economic status and ethnicity; we shall discuss the family in this chapter. The family is the second most important factor in ordering social space.

The early classical sociologists such as Marx, Durkheim, Weber, Simmel, Toennies, Troeltsch, and others were all concerned with industrial change in Europe and its consequences for community and social order. Karl Marx focused on the political economy; Max Weber explored the complexities of bureaucracy. In chapters seven and eight we discussed how urbanization brings about changes in economic and political institutions. Emile Durkheim, having seen drastic revolutionary changes in France that did not bode well for social solidarity, was concerned about social cohesion. In this chapter we shall examine changes in the structures, functions, and roles of the family. Economic and political power have tended to overshadow the importance of family relations and of networking and neighboring in communities.

First, two very different perspectives on how the family is changing require attention: these are the structural-functional and feminist perspectives, and they will act as guides to family functions and family roles. Later in the chapter we shall discuss threats to family solidarity and important studies that help us understand the contribution of family networks in urban neighborhoods and communities.

Changing Family Perspectives

Industrialization and urbanization came to Canada somewhat later than in Europe. In the early years of European settlement, Canada was largely a country of hewers of wood, drawers of water, and farmers of land, where large families were an asset and mobility was often not great. Canada increasingly became an industrial nation in the nineteenth and twentieth centuries, and now three out of four Canadians live in cities of 1000 or more. In a city, the structures and functions of families and the roles of individuals in the family change, and family solidarity is more at risk in the city (Gold, 1982:154-5; Eichler, 1988:31-58).

Parsons' Structural Functionalism

Talcott Parsons (1971) developed a four-fold typology for classifying societies, which greatly influenced early sociological thinking. He worked with two key "pattern variables": particularism-universalism and ascription-achievement (Gist and Fava, 1974:37-9). In the first variable, particularism relates to individuals in their specific situations; universalism is the opposite pole, and relates to people in broader and general situations. In the second variable, the ascriptive pole deals with characteristics over which the individual has no control: sex, age, race, or ethnicity; while the achievement pole refers to skills that can be developed and achieved, through education for example. Parsons said that these two variables were continua, and he plotted four cells or types, which he described as particularistic-ascriptive (preindustrial societies) particularistic-achievement, universalist-ascriptive, and universalistic-achievement (industrial urban societies).

A preindustrial *gemeinschaft* folk society is a small, rural community where face-to-face primary relations take place, where people all know and trust each other in particularist ways, and where their cultural traditions are so set that they could be thought of as largely unchangeable or ascribed. In the urban *gesellschaft* society there are more secondary relations, where people are increasingly dealt with in universalistic terms and categories as means to ends, and where achievement of projected goals or ends is important. According to Parsons, modern societies are increasingly moving from ascriptive-particularism towards universalism-achievement or an urban way of life. Folk societies in Africa and Asia may be moving through a variety of intermediate states before they become urban universalistic-achievement societies.

Talcott Parsons (Parsons and Bales, 1955) has also applied his concept of structural functionalism to the family, and others have discussed the family within that tradition. Structural functionalists assume that society "needs" stable families because they provide the norms and define the roles that enable society to function properly (Nett, 1988:273). Parsons says that in a folk society within a particularistic-ascriptive setting, traditional patriarchal families with clearly defined roles based on gender are functional to the perpetuation of stable family life (Gold, 1982:156-7). The male head of the household works outside the home and is responsible for the family's economic welfare, while the wife will handle the domestic work, bring up the children, and provide emotional support. Thus, the separation of roles based on gender is functional to the survival of the urban family (Nett, 1988:274). While this pattern often occurs among first-generation rural immigrants, the pattern changes as they become more urban and upwardly mobile.

In chapter two we saw that a majority of the populations in most countries in Africa and Asia still live in rural areas (Sjoberg, 1960). Children are an asset in agricultural economies because they can help with food gathering and/ or production. Ramu (1988a:42-84) studied the changes in rural families in India when they moved to urban settings, and found that households became more nuclear, and marital communications, family interaction, authority patterns, and role expectations changed. Most rural families in Canada (influenced by urbanism) are now more modified nuclear rather than extended types, so they are no longer similar to the non-industrial extended family represented in Figure 9-1 (Ramu, 1989a:139-86).

Many immigrant families such as the Portuguese, southern Italians, and Greeks who settle in Canadian cities come from rural areas. Gans (1962) calls them urban villagers. The Portuguese (Anderson, 1974; Anderson and Higgs, 1976) in Toronto are a good example of such immigrants. They came in the 1970s, many of them sponsored by their relatives so they did not have to compete educationally and occupationally under the point system. Having

Figure 9-1   Types of preindustrial rural and modern industrial urban families

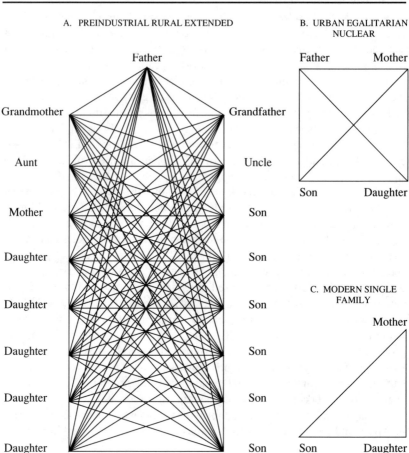

only low educational and occupational skills, their incomes were meagre, so they settled in the inner city where housing was affordable. They had the extended family structure illustrated in Figure 9-1.

In many preindustrial rural societies of Africa and Asia, as in Canadian rural families of the pioneer past, families are and were much larger.

The nuclear family (type B in Figure 9-1) consists of two generations only: parent(s) and two to four children. Husband/wife relationships tend increasingly to be egalitarian, and children are also beginning to have a considerable input in family decision making.

Type C, the single-parent family (more often headed by a mother than a father), illustrates how fragile the nuclear family structure can be. The single-parent family is becoming more common because of rising divorce rates and because more unmarried women are having children. Functions in single-parent families change; we shall discuss functions in the next section.

Internal family structures also change as families move from rural areas to the city. Rural preindustrial families tend to be patriarchal and hierarchical in structure: the male head of the household is dominant, the females tend to be submissive and the children are socialized to accept a lower place in the structure, as illustrated in Figure 9-1 (Deere and de Leal, 1982; Friedmann, 1981; Phillips, 1989:295). These traditional relationships have begun to change in Canadian rural areas, depending on the extent to which families have been exposed to more urban ways (Phillips, 1989:294-7).

Rural families also tend to have more segregated roles and spheres of work; men's and women's work are independent (Bott 1977:53). Women are in "charge" of the kitchen; men refer to outside work as "their" work, even though their wives often help outside. The line of authority is clear however, from father to mother to oldest children down to the youngest in line. Age also becomes a distinguishing factor. Such patriarchal, hierarchical family patterns are usually perpetuated for one or more generations by rural immigrants to the city.

As education, occupational status, and income rises, urban families become smaller, and some move to the suburbs. Family relations also change. The family becomes more democratized and egalitarian. Women increasingly work outside the home, and the status and roles of parents become more interchangeable. With fewer children, parents may take more interest in the activities of their children—for example they may drive them to hockey or ringette practices. If both parents are working outside the home, the children are required to become more independent. Both gender and age roles change towards what Bott (1971:54) calls joint organizational family roles. Family structure becomes a network rather than a hierarchy.

Recent Feminist Perspectives

Since the 1970s an extensive literature has developed on various feminist perspectives on the changing family (Keohane *et al*, 1982; Nett, 1986, Nett, 1988:15). Jaggar and Struhl (1978) wrote a book on five feminist frameworks (conservatism, liberalism, traditional Marxism, radical feminism, socialist feminist) that provide alternative theoretical accounts of the relations between women and men. *Conservatism* denies that women are oppressed, and claims that human nature is essentially the same in all times and places, that human interests, desires, abilities, and needs are determined by innate factors (Jaggar and Struhl, 1978:69). Human biology is considered a major factor in causing differences between the sexes, and these therefore cannot be changed. Feminists dispute this contention.

Liberal feminism had its origins in the "social contract" theories of the sixteenth and seventeenth centuries and the publication in 1792 of Mary Wollstonecraft's *A Vindication of the Rights of Women* (Jaggar and Struhl, 1978:70). Wollstonecraft declared that women's capacity to reason would be equal to that of men if they were given equal education, and therefore they would have equal opportunity to exercise their talents unhindered by restraints of law or custom. When discrimination has been eliminated, women will also be liberated.

Marxist feminists reject the importance of biology in gender differences, and point instead to the differences in functions imposed by the societies in which humans live. "Rejecting the biologism of conservatives, Marxists reject the liberal's belief that it is possible for people to have genuine equality of opportunity for the development of their potential while they remain within a class society where the many produce the wealth but the wealth and power end up in the hands of a few . . . " (Jaggar and Struhl, 1978:71.) Marxists locate the origins of women's oppression in the economic system, where the means of production are in the hands of the few (mostly men). The importance of political and economic power on the macro level, as discussed in chapters seven and eight, can now be seen as also important on the micro level.

Radical feminism insists that the oppression of women is fundamental to all societies and at all times in the past. It is the most difficult oppression to eradicate or change, it causes the most suffering to its victims, and it is a model for all other oppression (Jaggar and Struhl, 1978:71-72). There seems to be general agreement by radical feminists on women's oppression being widespread, fundamental, and difficult to change, but they differ on the extent of the suffering caused and whether it is a model for other forms of oppression.

Jaggar and Struhl (1978:72-73) summarize:

> *Socialist feminist* theory begins with basic acceptance of the historical materialist approach that was begun by Marx and Engels. It argues, however, that the traditional Marxist analysis needs to be enriched if it is to be thoroughly adequate for understanding the multifaceted nature of women's oppression. By placing an emphasis on understanding the cultural institutions (the family, heterosexual intercourse, etc.) that play a major role in oppressing women, this theory incorporates the central radical feminist insights; by insisting on analyzing these institutions within the context of class society, socialist feminism continues to employ a fundamentally Marxist method.

Socialist feminists recommend that problems such as abortion, poverty, and degradation need to be studied among the various social classes and among different racial groups to understand the variations in social class and male oppression. They agree that sexism is at least as fundamental as economic oppression (Cuneo, 1990:198-9). Socialist feminists see the family as an integral part of other economic, political, and social systems; they consider that domestic "unproductive" labor must be recognized and that household duties must be shared. There is an interconnectedness of home and work, private and public, personal and political, family and economic systems (Clement, 1988:74-5).

Meg Luxton's book, *More Than a Labour of Love* (1980), showed the interrelationships between women's roles in Flin Flon, Manitoba, a small city of 10,000 people. It was a case study of three generations of housewives, and showed how domestic labor in a mining town changed when industrial capitalism entered the area. Flin Flon was a company town, and both men and women were dependent on the company for work. For women, who could not work down the mine, their only alternatives were low-paying, insecure, and monotonous jobs, or marriage.

Fifty years ago there were no labor-saving devices, and housework was carried out in primitive conditions. As time spent on housework decreased with the use of vacuum cleaners and other devices, time spent on bringing up children increased, even though families were smaller (Luxton, 1980:82-4). Over three generations the number of women working outside the home changed: very few did so in the first generation, more were working in the second generation, and about half the women were in the labor force in the third generation. Despite these changes, household schedules were largely arranged around the rotating work shifts of the men, and wives, even when working outside the home, continued to be primarily responsible for the emotional well-being of their husbands, as well as coping with the housework and taking care of the children. Men helped relatively little in the household even when women were in the labor force, although this had improved somewhat by the third generation (Luxton, 1980:184-7).

Trade unions and pro-labor political parties provide for greater organizational support for men than for women. Women feel more alone in their struggle to obtain respect for the work they do in the home, and to get fulltime jobs on a steady basis (Cuneo, 1990:8-11). "Challenging the way domestic labor is organized means challenging the most basic structures of male-dominated industrial capitalist society." (Luxton, 1980:222.) Luxton (1980:231) concluded from her study that "working-class women are starting to realize that the present form of the family holds them back . . . The demands that these women are making to improve their daily lives require fundamental changes in the way society is organized." These struggles involve power relationships, part of the process of changing roles for all members of the family. We turn first to changing family functions.

Changing Family Functions

In our discussion of changing family structures we have already alluded to changing functions. In rural areas relatives and neighbors are close at hand. Family activities are highly visible, and norms, values, and behavior are exposed to daily scrutiny and observation. Such close social contexts provide ready help in need, as well as social pressure if deviation from the society's values and norms occurs (Eichler, 1988:109-10). To some extent such social scrutiny and pressures occur also in the city, especially in urban ethnic villages (Gans, 1962) described in chapter six. However, for most families, the urban environment is more open, and individuals and families have more freedom to make choices.

Structural-functional theorists assume that families serve such functions as the socialization of children and the provision of trust and affection, which only the family group can provide (Aberle *et al.*, 1950; Nett, 1988:273). According to Parsons and Bales (1955),the social class of the nuclear family was determined by the husband's occupation in the labor force. The husband had the instrumental role of providing economically, while the wife's expressive role was to maintain the household and nurture and socialize the children (Nett, 1988:274). These family functions have changed considerably, especially in cities.

Shift of the Workplace

The agricultural family lived in a household where the whole family was involved in the work necessary to the family's survival. The family was an economic, productive unit, and household and workplace occupied the same space. After the Industrial Revolution, machines were set up in factories, and work moved outside the household into factories, industries, and offices. The household became the home, a private place separate from work. Parents worked outside the home; children were educated in schools outside the home. Parsons' described WASP middle-class, suburban families of the 1950s. At this time it was mainly the husband/father who worked outside the home. Today, with the increasing labor force participation of women, the opportunities for the family to remain in touch during the day are limited. Small children may see their father or mother only briefly in the evening, after a hard day's work when all are tired and not at their best.

Education and training have been transferred to the school, where children learn in a formal setting and are taught by salaried teachers, not given hands-on training by their parents. Schools, however, offer children better opportunities to become independent. Children also learn in school to associate with a variety of people, to take direction from others, and to accept discipline, all of which will be required in their future work.

Transferral of Mate Selection

The selection of a mate has also been transferred from the control of the family to that of the individual (Gold, 1982:160-1). When the family was the unit of economic activity, the marriage of a family member was an economic trans-action, and was negotiated by the heads of the families concerned. In some societies a bride price was payable to the bride's family, the amount depending on the potential economic value of the bride to the family she was marrying into — for example, the agricultural produce she would generate in a society where it was customary for the wife to work on the land. In other societies a bride would be accompanied by a dowry, in part to ensure a means of future support for her. In these societies sons might be expected to marry for the economic benefit of their family, as for example marrying an heiress to restore the family fortunes. In societies that are becoming increasingly industrialized and urbanized, such as India, studies show that family control over mate selection decreases (Ramu, 1988; 19:207-27).

While parents may still influence which people their children date, such influence is usually indirect. Intermarriages between different ethnic, racial, religious, or socio-economic groups is increasing, because social control by parents over their children is more limited. Thus while urban families have become structurally more nuclear, at the same time they are becoming cultur-ally, religiously, or socio-economically more diverse, which can lead to insta-bility, but also to variety.

The Recreational Shift

Since work is more integrated into the regular life patterns of the preindustrial family, and since it is also carried out in closer proximity to the family residence, work patterns and leisure patterns are not as segmented as in the city. The craftsman or woman who is in charge of a personal business schedule can take time to attend to family matters or visit with clients as they come to buy products. To some extent Canadian farmers still cultivate such primary friendship relations as well, although as investment in machinery increases, as interest on loans and banks loom larger, they also become more profit- and goal-oriented, so that personal visits and relationships wane, giving way to tighter scheduling of time.

A generation or two ago it was not uncommon for a farmer to brag that he had never had a vacation in his life. Today farmers go to movies and concerts and take vacations away from home. In the past, rural "get-togethers" were often related to work activities: corn husking, barn raisings, rabbit hunts, or quilting bees. In preindustrial societies recreation often consisted of visiting neighbors, fishing, berry picking, and hunting. There was less need for people to get away from work activities because work had not controlled them as much during the week. Thus, the separation of family life, work, and recre-ation was not great.

Recreation in the city tends to shift to interests beyond the family context. Some activities, such as reading, boating, swimming, and tennis, can be done within the small context of nuclear relationships, but the need for more struc-tured foci seems to grow. Many want to get away from machines, schedules, and other people and retreat to the woods, parks, lakes, and nature. At the same time urbanites are so oriented to structure that they tend to be bored with unstructured visiting. Many engage in watching competitive sports at professional levels; a few actively participate at an amateur level. Children also take part in sports activities, where they have opportunities for social networking centered around a specific activity.

Recent technological devices such as television and VCRs have fostered spending some leisure time in the home. These devices provide a break from contacts at work or school, and permit family members to spend time not working or doing household duties. Pleasurable, relaxing activity seems to be what is required for urban leisure. Rural workers have more freedom than urban workers, who in leisure hours seek the freedom to do as they please.

Changes in Security and Insurance

The extended family or kin acted as a security network for the preindustrial family. Family type A shown in Figure 9-1 illustrates the security that three generations and numerous children provide. When a parent dies, grandparents, uncles, aunts, and older siblings can absorb much of the shock. If a mother dies, there is a large nurturing and childrearing network already operating that can fulfill her functions. Since many family members are involved in economic activities for the support of the family, such as work, hunting, gardening, farming, or craft work, family income does not cease with the loss of a father.

The nuclear family in the industrial urban setting is very vulnerable to death, accident, or bad times. The loss of even one member out of a total of four eliminates a quarter of the potential for nurturing and social interaction. The loss of a parent in the nuclear family may be devastating; the loss of the parent in a single-parent family when children are small, breaks up the family. Since the larger kinship network is usually also small and/or not nearby, families must resort to insurance against fire, hail, flood, unemployment, accident, death, and other disasters.

In non-industrial countries, a large proportion of the population is poor, and many large cities in Africa, Latin America, and Asia do not have welfare systems to take care of the needs of the poor. Industrialized countries such as Scandinavia, Britain, and Canada have social welfare networks, provide child welfare payments, unemployment and accident insurance, and old age security for families that can not adequately provide for themselves. But even in these countries, some families are living at subsistence levels. Single-parent families headed by women, and the elderly (again mostly women, because they live longer), make up a high percentage of the urban poor (Clark, 1978).

Changing Gender Roles

In the preindustrial, traditional society, the assumption was that everyone would marry, and there was considerable social pressure to marry. Getting married and having a family were an integral part of the whole social structure. Unmarried adults did not fit well, and there were pressures to have a traditional place in an extended family. As societies become more urban, traditional communities loosen. Women in particular become more independent, and in industrial urban western societies are increasingly able to make individual choices.

Changing Family Networks

In her discussion of the family and social networks, Elizabeth Bott (1971) says that the urban family does not have boundaries as in closed communities, but is rather a network that has links with a series of other networks. All the urban families she researched "maintained relationships with external people and institutions—with a place to work, with service institutions such as school, church, doctor, clinic, shops, with voluntary associations such as clubs, evening classes, and recreational institutions. They also maintained more informal relationships with colleagues, friends, neighbors, and relatives." (Bott, 1971:98.) Bott maintains that no urban family can survive without its network of external relationships. She suggests that family structures will need to adapt and readjust to these relationships (Blau, Blum, and Schwartz, 1982:45-61).

Bott presents three types of family organization — complementary, independent, and joint.

> In the complementary organization the activities of husband and wife are different and separate but fitted together to form a whole. In independent organization, activities are carried out separately by husband and wife without reference to each other, insofar as this is possible. In joint organization, activities are carried out by either partner at different times (Bott, 1971:53).

In her studies Bott found all three types of organization in every family studied, but the relative emphasis on each varied.

In the independent, segregated, conjugal role-relationship model, husband and wife had clear differentiation of tasks and different leisure pursuits and groupings of friends. As a result there was a highly segregated conjugal role-relationship. Bott reported that this model was found most often among families in unskilled or semiskilled manual occupations. Traditional farm families would fall into this category as well. There will be a clear division of labor into male tasks and female tasks. Spouses will say, "I did this" and "my car" rather than "we did this" and "our car."

Joint family organization is more common than the independent model. Husband and wife expect to carry out many activities together with a minimum of task differentiation and separation of interests. Bott (1971:54) found that as family occupations changed from semiskilled to professional, conjugal segregation diminished and the joint conjugal role-relationship model became more evident. Professional couples referred more often to joint decisions, and each sought the opinion and reaction of the other spouse. Joint family organization would be more common in families of higher socio-economic levels, especially in those who have become more urban and upwardly mobile.

Because of the need for ties with many social networks in the city, Granovetter (1973:1373) argues that there is also strength in having weak ties. While a strong core family network is needed, there is limited time and energy to invest in the many other social contacts that are available; hence, limited, weak ties are an asset, even essential. The contributions of Bott and Granovetter suggest that if urban Canadians plan to survive in the city, they must build many social networks involving some strong and some weak ties. Weak ties can be as important as strong ones. Barry Wellman and associates (1982;1983) have studied such networks in Canada; we shall explore these later.

The Single Independent Woman

In urban industrial western countries such as Canada, many single adult women never marry or marry and then divorce or separate. Both boys and girls receive an education, and girls do well in the educational system so that on average females are better educated than males; women can now be financially independent.

The feminist movement has created an increasing awareness of the inequalities faced by women, and pressures have been mounting everywhere to provide equal job opportunities for women (Clement, 1988:74-75). For example, while women have equal access to teaching children at the lower grade levels, they are still far from having parity of job opportunities at higher levels of teaching, especially at universities (Cuneo, 1990:9, 140). Such barriers to equal opportunities for women change slowly, but progress has been seen in the last few decades.

More single adult women are moving to the city than single men. In the city, women have more opportunities to compete for jobs, earn a steady income, develop independent careers without the discrimination of the past (MacKenzie, 1986:84), and buy their own home; in the city also they are able to distance themselves from social pressure to marry and have a family. Thus, many single women may have a career, unfettered by obligations towards husband and children. The single career woman is a good example of the individual independence possible in industrial cities, where pressures on single adults to marry have lessened. But a single person without a family does lack a support network in old age. When her parents pass away, she has no children to support her: for many the city can become a lonely place.

The Working Mother

A generation ago, the majority of couples accepted the "traditional roles" for husband and wife: the husband as the breadwinner and the home as the proper place for the wife (Nett, 1988:218). Over half of all married women are now in the labor force. In 1960, 95 percent of Canadians believed that women with small children should stay at home; in 1982 only 62 percent thought so (Boyd,

1984:13). In 1976, two-thirds of mothers with children under three years were at home full-time; by 1984, fewer than half were (Report of the Task Force on Child Care, 1986:8; Nett, 1988:218-9). Enormous changes are taking place in attitudes towards mothers working outside the home (Gold, 1982:168-9).

A number of social scientists have described some of the difficulties faced by the working mother in the labor force. Although technological devices have eased the heavy labor of housework, they have not greatly lessened the number of hours spent on it (Armstrong and Armstrong, 1984; Luxton and Rosenburg, 1986; Strong-Boag, 1986; Wilson, 1986). Table 9-1 shows the results of studies by Adler and Hawrylyshyn (1977:339), Harvey, (1975:12-16), and Meissner (1981:343-6); married women not working in the labor force on the average spend at least as much time working at home as a male working fulltime in the labor force. Women working in the labor force still spend more than twenty hours doing housework when they get home, even though men are beginning to share some of the work. Thus, the working mother is faced, in addition to a fulltime job, with the extra burden of hours of work at home representing half a fulltime job; and presumably some work remains undone (Eichler, 1988:45; Luxton, 1980:184-7).

Table 9-1 Reports of hours spent in household work and the labor force per week by married women and men

	REPORTS OF HOURS SPENT		
MARRIED WOMEN	ADLER AND HAWRYLYSHYN (1977)[a]	HARVEY (1975)[b]	MEISSNER (1981)[c]
Not in labor force	35-60	44.2	42.3
In labor force	20-37	26.6	20.3

[a]p. 339.
[b]pp. 12-16.
[c]pp. 343-6.

	HOURS SPENT BY		
	HUSBAND IN LABOR FORCE		HUSBAND NOT IN LABOR FORCE
MARRIED MEN	no children	child less than 5 years old	child less than 5 years old
Total household work[a]	15.0	17.2	44.1
Wife in labor market[b]	10.3	15.0[c]	—
Wife not in labor market[b]	10.5	15.6[c]	—

[a]Harvey and Clark (1975, p. 12-16). No control on wife's labor force status.
[b]Adler and Hawrylyshyn (1977, p. 339–Appendix Table 2).
[c]Data include one child 6 years of age or younger.

SOURCE: Douchitt (1984: 34:110)

While the status of housewife may be more tolerable for some women with low levels of education, many middle class women with a college education tend to aspire to challenging professional jobs. Middle class housewives may chafe at their working peers' implied attitude that they should be out working. Margaret Laurence (1973:10-18) portrayed the continually questioning, self-deprecating woman raising children at home and finding it hard to keep up with current intellectual trends. In contrast, Lopata (1971) and Eichler (1977) both reported that women obtained considerable satisfaction from the job of homemaker, feeling that they were appreciated by their family and that their work was at least as important as many jobs women in the work force held.

In the preindustrial, traditional society married women were surrounded by children and other women, and did work that added to the family income such as gardening, gathering and peparation of fruit, field work and making of clothes and household materials (wool, rugs, blankets). In comparison, many middle class women in the suburbs can feel trapped (Gordon, Gordon and Gunther, 1964). This however, seems to vary by individuals, place of residence in the city, recency of immigration, and social class.

Changing Male Roles

Nett (1988:219) says the standards for masculinity in our society have changed in the past generation, and better-educated, younger men and women in particular value traits in men that were formerly only acceptable in women. Research (Melville, 1983; Luxton, 1980) shows that the ideal male should be tender, considerate, easy-going, and responsive — more emotionally competent than in the past. The ability to love, and personal warmth are some of the expressive qualities that are now highly valued. It is too early to tell whether former masculine traits such as competitiveness, strength, dominance, and aggression are still necessary in the world of work, or whether that too is changing, especially as over half of the women in Canada today are in the labour force (Nett, 1988:219). Ehrenreich (1983) wonders to what extent the workplace drains its workers, and as women increasingly enter the workforce, whether they too will be less able to give of themselves emotionally, as men were unable to in the past. Can both expressive qualities and competition at work be maintained, and if so, to what extent? (Seward, 1990:343-62; Norris, 1990:33-59.

In 1983, 52 percent of married women and 82 percent of married men were in the labor force. To what extent do males and females share in household duties in an attempt at sharing the workload? Exchange theory would suggest that there should be more sharing, especially as women increasingly add to the family income; greater sharing would be in line with egalitarian ideals. Boyd (1984; 1990) and Douchitt (1984), who studied public opinion polls over a period of time, suggest that men do not share equally in the household work. Some of these findings are reflected in Table 9-1, which shows that husbands in the workforce without children spend on average about 10 to 15 hours doing housework, and very little more (15 to 17 hours per week) in families with small children (Adler and Hawrylyshyn, 1977; Harvey, 1975:336; Harvey and Clark, 1975:12-16; Meissner, 1981:343-6; Douchitt, 1984:110). Harvey and Clark, 1975:12-16) however, found that husbands not in the labor force, but with young children, worked a regular 44-hour week at home, just as women do when they stay home.

Elizabeth Bott (1971:53) found all three (complementary, independent, and joint) family types of organization in the city, but blue-collar immigrant families who have come from rural areas into the city are skewed more in the direction of independent roles of the spouses, while in middle class suburbs the tendency is more towards joint arrangements. The urban trend is away from traditional, independent family roles towards joint family roles, especially in the suburbs. Since the roles of males and females are not as clearly defined as in the traditional family, the potential for both sharing and interaction is greater, but so is the potential for conflict. In the next part we wish to explore the factors that may lead to family breakdown: changing roles must be important.

Threats to Family Solidarity

As family structures, functions, and roles change, so too do family problems. Preindustrial rural families were not free of problems, because patriarchal dominance, the struggle for economic survival, the difficulties involved in raising large families, and general family and community pressures took their toll. As families became smaller, as more and more family functions were shifted to other institutions, and as parental and children's roles changed, a reshaping of the family to a primary network has changed many of the problems families face.

Divorce and Separation

We would expect that as family structures change (as illustrated in Figure 9-1), families would be more vulnerable to breakdown (McKee *et al.*, 1983:20-38). Indeed separation and divorce rates show that that is the case. Whereas separation and divorce rates were very low in preindustrial rural societies, Burch (1985:12) shows that in 1984, about 11 percent of ever-married adults (10.1 of males and 12.4 of females) over eighteen years of age have been divorced at least once. Divorce rates escalated after less restrictive divorce laws were introduced in Canada in 1968 and in 1986, from about 225 in 1968 to 1150 per 100,000 population in 1983 (Nett, 1986:371). By 1981 well over one-third of all single adults were either separated or divorced (26.3 and 31.3 percent respectively) (Nett:1986:373).

What are the causes of marriage breakdown? Certainly easier grounds for divorce are one factor. Presumably, in the past, many couples stayed together even when they no longer wanted to, either because of religious or community pressures, or because of difficulties in obtaining a divorce. Shelton (1987:827-32) found a correlation among residential mobility rates, community size, and marriage dissolution. As city size increases, mobility and divorce also increase. South and Spitze (1986:51:583-90) found the same. Ambert (1980) suggests factors such as reduced religious influence, a secularized view of marriage, increased independence of women, a lack of psychological emancipation of men, increased longevity of both spouses, and more choices available to individuals are some reasons. Whereas in the past it was thought that families must be kept together at all costs, now the focus has changed to the importance of individual ties among husband, wife, and children. Couples expect greater personal satisfaction from marital bonds. This is not surprising when we see the high value placed on "love" and personal affection.

In Table 9-2 Kitson *et al.* (1985:255-93) list the five most often mentioned reasons for separation and divorce as reported in ten studies carried out since 1956 in the United States. The variety of reasons given and the variations among the studies are striking, but there are some common trends. Extramarital sex appears as a reason for marriage breakup in seven of the ten studies, and difficulties in communication between spouses appear in four of the studies. Both reasons are related to personal needs. What seems to have changed is that increasingly the focus is on personal independence and individual fulfilment (Hurley, 1987; Gibson, 1986). As Canadians become more urban, families become smaller and the ties among husband and wife and their children seem to become overloaded with excessive demands. In larger, extended families, demands could be spread over more members, and since greater value was placed on the family structure as a whole than on the individual family members, aspirations within the family were balanced and checked. It is true that modern nuclear families, if they work well (and many do), provide more richly for individual fulfilment. But when they do not work (and some do not), the likelihood of marriage breakup is greater. Families now seem to exist either in very good or very bad situations, whereas the traditional family tended to a more moderate but less challenging mode.

Spouse and Child Abuse

In rural areas the behavior of family members can easily be observed, and community pressures can be brought to bear if a family member is being abused. An extended family contains more adults than the modern, nuclear family, so it is more difficult for one adult to abuse a family member without restraint. Today's changes in family structure have provided a greater potential for violence within the family: husbands may abuse wives or children, a single parent may abuse the children because now there is no other adult around to restrain a family member who is out of control.

MacLeod (1987) estimates that two out of three Canadian women each year experience physical or psychological abuse, and most of it from live-in-lovers, husbands, or dates. There are very few cases of battered husbands. Many wives do not have the occupational skills to support themselves and prefer to stay with the children: they often endure abuse that otherwise they might not tolerate. Many have few alternatives. Shelters for battered women and children are limited, and they are set up only to provide temporary relief, which does not solve the long-term problem of an abusive husband and father. Now that so many married women work outside the home, both husband and wife often arrive home too tired to relate to their children adequately. Thus, child abuse is also increasing (Zuravin, 1988, 50:983-93; Ross, 1980). Spouses who stay at home with their children may be experiencing frustration and vent it in child abuse, especially in an urban environment where individual freedom is stressed and desired. Increases in family violence seem to be related to weaknesses of the nuclear family structure and to the need to make adjustments to changing roles.

Poverty Among Elderly Women

In traditional extended families, the elderly continued to be part of the family structure until death, although with a gradual decrease in workloads and withdrawal from leadership roles. However, elderly women could still help with cooking and caring for their grandchildren. Elderly men could care for animals and fill in when extra hands were needed on the farm. Thus the elderly continued to have family ties, a place of residence, and respect from others. These patterns, according to Arcury (1986, 11:55-76), prevailed in Kentucky in 1900 but had changed to more urban patterns even in rural Kentucky by 1980.

Technology, an important element in industrialization and urbanization, has helped to improve medical care and public health measures; as a result, people have a greater life expectancy. By 1981 the elderly comprised 9.1 percent of the population in Canada.

> Before 1951 the number of elderly men was always greater than the number of elderly women. However, after 1951 the sex ratio has reversed, so that by 1981 there were four elderly women for every three [elderly] men. In 1981 women over 85 outnumbered men two to one. (Driedger and Chappell, 1987:11.)

In 1981, one-half of the women over 65 were widowed; only one-sixth (14 percent) of the elderly men were widowers. Women outlive men on the average by about eight years; many elderly women, therefore, live on their own.

In Canada, women are subject to what some call double or triple jeopardy situations (Markides, 1983). "Jeopardy studies usually concentrate on the combined effects of two or more negatively perceived statuses such as age and ethnicity, or age, sex and ethnicity, or age, sex, ethnicity and social class." (Driedger and Chappell, 1987:18.) Scholars argue that occupying two or more stigmatized statuses has greater negative consequences than occupying only one (Dowd and Bengston, 1978; Palmore and Manton, 1973; Jackson, 1972).

Marshall and Rosenthal (1986:136) found that in 1981, married couples

Table 9-2 Top-ranked reasons for marital breakdown in selected surveys

	GOODE (1956) OPEN-ENDED	KITSON AND SUSSMAN (1982) OPEN-ENDED	BURNS (1984) CHECKLIST AND OPEN-ENDED	LEVINGER (1966) FEMALE PARENTS COURT-REQUIRED INTERVIEWS	KITSON AND SUSSMAN (1982) OPEN-ENDED, FEMALES
1. Non-support	Personality	Other (sexual incompatibility)	Mental cruelty	Lack of communication
2. Running around/out with the boys	Home life	Other (lack of communication)	Neglect of home/children	Internal gender role conflict
3. Drinking	Complaints not listed in Goode	Home life	Physical abuse	Extramarital sex
4. Authority	Authority	Non-support: finances	Financial problems	Untrustworthy; immature
5. Personality	Values	Extramarital sex	Extramarital sex	Drinking

ALBRECHT ET AL. (1983) CHECKLIST: ALL SUBJECTS	BLOOM & HODGES (1982) FEMALE PARENTS (RANK IMPORTANCE)	FLETCHER (1983) FEMALES OPEN-ENDED	GRANVOLD ET AL. (1979) CHECKLIST, FEMALES	KELLY (1982) OPEN-ENDED, FEMALES
1. Extramarital sex	Communication difficulties	General personality	Lack of communication	Feeling unloved
2. No longer in love	Lack of love	Specific personality problems	Conflicts over roles/responsibilities	Belittlement by spouse
3. Emotional problems	Verbal abuse	Negative attitudes of spouse	Lifestyle/values	Spouse hypercritical
4. Financial problems	Extramarital sex	Actions or specific behaviors	Extramarital sex	Sexual deprivation
5. Sexual problems	Interest in another person	Extramarital sex	Sexual problems	Anger/nagging

SOURCE: Kitson et al. (1985).

aged 66 and over had an average income of $17,900; unattached elderly men averaged $10,000; and unattached elderly women averaged $8,800. Elderly women have to live on small incomes: often, when a husband dies, his pension income dies with him. In 1981, one-fourth (27 percent) of the elderly in Canada over 65 lived alone; over half (60 percent) lived with their family; and 13 percent lived with others (Driedger and Chappell, 1987:71). Although many elderly people still live with their families, many live alone, particularly in the city. The urban elderly are often more independent, and if they are healthy and have the financial resources to live alone, they cherish their independence. However, when their health begins to fail, their independence becomes a liability. Urban nuclear families are less equipped and also less willing to have their elderly relatives live with them. The elderly are then more dependent on secondary institutions. The city is a challenging place for the young, but it is less hospitable towards the elderly, particularly to women, who have many more years to live by themselves.

Community Studies of Urban Family Networks

To further illustrate some of the theoretical points made so far, let us examine actual variations in family structures, functions, roles, and networks. We have selected studies of three ecological areas of the city — the suburb, the inner city, and an urban community in between (Michelson, 1976:77-86; Michelson, 1977:138-41). The study of a suburb — Crestwood Heights — is typical of many structural-functional studies done shortly after World War II. The urban study on East York uses a more contemporary, social-networks approach. Both studies were done in Toronto. The study of Native peoples in Winnipeg uses both the structural-functional and networks approaches to illustrate that family structures are often fluid, depending on the types of groups studied.

Classical: Crestwood Heights

Seeley, Sim, and Loosley (1956) made the first indepth Canadian study of a suburb in Toronto soon after World War II and published it in 1956. It has since become a classic. At the time of the study, Crestwood Heights (located on top of an escarpment or crest high above the rest of the city), was a new, upper middle class suburb comprised of Jewish (one-third) and non-Jewish residents who were upwardly mobile. The authors introduce their book by saying that " . . . the major institutional focus is upon child-rearing" and . . . "the goal is not for oneself alone but for one's children . . . " (Seeley et al., 1956:4,7). The authors did extensive participant observation and also submitted questionnaires to nearly 2000 children. The authors examined the quality of life in the suburb, the lifestyles and aspirations of the inhabitants, and the structures and functions of their social institutions, including the family and its socialization function.

Seeley et al. (1956:49-54) showed that the house in Crestwood Heights was property, stage, and home. Most of the residents owned their homes, and pressures to keep the property beautiful were considerable. The house acted as a "stage" for "productions" of formal hospitality. The front living room was designed for the gracious reception of guests; one five-year-old exclaimed, "Mummie, aren't you afraid when people come to our house that they'll think they are coming to a furniture store?" (Seeley *et al.*, 1956:50.) Living rooms were usually kept as "museums" for guests; here the best furniture, paintings, and art were displayed as symbols of status and upward mobility. The stage had always to be set and charmingly arranged, harmoniously matched in color. But it could also be rather cold and empty of life since children were usually forbidden to set foot in it. It was the kitchen and family room that were designed for family living and used as part of "home."

The aim was privacy for each member of the family, and was usually achieved because these homes were large and each child had its own room. One girl reported, "we scatter throughout the house to follow our interests." (Seeley, 1956:56.) In smaller, rural homes the family used to gather around the hot stove and the oil lamp; in suburban Crestwood Heights the electric light and warmth were spread evenly all over the house, so that family members were more dispersed. In suburbia in the 1940s, the home was the place where the female homemaker could act out her roles in a typically upper middle class fashion.

Native Households in Inner Winnipeg

In contrast to the upper middle class suburb in Toronto, Evelyn Peters (1984) carried out a study of Native Indian households in the inner city of Winnipeg. The Native households differed from the nuclear, conjugal families that predominated in the white urban population. "Native households frequently contain members other than the nuclear family, expanding and contracting as individuals in the extended family require shelter." (Peters, 1984:1.) Large numbers of Indians on the Canadian Prairies live on rural reserves; many come from the north into Winnipeg for shorter or longer periods of time. Larry Krotz (1980:25) has described the fluid living arrangements of the Native family in Manitoba, travelling between the reserve and Winnipeg.

Past studies by Dosman (1972:185), Nagler (1970:21), Ablon (1964), and others have shown that if Indians need help, they turn to relatives or friends, and expect help from them as a matter of right. When only a few Indians were living in the city, frequent visits of relatives or friends from the reserve for extended periods became a considerable burden for the urban Natives. Yet urban Indians felt obligated to provide this help, because should they themselves need to go back to the reserve, they would require and expect similar aid. In her study, Peters (1984) wanted to find to what extent this system of mutual aid still held in Winnipeg. In 1979 she interviewed a random sample of 176 Indian households in Winnipeg, 98 of which were single-parent (56 percent), and 78 were two-parent families. One-quarter of all inner city households were single-parent families (Clatworthy, 1980). Peters found that the average single-parent household contained 3.8 persons, including 2.6 children (46 percent under five or six), and 13 percent also included other relatives or friends. Two-parent households averaged 4.7 persons, with 2.6 children (53 percent under aged six); eleven percent included other relatives or friends.

There were important differences between the one- and two-parent families. The average household income for single-parent families was $5,654 ($1,488 per capita); 87 percent of these families were on welfare, and only 14 percent of the heads of these families worked fulltime. Ninety-four percent were renting, and the average monthly rent was $214; 40 percent lived in apartments with an average person-per-room density of 0.80. Two-parent families fared considerably better; the average annual household income was $10,772 ($2,292 per capita); only 18 percent were on welfare; and 67 percent of the heads of the household worked fulltime. Eighty-six percent rented, 32 percent lived in apartments, and the average person-per-room was 0.95 (Peters, 1984:10,11). Twenty-six (15 percent) of the households interviewed were extended families. More than two-thirds of the households had overnight visitors during a three-month period; an average Indian household accommodated one additional person every sixth day (Peters, 1984:16).

Peters' (1984:19) study showed that adult children who are not parents make relatively little contribution to the household budget (most of these households receive welfare or mother's allowance). Where adult children had their own children, they also received mother's allowance and welfare, so that finances were often pooled. Some parents also worked to bring in added income while someone else did the babysitting.

Peters (1984:27, 28) found that there was frequent movement back and forth between the reserve and the city. Many seemed to "try out" the city before they stayed. Some came in only to use facilities and services: going to the hospital or the dentist; shopping; going to school; or looking for a job. Others migrated seasonally, working up north in the summer and coming back to Winnipeg in the winter (Nagler, 1970; White, 1980). Men were often less well off because they found it difficult to get jobs, and if they did have a job they were paid low wages. Mothers with young children were better off because they received welfare payments and mother's allowances. This situation worked against long-lasting conjugal relationships. Half of the Indians lived in poor housing. Two percent of Winnipeg's inner city housing was in very poor repair, and 27 percent of the households studied lived in such housing. "More native households have single female parents as head; more households are extended; and household composition exhibits considerable instability." (Peters, 1984:35.) In contrast to the suburbs, inner city people live in poverty, and Native Indians in Winnipeg live in the greatest poverty and have many problems.

Urban Networks in East York

Barry Wellman (1982) studied families in East York, Toronto, from a social networks perspective. This approach is similar to Elizabeth Bott's approach discussed in the second half of this chapter. Both studies were done in Toronto, but in different areas and 25 to 30 years apart. The study of Indians in inner Winnipeg illustrates that such urban families are not necessarily constrained by the boundaries of the urban area, and that there is considerable mobility and fluidity in family network ties. Wellman's East York study shows that suburban families are woven more around personal ties than around neighborhoods.

Wellman and associates (1982,1983) surveyed a random sample of 845 people living in East York, an inner suburb of Toronto; in 1968 these comprised mostly people of British background. They repeated the study in 1978; by this time the community had changed considerably, and many Greeks, Italians, and East Indians had moved into the area. The researchers focused on personal network ties rather than on spatial neighborhood patterns. They found in 1978 that migrants into the city rarely come to the city alone and disconnected, but rather use links with kin and former friends to establish themselves. Wellman (1982:8) found that three-fourths of the social ties of the people they studied stretched beyond the boundaries of the East York community. While half of the social ties were with kin, especially parents and adult children, the other half were with friends, neighbors, and workmates.

Wellman (1982:15) found that:

> "Singles" living alone resemble "Community Lost" depictions of urban life — transitory, sparsely-knit, with few links to friends and kin — while the networks of "houseworkers" and husbands raising children resemble "Community Saved" depictions — neighborhood and kinship-based support groups exchanging much emotional aid, small services and household items.

Industrialization and urbanization tend to disconnect ties with workmates and relatives, and replace them with a variety of interest groups, giving suburbanites many choices among social contacts and activities. Urban living has become a "McDonaldization" of life, according to Slater (1970), where members purchase clothing, food, emotional support, and comfort, and where they can hire institutions to care for their young, their infirm, and their elderly.

Neighbors, another traditional support, rarely provided a base for intimate relationships, but were founded rather on close physical access, and provided companionship and limited aid (Wellman et al., 1983:17).

East Yorkers' personal communities are sizeable and diverse, but their interactions did not take place in public view. This may be why earlier studies, more oriented to ecology and institutions, mistook the meaning of the empty streets of the suburbs and thought they implied a lack of community. Suburbanites tended to meet inside their homes; they used the telephone widely; and many also met in their cottages — secondary homes away from the city (Wellman et al., 1983:23). Few East Yorkers were active in voluntary organizations, and less than one-fourth of all their active ties took place on neighborhood streets or verandas. Their lifestyle was a form of privatization of community life.

Most people with whom East Yorkers had active ties lived more than fifteen kilometres away; only 22 percent lived within one to two kilometres. One-third of all their active and intimate ties lived more than forty kilometres away. East Yorkers usually could walk to visit kin or friends. Wellman and associates (1983:29-30) conclude that most East Yorkers had at the core of their networks a good many stable, traditional ties that have endured for twenty or more years; these included kin, childhood friends, and neighbors in that order of importance. Kin loomed large in supplying emotional support, advice on family problems, and general support. As in rural communities or in the inner city, suburbanites need social supports, and the family played an important role in supplying them, but for additional supports personal networks have largely replaced local-area communities.

Summary

The family is the primary social group, and its function is to socialize people to the language, culture, values, and norms of their society. In urban families changes take place in family structure, functions, roles, and in the kinds of problems faced by the family.

Parsons is the best known structural-functionalist sociologist; he suggested that all societies begin as folk societies, where a focus on particularism and ascription prevail. As societies urbanize, they experience more variety, and there is more room for individual achievement and initiative; all these contribute to change. Families change from large, extended structures to small, nuclear structures, and they also change from patriarchal hierarchies to ones having egalitarian relationships. Recent feminist studies vary in their perspectives, which may be liberal, Marxist, radical, or socialist. All, however, are concerned with the status, roles, and rights of women, and with power relationships between the sexes in the workplace, in politics, and in social institutions and organizations.

The functions of the family change as structures change. In traditional families work takes place within the household, while in the city the workplace shifts away from the home. Mate selection is the responsibility of parents in folk societies, but becomes the choice of individuals in the city. Recreation and leisure patterns also shift: from informal family fun to scheduled, professional sports and performances, and to activities outside the home. Insurance is paid for in the city, whereas the extended family acted as the security umbrella.

Urban family roles also change, and Elizabeth Bott suggests that the urban family can better be discussed from the perspective of social networks, which is more compatible with feminist concerns, than from a structural-functional perspective. In traditional, rural societies women are dependent on the family, whereas in the city the single woman can set up her own household and support herself — although not always without difficulty. Women are still disadvantaged in the workplace, and parity is difficult to achieve. More and more married women are entering the workforce, adding a second income to the family. Children become more independent as a result. The men's roles also change as they are expected to share household duties and childcare.

These family changes are accompanied by problems of modern urban living. Separation and divorce rates have increased because nuclear families overload bonds among family members. In small nuclear families, there is greater potential for spouse and child abuse. The elderly find more independence in the city, but because women live much longer than men, elderly women are more often faced with poverty and lack of support.

A study of Native households in Winnipeg shows that inner city families are changing in both structure and function. Studies in the 1950s and 1980s of suburbs in Toronto show that families tend to have greater social networks. Urban social ties are less confined to geographical areas, and as urban communication increases, networks can bridge considerable distances, keeping urban family members in touch with each other.

10. Metropolitan Problems

With the momentous changes taking place in metropolitan areas today we may also expect many problems. The uneven development of technology serves some areas better than others: large-scale movements of populations create imbalances; the unequal distribution of economic opportunities provides inequalities in the quality of life; and civil rights are also unevenly distributed. Since in many countries such as Canada, three out of four people are now living in urban areas, urban problems are usually also problems for the general society. However, the city does create unique problems and these will be discussed in this chapter (Lithwick, 1970; Roussopoulos, 1982:11-34).

Perspectives vary on what the most pressing urban problems are, and what causes them. A review of the literature shows that studies may focus on economic, technological problems such as transportation, pollution, and urban blight, or on problems of social class including poverty, poor housing, and inequalities, or on other social problems such as crime, discrimination against minorities, and social deviance of individuals.

Perspectives on Urban Problems

Two perspectives on how and why urban problems develop are worth reviewing. The first is in continuity with early urban ecological thought and revolves around functionalist urban ecology. The second is based on Marxist analysis, and is concerned with social dynamics and interrelationships that involve power and social class (Roussopoulos, 1982).

Functionalist Urban Ecology

Amos Hawley (1981, 1986) is an eminent urban ecologist associated with the functionalist urban ecology approach. ''Under his influence the understanding of the basic forces that shape the patterns of human settlement have shifted from an emphasis on competition for space to a concern with interdependence, systemness, and equilibrium.'' (Flanagan, 1990:213.) Hawley (1981, 1986) continues some of the spatial emphases of the Chicago School, combined with the structural functional systemic contributions of Talcott Parsons (1951). Functionalism as expounded by Parsons is rooted in Durkheim's concept of organic solidarity, and focuses on the balance and equilibrium among the various components of the societal system.

Hawley's (1986:29-50) urban ecological theory is strongly based on Parsonian ideas of the urban social system, involving both spatial and social interdependence in interlocking and symbiotic patterns that together create an ecosystem. Using this approach, urban problems emerge when spatial areas deteriorate, when housing and facilities age, when means of transportation can no longer cope, and when in general the ecosystem becomes increasingly dysfunctional, disorganized, and unbalanced.

Other sociologists, such as Wilson (1984:280-90), have turned from a focus on internal spatial patterns of one urban system to compare the relationships among cities. In chapter seven especially, we compared the 25 metropolitan centers in Canada and found that Toronto and Montreal dominate, and that the other centers, with less economic power, tend to be positioned towards the periphery. Thus, interurban linkages within a nation become an important large system, in which cities are linked together in a hierarchical structure according to the financial, commercial, and political institutions they house (Flanagan, 1990:214-15). Corporate head offices will make decisions based on where the centers of influence lie, and they will locate in the functional and symbolic center of such activity.

Using Wilson's (1984) ideas of intermetropolitan, interurban, and intraurban interdependencies, we can discuss the dominance of some urban places over others. As illustrated in chapter seven, the most influential cities are those that have high concentrations of wholesaling and manufacturing, and are the locus of corporate centers of decision-making concerning employment, credit, capital flows, and dissemination of information. As shown in chapter eight, Winnipeg was such an influential city when it was the gateway to the West, but later lost that position to Vancouver and is increasingly also losing its dominance over the Prairies to Edmonton and Calgary. Montreal used to be the most influential city in the nation, but is losing this dominance increasingly to Toronto. However, as populations in such large urban centers grow, the metropolis also pays a price. Migrants and immigrants are strongly drawn to such centers because they offer job opportunities; as a result the population becomes more heterogeneous ethnically and racially, but transportation and housing facilities are overloaded, and social institutions are strained as pressures mount on every side.

Class in the Political Economy

Recently, many urban scholars feel that the functionalist urban ecologists have not been able to develop conceptual theories that address the many problems of troubled giant megalopoli (Roussopoulos, 1982). Serious urban race riots in the 1960s, the economic decline of central cities, housing shortages, and unemployment attracted "critical theorists in a Marxist vein" to examine what the problems were (Flanagan, 1990:216):

According to the Marxists, the failure of conventional approaches to urban sociology was due to a "fetishism of space" that ignored class analysis and the process of capital accumulation, the central concerns of Marxist thought. In this view it makes no sense to speak in terms of the suburbs versus the cities, or of the competition between Chicago and St Louis.

Larry Sawers (1984:4-7) thinks that competition between areas of a city or between cities is a "fundamental distortion of reality." Conflict takes place between groups of people with different interests; urban problems are merely a reflection of the larger social and economic problems in society. Class relations, not space, is the most important source of conflict in the city. Earlier, Manuel Castells (1972) in his work *The Urban Question* claimed that Louis Wirth's works on urban life were flawed because his assumptions were incorrect. Castells (1972:81) says it is not the urban environment that produces differential urban cultures, but industrialization. Excessive individualism and fragmentation of roles and values are a result of an industrial system based on individual enterprise, competition, the profit motive, and inheritance—all part of *laissez faire* capitalism. The various Marxist analyses have developed around capital accumulation and class conflict: two aspects of the capitalist profit drive and production process.

Harvey (1985:1) suggests that production, circulation, consumption, and exchange are part of a circulation of money where the urban environment is built, destroyed, and rebuilt for the sake of circulating capital and profits. This is a process of "creative destruction," in which capital will circulate, and in each cycle profits can be made. Thus, the desired end is not to provide offices and homes for people who need them, but to circulate capital for profit (Flanagan, 1990:218-19). Homebuilders will buy land and develop homes in suburbs because it is more profitable to do so on the periphery of the city than it is in the center of the city. In the fastest growing metropolitan centers, such as Calgary, Edmonton, and Toronto, there is a temptation to speculate in land, materials, and buildings in the expectation that prices will rise and provide a better return on investments.

Sawers (1984) focuses on class conflict. Capitalists compete to sell their products or services at a profit, while labor wants affordable consumer goods, controlled and reasonable rents, safe vehicles to drive, plenty of land for reasonably priced housing, and universal health care.

> Living labor confronts the power of these corporate giants . . . . When workers demand higher wages and better working conditions, and the corporate power refuses, relying on its size, financial and political strength, and most of all on its ability to deny the workers a means of living, it has appropriated this strength from the sweat and blood of past workers. When a company moves from a city to a place where it can find labor that will work for less, it takes the productive capacity built by its workers away from them—creating unemployment, eroding the tax base, leading ultimately to urban crisis (Tabb and Sawers, 1978:9).

The mainstream functionalist and Marxist traditions differ in their basic assumptions. The early ecologists thought competitive land-use patterns were the cause of urban problems, while Marxists assume that the use of capital and the profit motive are at the crux of urban social problems. Many recent urban sociologists think of themselves as working in a "political economy" tradition, in which economic and political forces combine to shape the urban society. In the process, economic and political power tend to overwhelm family and community interests.

Theories of Disorganization, Conflict, and Deviance

Merton and Nisbet (1976) suggest that social problems can be discussed from the three perspectives of social disorganization, social conflict, and social deviance. Each of these three approaches begins with assumptions and perspectives that require examination.

Social disorganization is clearly linked to the structural-functional perspective; its origins can be traced to Emile Durkheim and his work on mechanical and organic solidarity, division of labor, and anomie. According to Durkheim, mechanical solidarity is common in preindustrial and rural communities, where the members engage in similar tasks, have common beliefs, and depend on strong kinship and neighborly social bonds. People relate to each other in face-to-face primary interactions; boundaries are more clearly defined; and adherence to folkways and social cohesion are constantly monitored. However, as societies become more complex, as division of labor increases, and as specialization results in greater differentiation among people living in industrial urban societies, the dependence on others to provide some of the necessities of life increases; Durkheim (1893) called this dependence organic solidarity. Such differentiation also brings with it the potential for greater social disorganization or anomie (normlessness).

Robert Park, Louis Wirth, and Ernest Burgess of the Chicago School extended some of the ideas of Europeans, such as Ferdinand Toennies, by suggesting that as small, primary, *gemeinschaft* communities get larger, they turn into urban, complex societies where secondary relations are more common. As such communities become more diverse and less cohesive, they develop differing values and norms, social relations tend to become less functional, and there is greater potential for social disorganization. Talcott Parsons concluded that as social systems become more complex, they will lose some of their equilibrium and become dysfunctional.

According to social disorganizational theorists, it is when social structures are not well organized that they become dysfunctional and fail to do their work. Thus, housing in the core city deteriorates and no longer provides adequate or appropriate shelter. Residents of these slum areas are not sufficiently educated and trained for jobs, therefore they cannot remain adequately employed, and without proper incomes families become impoverished. The assumption is that the social structures have failed: if new housing, new schools, and new communities are built, this will create an environment where social organizations will again carry out their designated functions. Social equilibrium needs to be restored.

Social conflict theorists do not agree that the problem lies in spatial and social structures. To solve urban problems, they say, the society's social, economic, and political values must be changed, so that institutions and structures will serve the people. Lewis Coser (1956) followed Georg Simmel (1955) in suggesting that social conflict is functional rather than dysfunctional: rather than tearing apart the social fabric, conflict may serve to strengthen the boundaries of groups as they compete with each other. Thus, group-binding, group-preserving functions may be aroused as threats from other groups emerge. This can increase group cohesiveness, clarify group goals, solidify ideologies, and create the will to perpetuate values that are deemed important (Coser, 1956).

Conflict may take place between labor unions and management, resulting in strikes and disruptions. Riots by minorities or by the poor in ghettoes draw attention to lack of jobs or to oppressive institutions (Sullivan *et al.*, 1980:70-1). Race riots were common, especially in the 1960s in the United States, and the Oka standoff between Aboriginals and the Quebec police in 1990 is a good recent example. The Oka incident revolved around aboriginal land that had not been ceded, aboriginal land claims that had not been negotiated, and aboriginal rights that were being ignored. Those in power regarded the conflict as a problem in the development of resources; the Indians considered it an opportunity to insist on their rights and solve long-term land claims. The goals of each side were different; in such conflicts the powerful usually win.

The struggle for power pits groups in the city against each other. Marxists contend that this struggle between opposing forces is basically between those who have economic and political power — the bourgeoisie — and those who have only their time and labor to offer — the proletariat. The conflict may manifest itself in many forms. Poverty is a result of the disproportionate distribution of jobs, pay, and resources; racial strife is related to inequalities between white haves and non-white have-nots; crime stems from the have-nots trying to get a larger share of property and power. Conflict is seen as inevitable as long as societies contain stratified groups, and inequalities between groups is a result of the western capitalist political economy.

Urban deviance is a third approach to examining the problems of the city. Societies develop *mores* and norms that are embodied in criminal and other laws. If these laws are broken, the survival of society is threatened (Stebbins, 1988:2-7; Hagan, 1990). Murder is deviance at its most intolerable level. In addition, there are laws against theft, burglary, forgery, rape, assault, embezzlement, confidence games, and fraud, among others (Stebbins, 1988; Sacco, 1988). The right to private property, to live safely free from bodily harm, and to voluntary sexual activity are all human rights that must not be violated.

Urbanites are usually more tolerant of differences and nonconformity in people than are people living in traditional communities (W.J. Wilson, 1987). Scholars of urban deviance drew their arguments from Simmel (1955) and Wirth (1964), concluding that urbanites draw sharper distinctions between friends and strangers, and are much more likely to treat the latter (and their nonconformities) with indifference (Gillis, 1990:497). This often results in "bystander apathy" in the city, which attracts both creative and bizarre expressions of behavior such as the beatniks of the 1950s and the hippies of the 1960s (Gillis, 1990:498). Such different lifestyles would be considered deviant in rural areas, but are tolerated in large cities. However, illegal activities such as murder, forgery, violent crimes, and crimes against property clearly violate norms on which all or most agree, and these crimes are clearly seen therefore as immoral and illegal. We shall have opportunities to discuss some of these later. Alcoholism, drug addiction, prostitution, rape, and even mental disorders are usually considered forms of deviant behavior.

The Ecological and Demographic Contexts

Urban ecologists of the Chicago School, such as Park, Burgess, McKenzie, and Wirth, found that the older, inner city of Chicago had many problems compared to the outer suburbs. Many scholars of urban areas, such as Thomas and Znaniecki (1918-20), who studied ethnic, Polish groups, Anderson (1923), who studied single men, Thrasher (1963), who studied juvenile gangs and crime, and others who studied Blacks and the racial factor, carried out most of their research in the inner city of Chicago. Since Chicago was studied so intensively, and since studies in other cities were often not available, the "Chicago model" became a guide for hypotheses and theories on how all cities in the United States functioned. Later, other sociologists working in the New England area provided some comparisons with other cities such as Boston and New York. Sometimes the patterns were confirmed, but sometimes there were important differences.

Since urban research in Canada did not begin until later, we need also to examine whether 1) the early Chicago findings still hold; 2) whether American urban patterns also apply to Canada; 3) whether early comparisons between the inner and outer city are still valid today; and 4) whether there are similarities and differences among cities. Urban problems need to be examined in this larger ecological and demographic context, which will help to explain some of the persistent problems as well as new and emerging problems of the contemporary city in Canada. In this section we shall look at inner-outer-city comparisons, changing household patterns, the ethnic factor, and the social class factor. These structural patterns will help explain why some social, industrial, and ecological problems occur. We will also see whether the early ecological approach, Marxian social economy, and the structural-functional framework all help to gain a larger perspective than using only one approach.

Inner- and Outer-City Comparisons

Between 1951 and 1986, populations in inner cities have declined steadily, from 16 percent of the total population in the metropolitan area in 1951 to 4 percent by 1986 (Ram, Norris, and Skof, 1989:17). In Table 10-1 we see that there has been a loss of population in the inner city of 12 Canadian cities in

Table 10-1 Population of inner cities and as a percentage of total metropolitan areas, 1951-1986

CMA	INNER-CITY POPULATION					INNER CITY AS % OF TOTAL METROPOLITAN AREA				
	'000					%				
	1951	1961	1971	1981	1986	1951	1961	1971	1981	1986
Toronto	143.5	127.1	124.8	114.7	128.2	12.8	7.0	4.7	3.8	3.7
Montréal	219.7	163.0	128.0	93.5	93.0	15.7	7.7	4.7	3.3	3.2
Vancouver	83.9	70.4	72.6	71.6	74.0	15.8	8.9	6.7	5.6	5.4
Ottawa-Hull	80.9	72.1	57.5	43.0	43.6	28.7	16.8	9.5	6.0	5.3
Edmonton	20.4	17.8	20.0	17.8	18.3	11.8	5.3	4.0	2.7	2.3
Calgary	22.0	17.0	17.8	17.3	18.8	15.8	6.1	4.4	2.9	2.8
Winnipeg	45.4	38.2	31.7	26.1	28.3	12.8	8.0	5.9	4.5	4.5
Québec	50.6	44.3	32.9	21.0	21.9	18.4	12.4	6.8	3.6	3.6
Halifax	24.8	23.1	14.6	10.1	10.5	18.5	12.5	6.6	3.6	3.5
Saskatoon	6.5	5.3	4.4	3.8	4.4	12.2	5.6	3.5	2.5	2.2
Regina	16.8	14.3	11.8	8.3	8.6	23.6	12.7	8.4	5.0	4.6
Saint John	13.2	13.7	12.2	7.1	6.8	16.9	14.3	11.5	6.3	5.6
Total	727.8	606.0	528.3	434.2	456.4	15.8	8.5	5.5	4.0	3.8

SOURCE: 1951-1981 Censuses of Canada, published data for census tracts, and 1986 Census of Canada, unpublished data. Ram *et al* (1989: 22).

both actual numbers and in the proportion of the total metropolitan population, from 728,000 representing 16 percent in 1951, to 456,000 representing only 4 percent in 1986. It is clear, then, that the loss of population in the inner city has been large. To provide the reader with some sense of what is meant by an inner-city, we also present the inner city maps of Toronto, Montreal, and Vancouver that Ram, Norris, and Skof (1989:14) used to make the comparisons shown in Figure 10-1.

Comparing the twelve metropolitan areas in Table 10-1, we see that inner city losses vary considerably. All except two of the smaller centers have lost inner city population; some, such as Montreal, Quebec City, and Halifax, have lost over half their population in 35 years. These are older eastern cities.

Changing Family and Household Patterns

In chapter nine we discussed the changes in urban family structures, and in Table 10-2 we illustrate one of these patterns. People living alone comprised 15 percent of the households in these twelve inner cities in 1951, but this had increased to over one-half (56 percent) by 1986 (Ram, Norris and Skof, 1989:22). This four-fold increase also occurred in the outer urban areas (5 to 22 percent), but the number of households is much smaller. There are increasing concentrations of young, single people in the inner cities, using the cheaper housing there as a "staging area" before they marry and move to the suburbs to raise their families. The divorced population is also increasing there, and there are also large populations of the elderly and widowed in the inner cities. By 1989, over half the population of the inner cities of ten of these urban areas was single, an enormous increase since 1951. Housing in inner cities seems to be more suitable for singles, and they are also closer to core area facilities and work. One-half (49 percent) of the inner city families were without children, compared to only one-third in the suburbs.

Inner cities also tend to have a much higher proportion of lone-parent families (22 percent) compared to the 14 percent in outlying areas (Ram, Norris and Skof, 1989:24). But metropolitan areas vary greatly in the number of lone-parent families, from only 15 percent in Calgary's inner city to as high as 33 percent in Saint John. These differences are not as great among the outer areas — the range is from 12 to 15 percent in 1986.

The Ethnic Factor

In chapter six we illustrated the importance of the ethnic mosaic in ethnic group segregation in the cities of Canada. Variations in ethnic segregation are also evident within the city and among cities. In Table 10-3 we see that the foreign-born population in twelve centers constituted one-fourth (27 percent) of the total inner city population, and one-fifth (21 percent) of the total population in the outer areas in 1961 (Ram, Norris and Skof, 1989:25). These proportions remained quite stable through to 1986, with a slight increase in

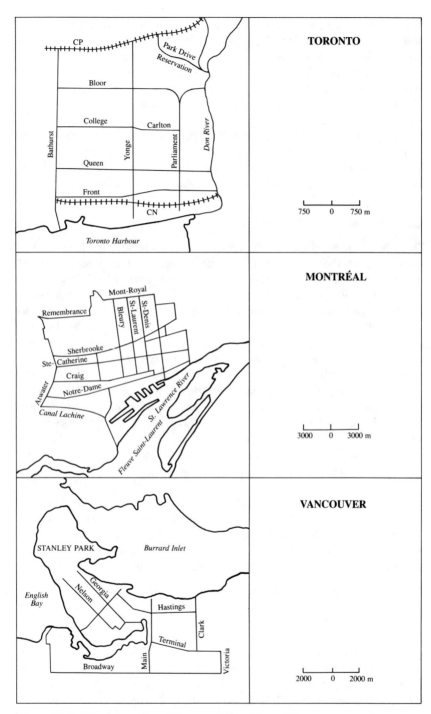

Figure 10-1 The inner cities of Toronto, Montréal, and Vancouver
SOURCE: Ram *et al.* (1989: 14).

Table 10-2 Percentage of total private households with persons living alone, inner cities and remainder, 1951-1986

CMA	INNER-CITY					REMAINDER				
	1951	1961	1971	1981	1986	1951	1961	1971	1981	1986
Toronto	9.8	22.5	34.7	51.4	48.9	4.2	7.3	12.2	20.0	19.9
Montréal	14.5	28.0	42.7	56.5	55.9	3.3	7.0	13.1	22.0	23.7
Vancouver	20.4	33.6	47.0	62.4	63.7	8.3	10.9	15.9	23.7	24.2
Ottawa-Hull	10.4	20.9	36.2	54.6	53.4	3.4	5.1	9.9	20.3	20.5
Edmonton	25.6	38.7	49.8	59.9	60.1	6.3	8.0	12.1	19.6	20.9
Calgary	25.4	43.1	51.6	64.0	63.4	8.2	9.3	12.5	18.3	20.8
Winnipeg	17.9	33.4	47.4	58.8	57.2	4.4	7.0	13.6	23.7	23.9
Québec	9.6	19.5	36.1	53.9	53.9	2.4	4.5	9.8	18.5	20.5
Halifax	8.6	12.0	26.2	45.2	45.4	4.3	5.8	9.3	18.5	18.2
Saskatoon	26.2	40.9	54.6	60.6	60.9	7.6	9.0	15.3	24.3	22.8
Regina	20.4	33.8	50.3	64.5	65.7	5.4	6.3	12.1	20.2	20.2
Saint John	11.9	18.9	26.6	40.7	45.6	5.6	7.4	10.3	17.3	17.9
Total	14.7	27.3	41.4	56.4	55.8	4.7	7.5	12.7	21.0	21.8

SOURCE: 1951-1981 Censuses of Canada, published data for census tracts, and 1986 Census of Canada, unpublished data. From Ram (1989: 24).

Table 10-3 Immigrant population as a percentage of total population, inner cities and remainder, 1961-1986

CMA	INNER-CITY				REMAINDER			
	1961	1971	1981	1986	1961	1971	1981	1986
Toronto	40.3	41.0	40.9	39.1	32.7	33.6	37.9	36.3
Montréal	19.5	22.8	27.3	27.1	14.9	14.4	15.8	15.6
Vancouver	48.1	41.4	41.1	37.9	26.8	25.4	29.1	28.4
Ottawa-Hull	13.0	16.0	20.4	19.8	12.0	12.1	13.9	13.7
Edmonton	37.2	26.9	28.3	25.4	22.6	18.0	19.6	18.4
Calgary	41.8	28.8	30.4	32.1	23.6	20.1	21.1	20.7
Winnipeg	33.0	30.4	34.5	34.4	22.9	19.2	18.7	17.5
Québec	3.3	3.1	4.3	5.8	1.9	2.2	2.2	2.3
Halifax	6.4	8.2	8.9	10.4	7.1	7.2	7.3	7.1
Saskatoon	36.2	30.5	24.3	21.4	16.9	13.3	11.4	9.3
Regina	31.1	24.2	24.5	18.7	15.5	12.1	10.0	9.1
Saint John	7.1	6.2	6.3	6.1	5.4	4.7	5.2	4.7
Total	27.0	28.0	31.3	30.2	21.1	20.6	22.8	22.2

SOURCE: 1961-1981 Censuses of Canada, published data for census tracts, and 1986 Census of Canada, unpublished data. Ram (1989: 25).

the inner cities (to 30 percent). There were some interesting variations among the twelve centers, however: the foreign-born increased during these 25 years in the inner cities of Montreal and Ottawa-Hull; decreased in Vancouver, Edmonton, Calgary, Saskatoon, and Regina; and remained fairly stable in the other five centers. The range of foreign-born in the inner city in 1989 also varied, from as few as 6 percent in Quebec City to as many as 39 percent in Toronto.

To compare the concentration of ethnic groups, Ram and associates (1989:27) developed an index of concentration in the inner and outer areas of the twelve CMAS in 1961, 1971, 1981, and 1986. One hundred represented an identical concentration of non-British and non-French ethnic groups in both the inner and outer areas; an index over 100 indicated greater concentration in the inner city, and under 100 represented a greater concentration in the outer city. Only Saskatoon and Edmonton had scores slightly under 100 in 1986; the others were all over 100, with Quebec City scoring 203 and Montreal 138. These two Quebec CMAS are dominated by French Canadian populations that tend to be highly segregated from the remaining population. In 1986, three-fourths of the residents of the inner city in Winnipeg were from non-charter ethnic groups; this inner city, which includes high concentrations of Indians, had the highest index of the twelve cities studied. We expect that such high concentrations of visible minorities and foreign-born immigrants will create racial problems in the inner city, which we want to examine later.

Class and Socio-Economic Factors

Of the three indicators of socio-economic status, income was most often used to portray status in the inner city. In Table 10-4 we see that in 1970 the average inner city income was $21,056, 70 percent of that earned ($30,003) in the outer city. This ranged from 64 percent in Halifax to 79 percent in Saint John. By 1985 inner city income had declined to 62 percent of outer city income, ranging from 44 percent in Winnipeg to 82 percent in Saskatoon. Winnipeg has the largest concentration of Indians in its inner city; Halifax has a large concentration of Blacks. Inner city incomes actually dropped in Winnipeg and Saint John between 1970 and 1985, while incomes in the remainder of these twelve cities rose modestly. Such declines are significant when we consider that inflation increased substantially during these fifteen years. In all twelve cities, inner city incomes were substantially lower than in the suburbs.

Differences in home ownership were also substantial; only 14 percent of inner city residents (5 percent in Calgary) owned their homes, compared to 57 percent in the suburbs. Over one-half of the inner city residents in Winnipeg (56 percent) and Saint John (55 percent) in 1985 earned less than $20,000 per family; the average was 39 percent for the twelve cities combined. Income levels and home ownership figures tend to support the conclusions of the early Chicago School studies concerning the inner city.

Table 10-4 Median income of census families in contant 1985 dollars, inner cities and remainder, 1970 and 1985

	1970			1985		
CITY	INNER CITY	REMAINDER	$\frac{\text{INNER CITY}}{\text{REMAINDER}} \times 100$	INNER CITY	REMAINDER	$\frac{\text{INNER CITY}}{\text{REMAINDER}} \times 100$
	$	$	%	$	$	%
Toronto	22 689	32 624	70	30 622	41 723	73
Montréal	18 715	27 971	67	24 445	34 646	71
Vancouver	21 620	29 960	72	23 197	38 076	61
Ottawa-Hull	23 977	34 007	71	31 282	43 107	73
Edmonton	23 170	29 997	77	27 367	38 781	71
Calgary	21 258	30 727	69	24 594	41 104	60
Winnipeg	18 552	28 188	66	16 026	36 364	44
Québec	20 129	27 301	74	21 796	35 284	62
Halifax	18 232	28 393	64	23 747	36 815	65
Saskatoon	21 067	26 541	79	29 536	35 832	82
Regina	19 785	27 606	72	25 422	39 324	65
Saint John	19 825	25 063	79	18 200	31 564	58
Total	21 056	30 003	70	23 639	38 361	62

SOURCE: 1971 and 1986 Censuses of Canada, unpublished data. Ram (1989: 32).

However, inner city education and occupation statistics illustrate a new trend that needs examination. In 1986 education levels of residents in the inner city was higher (36 percent with some university) than in the outer cities (23 percent). This is a major change since 1971, when these levels were 17 and 14 percent respectively. This trend to higher education levels in the inner city is confirmed in ten of the twelve CMAs, the exceptions being Winnipeg and Saskatoon. There were more degree holders in 1989 in the inner city (21 percent) than in the suburbs (12 percent). This is a major change since 1971, when seven of the twelve CMAs had more highly educated residents in the suburbs than in the inner city. The influx of better educated, single young people in search of cheap, older housing, and older residents moving into newly built condominiums, seems to be raising the educational level in the inner city.

Similar trends are happening in occupations. There were about the same proportions of people in professional/managerial jobs in both parts of the city in 1971 (24 and 22 percent), but by 1986 there had been a major change: 37 percent residing in the inner city had professional/managerial jobs, compared to only 28 percent in the remainder of the city. These proportions did not vary by gender. Service occupations were more heavily located in both 1971 and 1986 in the inner city, where such jobs are more numerous. These new trends

— more highly educated residents and higher level occupational groups — are new phenomena that will cause changes in the patterns of urban social problems in Canada in the future. These patterns are not necessarily the same as in the United States, nor are they similar to the early urban problems studied in Chicago.

Having examined some of the ecological patterns of shifts in urban population, let us now turn to a sampling of some urban problems, the major focus of this chapter. We hope that this ecological demographic review will have provided a useful context to help in understanding the rise of and nature of urban problems in the 1990s.

Economic and Ecological Urban Problems

In this section we are going to discuss the problems that arise from the economic and political structures of urban industrial society. We can only outline a few of these structural problems. We have chosen to deal with urban poverty, which is evidence of economic and political powerlessness; lack of adequate housing and urban blight; air, water, and noise pollution; transportation problems; and urban sprawl.

Urban Poverty and Powerlessness

Rural poverty is as common as urban poverty, but the contrast of wealth and poverty are much more visible in the city, where the rich and the poor may well live in proximity to each other, particularly in Third World countries (Richardson, 1972:173-200; Fingard, 1977). Within cities, poverty is more common in the inner city, as we illustrated in Table 10-4. Recent immigrants, racial minorities, and single women are among the poor concentrated in the inner city.

S.D. Clark (1978) describes the life of some of the rural poor in northeastern New Brunswick and northern Ontario and Quebec. Many trek to nearby cities, including French Canadians from New Brunswick and Quebec, and Indians from the northern Prairies. Clark (1978:139-57) describes the heavy immigration of the Irish to Toronto during the 1840s and 1850s; they were among the poorest in Toronto then. More recently, immigrants from eastern Europe and Italy hold that position. The highest incidence of poverty can be found in the downtown area of Toronto, which has the largest non-British population (Clark, 1978:142).

There are several theories that attempt to explain the causes of poverty. Each has its supporters and detractors. Oscar Lewis (1966) assumed that poverty is a feature of a highly stratified, competitive economic system that includes high rates of unemployment and underemployment for unskilled labor, low wages, and a failure to provide for social, political, and economic integration (Flanagan, 1990:240). Lewis (1966) held that the poor tend to adapt culturally to economic disappointment and defeat, and they create a system of values and attitudes that they pass on to their children; Lewis called this the "culture of poverty." Poverty becomes a way of life because internalized values create a vicious cycle of being poor to which each generation is socialized and trained. This theory seems to link up with Robert Park's thinking that populations in natural areas generate their own moral order; which was further developed in his study of Blacks in Chicago by Gerald Suttles (1968) in the social order of the slum.

Flanagan (1990:241) summarizes some 70 of Lewis' psychological and social characteristics of the poor: 1) strongly fatalistic; 2) weak ego development and incapacity for self-control; 3) living for the moment; 4) little ability to defer gratification or plan for the future; 5) knowledge only of their own limited neighborhood; and 6) lack of class consciousness. These characteristics do not promote a desire for personal or community improvement. Lewis saw them as deeply ingrained habits that tended to retard the ability to compete in the larger society.

There were many critics of the culture of poverty thesis; one was Valentine (1968:144), who said it blamed the poor too much and avoided the recognition of need for change in the structures of society. Ryan (1971) claimed that these were only the excuses of the middle class, who were not willing to face up to the fact that capitalism did not work for all, and that the lack of money was one of the problems of the poor. It is not their culture that keeps people poor, but a structure of poverty that is built into western society as a permanent feature of the problems of distribution of rewards: this feature is unemployment or underemployment. Lack of employment opportunities, technological skills, and education and training tend to separate the poor from those who can compete. Many higher-paying industrial jobs have moved from the inner city, leaving a preponderance of jobs in the service sector, which do not pay well, to the unskilled.

Spates and Macionis (1987:321) found in 1984 that 16 percent of families below the poverty line in American metropolitan centers were located in inner cities, and only half (8 percent) as many outside the inner cities. They also found that 11 percent of the Whites in inner cities, 30 percent of the Hispanics, and 34 of the Blacks were below the poverty line (Spates and Macionis, 1987:323). More than three times as many visible minorities as Whites in inner cities were poor. Outside the inner cities there were fewer proportions of poor: 7 percent Whites, 21 percent Hispanics, and 22 percent Blacks. These American data clearly show that poverty is more common in inner cities, and it is also more common among visible minorities. The poor are powerless to change the economic and political structures. Power is located in the hands of those who also have financial resources. How this power should be restructured to change the plight of the poor depends on the perspective taken. Marxists would say that a better distribution of income is needed, while structural functionalists would say that the present structures need to be balanced to provide greater benefits to all, but that inequality is an inevitable part of all industrial urban societies.

Housing and Urban Blight

A blighted area is one that has lost its attractiveness, and also some of its functions. Blight is common in the older sections of the city, often towards the center (Kowaluk, 1982:64-71). Physical deterioration usually occurs in conjunction with obsolescence of buildings. Non-resident owners let properties decay, hoping to sell the land at a handsome profit when land values rise. "Another source of influence on the physical deterioration of buildings lies in the agencies that are in the land business of lending money for home construction and improvement — banks, building and loan associations, and insurance firms. These agencies have followed policies of 'blacklisting' areas . . . " (Hawley, 1981:267). Withholding mortgages leaves the buildings in an area to deteriorate.

Inner city problems derive principally from three sources: 1) changes in the technological-economic-social structure of cities, making buildings and functions obsolete; 2) physical changes that occur in the process of urbanization, which is more complicated in the inner city; and 3) municipal financial problems and fragmentation of municipal government, which usually works to the disadvantage of inner city governments (Nader, 1975:337). The inner city is frequently the product of nineteenth century technology, where it was essential to concentrate uses; the suburbs developed later, when dispersed activities were possible and desirable.

Owners are discouraged from redeveloping their inner city property because new buildings will carry higher taxes; housing for low-income renters is unprofitable and is fraught with great risks; and often a delay in redevelopment helps to increase the potential for profit because land values may rise. The availability of older housing that has deteriorated has its benefits for the poor. They have cheap housing, commercial buildings are often available for inexpensive meeting places such as neighborhood meetings, theater and dance groups, and store-front churches. There are also disadvantages, in that such dilapidated buildings are fire and health hazards. Those who can afford it move to the suburbs where housing is newer, where communities have more up-to-date facilities, and where residents have better incomes and education to maintain a creative environment.

Transportation Problems

Cities that developed before the end of the nineteenth century were dependent on walking or on animal-drawn transportation. When steam power made rail transportation possible, populations clustered near railroads for easy access to work and shopping. Coal-burning steam engines added to the noise and air pollution of the city (Geisler, 1982:81-91).

The motor vehicle was developed early in the twentieth century, but did not begin to dominate urban areas until after World War II. It facilitated the move to the suburbs for those who could afford it (Richardson, 1972:129-41). However, most of these suburbanites still worked in the central city. More expressways provide faster access to the center, but removal of homes to make space for them seriously cuts into the tax base for running the city. When cities cannot keep up with building more or wider expressways, traffic congestion, especially during rush hours, becomes a problem as more and more people try to drive into the city, often only one person per car.

To deal with the traffic problem, municipal governments debate the need for new public transit schemes (Jacobs, 1971:204-10). Modern bus and rail transit systems are more economical and more efficient than cars, but can cities persuade commuters to use these public facilities? Very large metropolitan centers such as New York, London, Tokyo, and Moscow have efficient and fast subway systems that function well and are used extensively. The Bay Area Rapid Transit (BART) was completed in the San Francisco-Oakland Bay area in the 1970s; it is an example of good modern systems that are still being built. Commuters on BART are assured of fast, clean, and comfortable transportation. Older systems, Chicago's for example, have become slow. As a result, fewer people use them, and the systems no longer pay for themselves (Bello, 1958:49). A vicious cycle is set up: old systems that commuters do not want to ride bring in less revenues, and so there is less money for buying newer and better facilities.

As more cars enter the central city, parking becomes a problem. Larger parking facilities are built to stack cars higher and higher. Not only does it take longer to retrieve the cars, but these car-park skyscrapers empty their contents into the streets at the end of each day, flooding their capacity. Amsterdam has managed better than most cities to keep a balance among foot, bicycle, bus, rail, water, subway, and automobile traffic. Canadian cities, particularly those on the Prairies, depend too much on the automobile for transportation.

Environmental Pollution

Large metropolitan populations make intensive use of the environment. They impose strain on water resources, add pollutants to the air, and accumulate huge piles of solid and liquid wastes. They consume large amounts of fuels for transportation, heating and cooling buildings, and for industrial uses; and they use up huge amounts of raw materials for manufacturing, packaging, and in the construction of streets, buildings, technical equipment, and facilities (Hawley, 1981:263-4).

Many cities are built on the shores of oceans, seas, lakes, or rivers, some of which provide ready access to fresh water. However, these waterways also provide ready means for the disposal of sewage, so that purification is necessary if the water is to remain safe for drinking. Pollution stemming from industrial water use adds to problems. The costs of purification also escalate over time. Many rivers and lakes in North America are dead, and many can no longer be used as beaches and resort areas. In Europe, rivers such as the Thames in England and the Rhine in northeastern Europe became heavily polluted. Many urban centers on the Atlantic east coast have polluted harbors, such as New York and Boston. Even the oceans are polluted. Sea-going vessels transporting large volumes of fuel increase the risks of oil spills, as the Valdez Exxon Oil disaster in the Gulf of Alaska demonstrated.

Air pollution is just as serious as water pollution; most of it is caused by the use of combustion engines and by industry. Los Angeles, the city most influenced ecologically in its growth patterns by the automobile, is greatly affected by air pollution, particularly because the emissions from the large number of cars became trapped between the Pacific Ocean and the mountains. Air pollution controls have been devised, fuel emissions by cars have been reduced, but the population is also growing. Mexico City, presently the largest urban center, rests high on its plateau in a haze that can be seen from the air by plane passengers as they are arriving. Offensive odors, soiled clothes, irritation to eyes, and damage to the paint on houses, to rubber tires, metal products, fabrics, monuments, and plant life are all the results of air pollutants (Hawley, 1980:265). The heavily industrialized midwestern United States and southern Ontario in particular give rise to air and water pollution. Industrialized countries are faced with monumental financial outlays to control air and water pollution. So far most have only brought themselves to study these problems.

Noise pollution is caused by industry, machines, automobiles, and communication devices. Traffic on expressways can be heard for miles, and residential areas try to reduce traffic noise by building earth or fence sound barriers. Constant traffic noise subtracts substantially from the quality of life. Other sources of noise pollution are from transistor radios, calling devices, and cellular telephones, which disturb and pollute for everyone in close proximity to their users.

Urban Sprawl

Lest we think that all urban problems are located in the inner city, let us at least briefly look at a problem that affects the outlying areas of cities—urban sprawl. Upwardly mobile residents move to the outer suburbs or beyond, seeking the utopian advantages of both town and country. New businesses also start up on the outer edges of the city where premises are less costly, and manufacturing moves out there to expand. All these shifts to the outlying areas are made possible by the flexibility of automobile transportation. Land speculators and developers buy up land outside urban municipal jurisdictions to accommodate this expansion and in search of profits. Depending on the land use controls in an area, these new developments may create urban sprawl. Urban sprawl makes for bad aesthetics as well as bad economics (Whyte, 1958:115-17). Good farm land often is paved over. If planning is haphazard, and there are gaps between city boundaries and new developments, gas, water, sewage, and electrical services become expensive because the volume of use may be low in proportion to the costs of installation. Land speculation often results in areas of development leapfrogging over pockets of resistance, making the orderly development of communities difficult (Whyte, 1958:18-20).

Suburbs can become gigantic, centerless bedroom developments that may offer advantages to families with small children, but are boring for teenagers and youth because they lack clubs, sports arenas, and opportunities for social interaction. Some suburban youth may turn to alcohol and drug abuse. All family members, including youth, are almost totally dependent on automobiles; people may work in one suburb, live in another, and shop routinely in several others. It is difficult to provide adequate public transportation for these scattered industries, businesses, and schools. This is why many youth and adults who have finished raising their families move to the central city where they have easy access to services and facilities (Horton, Leslie, and Larson, 1985:290). Many suburban homeowners find that the costs of running a large suburban home and traffic congestion become burdens that they exchange for an apartment downtown.

Deviance and Problems of Disorganization

While poverty, urban blight, problems of transportation, environmental pollution, and urban sprawl are macro sources of disorganization and conflict, let us now examine some problems at the micro level—social problems such as crime and racial discrimination. We shall select only a few samples to illustrate the kinds of problems there are, and how they vary from city to city.

Crime as Personal and Social Deviance

Some of the Chicago sociologists, such as Anderson, Thrasher, and Sutherland, found homeless men, gangs, and criminals in the inner city of Chicago, and their books *The Hobo*, *The Gang*, and *The Professional Thief* have become classics (Michelson, 1976). Flanagan (1990:269) shows that crime rates in the United States vary by size of city. The assumption of many early sociologists was that crime would be lowest in rural areas where community ties were strongest, and that crime would increase with size of city (Glaser, 1970). They thought that personal and community ties would be difficult to maintain in a large city, where the tendency is towards secondary relationships. They also assumed that poverty was a source of crime (Hagan, 1990; Sampson, 1986:271-311).

In Table 10-5 we see that indeed rates of violent crimes and property crimes increase with size of city in the United States. Overall, violent crime rates in populations less than 10,000 are 272 per 100,000, while the rate in cities over 250,000 is five times as great, although there is less robbery and even less aggravated assault per capita in large cities. For the property crime rate, the average figure in large cities is double the rate in small cities, as are the rates for burglary and theft; motor vehicle theft is much greater per capita in large cities. These crime rates clearly support the findings of the early American sociologists.

However, we cannot assume that these findings also apply to Canada. In

Table 10-5 Violent and property crimes rates by city size in the United States, 1987

	VIOLENT CRIME[a]				
CITY SIZE	TOTAL	MURDER	FORCIBLE RAPE	ROBBERY	AGGRAVATED ASSAULT
250 000 or more	1344	19	78	684	563
100 000-249 999	802	10	52	298	441
50 000-99 999	536	6	36	186	307
25 000-49 999	420	5	28	124	263
10 000-24 999	307	4	20	70	214
Less than 10 000	272	4	17	41	211

	PROPERTY CRIME[a]			
CITY SIZE	TOTAL	BURGLARY	LARCENY-THEFT	MOTOR VEHICLE THEFT
250 000 or more	7606	2156	4339	1111
100 000-249 999	7002	1949	4471	582
50 000-99 999	5499	1456	3521	522
25 000-49 999	5130	1265	3480	385
10 000-24 999	4247	1000	2965	283
Less than 10 000	3946	881	2850	315

[a]Offences known by the police per 100 000 population.
SOURCE: *Statistical Abstract of the United States, 1987* (1986: 157) Table 265.

Figure 10-2 we see that the rates for homicide, total violent crime, and total property crimes do not vary greatly by urban size in Canada as they do in the United States. However robbery does follow the American pattern, increasing with city size, and this also is true for prostitution as cities rise above 50,000 population.

While city size seems to be less of a factor in crime rates in Canada than in the United States, there are regional differences in Canada. In Table 10-6 we have ranked the 24 metropolitan areas of Canada by criminal code violations in 1988 and find that size is not as great a factor as region. Eastern urban centers generally have lower total crime rates, while west coast cities, particularly Victoria and Vancouver, have the highest crime rates. Urban centers in the West are among the highest in violent, property, and all other crimes. Have eastern cities been able to consolidate their social organization better than the West? Since the Maritime provinces were predominantly British, and French were the majority in Quebec, and the West has been ethnically much more heterogeneous, is homogeneity of ethnicity a factor in crime rates? While Toronto and Ontario were predominantly of British origin earlier, they are now becoming more ethnically heterogeneous — will this tend to raise crime rates, particularly in Toronto which is becoming very diverse ethnically and racially?

Figure 10-2   Canadian crime rates by city size expressed as ratio of small-town
rates, 1978

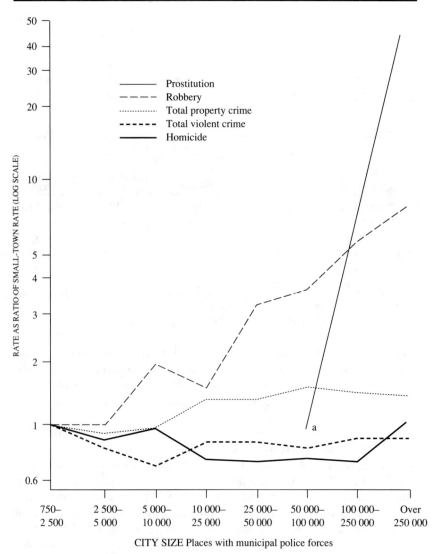

CITY SIZE Places with municipal police forces

^a Too few prostitution crimes in cities below 50 000
SOURCE: Fischer (1984:106).

We have not been able to break down our data for inner and outer city
areas, but it is interesting to note that York, a suburb of Toronto, has by far
the lowest violent crime rates of all types. Goldberg and Mercer (1986:220-
1) found in 1976 that property crime rates for total metropolitan areas in

Canada did not very greatly by city size; however, the central city rates went up with increases in city size. They also found that the ratio of crimes per 100,000 population was greater in inner cities than in the rest of the outer cities.

Ethnic and Racial Discrimination

In chapter six we discussed ethnic and racial segregation and plotted concentrations of Chinese, Jews, Greeks, Italians, Portuguese, and Indo-Pakistanis in the central areas of Toronto, Montreal, and Vancouver (Figure 6-2). The Chinese in particular are well represented in the inner cities of the three centers shown in Figure 10-1. In Table 6-3 we showed that the Native peoples were usually the most segregated group, and were located in the inner cities (Frideres, 1988:205-29). Table 6-4 shows that dissimilarity indices and Gini indices were highest for Jews in all three of the largest metropolitan centers in Canada, and Chinese and Indo-Pakistani index ranges were also high, especially in Montreal. Segregation scores in Winnipeg were also high for Jewish and French groups (Table 6-5). To what extent are such ethnic segregation patterns also associated with prejudice and discrimination?

Using a Bogardus scale, Driedger and Mezoff (1980) asked students in nine Winnipeg High Schools to what extent they were willing to relate to 20 ethnic groups. Their findings are shown in Table 10-7. (The Bogardus scale measures willingness to be close to or far removed from others.) It is clear that Winnipeg students were much more willing to marry a person of Caucasian origin than one from a visible minority. A willingness to allow some groups into the country only as visitors, or to debar them altogether, shows intolerance. Table 10-7 clearly illustrates that there is a degree (11 percent) of anti-Semitism in Canada (Driedger and Mezoff, 1980:1-17). Driedger and Clifton (1984) found that in Winnipeg, negative stereotypes towards the Jews were present, and two-thirds of the Jewish university students reported that they were experiencing discrimination (Driedger and Mezoff, 1980). Since Jewish students, however, had high socio-economic status, this discrimination was not based on social class. Religion seemed to be the important differential. Similar patterns of willingness to relate to Chinese, Germans, Italians, Jews, Portuguese, Ukrainians, and West Indians were found by Breton et al. (1990:200) in Toronto: it was highest for northern Europeans, and lowest for visible minorities. Most Torontonians (range of 67 to 92 percent) were willing to accept these groups as neighbors, however.

Breton and associates (1990:208) also asked minorities to report their experiences of discrimination at work; their findings are shown in Table 10-8. A majority of West Indians (57 percent) perceived discrimination in pay and work, and one-third of the Chinese (37 percent) and Portuguese (33 percent) also reported serious problems at work in Toronto. Two-thirds or more (61 to 76 percent) of the groups thought the West Indians experienced discrimination, and one-third to one-half (37 to 53 percent) thought the Chinese

Table 10-6 Violent, property, and other crimes in 24 Canadian metropolitan centers, 1988

METROPOLITAN CENTERS	RANK	ASSAULT	ROBBERY	VIOLENT CRIMES TOTAL	BREAK & ENTER	FRAUD	THEFT	PROPERTY CRIMES TOTAL	OTHER CRIMES TOTAL	CRIMINAL CODE TOTAL
Victoria	1	1706	214	1967	2583	1058	7740	12064	5270	19301
Vancouver	2	1231	406	1665	2800	391	7195	11217	4606	17488
Edmonton	3	1094	169	1377	2368	593	7095	10817	3839	16033
Regina	4	772	135	961	3017	943	6211	10777	3120	14858
Halifax	5	1081	172	1274	2057	895	6226	9486	3477	14237
Saskatoon	6	773	95	984	2092	909	6289	9911	3232	14127
Thunder Bay	7	1177	67	1327	1436	796	4611	7401	3661	12382
Windsor	8	1070	84	1173	1463	362	4733	7116	3996	12285
Ottawa	9	574	148	1038	1784	531	4755	7599	2838	11475
Winnipeg	10	629	199	865	2069	569	4793	7976	2534	11375
Montreal	11	857	424	1299	2269	524	3895	7539	2509	11347
Quebec	12	521	326	869	2703	1119	4141	8454	1940	11261
London	13	869	50	922	1346	570	4020	6236	3729	10887
Hamilton	14	1127	64	1213	1281	549	3464	5708	2864	9785
Toronto	15	979	161	1163	1079	580	3362	5633	2932	9728
Calgary	16	482	96	592	1463	382	4482	6772	2128	9492
Sudbury	17	617	46	696	1657	264	2926	5555	2251	8502
Trois Rivières	18	615	98	725	1677	387	2938	5371	2259	8355
Saint John	19	871	56	937	973	548	2764	4721	2537	8195
Sherbrooke	20	347	83	437	2294	610	2726	5945	1769	8151
Waterloo	21	756	37	800	1106	384	3324	5123	2072	7995
St. John's	22	780	11	820	796	479	2584	4139	2664	7623
Jonquière	23	537	38	583	1361	357	1983	3944	1018	5545
York	24	306	16	329	836	308	1879	3238	1198	4765

Table 10-7 The degree of distance that Winnipeg high school students prefer to maintain between themselves and twenty groups of European and non-European origin (percentage)

ETHNIC GROUPS[a]	MARRY	HAVE AS CLOSE FRIEND	SOCIAL DISTANCE SCALE (BOGARDUS) HAVE AS NEIGHBOR	WORK WITH ON JOB	HAVE AS ACQUAINTANCE	WILLINGNESS TO HAVE AS VISITOR ONLY	WOULD DEBAR FROM NATION	NUMBER[a] WHO RESPONDED
EUROPEAN ORIGIN								
American	75	14	5	2	2	2	2	2220
British	65	20	6	4	2	3	1	1849
Scandinavian	56	24	8	6	3	2	1	2265
Dutch	53	25	11	5	4	1[b]	1	2328
Polish	51	26	9	6	4	2	2	2223
Ukrainian	50	28	9	6	4	2	2	1764
French	50	24	9	6	6	2	5	1912
German	48	25	11	7	4	3	2	2002
Italian	44	28	10	7	6	3	3	2163
Russian	41	27	11	7	6	3	5	2163
Jewish	28	34	12	7	9	4	7	1883
NON-EUROPEAN ORIGIN								
Negro (Blacks)	29	49	11	6	3	1	1	2256
Mexican	29	37	14	8	6	4	1	2262
Japanese	26	44	14	7	6	2	2	2209
Filipino	26	40	13	9	6	4	2	2147
Chinese	25	45	13	7	5	2	2	2328
West Indian	23	43	13	9	8	3	3	2131
East Indian	23	42	13	10	8	3	2	2190
Native Indian	22	41	10	10	10	3	4	2145
Eskimo (Inuit)	19	45	13	10	8	3	2	2160

[a] Ingroup evaluations were deleted (e.g. the British in the sample did not evaluate their own group, etc.)   [b] The N's in any one cell never dropped below 20.

SOURCE: Driedger and Mezoff (1980:8).

Table 10-8 Perception and experience of discrimination by members of minority groups (percentages)

	CHINESE	GERMAN	ITALIAN	JEWISH	PORTUGUESE	UKRAINIAN	WEST INDIAN
A. Discrimination re: job, pay, and work conditions:							
A very and somewhat serious problem	37	3	20	15	33	8	57
Not too serious	42	17	37	46	26	30	23
Not a problem	17	75	41	35	33	58	14
Don't know	3	4	2	4	8	3	6
N—weighted[a]	(57)	(178)	(429)	(168)	(67)	(89)	(118)
B. Employers perceived as discriminating a lot or somewhat:							
By group itself	53	18	30	40	30	24	66
By Majority Canadians[b]	47	17	38	39	49	16	76
By minority groups[b]	37	18	32	28	37	16	61
C. Have experienced discrimination when trying to find a job	17	5	7	12	5	10	22

[a]The N's are the same for sections A and C of the table.
[b]The weighted N for Majority Canadians is 787. For the minority groups combined, the N varies between 1097 and 1107.
SOURCE: Breton *et al.* (1990:208).

in Toronto had similar problems of discrimination. It is clear from the Toronto study that visible minorities are discriminated against in Toronto, which is becoming the most ethnically and racially diverse metropolis in Canada (Henry and Ginzberg, 1985). With a population of 3.4 million, Toronto may be headed in the direction of many larger American urban centers, where racial prejudice, especially against Blacks, is serious. As shown in Table 10-3, ethnic minorities tend to be more heavily concentrated in the inner city.

Summary

Early urban sociologists of the Chicago School developed the ecological approach to the study of the city, assuming that the spatial distribution of populations was important to differentiating urban lifestyles. Later, some sociologists stressed the impact of power and social class on urban problems. Theorists of social problems have used these approaches in their discussion of social disorganization, social conflict, and deviance in the metropolis.

To provide a context for the discussion of urban problems, we focused on ecological and demographic comparisons of the inner and outer cities of a dozen CMAs in Canada. Inner city populations have declined since 1951, while suburban populations have grown. Inner city single-person households have increased fourfold during the past 35 years. Immigrant and racial groups are highly concentrated in the inner cities, and their incomes are only 70 to 62 percent of the incomes of those living in other parts of the metropolis. Surprisingly, educational levels have risen in the inner cities as young adults and the elderly move back into the city from the suburbs. Clearly, inner city demographics suggest that there is a greater potential there for problems than in the suburbs.

Urban poverty and powerlessness are rampant in many inner cities of Canada, as are urban blight and dilapidated housing. Suburbanites who work in the central cities press for more expressways, but these would reduce the tax base, and already there are far too many cars on the roads, resulting in traffic congestion. Exhaust from these cars and emissions from factories lead to air pollution. Water is polluted by industrial use and by sewage, and many urban centers must employ expensive water treatment techniques. Noise pollution is also a hazard to the quality of urban life. In addition to these inner city problems, suburban sprawl, land speculation and lack of control and planning, and traffic congestion occur on the outer edges of the city.

Inner city conditions provide spawning grounds for many types of crime. In the United States, the larger the city, the higher the rates of murder, rape, robbery, assault, burglary, and theft. Crime rates vary in Canada, and high rates seem to be grouped by region. Studies in Winnipeg and Toronto show that there is racial discrimination, particularly among visible racial minorities. West Indian, Chinese, and Jewish minorities in particular reported discrimination at work.

11. City Planning

Many cities around the world have a feature that identifies them and is often an important symbol as well: the skyline of Manhattan Island and the Statue of Liberty in New York; San Francisco's Golden Gate Bridge; Big Ben and the parliament buildings in London; the Eiffel Tower in Paris; the statue of Christ of the Andes in Rio de Janeiro; the citadels in Quebec City and Halifax; the Olympic Stadium in Montreal, and the CN Tower of Toronto.

In this chapter we want to introduce some of the ideal urban forms proposed by planners, and some of the strategies they used in their attempt to provide for better living conditions and beautification of the city. What criteria should be used in assessing the quality of urban life, and what are the essential objectives in urban planning? Master plans have been devised for population growth, land use, transportation services, and utilities, as well as for financial planning. Parks, the separation of industrial and residential areas, and communities designed to meet human needs are crucial to the quality of urban life. Housing must be available that will meet the needs of people of all income levels; it should be functional for all stages of family life, and able to be used in a variety of activities, serving diverse socio-economic, ethnic, and social needs.

Finding Ideal Urban Forms

Rapid industrialization began in Britain about 1800, in the United States about 1840, and in Canada about 1880. It brought with it rapid urbanization, particularly in London, New York, and Toronto, although metropolitan expansion in Canada has mostly occurred since the 1950s. Modern urban planning did not begin until the 1870s, and originated in Sweden. Gerald Hodge (1986:55) has traced the evolution of community planning concepts since 1890; we show this in Figure 11-1.

Hodge (1986:55) shows that planning for cities at the turn of the century arose from two areas of concern: 1) deterioration of living conditions, and 2) deterioration of the appearance of cities. Different remedies and forms of community planning sprang from these two concerns.

> Out of concern over living conditions came the notion of Garden Cities, wholly new communities designed to allow new patterns of living in less congested

surroundings. Out of the concern over the appearance of cities came the notion of the City Beautiful, the re-design of major streets and public areas in existing cities (Hodge, 1986:55).

Over time these two emphases became merged; planners attempted to design garden suburbs after 1900, resource towns after the 1920s, and Greenbelt towns after the 1930s. A focus on planning neighborhood units emerged after World War I, and we are still working at designing essentials for neighborhoods and communities today. Planners are trying to meld ways to provide better living conditions and better appearance in Canadian cities. We begin by examining some of the models of Howard, Le Corbusier, and Frank Lloyd Wright.

Howard's Garden City Concept

Ebenezer Howard introduced the Garden City concept in 1898, suggesting that the advantages of country and town be combined into a town-country plan (Howard, 1965). The benefits of the country: open land and forests, fresh air, abundance of water and sunshine—should be linked with the benefits of urban life: opportunities for socializing, entertainment, job opportunities and high wages, and such features as well-lit streets (Howard, 1965). The combination of natural beauty and social opportunity was intended to eliminate the disadvantages of country living: unemployment, long hours of work for low wages, lack of entertainment, and distance from work: and to avoid the disadvantages of urban life: high rents, pollution, and slums (LaGory and Pipkin, 1981:292). The idea of garden cities was an ambitious plan to overcome the stratifications of British society with its extremes of wealth and poverty (Fishman, 1977:3038; Sewell, 1977:19-27).

Figure 11-1   Evolution of urban community planning concepts since 1890

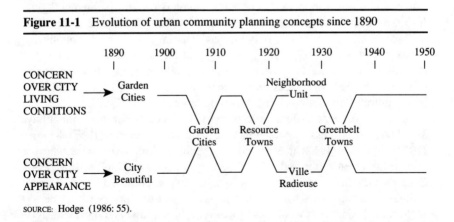

SOURCE: Hodge (1986: 55).

Figure 11-2 shows the garden city plan within its rural belt. The city would be surrounded by farms, pastures, and fields, and an agricultural college would be located in this belt. The agricultural belt would cover an area of about 2000 ha. The population of the town would be about 30,000. The town would cover an area of 100 acres, and some of this land would be set aside for industry and commerce to provide jobs for the town's residents. Land uses would be arranged in a way to allow for maximum convenience in moving around the garden city, and a means of transportation between the central city and the garden city would be provided (Hodge, 1986:57).

Each house in the garden city would have its own garden, each neighborhood its own area for schools, playgrounds, and churches, and all of these would be surrounded by "gardens" (Hodge, 1986:57). Figure 11-2 shows a detail of the city proper, with its radial ring roads and centrally located park and municipal buildings, and a glass-enclosed shopping mall for all kinds of weather. After the city had grown to a certain size, additional people would be siphoned off to a new garden city. Eventually these new garden cities would surround the first garden city. Howard's ideas were turned into reality with the building of two garden cities north of London, the first named Letchworth, built in 1903, and the second, built in 1919 and called Welwyn (Hodge, 1986:57). Howard's garden cities were designed before the automobile became a widespread form of transportation. Since the advent of the automobile, planning has changed to meet new needs.

Frank Lloyd Wright's Broadacre

The American architect Frank Lloyd Wright continued the attempt to blend rural and urban features in several of his books: *When Democracy Builds* (1945), and *The Living City* (1958). In these works he advocated spatial dispersion, made possible by the use of the automobile (LaGory and Pipkin, 1981:292). As did Howard, Wright valued low urban density, and this is evident in his plan for an ideal community called Broadacre, shown in Figure 11-3. This design is intended for a semi-agrarian lifestyle (an acre of farmland for each dwelling), and a centrally located shopping center, made possible by the car. Eliot-Hurst (1975:299) was critical of the Broadacre plan, saying it is really an urban concept, where the automobile is needed to connect the residences to the workplaces, where there is little concern for sprawl; one poor feature of the design is that it uses up large areas of farmland.

Wright's Broadacre does little to provide a center for the community. Wright did not address the economic base of the plan. Reisman (1957), Kramer (1972), and Gans (1962) have criticisms of this plan similar to those of suburbia with its homogenization and cultural poverty (LaGory and Pipkin, 1981:294). Such decentralized communities would be very expensive to provide with utilities, and fuel costs for automobiles at present-day prices would be too high; today's concerns would also focus on urban sprawl and on saving agricultural land.

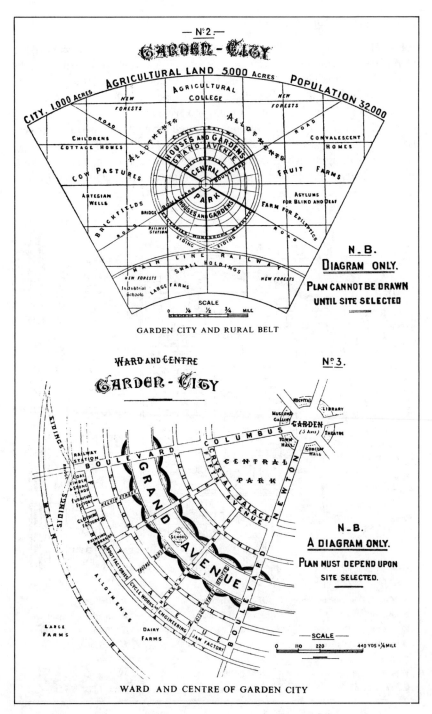

Figure 11-2 Arrangement of land uses in Ebenezer Howard's garden city, 1898
SOURCE: Howard (1965)

Le Corbusier's High-Density Settings

While Howard and Wright wanted to decentralize the city, Swiss-born Le Corbusier, working in France, held the opposite view. He designed for high-density housing in large cities (Flanagan, 1990:284-7). Le Corbusier wanted better housing for all, and was diametrically opposed to the elitist concepts of Howard and Wright. He wanted a tightly focused and centralized urban plan, with high-density, high-rise buildings scattered through open parklike spaces. He expounded his ideas in *The City of Tomorrow* (1929) and *The Radiant City* (1933). His design was followed in many countries: Sweden, France, India, and in Calgary's downtown; it is shown in Figure 11-4 (LaGory and Pipkin, 1981:294).

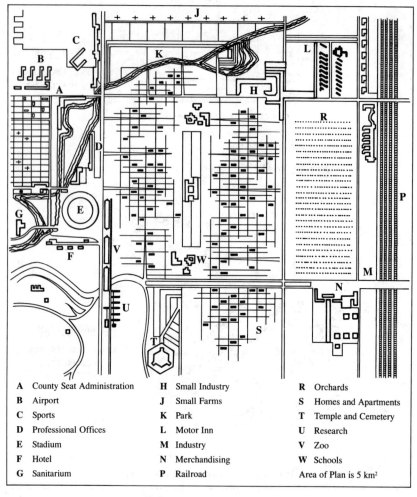

A	County Seat Administration	**H**	Small Industry	**R**	Orchards
B	Airport	**J**	Small Farms	**S**	Homes and Apartments
C	Sports	**K**	Park	**T**	Temple and Cemetery
D	Professional Offices	**L**	Motor Inn	**U**	Research
E	Stadium	**M**	Industry	**V**	Zoo
F	Hotel	**N**	Merchandising	**W**	Schools
G	Sanitarium	**P**	Railroad		Area of Plan is 5 km²

Figure 11-3 Frank Lloyd Wright's Broadacre
SOURCE: Gallion and Eisner (1975).

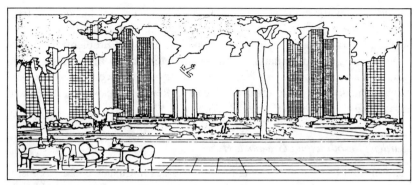

Figure 11-4 Le Corbusier's view of the contemporary city, 1922
SOURCE: Le Corbusier Foundation.

Le Corbusier's downtown business space occupies several sixty-storey office buildings in the center; most of the residential space is in eight-storey apartment buildings surrounded by parks. By using high-rise buildings he conserved space, and provided light, air, and natural beauty in parks. His plan allowed for urban centers of up to three million people. Some areas of London that were rebuilding in the 1950s and 1960s adopted his plan (Hall, 1975:76). Critics say that a sense of neighborhood in which children's play could be supervised is greatly inhibited by this plan. Also, Le Corbusier was obsessed with geometric forms, and many find his designs too rigid. Critics say he was more concerned with form than with function. Planners also found that it was difficult to find the land for such large plans, particularly in cities where politics and economics did not make such large plans practical.

The City Beautiful Movement

Having presented some ideal plans for cities, let us now concentrate on concerns about urban appearance, and how designs to improve appearance could be adjusted and applied in already existing urban areas. In 1893 Chicago hosted the World Columbian Exposition, and the design of the grounds and buildings of this Expo stimulated an interest in beautifying American cities. For the exposition, John Root and Daniel Burnham, two Chicago architects, conceived a setting of buildings, statues, canals, and lagoons on the shores of Lake Michigan (Hodge, 1986:58). Their aesthetic principles influenced the design of city halls, public libraries, banks, railroad stations, civic centers, boulevards, and university campuses — all still very evident in Chicago on Lakeshore Drive.

Canadian architects, engineers, and surveyors were also influenced by the plans of this creative world fair. A city-wide plan was begun in Toronto in 1906, involving a system of parks, diagonal streets, and parkways; this plan was also used for Berlin (now Kitchener) in 1914; in 1915 plans for Ottawa and Hull were also developed (Hodge, 1986:59). The City Beautiful drive included plans for monumental buildings, civic centers, public squares, tree-lined avenues, and walkways. Critics say that the City Beautiful movement worked mostly on adornment, and did not tackle the real problems of the city such as housing and sanitation. Those who defend it say that "classic" and powerful aesthetic principles, such as symmetry, coherence, perspective, and monumentality that have endured since the Renaissance were adapted and introduced in new ways (Hodge, 1986:59).

Garden, Resource and Greenbelt Hybrids

Garden suburbs used in planning residential areas in Canada could be considered a hybrid of the garden city and the City Beautiful. Raymond Unwin's Hampstead garden suburb in London, England was a forerunner; it had curved streets, parks, and open spaces. This type of design is now popular in North America. Notable garden developments in Canada are Shaughnessy Heights in Vancouver, Mount Royal in Calgary, Rosedale and Forest Hill in Toronto, Rockliffe in Ottawa, and Westmount in Montreal (Hodge, 1986:62).

Many new resource towns in the frontiers of Canada near mines, mills, smelters, or factories include conscious attempts to create attractive, healthful communities. Prince Rupert, B.C. was among the first in 1904; it had main avenues, circles, crescents, and public sites designed for a population of up to 100,000. Thompson, Manitoba, which has grown to be the third largest city in Manitoba, was designed as a company town by Inco Nickel Company.

Between the world wars, "new town" plans were made by Henry Wright and Clarence Stein, based on the ideas of Ebenezer Howard and Raymond Unwin; the first was built at the edge of New York City (Hodge, 1986:66). Radburn, one of the first new towns designed for the age of the motor vehicle, was begun in 1928: it included superblocks through which only local traffic could pass, specialized roads for service vehicles, a separation of pedestrians and automobiles, and houses that faced gardens and parks, not streets (Hodge, 1986:66-7). During the Depression of the 1930s, similar projects, called greenbelt towns, were built in the United States and Canada.

Brasilia, a New Inland Capital

Perhaps the most dramatic town plan of modern times is Brasilia, the capital of Brazil. The population in Brazil had been concentrated mostly on the eastern shores of the Atlantic ever since the seafaring Portuguese established their colony in South America, in clusters around Rio de Janeiro and Sao Paulo. Brazilians had dreamed since the independence of Brazil in 1822 of developing an inland capital to explore and expand settlement of the interior (Hodge, 1986:11-12). In 1956, a competition was held for a plan to build such a capital nearly 1000 km inland, northwest of Rio de Janeiro. Lucio Costa's plan was chosen, and fine buildings were designed by architect Oscar Niemeyer. The first phase of the city was completed in 1960 (Hodge, 1986:12).

As seen in Figure 11-5, the city was planned in the form of a curved cruciform, somewhat similar to an aircraft or bird with its wings spread forward. The residential areas surround the wings. The main square (a) is located at the tail end, and the president's residence (b) is located farther down in a more secluded place. The foreign embassies (c) are located to the left between the residential wings (d); other residential areas are clustered (e) on the other side in a variety of designs. The recreational area (f) is located at the top end or nose of the fuselage, the university (g) is to the right, and the cemetery (h), airport (j), and main traffic interchange are interspersed. This is one of the most extensive and best known plans developed in the second half of this century.

The excitement of building a new city with non-stop growth for thirty years has both advantages and drawbacks. Brasilia has little air pollution; it is easy to move around within the city; but it is too dependent on cars; prices are high because food and supplies must be shipped inland to an area where economic

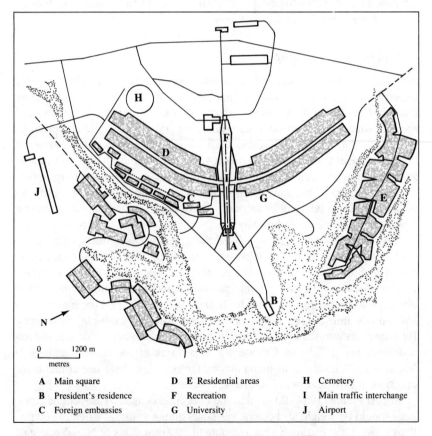

A	Main square	D	E	Residential areas	H	Cemetery
B	President's residence	F		Recreation	I	Main traffic interchange
C	Foreign embassies	G		University	J	Airport

Figure 11-5 Plan for Brasilia, the new capital of Brazil, 1957
SOURCE: Hodge (1986: 12).

velopment and population concentrations are sparse. The office buildings wntown buzz with air conditioners and guzzle energy — planners had not expected the energy crises that developed after the city was built. Brasilia has also had difficulties attracting federal employees into the isolated interior away from the more exciting Rio de Janiero, where the capital was formerly located. Perhaps, as the interior of Brazil develops (Ottawa has had similar problems), Brasilia will become more of a natural outgrowth of its region, which it has not been so far. Brasilia is an excellent example of how, no matter how wonderful an urban plan might be, an urban area must have a natural context and be an outgrowth or product of its own environment, developed over time.

Strategies for Urban Planning

How do we decide which criteria should be used in designing greater quality of urban life (Eyles, 1990)? Even if we can agree on desirable criteria, what strategies can be employed actually to bring such desirable features into being? Criteria and strategies together may then be combined to help plan healthy cities (Duhl, 1986; O'Neill, 1990:33-48).

Urban Quality of Life Criteria

With only 25 metropolitan centers spread across a ribbon of 5000 km, only three of which have over one million population, it is difficult to compare cities in Canada. With so many variations in size, regions, functions, and specializations, there are too few in each category to make valid comparisons (Kiernan, 1990:11-22). However, the United States, with a population ten times the size of Canada's and having roughly ten times as many urban centers as Canada, has provided more interesting comparisons. It soon becomes apparent that the criteria that must be taken into account are so varied that they are difficult to determine. San Francisco, for example, is often thought to be one of America's best cities — but why?

Boyer and Savageau (1984) ranked the 329 American Metropolitan Standard Areas (MSAS) of the 1980 census according to their quality of life. To do this they chose nine criteria — climate, housing, health care, crime, transportation, education, the arts, recreation, and economics (many of these were discussed as problems in chapter ten). They calculated a ranking for each city based on the nine criteria and found that New York, for example, ranked first for transportation, the arts, and health care, but last (worst) on crime (Spates and Macionis, 1987). In Canada we often think of the natural settings of Victoria and Vancouver as being among the best, but if we use crime as the criterion, they would rank last (Table 10-6).

Robert Pierce (1984) thinks that the nine criteria used by Boyer and Savageau should be weighted, because residents do not value all of them equally. Pierce found, for example, that a sample of 1000 residents of New York State valued good climate, absence of crime, economic opportunities, and good housing higher than the other five criteria. With a weighting system that took these findings into account, Pierce (1984) found that smaller cities ranked higher than large ones because they could meet people's needs better. It is clear that the choice of criteria and the weighting among criteria chosen will greatly affect the rankings for urban quality of life.

Ben-Chieh Liu (1976) studied 243 MSAs in the United States, focusing on the five key dimensions: economics, politics, the environment, health and education, and social relationships; the breakdown of these dimensions is outlined in Table 11-1. Liu chose these dimensions because they were universal, commonly understood, had policy implications, and were both flexible and amenable to study (Liu, 1976:53-4). The economic dimension deals with the problems discussed in chapter ten, such as income (poverty). The political dimension deals with opportunities for good jobs, and with communications; problems of pollution are addressed by the environmental dimension. Poverty and pollution are related to access to health services, and education has to do with training for jobs and a means of competing for work. The social and community living conditions deal with socio-economic status and ethnic and racial minority status.

Liu (1976:88) weighted some 1120 variables of city life on the basis of respondent satisfaction with physical, psychological, and social conditions. He divided the 243 American cities into large, medium, and small by size, and worked out total scores rating the centers from A to E, with "A" representing outstanding quality of life, and "E" as substandard. For example, San Francisco was rated outstanding with an "A," and Philadelphia, New Orleans, and Miami were rated substandard. In Table 11-2 we show the rankings of some of Liu's (1976) large MSAs, based on the five quality-of-life dimensions and controlling for four regions of the United States. It would be difficult to compare cities in Canada, with so few urban centers, using five dimensions and 120 variables, and controlling for regions. Someone should use Liu's system and add Canada's 25 metropoli to his 243 American centers to see how Canadian cities compare.

Liu's findings show that western cities, which are younger, smaller, and less industrialized, rate higher on quality-of-life. Smaller cities are likely to provide, overall, a more humane and satisfying urban life (Spates and Macionis, 1987:462-5). Once cities grow larger than three million, problems of crime, pollution, lack of health care and education, and poor social life tend to increase, which suggest that there is a maximum size to which cities should ideally grow. These problems are often more severe in the inner cities, causing many who can afford it to flee to the suburbs, where commuting costs and less intense vitality become a problem. Large cities also provide opportunity for more income, and people keep coming to such cities in droves; this increasingly seems to be a problem in Toronto, with a population rising to 3.4 million in 1986.

Strategies and Objectives of Planning

While Boyer and Savageau, Pierce, and Liu may use different means of

Table 11-1 Some of Liu's factors for measuring quality-of-life dimensions

ECONOMIC DIMENSION

Individual Economic Well-Being
1. Personal income per capita
2. Savings per capita
3. Percent of owner-occupied homes

Collective Economic Well-Being
1. Percent of families above poverty level
2. Degree of economic concentration in city
3. Production value per worker: construction

POLITICAL DIMENSION

Individual Activities
1. Availability of information: local Sunday paper distribution per 1000 population
2. Percent of homes with TV available
3. Local radio stations per 1000 population

Local Government Factors
1. Professionalism: average monthly earnings: teachers
2. Professionalism: average monthly earnings: other full-time employees
3. Professionalism: entrance salary: patrolmen

ENVIRONMENTAL DIMENSION

Individual and Institutional Environment
1. Air pollution: average level: total suspended particles
2. Air pollution: average level: sulphur dioxide
3. Visual pollution: average annual inversion frequency

Natural Environment
1. Mean annual inversion frequency
2. Possible annual days of sunshine
3. Number of days with thunderstorms

HEALTH AND EDUCATION DIMENSION

Health: Individual Aspects
1. Infant mortality per 1000 live births
2. Death rate per 1000 population
Education: Individual Aspects
1. Median school years: persons over 25
2. Percent, 4 years high school or more: persons over 25

Health: Collective Aspects
1. Dentists per 1000 population
2. Physicians per 1000 population
Education: Collective Aspects
1. Per capita local government expenditures
2. Percent of persons with 4 years of college or more: persons over 25

SOCIAL DIMENSION

Possibilities for Individual Development
1. Labor force participation rate
2. Mean income per family member
3. Percent of married couples with own home

Community Living Conditions
General Conditions
1. Percent homes with plumbing
2. Percent homes with more than 1 person per room
3. Percent homes with telephone available

Individual Equity	Facilities
1. Race: ratio of black-white income level	1. Number of banks per 1000 population
2. Race: ratio of black-white employment level	2. Number of retail trade establishments per 1000 population
3. Race: ratio of black-white professional employment level	3. Number of books in public library per 1000 population

SOURCE: Adapted from Liu (1976: 54-79): Spates and Macionis (1987: 459).

assessing the quality of life in cities, they all point to seven general characteristics, which Spates and Macionis (1987:466) summarize: 1) a nonexploitative relationship to the environment; 2) governmental leaders committed to the common good; 3) a thriving economy; 4) adequate health, transportation, housing, artistic, and educational facilities; 5) an open system providing equality to all; 6) residents committed to quality of life; and 7) a relatively small size so that traits can be balanced and controlled.

Palen (1987:438-9) suggests that approaches to social planning and problem solving range from using existing social mechanisms in conventional ways to radical restructuring of the entire system. Our discussion in chapter ten of the structural-functionalist and Marxist approaches already suggested differences in urban problem-solving. In Table 11-3 we summarize three approaches to planning and necessary action.

Conventional approaches assume that the system is adequate — it is individuals who often do not function sufficiently well to make the system work properly. To solve problems, people using these approaches tend to replace personnel, or reassess priorities to see whether resources and priorities should be reordered. Reformers are usually committed to many of the goals and ideals of society, but advocate new methods and means of getting better results, involving some reordering of the structure. Radical approaches differ in that they question the goals, the means, and the structures themselves. They do not believe that "technology saves," but that social structures perpetuate values that keep the poor from having access to opportunities and being able to compete.

Gerald Hodge (1986:362-4) has divided Canadian planning into three periods. The formative period (1890 to 1930) started with Herbert Ames' study of Montreal slums. The transitional period (1930 to 1955) spanned the Depression and World War II. The modern period (1955 to present) began soon after the last world war.

While the strategies for urban planning may vary, the objectives tend to be similar (Gold, 1982:340-2). Let us summarize:

1. Providing best possible environment for urban living
2. Strengthening the urban economy
3. Overcoming problems of urban growth and change in the past
4. Anticipating and projecting growth in the future and preparing facilities to meet future needs

Table 11-2 Rankings and ratings of selected large MSAs on five quality-of-life dimensions

| | DIMENSIONS | | | | | | | | | |
| | ECONOMIC | | POLITICAL | | ENVIRONMENTAL | | HEALTH/EDUCATION | | SOCIAL | |
CITY	RANKING	RATING	RANKING	RATING	RANKING	RATING	RANKING	RATING	RANKING	RATING
TOP 5 WESTERN*										
Portland, Ore.	3	A	8	A	11	A	9	A	1	A
Sacramento, Calif.	40	C	7	A	1	A	8	A	5	A
Seattle-Everett, Wash.	20	B	19	B	2	A	6	A	2	A
San Jose, Calif.	36	C	25	B	7	A	1	A	15	B
Denver, Colo.	33	C	16	B	24	C	3	A	4	A
TOP 5 MIDWESTERN										
Minneapolis-St. Paul, Minn.	25	B	9	A	20	B	7	A	9	A
Milwaukee, Wis.	16	B	12	A	32	C	19	B	8	A
Grand Rapids, Mich.	14	B	5	A	31	C	21	B	30	C
Columbus, Ohio	35	C	21	B	38	C	23	B	14	B
Cleveland, Ohio	4	A	28	C	60	E	32	C	24	B
TOP 5 NORTHEASTERN										
Rochester, N.Y.	11	A	3	A	13	B	13	A	50	D
Hartford, Conn.	22	B	6	A	40	C	5	A	23	B
Buffalo, N.Y.	32	C	1	A	45	D	25	B	18	B
Albany-Schenectedy-Troy, N.Y.	47	D	2	A	53	D	14	B	25	B
Syracuse, N.Y.	51	D	4	A	42	D	15	B	20	B
TOP 5 SOUTHERN										
Houston, Tex.	2	A	53	E	26	C	33	C	29	C
Dallas, Tex.	1	A	64	E	21	B	39	D	35	C
Richmond, Va.†	10	A	39	C	41	D	50	D	60	E
Atlanta, Ga.†	7	A	56	E	52	D	37	D	44	D
Fort Lauderdale-Hollywood, Fla.†	12	A	47	D	36	C	58	E	26	B

*As ranked by Liu's "Overall" Quality of Life Index (see Table 15-2).   †Ranked lower than 34 nationwide.

SOURCE: Adapted from Liu (1976: Tables 1–5); Spates and Macionis (1987: 461).

Table 11-3 Strategies for urban planning and problem solving

ASSUMPTIONS REGARDING PROBLEM SOLVING	GENERAL APPROACH TO PLANNING	RESULTING ACTION TAKEN
Most, if not all, problems can be solved by existing mechanisms	Conventional approaches (system needs minor modifications, fine tuning, or both)	New leadership, better administration, shift in priorities, new legislation
Some problems cannot be solved by existing mechanisms	Reformist approaches (system needs some major modification; likely to see system itself as source of problems)	Mobilization of power bases outside existing party structures, quasi-legal protests, civil disobedience
Most, if not all, problems cannot be solved by existing mechanisms	Radical approaches (system needs major revision or replacement)	Rejection of societal goals, extreme countercultural movements, revolution, planned violence

SOURCE: Palen and Flaming (1972: 335).

5. Minimizing the economic and social shock in new developments
6. Achieving beauty and functional urban features in new plans
7. Strengthening the democratic processes needed to facilitate change

Elements of a Master Plan

Planning agencies like to develop a metropolitan development plan as a blueprint to encourage planners to study seriously the overall development of a city and project directions for the future (Porteous, 1977:347). Such a plan can serve as a basis for budget planning and taxation, and it provides a sense of direction (Butler, 1976:479-83). Planners in metropolitan Winnipeg developed a comprehensive development plan that was accepted by the metropolitan council in 1968 (Metro Winnipeg Plan, 1968). Their ambitious plans spawned numerous substudies, which soon escalated into greater financial requirements so that councillors began to balk at the expensive "vision." Later, *Plan Winnipeg: An Introduction to the Greater Winnipeg Development Plan Review*, was published in 1981; it was only 16 pages long, even though it too was a comprehensive plan. The 1990 guidelines for downtown Winnipeg (1990) are again more substantial (Lane, 1989; Winnipeg Core Area, 1985, 1986, 1987, 1990). For many reasons master plans are less popular now than they were in the 1960s, but the basic elements are usually the same, so let us introduce them briefly.

Population Base Studies.

A population base study examines the basic demographic trends such as birth rates, death rates, and in- and out-migration rates, to provide a profile of how fast the population has been growing over several decades. Projections are then made to predict future growth, so that the residential, economic, political, social, and ecological demands of the population can be met in the future. The population density of the central city and the suburbs are compared, to give some sense of where populations are moving within the urban area, so that the needs for schools, parks, shopping centers, and other facilities can be provided for. Data on the age patterns, sex, and marital status of the population, size of households, employment patterns, vital statistics, population density, housing characteristics, and net migration are all used to project trends. These basic population studies also compare municipalities by age and by ethnic, racial, and socio-economic status groups to gain some sense of which groupings of population tend to cluster together so that differential needs can be taken into account.

Land-Use Plan

Next to people, the most important urban resource is land. In planning for land use, some of the objectives are to designate areas for the various urban activities, allow for social and economic factors to influence the physical form of the community, provide flexibility so that changes in technology can be accommodated, and develop a system for regulating and controlling land use.

Maps are needed to plot how land is currently used, and to identify areas for the various kinds of land use in the future. Zoning laws are needed to enforce the land use plans. Land use includes residential areas, both low and high density, commercial and industrial areas, parks and recreation, schools, public buildings, and vacant areas. Existing buildings may be rated as good, fair, poor, and very poor, using criteria such as age, size, physical condition, and the like. Separating good living areas from commercial and industrial areas is essential, and streets and transportation routes must be designed so that they do not encroach on residential living space.

Traffic and Transportation Facilities

Movement among the various land use areas, especially in larger urban centers, depends upon efficient circulation of traffic. One factor in providing a good quality of life is finding ways to allow people to live in pleasant areas such as suburbs, while arranging ways for them to get to work, which is usually some distance away, without delays. As populations increase, it is necessary also to provide major traffic arteries that can handle both volume and speed, and these requirements have led to the construction of expressways, especially in the United States. However, such trafficways tend to segment the city into sections and to fragment living areas. The use of public transportation—buses, railways, and subways—have been effective in large cities such as New York, Moscow, Tokyo, and most recently San Francisco, but tremendous costs are involved.

Many urban areas have designed major traffic arteries on the periphery, as outer traffic circles or perimeter highways, to stream traffic around large urban areas so that it does not fragment the city as much. Such periphery roads can also act as boundaries to restrict urban sprawl outside the metropolitan perimeter. On the other hand, persuading national, provincial, and municipal governments to co-operate in such large highway projects is often a complicated process.

Terminal Facilities

Railroad terminals entered most cities a century ago; some of these now need to be moved out of the center, as Saskatoon did a few decades ago, or as the Canadian National Railway yards were partially redirected in Winnipeg recently. Enormous costs are involved, and federal help is usually needed. Saskatoon replaced the railway terminal in the heart of the central business district with business development when the city was still small. Winnipeg, as part of a larger Winnipeg Core Area Initiative (1985, 1986), has reclaimed some of the historic fort area by replacing railyards with The Forks Development Project (1987). The old Canadian National Railway station remains as a passenger depot used by VIA passenger trains, and a historic park-recreational-business area has replaced the railyards (Lyon and Fenton, 1984).

Airport facilities are usually built quite close to smaller cities, with the result that when cities expand, the airports become engulfed by urban expansion, creating problems of congestion, overhead aircraft noise, and restrictions on heights of new buildings. Some of these smaller airports are often converted to use by local air traffic, and new airports are built considerable distances from the metropolis, such as Dorval near Montreal and Edmonton's international airport, both of which are as much as 40 or 50 km from the city center. Bus terminals usually remain near the center of the city for easy access by foot or taxi. Trucking firms are getting larger, and they tend to locate their terminals and warehousing on the periphery for easier access to expressways between metropoli. Most transportation terminals require vast parking facilities for cars, which make their location outside cities increasingly more attractive. These facilities on the periphery usually encourage urban sprawl, creating future problems of control over land use.

Utility Services

Utilities such as water, gas, and electricity, storm and sanitary sewers, and telephone and communications facilities are among the essential elements of a city structure upon which all residential, business, and recreational activities depend. The provision of these utilities is crucial for the health, convenience, and economy of a growing urban area. Materials used for sewers change, so that facilities laid a hundred years ago in old sections of the city may have become obsolete; or their capacity is no longer sufficient to avoid flooding. The locations of sewers require easements so that in future relocations or replacements, the effects on private and public properties will be minimized. Telephone and electrical lines formerly were carried on poles and wires above ground; increasingly they are being laid underground to avoid unsightly clutter. But making repairs to underground lines is a problem. Urban sprawl should be contained to allow for systematic extensions of existing utilities; in this way new residents would be paying for these extensions as the areas serviced were being occupied.

A Financial Plan

One of the problems in city planning is that planners have not given adequate attention to the financial costs of their plans, and even when they have, city councils are often reluctant to designate adequate funds. A master financial plan requires extensive allowances for commercial and economic development; analysis of the financial structure of the urban area; an evaluation of how units of government will need to co-operate; and a schedule for how income is to be generated. Priorities must be established, and the stages of development projected. For larger projects, the total costs can be spread over a number of years. It is important to win support from politicians and citizens through open discussion and information.

The political situation varies from one city to another, as illustrated in chapter eight. A unicity form of government such as that in Winnipeg (1983) can rely on the resources of its wealthy suburbs to help finance projects such as parks and public facilities. A complex structure, such as that in Montreal, with its many unco-ordinated urban municipal governments, nevertheless was able in the past to bring into being large projects such as Expo 67 and the Olympic games through the charismatic and powerful leadership of Mayor Drapeau. The fast growing metropolis of Toronto has an economic advantage in its highly industrial, southern Ontario hinterland, so that it has become a magnet to which many have been drawn. Such fast economic growth and industrial stimulation also has its drawbacks such as escalating housing prices, and it is to these we wish to turn in the last section of this chapter.

Industrial Areas

Earlier, industry was often located in the center of the city near railroad depots and warehousing. As a result of high urban taxes, the lack of spacious industrial sites, and less dependence on rail transportation because of the trucking business, industries have for the most part moved out of the central area of modern cities. Thus revenues and taxes from industry are lost to many central cities. Some light industries remain in the central city. With improved controls on noise, dust, fumes, and smoke, distinctions between light and heavy industries are no longer as clear cut, but industries are increasingly segregated in industrial areas away from residential areas. Most cities have now zoned large tracts of land with access to transportation for industrial parks. Pressure has come from the public to clean up environmental problems, and more efforts are being made to monitor and control industrial wastes and pollution. However in some cities, such as Hamilton, Sudbury, and Pittsburg, which are so dominated by industry, and in some smaller cities that exist as company towns, it is difficult to enforce environmental controls. On the other hand, most cities try to attract industry to contribute to their financial needs through jobs and taxes, so there is a tension between the benefits of industry and control of its potentially harmful effects. Zoning is an important issue in planning (Goldberg and Harwood, 1980).

Commercial Areas

Cities serve as centers of employment, trade, and services. The services used to be concentrated in the central business district, but since World War II smaller strip-shopping areas and large shopping malls have mushroomed everywhere. Thoroughfares are not now necessarily the major shopping areas, and planning accessibility to easy shopping requires a flexible mix of roads adapted to the needs of the automobile. Spacing shopping facilities for daily and weekly shopping patterns so that they are conveniently close to residential areas but not disruptive by causing noise or congestion is a challenge. Convenience stores, which often stay open 24 hours, fast-food services, car and television repair services, dry cleaning establishments, and drugstores are part of what most modern urbanites consider essential today, but they must be compatible with neighboring residential land uses.

Parks, Playgrounds, Schools, Cultural Facilities

Parks and playgrounds can usually be linked with schools so that space can be shared for recreational facilities. Population studies are essential for forecasting enrollments by area to serve as a basis for allocating school sites. Such studies help school boards to fulfill their responsibilities to provide educational facilities at all levels. New housing developments must be encouraged to include spaces for parks, recreation, and schools as part of the package. Some developers tend to look too much to profits, paying too little attention to recreational, educational, and cultural facilities — all important to the quality of life.

Thriving urban centers also need large, centrally located facilities such as auditoriums, sports stadiums, outdoor and indoor theatres, and art, folk, and historical museums to add to the general civic and cultural life of a large urban community. Such facilities also help to attract travelling celebrities, musicians, and sports organizations. As metropolitan centers become known for their cultural interests, musical, operatic, symphonic, dramatic, artistic, and other groups will visit the city. These in turn provide additional attractions for conventions and conferences, all of which are good for business.

Neighborhood Planning

There is an extensive literature on neighborhood planning (Porteous, 1977; Hodge, 1986). Residential neighborhoods are perhaps the most essential part of an urban master plan. Good homes need not only good structural design, but a good social context. Utilities, schools, recreation facilities, churches, shopping areas, and access to other parts of the city are all important. A variety of housing structures, including single-family homes of one or several storeys and multiple-family dwellings, are needed (Department of Environmental Planning, 1980, 1982a, 1982b, 1983).

Much attention is being given to the preservation of existing neighborhoods in order to prevent urban blight in older areas. New suburban developments need to create neighborhoods: strangers move together to create new community organizations such as clubs, sports associations, business relationships, professional contacts. Such social relations do not happen without social, educational, spatial, economic, and political planning.

Planning Quality Neighborhoods and Communities

Having discussed some planners' ideals for communities, and some of the strategies, objectives, and elements of the urban plan, let us now focus specifically on the neighborhood (Bookchin, 1986:118-63). The neighborhood is the most basic unit of the urban environment: here children grow up, people retreat after work, and the elderly spend their last days. How can we create neighborhoods, what are some housing criteria that will enhance the quality of life, and how can we also exercise our social responsibilities to those who need public help in housing?

Creating Neighborhoods and Communities

A neighborhood is the geographic space in which one feels at home (Porteous, 1977:68). Neighbors live in close spatial proximity to home base; they are neither prescribed as colleagues at work are, nor chosen as friends are, but determined because they live in the same place (Porteous, 1977:69). Neighbors recognize each other on meeting, but do not have closer contacts unless they are also friends. When there has been a disaster such as a death, crime, or a fire, and when there is a need for collective political action, neighbors will usually band together. The neighborhood unit is useful in planning. Planned neighborhoods go at least as far back as Ebenezer Howard's (1898) garden city, discussed earlier; other planners, such as Frank Lloyd Wright, Le Corbusier, and Lewis Mumford all planned with neighborhoods in mind.

The need for greater attention to urban neighborhood development has occupied planners for more than sixty years in North America, beginning with Clarence Perry (1929), who advocated the study of "neighborhood units." James Dahir built on Perry's ideas, suggesting that neighborhood units require unity characterized by four basic factors: 1) a centrally located elementary school within a walking distance of less than a kilometre; 2) neighborhood parks and playgrounds comprising 10 percent of the area; 3) local shops to meet daily needs at accessible points on the periphery; and 4) a residential environment of harmonious architecture, trees, centrally located community buildings, and thoroughfares that surround the community and define its perimeters (Theobald, 1949:16). These features have been criticized but have persisted in city planning (Hodge, 1986:65).

Paul Theobald (1949:2-9) tried to include Dahir's factors in his diagram (shown in Figure 11-6). Raymond Currie (1986, 1989) and others have also tried to use these features to construct plans for cities such as Winnipeg. The neighborhood becomes the natural basic planning unit, centered around communal interests whose focal point is in the elementary school. The size of the neighborhood depends on the size of the school and the number of families who have children in the school. As shown in Figure 11-6, neighborhoods can then be combined to share a high school, where a community center may begin, assuming that older, high school students can walk over a kilometre to school, if necessary.

William H. Whyte's (1954:140-3, 204-12) study of Park Forest, Illinois, illustrates the patterns of neighborhood friendships and their relationship to space. Children and their play patterns, the setting of driveways and stoops, and the location of residents in the block all greatly affected potential friendships. According to Whyte's conception, "The city planner . . . has the power to determine the nature of intensity of people's social lives." (Michelson, 1976:180-3.)

Housing Criteria for Quality Living

Jonas Lehrman and A.N. Sengupta (1969) undertook an investigation for the Corporation of Winnipeg to determine what criteria were essential for a quality residential environment. They presented seven criteria: privacy, identity, comfort, choice, adaptability, accessibility, and interaction. The overwhelming problem they wanted to solve was how to live with high densities and close proximities without losing humanity.

Privacy implies protection from unwanted intrusion. Is the housing cluster and the individual dwelling sufficiently protected against sound disturbances such as traffic, delivery vehicles, parking spaces, neighbors, and children's play areas? Plans need to safeguard audio, visual, and physical privacy without sacrificing access to facilities, yet at the same time allowing for interaction with people (Lehrman and Sengupta 1969:14-29). The balance between withdrawal and isolation is crucial. They assume that the need for privacy is universal, but this need must be interpreted in the context of time, place, and culture so that a balance can be achieved. With upward mobility, people want to be more selective in their interactions. They rely on their homes to help them monitor personal contacts.

Identity, according to Peter Smithson, has to do with "feeling that you are

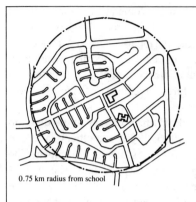

0.75 km radius from school

THE NEIGHBORHOOD is the natural basic planning unit which permits the greatest economy and freedom in the layout of blocks, streets, shopping centers, schools, recreation spaces, houses. It centers around communal interests, whose focal point is the elementary school. Ultimate size of each neighborhood may be measured by the number of families whose children will fill an efficiently run school. Each neighborhood requires well-defined borders to preserve and protect its unity and special character. Topographical limits or planted areas may determine these.

THE COMMUNITY is composed of one or more neighborhoods separated by open green spaces but bound together by secondary roads. The development of a community requires common interests vital to residents. Size depends primarily on predominating interest or need—usually high school community center—and on the most workable and economical organization for that function. (Clarence Stein)

Figure 11-6 Models showing neighborhood and community planning
SOURCE: Theobald (1949: 2–9).

somebody living somewhere.'' (Lehrman and Sengupta, 1969:30.) There needs to be a ''sense of place'' that a person can take pride in and where self-expression is possible. Again, differences exist between individuals, families, societies, and cultures. People who live in slums may be attached to their homes, so middle-class planners must recognize that bulldozing a slum means destroying many people's homes. A balance is needed between individual creativity and conformity to the neighborhood setting. Is there architectural variety among the houses? Are existing natural features used to good advantage? Are there controlled access points into the neighborhood? Are residences related so they contribute to each other's appearance and together present an image of uniqueness? Does the community have a landmark and special activities, and does it create identity?

Comfort, allied with convenience, is marked by ease, safety, health, and commodiousness (Lehrman and Sengupta, 1969:49). Air and noise pollution, accidents, fires, and floods are sources of discomfort. Easy access to a wide range of facilities and services, including outdoor and indoor recreation, public transportation, stores, schools, and institutions such as churches, libraries, and nurseries are sources of comfort.

Choice of site, density, dwelling type, and facilities are related to variety from which to choose. Is there a good selection of street activity for children and adults? A variety of choices in both work and leisure are important. Does the neighborhood provide variety for different age groups, family arrangements, social and income groups? Are there rental homes and homes that can be bought? Residential areas tend to be designed for specific groups such as families, singles, or older citizens. Price ranges also vary. People must have a choice of neighborhoods because some will be able to afford more than others. Ethnic, religious, and cultural needs will also vary.

Adaptability includes the opportunity to respond to change without loss of identity. Living involves continuous change, and thus elements of comfort, choice, and the need for identity and privacy may also change. Upward socio-economic mobility is part of these changing needs in the family life cycle (singles, adults, parents with children, parents whose children have left home, and the elderly). To what extent can the dwelling itself be adapted to changing family needs? Can space be adapted as the needs for space change? Can additional cars and boats be accommodated? Neighborhoods also change as cohorts of owners and renters move through the aging process. Can maintenance costs be anticipated and absorbed? Residential mobility is extensive, so movers need to adjust to new communities they move to, and non-movers need to adjust to newcomers.

Accessibility is concerned with ease of movement between home and locations outside, as well as within the neighborhood. Hans Blumenfeld (1967) put the dilemma well:

> Why do we want to move people, goods, and messages? Why can't people stay put? Why don't we all adopt the wisdom of Voltaire's *Candide* and just cultivate our own garden?

Access is linked to the other five criteria mentioned so far. Is there sufficient space for parking, and for service and delivery vehicles, repair and maintenance crews, fire trucks, ambulances? Can conditions brought by wind, rain, ice, and snow be handled properly? Is there public transportation if needed, and can major highways be reached easily? Privacy and accessibility are really opposites that must be blended together into a structure where they complement each other.

Interaction has to do with social networks, whereas accessibility has to do with spatial arrangements. There must be dialogue between people as well as between people and their environment. People in an urban environment cannot have interactive relationships in all their activities — people do not have intimate interchanges with store clerks, for example. Does the residential area have a suitable layout of bays and streets so that spatial arrangements will facilitate interaction?

These seven criteria of Lehrman and Sengupta (1965), if combined in residential housing areas, should go a long way towards developing satisfactory neighborhoods and communities in the city.

William Michelson (1976, 1977) has done extensive research on the effects of housing on social life in Toronto. "A giraffe cannot live in a home that was built for a flounder." (Michelson, 1977:12.) His studies measure feelings about new homes, housing types, new locations, new neighborhoods, and people's satisfactions and dissatisfactions with their housing. It is a comprehensive five-year study showing why people moved, how they moved, and their patterns of social interaction in different locations.

Public Housing and Social Responsibilities

The housing criteria discussed so far are focused on middle-class or higher income urbanites who, to varying degrees, can afford to buy or rent quality housing. What about the needs of urban residents who are on welfare; many of them single-parent families with women as heads of households (Flanagan, 1990:294-7)? These people need low-cost housing with subsidized rents, usually built by governments with public funds. However, some local government housing projects, such as Pruitt-Igoe, a project of eleven-storey apartment houses in St Louis, were not successful because they lacked clearly defined neighborhoods; Pruitt-Igoe was dynamited in the 1970s (Palen, 1972:274).

The first planned public housing in Toronto was Regent Park North in the central city, built in 1948 (McMillan, 1990:56). Regent Park, a massive low-rental public housing project, was considered a progressive beginning to the social engineering of slum-clearing projects in various parts of Canada. Since then, Toronto has developed additional projects: Lawrence Heights in 1957, Moss Park in 1960, Alexandra Park in 1965, and Cabbagetown; all are shown in Table 11-4 (McMillan, 1990:56). All except Lawrence Heights are located in the central city of Toronto (Sewell, 1977b:28-38).

Table 11-4 Comparison of public housing projects in Toronto, 1981

	CITY OF TORONTO	REGENT PARK (BUILT 1948)		LAWRENCE HEIGHTS (BUILT 1957)	MOSS PARK (BUILT 1960)	ALEXANDRA PARK (BUILT 1965)	CABBAGETOWN
POPULATION							
Population	599 220	9 970		3 770	4 600	3 839	4 180
% under 5 years	5	10		8	4	6	4
% under 15 years	16	30		30	9	22	12
% 65 and over	13	8		9	18	14	5
Population 15 and over – % women	52	57		60	44	52	47
men	48	43		40	56	48	53
HOUSEHOLDS AND FAMILIES							
Average persons per household	2.4	2.9		3.2	1.7	3.0	2.3
Average persons per room	0.5	0.7		0.7	0.5	0.7	0.4
% with more than one family	2.3	1.3		:::	:::	3.9	
% of lone-parent families	15	69		55	29	29	18
HOME LANGUAGE							
Neither English nor French (%)	25	15		–	–	41	–
LABOUR FORCE							
Participation rate (%) – men	79	54		59	63	63	83
women	61	39		48	45	47	66
Unemployment rate (%) – men	5	13		7	11	6	7
women	5	12		8	4	2	2
INCOME (1980)		NORTH	SOUTH				
Median household income	19 900	5 900	9 400	12 800[1]	8 700	10 400	19 700/28 100[2]
Median employment income – men	14 500	6 400	7 800	–	12 000	10 200	15 700/17 000
women	8 800	6 100	7 400	–	10 700	5 600	9 500/ 9 200
% living below the Low-Income Cut-Offs – families	17	69		–	37	47	12
– individuals	34	79		–	58	66	40

–Not available or too small to report. [1]Average household income. [2]For median income, Cabbagetown is divided into two areas.

SOURCE: Statistics Canada, 1981 Census Canada. McMillan (1990: 62).

Regent Park replaced a slum; in 1948 when it was built, the population was largely of British ethnic origin: large Black and Asian communities had arrived by 1981. Forty percent of the residents were children under 15 years of age, 69 percent were lone-parent families. Median household incomes ($5,900) were less than one-third that of households in Toronto ($19,900) in 1981, and only 54 percent of the men and 39 percent of the women were working in the labor force (McMillan, 1990:56-62). Regent Park was a complex of 1,000 units of low-rise apartment blocks.

Lawrence Heights, a suburban development of 19 low-rise, 3 1/2-storey, walk-up apartments, was built in 1957 in North York outside the central city. About half the residents were of non-British origin. Median household incomes were half as high as in Toronto, and only about half the residents were employed in the labor force. In 1960 to 1964, three 15-storey buildings with 900 units were also built near Regent Park; this project was called *Moss Park* (McMillan, 1990:56-62). The social statistics were very similar to those of Lawrence Heights; however, Moss Park had the highest concentration of elderly — 18 percent 65 years and older. About half (37 to 58 percent) lived below the poverty line.

Work on *Alexandra Park*, a fourth project, began in 1965. It was also in the inner city, and involved the rehabilitation of some houses and the replacement of others. This project had the highest ethnic diversity: 41 percent spoke non-official languages at home — but there were not nearly as many lone-parent families (29 percent), although still double that of the city of Toronto. *Cabbagetown*, a fifth project, is also in the central city area, but consists of a stylish neighborhood of privately renovated housing. Residents have few children, there are few lone-parent families, and incomes are similar to the average in Toronto. The residents have the highest level of employment of all the projects, and relatively few below the poverty line. Such mammoth public housing projects are no longer built; the emphasis in Toronto today is more on assisted housing by church, service, or other non-profit groups (McMillan, 1990:61). Public housing projects are too expensive for most centers, and their success is still being reviewed. The Milton-Park struggles to develop citizen housing in Montreal illustrates the persistence needed to bring about housing for the less affluent (Helman, 1987).

Summary

Urban planning is only a hundred years old, although there was evidence of planning in New France along the St. Lawrence and in the Maritimes earlier. Concerns for better living conditions and for creating a beautiful urban environment resulted in early, ideal plans for garden suburbs, resource towns, and greenbelts, such as Howard's garden city, Wright's Broadacre, and Le Corbusier's high-density settings. Brazil's new inland capital, Brasilia, is an excellent example of modern ideal planning.

Strategies for planning have changed from "ideal" models to attempts to understand the multiple variables and factors that must be combined and adjusted to the circumstances at a given time and place. Ben-Chieh Liu's studies of 243 MSAs in the USA suggested that quality-of-life revolved around five dimensions: economic, political, environmental, health and education, and community factors. Respondents to his survey showed that the different cities in his study rated differently on the numerous variables, and resulted in a wide range of rankings. Objectives of city planning are to provide the best possible environment, strengthen the economy, overcome existing problems, anticipate growth needs, minimize social shock, achieve beauty, and strengthen the democratic processes necessary to facilitate and support the needed changes.

While urban master plans are used less than in the past, they do highlight some ten elements that go into a comprehensive strategy. Population trends and land use provide basic information on projections for future needs. Transportation facilities, utilities, and services are increasingly important in a fast-moving environment. Plans must facilitate quality industrial and commercial areas, and arrange for parks, schools, and residential areas. Adequate funds are absolutely essential to build better communities.

The early ideal plans for urban living were largely focused on creating residential spaces that functioned better. People who occupy these spaces must create neighborhoods and communities that will permit social interaction, neighboring, and a sense of community. Housing should provide privacy, identity, comfort, choice, adaptability, accessibility, and interaction for those who can afford it. For those who have inadequate means, social agencies must provide public housing with at least minimal standards of good living.

The mobility, the problems, the pace of change, all make modern urban planning difficult, but also more satisfying if the quality of life can be enhanced. In industrial cities it is always easier to plan for those who have the means to purchase the best technology and the most creative plans. For the poor, overcrowding, pollution, and lack of economic opportunities make planning much more difficult.

References

Aberle, D. *et al.*
1950   "The Functional Prerequistes of a Society." *Ethics* 60:100-11.

Ablon, Joan
1964   "Relocated American Indians in the San Francisco Bay Area: Social Interaction and Indian Identity." *Human Organization* 23:296-304.

Abdul-Karim, Yusuf
1983   "The Ecological Structure of Halifax, 1971-1976." M.A. thesis, University of New Brunswick.

Adams, Robert M.
1960   "The Origin of Cities." *Scientific American* 203:155-72.

Adler, H.J., and O. Hawrylyshyn
1977   "Estimates of the Value of Household Work, Canada, 1961 and 1971." Ottawa: Office of the Senior Advisor on Integration. Ottawa: Statistics Canada.

Akyeampong, Ernest
1986   "'Involuntary' Part-Time Employment in Canada, 1975-1985." *The Labour Force*. Statistics Canada (December): 143-79.

Alihan, Milla
1938   *Social Ecology*. New York: Columbia University Press.

Ambert, A.M.
1980   *Divorce in Canada*. Toronto: Academic Press Canada.

Anderson, Alan B. and James S. Frideres
1976   *Ethnicity in Canada: Theoretical Perspectives*. Toronto: Butterworths.

Anderson, Grace M.
1974   *Networks of Contact: The Portuguese and Toronto*. Waterloo, Ontario: Wilfrid Laurier University Publications.

Anderson, Grace M. and David Higgs
1976   *A Future to Inherit: The Portuguese Communities of Canada*. Toronto: McClelland and Stewart.

Anderson, Nels
1923   *The Hobo: The Sociology of Homeless Men*. Chicago: University of Chicago Press.

Anderson, Nels
1934   *The Homeless in New York City*. New York: Unpublished manuscript for the Board of Charity, 470 pp.

Anderson, Nels
1940   *Men on the Move*. Chicago: University of Chicago Press.

Andrew, Caroline
1983   "Ottawa-Hull." In Warren Magnusson and Andrew Sancton (eds.), *City Politics in Canada*. Toronto: University of Toronto Press.

Arcury, Thomas A.
1986   "Rural Elderly Household Life—Course Transitions, 1900 and 1980 Compared." *Journal of Family History* 11:55-76.

Armstrong, Frederick H.
1981   "Ethnicity in the Formation of the Family Compact: A Case Study in the Growth of the Canadian Establishment." In Jorgen Dahlie and Tessa Fernando (eds.), *Ethnicity, Power and Politics in Canada*. Toronto: Methuen.

Armstrong, Pat
1984 *Labour Pains: Women's Work in Crisis*. Toronto: The Women's Press.
Armstrong, Pat, and Hugh Armstrong
1983 *A Working Majority: What Women Must Do For Pay*. Ottawa: Canadian Advisory Council on the Status of Women.
Armstrong, Pat, and Hugh Armstrong
1984 *The Double Ghetto*. Revised edition. Toronto: McClelland and Stewart.
Artibise, Alan F.J.
1975 *Winnipeg: A Social History of Urban Growth, 1874-1914*. Montreal: McGill-Queen's University Press.
Artibise, Alan F.J.
1977 *Winnipeg: An Illustrated History*. Toronto: Lorimer.
Balakrishnan, T.R.
1976 "Ethnic Residential Segregation in the Metropolitan Areas of Canada." *Canadian Journal of Sociology* 1:481-98.
Balakrishnan, T.R.
1982 "Changing Patterns of Ethnic Residential Segregation in the Metropolitan Areas of Canada." *Canadian Review of Sociology and Anthropology* 19:92-110.
Balakrishnan, T.R., and George K. Jarvis
1976 "Socioeconomic Differentiation in Urban Canada." *Canadian Review of Sociology and Anthropology* 13:204-16.
Balakrishnan, T.R. and George K. Jarvis
1979 "Changing Patterns of Spatial Differentiation in Urban Canada, 1961-1971." *Canadian Review of Sociology and Anthropology* 16: 218-27.
Balakrishnan, T.R., and John Kralt
1987 "Segregation of Visible Minorities in Montreal, Toronto and Vancouver." In Leo Driedger (ed.), *Ethnic Canada: Identities and Inequalities*. Toronto: Copp Clark Pitman.
Balakrishnan, T.R., and E. Selvanathan
1990 "Ethnic Segregation in Metropolitan Canada." In S.S. Halli, Frank Trovato and Leo Driedger (eds.), *Ethnic Demography*. Ottawa: Carleton University Press.
Bell, David, and Lorne Tepperman
1979 *The Roots of Disunity*. Toronto: McClelland and Stewart.
Bell, Wendell
1954 "A Probability Model for the Measurement of Ecological Segregation." *Social Forces* 32:357-64.
Bell, Wendell, and Robert V. Robinson
1980 "Cognitive Maps of Class and Racial Inequalities in England and the United States." *American Journal of Sociology* 86: 320-49.
Bellan, R.C.
1978 *Winnipeg First Century: An Economic History*. Winnipeg: Queenston House.
Bello, Francis
1958 "The City and the Car." In The Editors of Fortune, *The Exploding Metropolis*. Garden City, New York: Doubleday, pp. 32-61.
Berg, Ivar
1979 *Industrial Sociology*. Englewood Cliffs, N.J.: Prentice-Hall.
Berry, Brian J.
1964 "Cities as Systems Within Systems of Cities." In John Friedman and William Alonso (eds.), *Regional Development and Planning; A Reader*. Cambridge: MIT Press.
Berry, Brian J.L., and Philip H. Rees
1969 "The Factorial Ecology of Calcutta." *American Journal of Sociology* 74:445-91.
Bestor, Theodore C.
1985 "Tradition and Japanese Social Organization: Institutional Development in a Tokyo Neighborhood." *Ethnicity* 24:121-35.

Bestor, Theodore C.
1987 *Japanese Urban Life.* Stanford: Stanford University Press.
Blau, Peter M., Terry C. Blum, and Joseph E. Schwartz
1982 "Heterogeneity and Intermarriage." *American Sociological Review* 47:45-61.
Blumenfeld, Hans (ed.)
1967 *The Modern Metropolis.* Montreal: Harvest House.
Bonlet, Jac-Andre and Laval Lavallee
1984 *The Changing Economic Status of Women.* Ottawa: Supply and Services Canada.
Bookchin, Murray
1986 *The Limits of the City.* Montreal: Black Rose Books.
Boskoff, Alvin
1962 *The Sociology of Urban Regions.* New York: Appleton-Century-Crofts.
Bott, Elizabeth
1971 *Family and Social Network: Roles, Norms and External Relationships in Ordinary Urban Families.* Second edition. New York: Free Press.
Bourne, L.S.
1975 *Urban Systems: Strategies for Regulation.* Oxford: Clarendon Press.
Bourne, L.S., and R.D. MacKinnon
1972 *Urban Systems Development in Central Canada: Selected Papers.* Toronto: University of Toronto Press.
Boyd, Monica
1984 *Canadian Attitudes Toward Women: Thirty Years of Change.* Ottawa: Supply and Services Canada.
Boyd, Monica
1990 'Immigrant Women: Language and Socio-economic Inequalities and Policy Issues." In Shiva Halli, Frank Trovato, and Leo Driedger, (eds.), *Ethnic Demography.* Ottawa: Carleton University Press.
Boyer, Richard, and David Savageau
1984 *Places Rated Almanac.* Chicago: Rand McNally.
Braidwood, Robert J.
1957 "Jericho and its Setting in Near Eastern History." *Antiquity* 31:73-81.
Braidwood, Robert J.
1960 "The Agricultural Revolution." *Scientific American* Reprint.
Breasted, James H., Carl F. Huth, and G. Harding
1961 *European History Atlas: Ancient, Medieval and Modern European and World History.* Chicago: Denoyer-Geppert.
Breeze, Gerald
1966 *Urbanization in Newly Developing Countries.* Englewood Cliffs, N.J.: Prentice-Hall.
Breton, Raymond, Wsevolod W. Isajiw, Warren Kalbach, and Jeffrey G. Reitz
1981 "Ethnic Pluralism in an Urban Setting: Conceptual and Technical Overview of a Research Project." Research Paper No. 121, Center for Urban and Community Studies, University of Toronto.
Breton, Raymond, Wsevolod W. Isajiw, Warren Kalbach, and Jeffrey Reitz
1990 *Ethnic Identity and Equality: Varieties of Experience in a Canadian City.* Toronto: University of Toronto Press.
Browning, Harley L.
1958 "Recent Trends in Latin American Urbanization." *Annals of the American Academy of Political and Social Science* 316: March.
Burch, Thomas
1985 *Family History Survey: Preliminary Findings.* Ottawa: Statistics Canada.
Burgess, Ernest W.
1925 "The Growth of the City." In Robert E. Park and Ernest W. Burgess (eds.), *The City.* Chicago: University of Chicago Press.

Burgess, Ernest W.
1927 "The Determination of Gradients in the Growth of a City." *Publication of the American Sociological Society* 21:178-84.

Burgess, Ernest W.
1967 "The Growth of the City: An Introduction to a Research Report." In Robert E. Park and Ernest W. Burgess (eds.). *The City*. Chicago: University of Chicago Press.

Burke, Mary Anne
1990a "Loss of Prime Agricultural Land." In Craig McKie and Keith Thompson (eds.), *Canadian Social Trends*. Toronto: Thompson Educational Publishing.

Burke, Mary Anne
1990b "Urban Canada." In Craig McKie and Keith Thompson (eds.), *Canadian Social Trends*. Toronto: Thompson Educational Publishing.

Burstein, M., N. Tienharra, P. Hewson, and B. Warrander
1975 *Canadian Work Values: Findings of a Work Ethic Survey and a Job Satisfaction Survey*. Ottawa: Information Canada.

Butler, Edgar
1976 *Urban Sociology: A Systematic Approach*. New York: Harper and Row.

Calzavara, Liviana
1988 "Trends and Policy in Employment Opportunities for Women." In James Curtis *et al.* (eds.), *Social Inequality in Canada: Patterns, Problems, Policies*. Scarborough, Ontario: Prentice-Hall.

Chalaby, Abbas
1981 *Egypt*. Firenze, Italy: Editrice Bonenchi Publishers.

Cameron, David, and Peter Aucoin
1983 "Halifax." In Warren Magnusson and Andrew Sancton (eds.), *City Politics in Canada*. Toronto: University of Toronto Press.

Carswell, John
1981 "An Introduction: Cities Lost and Found." In Robert Breeden (ed.), *Splendors of the Past: Lost Cities of the Ancient World*. Washington, D.C.: National Geographic Society.

Carver, Humphrey
1948 *Houses for Canadians*. Toronto: University of Toronto Press.

Castells, Manuel
1972 *The Urban Question*. London: Edward Arnold.

Census of Canada
1981 Census of Canada, Catalogue 10.

Chaison, Gary N.
1982 "Unions: Growth, Structure and Internal Dynamics." In John Anderson and Morley Gunderson (eds.), *Union-Management Relations in Canada*. Don Mills, Ontario: Addison-Wesley.

Chelte, Anthony F., James Wright, and Curt Tausky
1982 "Did Job Satisfaction Really Drop During the 1970s?" *Monthy Labor Review* 105:33-36.

Childe, Gordon
1946 *What Happened in History?* London: Penguin.

Childe, V. Gordon
1950 "The Urban Revolution." *Town Planning Review* 21:3-17.

Childe, V. Gordon
1951 *Man Makes Himself*. New York: Mentor Books.

Childe, V. Gordon
1957 "Civilization, Cities and Town." *Antiquity* 31:36-38.

Chirot, Daniel
1977 *Social Change in the Twentieth Century*. New York: Harcourt, Brace Jovanovich.

Chirot, Daniel
1986 *Social Change in the Modern Era*. New York: Harcourt, Brace Jovanovich.

City of Ottawa
1970 "Generalized Land Use, Ottawa City Center." Ottawa: Planning Department, City of Ottawa.

Clairmont, Donald H., and Dennis William Magill
1974 *Africville: The Life and Death of a Canadian Black Community.* Toronto: McClelland and Stewart.

Clark, S.D.
1966 *The Suburban Society.* Toronto: University of Toronto Press.

Clark, Samuel D.
1978 *The New Urban Poor.* Toronto: McGraw-Hill Ryerson.

Clatworthy, Stewart J.
1980 *The Demographic Composition and Economic Circumstances of Winnipeg's Native Population.* Winnipeg: University of Winnipeg, Institute of Urban Studies.

Clement, Wallace
1975 *The Canadian Corporate Elite: An Analysis of Economic Power.* Toronto: McClelland and Stewart.

Clement, Wallace
1977 *Continental Corporate Power: Economic Linkages Between Canada and the United States.* Toronto: McClelland and Stewart.

Clement, Wallace
1986 *The Struggle to Organize: Resistance in Canada's Fishery.* Toronto: McClelland and Stewart.

Clement, Wallace
1988 *The Challenge of Class Analysis.* Ottawa: Carleton University Press.

Coale, Amsley J.
1973 "The Demographic Transition Reconsidered." *International Population Conference.* Lege, Belgium: International Union for the Scientific Study of Population.

Coleman, Richard P., and Les Rainwater
1978 *Social Standing in America: New Dimensions of Class.* New York: Basic Books.

Commoner, Barry
1971 *The Closing Circle: Nature, Man and Technology.* New York: Knopf.

Conrad, Geoffrey W.
1980 "The Incas." In Arthur Cotterell (ed.), *The Penguin Encyclopedia of Ancient Civilizations.* London: Penguin Books.

Corbusier, Le
1929 *City of Tomorrow.* London: Architectural Press.

Corbusier, Le
1933 *Radiant City.* Boulogne: Editions de L'Architecture d'Aujourd'hui.

Coser, Lewis
1956 *The Functions of Social Conflict.* New York: The Free Press.

Cotterell, Arthur
1980a "The Indus Civilization." In Arthur Cotterell (ed.), *The Penguin Encyclopedia of Ancient Civilizations.* London: Penguin Books.

Cotterell, Arthur
1980b "Shang." In Arthur Cotterell (ed.), *The Penguin Encyclopedia of Ancient Civilizations.* London: Penguin Books.

Cross, Michael S., and Gregory S. Kealey (eds.)
1985 *Modern Canada, 1930-1980s: Readings in Canadian Social History,* Volume 5. Toronto: McClelland and Stewart.

Culican, William
1980 "Phoenicia." In Arthur Cotterell (ed.), *The Penguin Encyclopedia of Ancient Civilizations.* London: Penguin Books.

Cuneo, Carl J.
1990 *Pay Equity: The Labour-Feminist Challenge.* Toronto: Oxford University Press.

Cunningham, Ralph
1971 "A Citizen's Contribution to the Spadina Expressway Debate." In Ralph R. Krueger and R. Charles Bryfogle (eds.), *Urban Problems: A Canadian Reader*. Toronto: Holt, Rinehart and Winston.

Currie, Raymond, and Charlene Thacker
1986 "Quality of the Urban Environment as Perceived by Residents of Slow and Fast Growth Cities." *Social Indicators Research* 18:95-118.

Currie, Raymond, and Shiva S. Halli
1989 "Mixed Motivations for Migration in the Urban Prairies: A Comparative Approach." *Social Indicators Research* 21:481-99.

Dahl, Robert A.
1958 "A Critique of the Ruling Elite Model." *American Political Science Review* 52:463-9.

Dakin, A.J.
1971 "In Defence of the Spadina Expressway." In Ralph R. Krueger and R. Charles Bryfogle (eds.), *Urban Problems: A Canadian Reader*. Toronto: Holt, Rinehart and Winston.

Darroch, Gordon A.
1983 "Occupational Structure, Assessed Wealth and Homeowning During Toronto's Early Industrialization 1861-1899." *Social History* 16:381-410.

Davies, W.K., and G. Barrow
1973 'Factorial Ecology of Three Prairie Cities." *Canadian Geographer* 17:327-53.

Davis, Kingsley
1955 "The Origin and Growth of Urbanization World." *American Journal of Sociology* 60:430.

Davis, Kingsley
1969 *World Urbanization 1950-1970*, Volume 1. Berkeley, Ca: Institute of International Studies.

Davis, Kingsley, and Hilda Hertz
1954 "Patterns of World Urbanization." *Report on the World Situation*. New York: Bureau of Social Affairs, United Nations Secretariat.

Dawson, Charles A.
1936 *Group Settlement: Ethnic Communities in Western Canada*. Toronto: Macmillan.

Dawson, Charles A., and W.E. Gettys
1929 *Introduction to Sociology*. New York: Ronald Press.

Deere, Carmen D., and Magdalena Leon de Leal
1982 "Women in Andean Agriculture." Women, Work and Development Series, No. 4. Geneva: ILO.

Department of Environmental Planning
1980 "Westminster: City Centre, Fort Rouge Community Committee Area." Land Development Series. Winnipeg: City of Winnipeg.

Department of Environmental Planning
1982a "Rossmere: East Kildonan, Transcona Community Committee Area." Land Development Series. Winnipeg: City of Winnipeg.

Department of Environmental Planning
1982b "Radisson: East Kildonan, Transcona Community Committee Area." Land Development Series. Winnipeg: City of Winnipeg.

Department of Environmental Planning
1983 "St. James Industrial: St. James, Assiniboia Community Committee Area." Land Development Series. Winnipeg: City of Winnipeg.

Dogan, Mattei
1988 "Giant Cities as Maritime Gateways." In Mattei Dogan and John D. Kasarda (eds.), *The Metropolis Era, A World of Giant Cities*, Volume 1. Newbury Park, Ca: Sage Publications.

Dogan, Mattei, and John D. Kasarda (eds.)
1988a *The Metropolis Era, A World of Giant Cities*, Volume 1, Newbury Park, Ca: Sage Publications.

Dogan, Mattei, and John D. Kasarda (eds.)
1988b *The Metropol Era, Mega-Cities*, Volume 2. Newbury Park, Ca: Sage Publications.

Dosman, E.J.
1972 *Indians: The Urban Dilemma*. Toronto: McClelland and Stewart.
Douchitt, R.
1984 "Canadian Family Time Use Data: Current Status and Future Prospects." *Canadian Economic Journal* 34:110.
Dowd, J.J., and V.L. Bengston
1978 "Aging in Minority Populations: An Examination of the Double Jeopardy Hypothesis." *Journal of Gerontology* 33:427-36.
Driedger, Leo
1978 "Ethnic Boundaries: A Comparison of Two Urban Neighborhoods." *Sociology and Social Research* 62:193-211.
Driedger, Leo
1979 "Mainenance of Urban Ethnic Boundaries: The French in St. Boniface." *Sociological Quarterly* 20:89-108.
Driedger, Leo
1980 "Jewish Boundary Maintenance of Urban Religious and Ethnic Boundaries." *Ethnic and Racial Studies* 3:67-88.
Driedger, Leo
1987 *Ethnic Canada: Identities and Inequalities*. Toronto: Copp Clark Pitman.
Driedger, Leo
1989 *The Ethnic Factor: Identity in Diversity*. Toronto: McGraw- Hill Ryerson.
Driedger, Leo, and Glenn Church
1974 "Residential Segregation and Institutional Completeness: A Comparison of Ethnic Minorities." *Canadian Review of Sociology and Anthropology* 11:30-52.
Driedger, Leo, and Richard Mezoff
1980 "Ethnic Prejudice and Discrimination in Winnipeg High Schools." *Canadian Journal of Sociology* 6:1-17.
Driedger, Leo, and Rodney A. Clifton
1984 *Canadian Review of Sociology and Anthropology* 21:287-301.
Driedger, Leo, and Neena Chappell
1987 *Aging and Ethnicity*. Toronto: Butterworths.
Driedger, Leo
1990 "Ethnic and Minority Relations." In Robert Hagedorn (ed.), *Sociology*. Fourth edition. Toronto: Holt, Rinehart and Winston.
Duhl, Leonard J.
1986 "The Healthy City: Its Function and Its Future." *Health Promotion* 1:55-60.

Duncan, Otis Dudley
1955 "Social Area Analysis." *American Journal of Sociology* 61:84-85.
Duncan, Otis D.
1961 "From Social System to Ecosystem." *Sociological Inquiry* 31:140-9.
Duncan, Otis D., and Albert J. Reiss
1956 *Social Characteristics of Urban and Rural Communities*. New York: Wiley.

Duncan, Otis D., and Albert J. Reiss
1958 "Suburbs and Urban Fringe." In William M. Dobriner (ed.), *The Suburban Community*. New York: G.P. Putnam's Sons.

Duncan, Otis Dudley, and Beverley Duncan
1957 *The Negro Population of Chicago: A Study of Residential Succession*. Chicago: Unversity of Chicago Press.
Durkheim, Emile
1893 *The Division of Labor in Society*. Glencoe, Il: The Free Press.

Ehrenreich, B.
1983 *The Hearts of Man*. Garden City, N.Y.: Anchor Press/Doubleday.

Eichler, Margrit
1977 "The Prestige of the Occupation of Housewife." In Patricia Marchak (ed.), *The Working Sexes*. Vancouver: University of British Columbia Press.

Eichler, Margrit
1988 *Families in Canada Today: Recent Changes and Their Policy Consequences*. Second edition. Toronto: Gage Publishing.

Eliot-Hurst, M.E.
1975 *I Came to the City: Essays and Comments on the Urban Scene*. Boston: Houghton-Mifflin.

Elmer, M.C.
1933 "Century-Old Ecological Studies in France." *American Journal of Sociology* 39:63-70.

Erwin, Delbert J.
1984 "Correlates of Urban Residential Structure." *Sociological Focus* 17:59-75.

Eyles, John
1990 "Objectifying the Subjective: The Measurement of Environmental Quality." *Social Indicators Research* 22:139-53.

Faris, R.E.L., and H. Warren Dunham
1939 *Mental Disorders in Urban Areas*. Chicago: University of Chicago Press.

Fingard, Judith
1977 "The Relief of the Unemployed: The Poor in Saint John, Halifax and St. John's, 1815-1860." In Gilbert A. Stelter and Alan F.J. Artibise (eds.), *The Canadian City: Essays in Urban History*. Ottawa: Carleton University Library.

Firey, Walter
1945 "Sentiments and Symbolism as Ecological Variables." *American Journal of Sociology* 10:140-8.

Firey, Walter
1947 *Land Use in Central Boston*. Cambridge, Ma: Harvard University Press.

Firey, Walter, and Gideon Sjoberg
1982 "Issues in Sociocultural Ecology." In George A. Theodorson (ed.), *Urban Patterns: Studies in Human Ecology*. Revised edition. University Park, Pa: Pennsylvania State University Press.

Fishbein, Seymour L.
1981 "The Sumerians of Mesopotamia." In Robert L. Breedon (ed.), *Splendors of the Past: Lost Cities of the Ancient World*. Washington, D.C.: National Geographic Society.

Fischer, Claude S.
1984 *The Urban Experience*. Second edition. New York: Harcourt, Brace Jovanovich.

Fishman, Robert
1977 *Urban Utopias of the Twentieth Century: Ebenezer Howard, Frank Lloyd Wright, and Le Corbusier*. New York: Basic Books.

Flanagan, William C.
1990 *Urban Sociology: Images and Structure*. Toronto: Allyn and Bacon.

Flon, Christine
1985 *The World Atlas of Archaeology*. New York: Portland House.

Freeman, R.B., and J.L. Medoff
1984 *What Do Unions Do?* New York: Basic Books.

Frideres, James S.
1988 *Native Peoples in Canada: Contemporary Conflicts*. Third edition. Scarborough, On: Prentice-Hall.

Friedmann, Harriet
1981 "Household Production and the National Economy: Concepts for the Analysis of Agrarian Formations." *Journal of Peasant Studies* 7:158-84.

Gallion, Arthur, and Simon Eisner
1975 *The Urban Pattern*. Third edition. New York: Van Nostrand.

Gans, Herbert J.
1962 *The Urban Villagers*. New York: Free Press.

Gans, Herbert J.
1962 "Urbanism and Suburbanism as Ways of Life: a Reevaluation of Definitions." In Arnold Rose (ed.), *Human Behavior and Social Processes*. Boston: Houghton, Mifflin.

Gans, Herbert J.
1967 *The Levittowners*. New York: Pantheon Books.

Garza, Gustavo
1978 "Mexico City: The Emerging Megalopolis." In Wayne Cornelius, Jr. and Robert Van Kemper (eds.), *Metropolitan Latin America: The Challenge and the Response*. Latin American Urban Research, Volume 6. Newbury Park, Ca: Sage Publications.

Gaylor, H.J.
1973 "Private Residential Development in the Inner City: The West End of Vancouver." In Lloyd Axworthy and James M. Gillies (eds.), *The City: Canada's Prospects, Canada's Problems*. Toronto: Butterworths.

Gee, Ellen
1986 "Population." In Robert Hagedorn (ed.), *Sociology*. Toronto: Holt, Rinehart and Winston.

Geisler, Stephen
1982 "The Crime Against Public Transporation." In Dimitrios Roussopoulos (ed.), *The City and Social Change*. Montreal: Black Rose Books.

Gendron, Bernard
1977 *Technology and the Human Tradition*. New York: St. Martin's Press.

Gibson, Nancy
1986 *Separation and Divorce: A Women's Survival Guide*. Edmonton: Hurtig.

Gillis, A.R.
1990 "Urbanization and Urbanism." In Robert Hagedorn (ed.), *Sociology*. Fourth edition. Toronto: Holt, Rinehart and Winston.

Gist, Noel P., and Sylvia Fleis Fava
1974 *Urban Society*. Sixth edition. New York: Thomas Y. Crowell.

Glaser, Daniel
1970 *Crime in the City*. New York: Harper and Row.

Gold, Harry
1982 *The Sociology of Urban Life*. Englewood Cliffs, N.J.: Prentice-Hall.

Goldberg, Michael, and Peter Horwood
1980 *Zoning: Its Cost and Relevance for the 1980s*. Vancouver: Fraser Institute.

Goldberg, Michel A., and John Mercer
1986 *The Myth of the North American City: Continentalism Challenged*. Vancouver: University of British Columbia Press.

Goode, W.J.
1956 *After Divorce*. Glencoe, Il: Free Press.

Gordon, Richard E., Katherine K. Gordon, and Max Gunther
1964 *The Split-Level Trap*. New York: Dell Publishing.

Grabb, Edward G.
1984 *Social Inequality: Classical and Contemporary Theorists*. Toronto: Holt, Rinehart and Winston.

Granovetter, Mark S.
1973 "The Strength of Weak Ties." *American Journal of Sociology* 78:1373.

Grant, George
1965 *Lament for a Nation*. Toronto: McClelland and Stewart.

Greer, Scott
1956 "Urbanism Reconsidered: A Comparative Study of Local Areas in a Metropolis." *American Sociological Review* 21:19-25.

Gutstein, Donald
1983 "Vancouver." In Warren Magnusson and Andrew Sancton (eds.), *City Politics in Canada*. Toronto: University of Toronto Press.

Hagan, John
1990 *The Disreputable Pleasures: Crime and Deviance in Canada*. Third edition. Toronto: McGraw-Hill Ryerson.
Hall, P.
1975 *Urban and Regional Planning*. London: David and Charles.
Hall, Peter
1984 *The World Cities*. Third edition. London: Weidenfeld and Nicolson.
Hamm, Bernd
1982 "Social Area Analysis and Factorial Ecology: A Review of Substantive Findings." In George A. Theodorson (ed.), *Urban Patterns: Studies in Human Ecology*, Revised Edition. University Park, Pa: Pennsylvania State University Press.
Hardwick, Walter G.
1974 *Vancouver*. Don Mills, On: Collier Macmillan.
Harris, Chauncey D., and Edward L. Ullman
1945 "The Nature of Cities." *Annals* 242:7-17.
Hatt, Paul
1946 "The Concept of Natural Area." *American Sociological Review* 11:423-7.
Harvey, A.S., and S. Clark
1975 "Descriptive Analysis of Halifax Time-Budget Data." Halifax: Institute of Public Affairs, Dalhousie University.
Harvey, David
1975 "The Political Economy of Urbanization in Advanced Capitalist Societies: The Case of the United States." In Gary Geppert and Harold M. Rose (eds.), *The Social Economy of Cities*. Beverley Hills, Ca: Sage.
Harvey, David
1985 *Consciousness and the Urban Experience: Studies in the History and Theory of Capitalist Urbanization*. Baltimore: Johns Hopkins University Press.
Hawley, Amos H.
1944 "Ecology and Human Ecology." *Social Forces* 22:398-405.
Hawley, Amos H.
1950 "Human Ecology, Space, Time and Urbanization." In Amos Hawley, *Human Ecology: A Theory of Community Structure*. New York: Ronald Press.
Hawley, Amos H.
1981 *Urban Society: An Ecological Approach*. Second edition. Toronto: Wiley.
Hawley, Amos H.
1986 *Human Ecology: A Theoretical Essay*. Chicago: University of Chicago Press.
Hawley, Amos H., and Otis Dudley Duncan
1957 "Social Areas and Analysis: A Critical Appraisal." *Land Economics* 33:337-44.
Hedley, R. Alan
1981 "Attachments to Work: A Cross-National Examination." *Comparative Research* 9:12.
Hedley, R. Alan
1986 "Industrialization and Work." In Robert Hagedorn (ed.), *Sociology*. Third edition. Toronto: Holt, Rinehart and Winston.
Hedley, R. Alan
1990 "Industrialization and Work." In Robert Hagedorn (ed.), *Sociology*. Fourth edition. Toronto: Holt, Rinehart and Winston.
Helman, Clattie
1987 *The Milton-Park Affair: Canada's Largest Citizen-Developer Confrontation*. Montreal: Véhicule Press.
Henry, Frances
1973 *Forgotten Canadians: The Blacks of Nova Scotia*. Don Mills, On: Longman Canada.
Henry, Frances, and Effie Ginzberg
1985 *Who Gets the Work: The Test of Racial Discrimination in Employment*. Toronto: The Urban Alliance on Race Relations.

Higgins, Donald J.H.
1986 *Local and Urban Politics in Canada*. Toronto: Gage Educational Publishing.
Hill, Frederick J.
1976 *Canadian Urban Trends*, Volume 2. Toronto: Copp Clark Publishing.
Hodge, Gerald
1986 *Planning Canadian Communities*. Toronto: Methuen.
Hollingshead, A.B.
1947 "A Re-Examination of Ecological Theory." *Sociology and Social Research* 31:194-204.
Hooker, J.T.
1980 "The Mycenaeans." In Arthur Cotterell (ed.), *The Penguin Encyclopedia of Ancient Civilizations*. London: Penguin Books.
Hooper, Diana, J.W. Simmons, and L.S. Bourne
1983 *The Changing Economic Basis of Canadian Urban Growth, 1971-81*. Toronto: Centre for Urban and Community Studies, University of Toronto.
Horton, Paul B., Gerald R. Leslie, and Richard F. Larson
1985 *The Sociology of Social Problems*. Eighth edition. Englewood Cliffs, N.J.: Prentice-Hall.
Howard, E.
1965 *Garden Cities of Tomorrow*. Cambridge, Ma: M.I.T. Press.
Hoyt, Homer
1959 *The Structure and Growth of Residential Neighborhoods in American Cities*. Washington, D.C.: Federal Housing Administration.
Hoyt, Homer
1982 *World Urbanization: Expanding Population in a Shrinking World*. Washington, D.C.: Urban Land Institute, Technical Bulletin No. 43.
Hughes, Everett C.
1943 *French Canada in Transition*. Chicago: University of Chicago Press.
Hunter, Alfred A.
1981 *Class Tells: On Social Inequality in Canada*. Toronto: Butterworths.
Hunter, Alfred A., and Abdul H. Latif
1973 "Stability and Change in the Ecological Structure of Winnipeg: A Multi-Method Approach." *Canadian Review of Sociology and Anthropology* 10:308-33.
Hurley, Dermot (ed.)
1987 *Separation, Divorce, and Remarriage: Psychological, Social and Legal Perspectives*. London, Ontario: King's College.
Innis, Harold A.
1930 *The Fur Trade in Canada: An Introduction to Canadian Economic History*. Toronto: Oxford University Press.
Innis, Harold A.
1951 *The Bias of Communication*. Toronto: University of Toronto Press.
Isajiw, W.W., and Leo Driedger
1987 "Ethnic Identity: Resource or Drawback for Social Mobility." Paper presented at the American Sociological Association meetings held in Chicago, August 17-21.
Jackson, J.J.
1972 "Comparative Life Styles of Family and Friend Relationships Among Black Women." *Family Coordinator* 21:477-85.
Jacobs, Jane
1958 "Downtown is for People." In Editors of Fortune (eds.), *The Exploding Metropolis*. Garden City, New York: Doubleday.
Jacobs, Jane
1963 *The Death and Life of Great American Cities*. New York: Vintage Books.
Jacobs, Jane
1971 "A City Getting Hooked on the Expressway Drug." In Ralph R. Krueger and R. Charles Bryfogle (eds.), *Urban Problems: A Canadian Reader*. Toronto: Holt, Rinehart and Winston.

Jacobson, Thokild
1980 "Sumer." In Arthur Cotterell (ed.), *The Penguin Encyclopedia of Ancient Civilizations*. London: Penguin Books.

Jagger, Alison M., and Paula Rothenberg Struhl
1978 *Feminist Frameworks: Alternative Theoretical Accounts of the Relations Between Men and Women*. New York: McGraw-Hill.

Johnston, R.J.
1976 "Residential Area Characteristics." In D.T. Herbert and R.J. Johnston (eds.), *Social Areas in Cities*, Volume I. New York: Wiley.

Kalbach, Warren E.
1980 "Historical and Generational Perspectives of Ethnic Residential Segregation in Toronto, Canada: 1851-1971." Research Paper No. 118. Centre for Urban and Community Studies, University of Toronto.

Kaliski, Stephen F.
1985 "Trends, Changes and Imbalance: A Survey of the Canadian Labour Market." In W. Craig Riddell (ed.), *Work and Pay: The Canadian Labour Market*. Toronto: University of Toronto Press.

Kallen, Evelyn
1977 *Spanning the Generations: A Study in Jewish Identity*. Don Mills, Ontario: Longman Canada.

Kaplan, Harold
1971 "Development Problems in Suburban Municipalities." In Ralph R. Krueger and R. Charles Bryfogle (eds.), *Urban Problems: A Canadian Reader*. Toronto: Holt, Rinehart and Winston, pp. 128-32.

Kawaluk, Lucia
1982 "On Housing." In Dimitrios Roussopoulos (ed.), *The City and Radical Change*. Montreal: Black Rose Books.

Kenyon, Kathleen M.
1956 "Jericho and its Setting in Near Eastern History." *Antiquity* 30:184-97.

Kenyon, Kathleen
1957 "Reply to Robert Braidwood." *Antiquity* 31:82-84.

Keochane, Nannerl O., Michelle Z. Rosaldo, and Barbara C. Gelpi (eds.)
1982 *Feminist Theory: A Critique of Ideology*. Chicago: University of Chicago Press.

Kiernan, Matthew J., and David C. Walker
1983 "Winnipeg." In Warren Magnusson and Andrew Sancton (eds.), *City Politics in Canada*. Toronto: University of Toronto Press.

Kiernan, Matthew J.
1990 "Urban Planning in Canada: A Synopsis and Some Future Directions." *Plan Canada* 30:11-22.

Kitson, G.C., K.B. Bahri, and M.J. Roach
1985 "Who Divorces and Why: A Review." *Journal of Family Issues* 6:255-93.

Kneedler, Grace M.
1951 "Functional Types of Cities." In Paul K. Hatt and Albert J. Reiss (eds.), *Reader in Urban Sociology*. New York: Free Press of Glencoe.

Krahn, Harvey L., and Graham S. Lowe
1988 *Work Industry and Canadian Society*. Scarborough, Ontario: Nelson Canada.

Kralt, John
1986a *Atlas of Residential Concentration for the Census Metropolitan Area of Montreal*. Ottawa: Minister of Supply and Services.

Kralt, John
1986b *Atlas of Residential Concentration for the Census Metropolitan Area of Toronto*. Ottawa: Minister of Supply and Services.

Kralt, John
1986c *Atlas of Residential Concentration for the Census Metropolitan Area of Vancouver*. Ottawa: Minister of Supply and Services.

Kramer, J. (ed.)
1972 *North American Suburbs*. Berkeley: Blendessary.

Kramer, Samuel Noah
1956 *History Began at Sumer*. Garden City, New York: Doubleday Anchor Books.

Krauter, Joseph F.
1968 "Civil Liberties and the Canadian Minorities." Unpublished Ph.D. Dissertation, University of Illinois.

Krauter, Joseph F., and K. Davis
1978 *Minority Canadians: Ethnic Groups*. Toronto: Methuen.

Krotz, L.
1980 *Urban Indians: The Strangers in Canadian Cities*. Edmonton: Hurtig Publishers.

Kumar, Pradeep
1986 "Union Growth in Canada: Retrospect and Prospect." In W. Craig Riddell (ed.), *Canadian Labour Relations*. Toronto: University of Toronto Press.

LaGory, Mark, and John Pipkin
1981 *Urban Social Space*. Belmont, Ca: Wadsworth Publishing.

Lai, David Chuen-yan
1980 "The Population Structure of North American Chinatowns in the Mid-Twentieth Century: A Case Study." In K. Victor Ujimoto and Gordon Hirabayashi (eds.), *Visible Minorities and Multi-culturalism: Asians in Canada*. Toronto: Butterworths.

Lai, David Chuen-yan
1988 *Chinatowns: Towns Within Cities in Canada*. Vancouver: University of British Columbia Press.

Lane, Barbara J.
1989 *Canadian Healthy Communities Project: A Conceptual Model for Winnipeg*. Winnipeg: Institute of Urban Studies, University of Winnipeg.

Lapierre, Dominique
1985 *The City of Joy*. New York: Warner Books and Doubleday.

Latif, Abdul H.
1973 "Factor Structure and Change Analysis of Alexandria, Egypt: 1947-1960." In Kent P. Schwirian (ed.), *Comparative Urban Structure: Studies in the Ecology of Cities*. New York: D.C. Heath.

Laurence, Margaret
1973 *The Fire-Dwellers*. Toronto: McClelland and Stewart.

Lehrman, Jonas, and A.N. Sengupta
1969 *Housing Criteria*. Winnipeg: Metropolitan Corporation of Greater Winnipeg.

Levin, Yale, and Alfred Lindesmith
1937 "English Ecology and Criminiology of the Past Century." *Journal of Criminal Law and Criminology* 27:801-16.

Lewis, Oscar
1966 "The Culture of Poverty." *The Scientific American 215* 4:19-25.

Li, Peter S.
1988 *The Chinese in Canada*. Toronto: Oxford University Press.

Lieberson, Stanley
1970 *Language and Ethnic Relations in Canada*. Toronto: Wiley.

Liebeschuetz, Wolfgang
1980 "The Early Roman Empire." In Arthur Cotterell (ed.), *The Penguin Encyclopedia of Ancient Civilizations*. London: Penguin Books.

Lightbody, James
1983 "Edmonton." In Warren Magnusson and Andrew Sancton (eds.), *City Politics in Canada*. Toronto: University of Toronto Press.

Lipset, Seymour Martin
1987 "Comparing Canadian and American Unions." *Society* 24:60-70.

Lithwick, N.H.
1970 *Urban Canada: Problems and Prospects*. Ottawa: Central Mortgage and Housing Corporation.
Liu, Ben-Chieh
1976 *Quality of Life Indicators in U.S. Metropolitan Areas*. New York: Praeger.
Lopata, Helen Z.
1971 *Occupation: Housewife*. New York: Oxford University Press.
Lorimer, James, and Myfanwy Phillips
1971 *Working People: Life in a Downtown Neighborhood*. Toronto: James Lewis and Samuel.
Lower Mainland Regional Planning Council of Board of British Columbia
1971 "The Economic Costs of Urban Sprawl." In Ralph R. Krueger and R. Charles Bryfogle (eds.), *Urban Problems: A Canadian Reader*. Toronto: Holt, Rinehart and Winston.
Lundgren, Robert
1973 "The Remaking of Gastown." In Lloyd Axworthy and James M. Gillies (eds.), *The City: Canada's Prospects, Canada's Problems*. Toronto: Butterworths.
Luxton, M.
1980 *More Than a Labour of Love*. Toronto: The Women's Press.
Luxton, M., and H. Rosenberg
1986 *Through the Kitchen Window*. Toronto: Garmond Press.
Lynd, Robert
1929 *Middletown*. New York: Harcourt, Brace Jovanovich.
Lyon, Deborah, and Robert Fenton
1984 *The Development of Downtown Winnipeg: Historical Perspectives on Decline and Revitalization*. Winnipeg: Institute of Urban Studies, University of Winnipeg.
McGahan, Peter
1986 *Urban Sociology in Canada*. Second edition. Toronto: Butterworths.
McKee, D.C., B. Prentice, and P. Reed
1983 *Divorce: Law and the Family in Canada*. Ottawa: Minister of Supply and Services Canada.
McKenzie, R.D.
1923 *The Neighborhood: A Study of Local Life in the City of Columbus, Ohio*. Chicago: University of Chicago Press.
McKenzie, Roderick
1968 "The Ecological Approach to the Study of the Human Community." In Amos Hawley (ed.), *Roderick McKenzie: On Human Ecology*. Chicago: University of Chicago Press.
MacKenzie, Suzanne
1986 "Women's Responses to Economic Restructuring: Changing Gender Space." In Roberta Hamilton and Michelle Barrett (eds.), *The Politics of Diversity*. Montreal: Book Centre.
MacLeod L.
1987 *Battered But Not Beaten: Presenting Wife Abuse in Canada*. Ottawa: Canadian Advisory Council on the Status of Women.
McMillan, Susan
1990 "Forty Years of Social Housing in Toronto." In Craig McKie and Keith Thompson (eds.), *Canadian Social Trends*. Toronto: Thompson Educational Publishing.
Magnusson, Warren
1983 "Toronto." In Warren Magnusson and Andrew Sancton (eds.), *City Politics in Canada*. Toronto: University of Toronto Press.
Magnusson, Warren, and Andrew Sancton
1983 *City Politics in Canada*. Toronto: University of Toronto Press.
Mann, W.E.
1970 "The Lower Ward." In W.E. Mann (ed.), *The Underside of Toronto*. Toronto: McClelland and Stewart, pp. 33-64.
Markides, K.S.
1983 "Minority Aging." In M.W. Riley, B.B. Hess and K. Bond (eds.), *Aging in Society: Reviews of Recent Literature*. Hillsdale, N.J.: Lawrence Erlbaum.

Markus, R.A.
1980 "Early Christianity." In Arthur Cotterell (ed.), *The Penguin Encyclopedia of Ancient Civilizations*. London: Penguin Books.

Marshall, V.W., and C. Rosenthal
1986 "Aging and Later Life." In Robert Hagedorn (ed.), *Sociology*. Third edition. Toronto: Holt, Rinehart and Winston.

Meissner, M.
1981 "The Domestic Economy: Now You See It, Now You Don't." In M. Hersom and D. Smith (eds.), *Women and the Canadian Labour Force*. Proceedings and Papers from a workshop held at University of British Columbia.

Melville, K.
1983 *Marriage and Family Today*. Third edition. New York: Random House.

Merton, Robert K., and Robert Nisbet (eds.)
1976 *Contemporary Social Problems*. Fourth edition. New York: Harcourt Brace Jovanovich.

Metropolitan Corporation of Winnipeg
1966 *South Point Douglas: Economic Land Use Analysis*. Winnipeg: Planning Division, Metropolitan Corporation of Greater Winnipeg.

Metropolitan Corporation of Winnipeg
1967 *Metropolitan Urban Renewal Study: Final Report*. Winnipeg: Planning Division, Metropolitan Corporation of Greater Winnipeg.

Metropolitan Winnipeg
1968 *The Metropolitan Development Plan*. Winnipeg: The Metropolitan Corporation of Greater Winnipeg.

Metropolitan Corporation of Greater Winnipeg
1969 *Downtown Winnipeg*. Winnipeg: Planning Divison, Metropolitan Corporation of Greater Winnipeg.

Metropolitan Winnipeg
1981 *Plan Winnipeg: An Introduction to the Greater Winnipeg Development Plan Review*. Winnipeg: City of Winnipeg.

Michelson, William
1976 *Man and His Urban Environment: A Sociological Approach*. Don Mills, On: Addison-Wesley.

Michelson, William
1977 *Environmental Choice, Human Behavior, and Residential Satsifaction*. Don Mills, On: Oxford University Press.

Miller, Delbert, and William H. Form
1980 *Industrial Sociology: Work in Organizational Life*. Third edition. New York: Harper and Row.

Mills, C. Wright
1956 *The Power Elite*. New York: Oxford University Press.

Miner, Horace
1939 *St. Denis: A French-Canadian Parish*. Chicago: University of Chicago Press.

Mitchell, Rick
1989 *Canada's Population From Ocean to Ocean*. Ottawa: Minister of Supply and Services Canada.

Moogk, Peter
1971 *Building a House in New France*. Toronto: McClelland and Stewart.

Morris, R.N.
1968 *Urban Sociology*. London: George Allen and Urwin.

Morton, James
1974 *In the Sea of Sterile Mountains: The Chinese in British Columbia*. Vancouver: J.J. Douglas.

Morton, W.L.
1957 *Manitoba: A History*. Toronto: University of Toronto Press.

Mumford, Lewis
1964 *The Highway and the City*. Toronto: New American Library.

Murdie, Robert A.
1969 *Factorial Ecology of Metropolitan Toronto, 1951-1961*. Toronto: Department of Sociology
      Research Paper No. 116, University of Chicago.
Nader, George A.
1975 *Cities of Canada: Theoretical, Historical and Planning Perspectives*, Volume I. Toronto:
      Macmillan.
Nader, George A.
1976 *Cities of Canada: Profiles of Fifteen Metropolitan Centres*, Volume II. Toronto:
      Macmillan.
Nagler, Mark
1970 *Indians in the City*. Ottawa: Canadian Research Centre for Anthropology, St. Paul
      University.
Nagpaul, Hans
1988 "India's Giant Cities." In Mattei Dogan and John D. Kasarda (eds.), *The Metropolis Era,
      A World of Giant Cities*, Volume I. Newbury Park, Ca: Sage Publications.
Nakamura, Hachiro, and James W. White
1988 "Tokyo." In Mattei Dogan and John D. Kasarda (eds.), *The Metropolis Era, Mega-Cities*,
      Volume 2. Newbury Park, Ca: Sage Publications.
Nett, Emily
1986 "The Family." In Robert Hagedorn (ed.), *Sociology*. Third edition. Toronto: Holt, Rine-
      hart and Winston.
Nett, Emily
1988 *Canadian Families: Past and Present*. Toronto: Butterworths.
Nicholson, T.G., and Maurice H. Yeates
1969 "The Ecology and Spatial Structure of the Socio-Economic Characteristics of Winnipeg."
      Canadian Review of Sociology and Anthroplogy 6:162-79.

Norris, Mary Jane
1990 "The Demography of Aboriginal People in Canada." In Shiva Halli, Frank Trovato, and
      Leo Driedger, (eds.), *Ethnic Demography*. Ottawa: Carleton University Press.

Ogilvie, R.M.
1980 "Rome Before the Republic." In Arthur Cotterell (eds.), *The Penguin Encyclopedia of
      Ancient Civilizations*. London: Penguin Books.

O'Neill, Michel
1990 "Healthy Cities Indicators: A Few Lessions to Learn from Europe." In Joan Feather (ed.),
      Indicators for Healthy Communities. Saskatoon: Department of Community Health and
      Epidemiology, University of Saskatchewan.

Ostry, Sylvia
1968 *The Female Worker in Canada*. Ottawa: Queen's Printer.

Palen, J. John
1975 *The Urban World*. New York: McGraw-Hill.
Palen, J. John
1987 *The Urban World*. Third edition. Toronto: McGraw-Hill.
Palen, J. John, and Karl H. Flaming
1972 *Urban America*. New York: Holt, Rinehart and Winston.
Palmore, E.B., and K. Manton
1973 "Ageism Compared to Racism and Sexism." *Journal of Gerontology* 28:363-9.
Pannell, Clifton E.
1984 "China's Changing Cities: Urban View of the Past, Present and Future." In Norton S.
      Ginsburg and Bernard A. Lalor (eds.), *China: The 80s Era*. Boulder, Co: Westview Press.
Park, Robert
1936 "Human Ecology." *American Journal of Sociology* 42:1-15.
Park, Robert
1952 *Human Communities*. New York: Free Press.

Park, Robert
1967 "The City: Suggestions for the Investigation of Human Behavior in the Urban Environment." In Robert E. Park and Ernest W. Burgess (eds.), *The City*. Chicago: University of Chicago Press; originally published 1916.

Parsons, Talcott
1951 *The Social System*. Glencoe, Il: The Free Press.

Parsons, Talcott
1971 *The System of Modern Societies*. Englewood Cliffs, N.J.: Prentice-Hall.

Parsons, Talcott, and R.F. Bales
1955 *Family, Socialization and Interaction Process*. New York: Free Press.

Pederson, Paul O.
1967 *Modeller fur Befolkningsstrucktur oq Befolkings- sudvikling i Storbymorader Specielt med Henblik pa Storkobenhavn*. Copenhagen, Denmark: Stat Urban Planning Institute.

Perry, C.
1929 *The Neighborhood Unit*, Volume 7. New York: Regional Association.

Persons, Stow
1987 *Ethnic Studies at Chicago, 1905-1945*. Chicago: University of Chicago Press.

Peters, Evelyn J.
1984 "Native Households in Winnipeg: Strategies of Co-Residence and Financial Support." Research and Working Papers 5. Winnipeg: Institute of Urban Studies, University of Winnipeg.

Petrie, Anne
1982 *A Guidebook to Ethnic Vancouver*. Surrey, B.C.: Hancock House Publishers.

Phillips, Lynne
1989 "Gender Dynamics and Rural Household Strategies." *Canadian Review of Sociology and Anthropology* 26:294-310.

Pierce, Robert M.
1984 "Rating American Cities." Paper presented at the Annual Meeting of American Geographers in Washington, D.C.

Pirenne, Henri
1956 *Medieval Cities*, translated by Frank Halsey. Garden City, N.Y.: Doubleday Anchor Books.

Plunkett, Thomas J.
1968 *Urban Canada and Its Government: A Study of Municipal Organization*. Toronto: Macmillan of Canada.

Polsky, Nelson W.
1959 "The Sociology of Community Power A Reassessment." *Social Forces* 37:232-6.

Porteous, J. Douglas
1977 *Environment and Behavior: Planning and Everyday Urban Life*. Don Mills, On: Addison-Wesley Publishing.

Porter, John
1965 *The Vertical Mosaic: An Analysis of Social Class and Power in Canada*. Toronto: University of Toronto Press.

Ram, Bali, Mary Jane Norris, and Karl Skof
1989 *The Inner City in Transition: Focus on Canada*. Catalogue 98-123. Ottawa: Minister of Supply and Services.

Ramcharan, Subhas
1982 *Racism: Nonwhites in Canada*. Toronto: Butterworths.

Ramu, G.N.
1988a *Family Structure and Fertility: Emerging Patterns in an Indian City*. New Delhi: Sage.

Ramu, G.N.
1988b "Martial Roles and Power: Perceptions and Reality in the Urban Setting." *Journal of Comparative Family Studies* 19:207-27.

Ramu, G.N.
1989 *Women, Work and Marriage in Urban India: A Study of Dual- and Single-Earning Couples.*
New Delhi: Sage.

Ray, Michael
1977 *Canadian Urban Trends*, Volume 3. Toronto: Copp Clark Publishing.

Rea, J.E.
1973 *The Winnipeg General Strike.* Toronto: Holt, Rinehart and Winston.

Rees, Philip H.
1970 "Concepts of Social Space: Toward an Urban Social Geography." In Brian J. Berry and Frank E. Horton (eds.), *Geographic Perspectives on Urban Systems.* Englewood Cliffs, N.J.: Prentice-Hall.

Reid, Frank
1985 "Reductions in Work Time: An Assessment of Employment Sharing to Reduce Unemployment." In W. Craig Riddell (ed.), *Work and Pay: The Canadian Labour Market.* Toronto: University of Toronto Press.

Reisman, David
1953 *The Lonely Crowd.* New York: Doubleday Anchor.

Reisman, David
1957 "The Suburban Dislocation." *Annals of the American Academy of Political and Social Science* 314:123-46.

Reisman, David
1964 "The Suburban Dislocation." In David Reisman (ed.), *Abundance for What?* New York: Doubleday.

Reitz, Jeffrey G.
1981 "Ethnic Inequality and Segregation in Jobs." Research Paper No. 123, Centre for Urban and Community Research, University of Toronto.

Reitz, Jeffrey G.
1990 "Ethnic Concentrations in Labour Markets and Their Implications for Ethnic Inequality." In Raymond Breton *et al.* (eds.), *Ethnic Identity and Equality: Varieties of Experiences in a Canadian City.* Toronto: University of Toronto Press.

Report of the Task Force on Child Care
1986 Ottawa: Supplies and Services.

Richardson, Boyce
1972 *The Future of Canadian Cities.* Toronto: New Press.

Richardson, R. Jack
1986 "Economic Institutions and Power." In Lorne Tepperman and R. Jack Richardson (eds.), *The Social World.* Toronto: McGraw-Hill Ryerson.

Richmond, Anthony H.
1972 "Ethnic Residential Segregation in Metropolitan Toronto." Research Report, Ethnic Research Programme, York University.

Robinson, Barry William
1968 "Leisure: A Suburban Winnipeg Study." Winnipeg: Unpublished Masters Thesis, University of Manitoba.

Rosenbluth, Gideon
1954 "Industrial Concentrations in Canada and the United States." *Canadian Journal of Economic and Political Economy* 20:206.

Ross, Patricia D.
1980 "Sexual Abuse of Children Within the Family: Tools for Understanding and Intervention: Conference Proceedings." Vancouver: Justice Institute of British Columbia and Ministry of Human Resources Child Abuse Team.

Roussopoulos, Dimitrois (ed.)
1982 *The City and Radical Social Change.* Montreal: Black Rose Books.

Roy, Patricia E.
1980 *Vancouver: An Illustrated History.* Toronto: Lorimer.

Russwurm, Lorne H.
1971 "Urban Fringe and Urban Shadow." In Ralph R. Krueger and R. Charles Bryfogle (eds.), *Urban Problems: A Canadian Reader*. Toronto: Holt, Rinehart and Winston.

Ryan, William
1971 *Blaming the Victim*. New York: Vintage.

Sacco, Vincent F.
1988 *Deviance: Conformity and Control in Canadian Society*. Scarborough, On: Prentice-Hall.

Sampson, Robert J.
1986 "Crime in Cities: The Effects of Formal and Informal Social Control." In Albert J. Reiss, Jr. and Michael Towry (eds.), *Communities and Crime*. Chicago: University of Chicago Press.

Sancton, Andrew
1983 "Montreal." In Warren Magnusson and Andrew Sancton (eds.), *City Politics in Canada*. Toronto: University of Toronto Press.

Santley, Robert S.
1980 "Teotihuacan." In Arthur Cotterell (ed.), *The Penguin Encyclopedia of Ancient Civilizations*. London: Penguin Books.

Sawers, Larry
1984 "New Perspectives on the Urban Political Economy." In William K. Tabb and Larry Sawers (eds.), *Marxism and the Metropolis: New Perspectives in Urban Political Economy*. New York: Oxford University Press.

Schnore, Leo
1964 "Urban Structure and Suburban Selectivity." *Demography* 1:170.

Schnore, Leo
1972 *Class and Race in Cities and Suburbs*. Chicago: Markham.

Schteingart, Martha
1988 "Mexico City." In Mattei Dogan and John D. Kasarda (eds.), *The Metropolis Era, Mega-Cities*, Volume 2. Newbury Park, Ca: Sage Publications.

Schwab, William A.
1982 *Urban Sociology: A Human Ecological Perspective*. Don Mills, On: Addison-Wesley Publishing.

Seeley, J.R.
1959 "The Slum: Its Nature, Use and Users." *Journal of American Institute of Planners* 25:7-14.

Seeley, J.R., R.A. Sim, and E.W. Loosley
1956 *Crestwood Heights: A Study of the Culture of Suburban Life*. New York: Wiley.

Semple, R. Keith
1988 "Urban Dominance, Foreign Ownership, and Corporate Concentration." In James Curtis, Edward Grabb, Neil Guppy and Sid Gilbert (eds.), *Social Inequality in Canada: Patterns, Problems, Policies*. Scarborough, On: Prentice-Hall.

Semple, R. Keith, and W.R. Smith
1981 "Metropolitan Dominance and Foreign Ownership in the Canadian System." *Canadian Geographer* 25:4-26.

Semple, R. Keith, and M.B. Green
1983 "Interurban Corporate Headquarters Relocation in Canada." *Cahiers de geographie de Quebec* 27:389-406.

Seward, Shirley B.
1990 "Immigrant Women in the Clothing Industry." In Shiva Halli, Frank Trovato, and Leo Driedger, (eds.), *Ethnic Demography*. Ottawa: Carleton University Press.

Sewell, John
1977a "The Suburbs." *City Magazine* 2:19-27.

Sewell, John
1977b "Don Mills: E.P. Taylor and Canada's First Corporate Suburb." *City Magazine* 2:27-38.

Shaffir, William
1974 *Life in a Religious Community: The Lubavitcher Chassidim in Montreal*. Toronto: Holt, Rinehart and Winston.

Shaffir, William
1981 "Canada and the Jews: An Introduction." In M. Weinfeld, W. Shaffir, and I. Cotler (eds.), *The Canadian Jewish Mosaic*. Toronto: Wiley.

Shaw, Clifford, and Henry McKay
1942 *Juvenile Delinquency and Urban Areas*. Chicago: University of Chicago Press.

Shelton, Beth-Anne
1987 "Variations in Deviance Rates by Community Size: A Test of the Social Integration Explanation." *Journal of Marriage and the Family* 49:827-32.

Shevky, Eshref, and Marilyn Williams
1949 *The Social Areas of Los Angeles: Analysis and Typology*. Berkeley: University of California Press.

Shevky, Eshref, and Wendell Bell
1955 *Social Area Analysis: Theory, Illustrative Application and Computational Proceedings*. Westport, Connecticut: Greenwood Press.

Shore, Marlene
1987 *The Science of Social Redemption*. Toronto: University of Toronto Press.

Simmel, Georg
1955 *Conflict and the Web of Group-Affiliations*. New York: The Free Press.

Simmons, James W.
1974 *Canada as an Urban System: A Conceptual Framework*, Research Paper No. 62. Toronto: Centre for Urban and Community Studies, University of Toronto.

Simmons, James W.
1983a *The Canadian Urban System as a Political System, Part I: The Conceptual Framework*, Research Paper No. 141. Toronto: Centre for Urban and Community Studies, University of Toronto.

Simmons, James W.
1983b *The Canadian Urban System as a Political System, Part II: Empirical Dimensions*, Research Paper No. 142. Toronto: Centre for Urban and Community Research Studies, University of Toronto.

Simmons, James, and Robert Simmons
1974 *Urban Cities*. Second edition. Toronto: Copp Clark Publishing.

Sjoberg, Gideon
1960 *The Preindustrial City: Past and Present*. New York: The Free Press.

Slater, Philip
1970 *The Pursuit of Loneliness*. Boston: Beacon Press.

Smith, W. and Associates
1972 "Downtown Vancouver Transit Concepts." Vancouver: City of Vancouver.

Smucker, Joseph
1980 *Industrialization in Canada*. Scarborough, On: Prentice-Hall.

South, Scott J., and Glenna Spitze
1986 "Determinants of Divorce Over the Marital Life Course." *American Sociological Review* 51:583-90.

Spates, James L., and John J. Macionis
1987 *The Sociology of Cities*. Second edition. Belmont, Ca: Wadsworth.

Spectorsky, A.C.
1955 *The Exurbanites*. Philadelphia: J.B. Lippincott.

Statistics Canada
1982 *Statistics Canada Daily*, Tuesday, June 15. Ottawa: Minister of Supply and Services Canada.

Statistics Canada
1984a *Canada's Cities*. Ottawa: Minister of Supply and Services Canada.

Statistics Canada
1984b *Urban Growth in Canada*. Ottawa: Minister of Supply and Services.
Statistics Canada
1989 *Crime Indicators, July-September*. Ottawa: Canadian Center for Justice Statistics.
Statistics Canada
1989a *Dimensions*. Catalogue CS 93-156. Ottawa: Minister of Regional Industrial Expansion and Minister of State for Science and Industry.
Statistics Canada
1989b *Winnipeg: Metropolitan Atlas Series*. Ottawa: Minister of Supply and Services.
Stebbins, Robert A.
1988 *Deviance: Tolerable Differences*. Toronto: McGraw-Hill Ryerson.
Stokes, Charles
1962 "A Theory of Slums." *Land Economics* 48:187-97.
Stolnitz, George J.
1964 "The Demographic Transition: From High to Low Birth Rates." In Ronald Freedom (ed.), *Population: The Vital Revolution*. New York: Anchor.
Stone, Leroy O.
1967 *Urban Development in Canada*. Ottawa: Dominion Bureau of Statistics.
Stone, Nat
1990 "Calgary: A Statistical Profile." In Craig McKie and Keith Thompson, (eds.), *Canadian Social Trends*. Toronto: Thompson Educational Publishing.
Strong-Boag, V.
1986 "Keeping House in God's Country: Canadian Women at Work in the Home." In C. Heron and R. Storey, (eds.), *On the Job*. Montreal: McGill/Queen's University Press.
Sullivan, Thomas, Kenrick Thompson, Richard Wright, George Gross, and Dale Spady
1980 *Social Problems: Divergent Perspectives*. New York: Wiley.
Sutherland, Edwin H.
1937 *The Professional Thief*. Chicago: University of Chicago Press.
Suttles, Gerald D.
1968 *The Social Order of the Slum: Ethnicity and Territory in the Inner City*. Chicago: University of Chicago Press.
Sweetster, Frank
1965 "Factor Structures as Ecological Structure in Helsinki and Boston." *Acta Sociologica* 26:205-25.
Tabb, William K., and Larry Sawers
1978 "Editors' Introduction." In William K. Tabb and Larry Sawers (eds.), *Marxism and the Metropolis: New Perspectives in Urban Political Economy*. New York: Oxford University Press.
Talbert, Richard (ed.)
1985 *Atlas of Classical History*. London: Routledge.
The Forks Renewal Board
1987 "The Forks: The Junction of the Red and Assiniboine Rivers." Winnipeg: Winnipeg Core Area Initiative.
Theobald, Paul
1949 "Organic Neighborhood Planning." In Walter Cropius (ed.), *Housing and Town and Country Planning*. New York: United Nations Bulletin, No. 2.
Theodorson, George A. (ed.)
1982 *Urban Patterns: Studies in Human Ecology*. Revised edition. University, Pa: Pennsylvania University Press.
Thomas, Jim
1983 "Toward a Critical Ethnography." *Urban Life* 11:490.
Thomas, William I., and Florion Znaniecki
1918-20 *The Polish Peasant in Europe and America*. Volumes I-IV. Boston: Gorham Press.

Thomlinson, T.M.
1969 "The Development of a Riot Ideology Among Urban Negroes." In Allen D. Grimshaw (ed.), *Racial Violence in the United States*. Chicago, Aldine.

Thrasher, Frederick M.
1963 *The Gang*. Chicago: University of Chicago Press.

Tokyo-to- Somu-Kyoku Tokei-bu Jinko Tokei-ka (ed.)
1975 *Tokyo-to no Jinko no Aramashi*. Tokyo: Tokyo-to Koho-shitsu Fukyu-bu Tomin Shiryo-shitsu.

Toronto Star
1986 "Intercorporate Ownership." 30:January.

Unikel, Luis, Ruiz Chiapetto, and Gustavo Garza Villareal
1976 *El Desarrollo Urbano de Mexico: Diagnostico e Implicaciones Futuras*. Mexico City: Centro De Estudios Economicos y Demograficos, El Cole io de Mexico.

United Nations
1965 "World Survey of Urban and Rural Population Growth: Preliminary Report by Secretary General." New York: United Nations Economic and Social Council.

United Nations
1981 *Statistical Yearbook*. New York: United Nations.

United Nations
1983 *Demographic Yearbook, 1983*. 35th edition. New York: Department of Economic and Social Affairs.

United Nations
1984 *The World Population Situation in 1983*. New York: U.N. Department of International Economic and Social Affairs, Population Studies No. 85.

United Nations
1985 *World Population Prospects, Estimates, and Projects as Assessed in 1982*. New York: United Nations, Population Studies No. 86.

Urban Design Studio
1990 *Realizing the Potential: Design Guidelines for Downtown Winnipeg*. Winnipeg: Faculty of Architecture, University of Manitoba.

Valentine, Charles A.
1968 *Culture and Poverty: Critique and Counterproposals*. Chicago: University of Chicago Press.

Van Arsdal, Maurice D., Santo Comilleri, and Calvin F. Schmid
1958a "The Generality of Urban Social Area Indexes." *American Sociological Review* 33:277-84.

Van Arsdal, Maurice D., Santo Comilleri, and Calvin F. Schmid
1958b "An Application of the Shevky Social Area Indexes to a Model of Urban Society." *Social Forces* 37:26-32.

Van Arsdal, Maurice D., Santo Comilleri, and Calvin F. Schmid
1961 "An Investigation of the Utility of Urban Typology." *Pacific Sociological Review* 4:26-32.

van Cleef, Danny
1985 "Persons Working Long Hours." *The Labour Force*. Ottawa: Statistics Canada, pp. 87-94.

Von Hagen, Victor W.
1958 *The Aztec: Man and Tribe*. New York: Mentor Books.

Wallace, Samuel E.
1965 *Skid Row as a Way of Life*. New York: Harper and Row.

Waller, M., and Morton Weinfeld
1981 "The Jews of Quebec and 'Le Fait Français'." In M. Weinfeld, W. Shaffir, and I. Cotler (eds.), *The Canadian Jewish Mosaic*. Toronto: Wiley.

Wallerstein, Immanuel
1974 *The Modern World-System: Capitalist Agriculture and the Origins of the European World Economy in the Sixteenth Century.* New York: Academic Press.

Walters, Colin
1980 "Ancient Egypt." In Arthur Cotterell (ed.), *The Penguin Encyclopedia of Ancient Civilizations.* London: Penguin Books.

Ward, Peter M.
1981 "Mexico City." In Michael Pacione (ed.), *Problems and Planning in Third World Cities.* New York: St. Martin's Press.

Warmington, B.H.
1980 "Sicily and Magna Graecia." In Arthur Cotterell (ed.), *The Penguin Encyclopedia of Ancient Civilizations.* London: Penguin Books.

Weber, Max
1958 *The Protestant Ethic and the Spirit of Capitalism.* Translated by Talcott Parsons. New York: Charles Scribners.

Weeks, Wendy
1980 "Part-time Work: The Business View on Second-Class Jobs for Housewives and Mothers." *Atlantis* 5:69-86.

Weinfeld, Morton, and William Easton
1979 "The Jewish Community of Montreal: Survey Report." Montreal: Jewish Community Research Institute.

Wellman, Barry
1982 "Studying Personal Communities in East York." Research Paper No. 28. Toronto: Centre for Urban and Community Studies. University of Toronto.

Wellman, Barry, Peter Carrington, and Alan Hall
1983 "Networks as Personal Communities." Research Paper No. 144. Toronto: Centre for Urban and Community Studies, University of Toronto.

White, P.
1980 "Off-Reserve Research: A Discussion of Methodological and Theoretical Deficiencies and Information Gaps." Ottawa: Department of Indian Affairs.

White, Paul
1984 *The West European City: A Social Geography.* London: Longman.

Whitney, Keith
1970 "Skid Row." In W.E. Mann (ed.), *The Underside of Toronto.* Toronto: McClelland and Stewart.

Whyte, William Foote
1943 *Street Corner Society.* Chicago: University of Chicago Press.

Whyte, William H.
1954 "The Web of Word of Mouth." *Fortune* 50:140-3.

Whyte, William H.
1956 *The Organization Man.* New York: Doubleday.

Whyte, William H.
1958 "Urban Sprawl." In Fortune Editors, *The Exploding Metropolis.* New York: Doubleday.

Wickberg, Edgar (ed.)
1982 *From China to Canada: A History of the Chinese Communities in Canada.* Toronto: McClelland and Stewart.

Wier, Thomas R.
1961 "A Survey of the Daytime Population of Winnipeg." In Norman Pearson *et al.* (eds.), *The Canadian City: A Synposium.* Montreal: Canadian Federation of Mayors and Municipalities.

Willets, R.F.
1980 "The Graeco-Roman City." In Arthur Cotterell (ed.), *The Penguin Encyclopedia of Ancient Civilizations.* London: Penguin Books.

Wilson, S.J.
1986 *Women, The Family and the Economy*. Revised edition. Toronto: McGraw-Hill Ryerson.

Wilson, William Julius
1984 "The Urban Underclass." In Leslie W. Dunbar (ed.), *Minority Report: What Happened to Blacks, Hispanics, American Indians and Other Minorities in the Eighties*. New York: Pantheon.

Wilson, William Julius
1987 *The Truly Disadvantaged: The Inner City, The Underclass, and Public Policy*. Chicago: University of Chicago Press.

Winnipeg Core Area Initiative
1985 *Winnipeg Core Area Initiative: Proposed Canada-Manitoba-Winnipeg Tripartite Agreement, 1986-1991*. Winnipeg: Winnipeg Core Area Initiative.

Winnipeg Core Area Initiative
1986 *Mid-Term Program Evaluations*. Winnipeg: Winnipeg Core Area Agreement.

Wirth, Louis
1928 *The Ghetto*. Chicago: University of Chicago Press.

Wirth, Louis
1938 "Urbanism as a Way of Life." *American Journal of Sociology* 44:1-24.

Wirth, Louis
1964 *Louis Wirth: On Cities and Social Life*. In Albert J. Reiss, (ed.). Chicago: University of Chicago Press.

Wooley, C. Leonard
1965 *Ur of the Chaldees*. New York: Norton.

World Bank
1985 *World Development Report*. Washington, D.C.: World Bank.

Wright, Frank Lloyd
1945 *When Democracy Builds*. Chicago: University of Chicago Press.

Wright, Frank Lloyd
1958 *The Living City*. New York: Horizon Press.

Yeates, Maurice
1980 *North American Urban Patterns*. New York: Wiley.

Zeitlin, Irving M.
1972 *Captialism and Imperialism*. Chicago: Markham.

Zuravin, Susan J.
1988 "Fertility Patterns: Their Relationships to Child Physical Abuse and Child Neglect." *Journal of Marriage and the Family* 50:983-93.

Index